Fourth Edition

Media Management

A Casebook Approach

Cover design by Maridou Tomai.

Lawrence Erlbaum Associates
Taylor & Francis Group
270 Madison Avenue
New York, NY 10016

Lawrence Erlbaum Associates
Taylor & Francis Group
2 Park Square
Milton Park, Abingdon
Oxon OX14 4RN

DEDICATIONS

Thanks to Harold Sohn for cheerfully finding things to do while I spent hours at my computer finishing yet another writing project.

And to University of Nevada at Las Vegas for its support and resources during the writing of this book.

Ardyth Broadrick Sohn

To Rob and Ian

To Donna Daniels and everyone in the Reference Department at the David W. Mullins Library.

And to everyone at the MultiMedia Resource Center at the University of Arkansas for the great job they do for me and my students.

Jan LeBlanc Wicks

To Leslie

Stephen Lacy

Thanks to Lee for his endless help and support over the years.

Thanks also to the many media professionals from around the world who have shared with me through workshops and research their insights into the challenges facing this changing industry.

C. Ann Hollifield

To Kathleen

George Sylvie

Contents

PREFACE

Writing a book is a team effort. Nowhere is that more true than this fourth edition of *Media Management: A Casebook Approach*.

When five intelligent people get together, you never know what will happen—unless four of those people are Steve Lacy, Ardy Sohn, Ann Hollifield, and Jan Wicks. Putting their collective heads together, they have easily made this the best of the four editions—not only because it is more up to date than earlier editions but also because it is simply better.

For example, instructors who favor this text will note that, as compared to previous editions, we spend more time in this fourth edition discussing groups, vision, change, diversity, and management styles—and that is a good thing. As a result, instructors who emphasize change and current trends in management will find that this text complements their styles and that their students—especially those using this edition as a fifth edition is being written—appreciate a text that maintains its freshness.

The authors took deliberate steps to increase the number of media-sensitive examples within each section of the text itself (e.g., in addition to the traditional, chapter ending cases). We believe that no reader should find him- or herself without some context, especially in the jargon heavy or technical areas. This is just the beginning of the many changes that each chapter includes. To detail all of them would take an entire chapter itself, so here are the highlights.

First, we have emphasized action. Of course, we kept our introductory chapter on decision making, focusing on its key role. We added, however, an ending chapter on knowledge management, not simply because that area has grown in the management literature. The chapter reinforces the authors' beliefs that good decisions are easier said than done; it deals with the harsh, practical realities of daily managing and the nettlesome problems it tends to generate. To further acknowledge daily realities, the law and leadership chapters now include healthy doses of information about ethics.

Second, we have emphasized reality. In addition to the previously mentioned improvements, we have added structural and contingency frameworks on leadership in chapter 2, which also takes a serious look at leadership and change. Moreover, we acknowledge the reality that most of our readers are years away from being in a position of management. So, not only are the cases detailed, as usual, but also the text often includes management scenarios in which more than one participant is a new employee or intern. This approach not only makes the text more relevant to students, but it also prepares them to understand the organizationally influenced motivations of their employers to be. Finally, this change acknowledges that, while managers manage their subordinates, they must also learn to deal with their superiors. We also took the reality approach to the global media chapter, de-emphasizing its previous, abstract focus on structure and adding a practical primer in global markets, technology, and policy. We do not ignore the structural issues, but we pay more attention to hands-on concerns.

Third, we delve more deeply into the aspects of change, be it through innovation, idea, machine, or another form. For example, the traditional technology chapter discusses influences, then goes on to provide insights into the buzzword *du jour*: convergence. The succeeding chapter 6 on law supplies additional focus on this area via discussion of the changing nature of laws and media management. If that were not enough, chapter 7 provides ample opportunity to explore the role of change in planning, especially through an ongoing look at a 20-year-old media company trying to plan its future in the current environment.

Fourth, we have emphasized analysis. Of course, the emphasis stands out in our case studies, the crown jewels of which are the extended case studies that require the reader to build on his or her knowledge of all the chapters. For example, market analysis skills—while introduced in chapter 8 and given a research framework in chapter 9—constitute vital, problem-solving tools in the extended cases. As usual, the cases are realistic, but even more so in this edition. Both depend on students' abilities to mine information resources and to extrapolate data. More importantly, the cases—while compelling reading—integrate many of the modern, nitty-gritty issues (e.g., diversity, group cultures, progressive discipline, training, and market-driven journalism) that media managers currently face.

Finally, we have taken great pains to make this edition especially readable. That may not sound like much in the way of an objective, but after three editions and 15 years, we acknowledged—thanks to previous readers' comments—that management can be deathly dull if you do not go to pains to make it relevant. So the reader will note that each chapter makes some small acknowledgement (via relevant transition) to its predecessor and that each chapter's summary attempts to reference its major points. To round it off, we used a narrative style that strongly adheres to active phrasing and conversational tone that we believe students will appreciate.

We hope you like this edition. We had fun writing it, and we hope it shows.

George Sylvie
University of Texas at Austin

1

MANAGERIAL DECISION MAKING

Managers carry out a wide range of organizational activities. They budget, evaluate employees, plan product changes, give raises, and more. All of these activities require decisions, and managers need to know how to make good decisions if their organizations are to achieve their goals. Simon (1960), the most noted scholar in the area of decision making, equated the decision process with management.

Decision making is so central to management that most managers do not think about the process by which they decide. However, this book assumes that managers must think about the process they use to solve problems if they want to improve as managers. Part of the problem that managers face in evaluating their behavior is that scholars have identified multiple approaches toward decision making. The traditionally dominant approach is called *rational decision making,* which sees decision making as a formal, step-by-step process used to achieve organizational goals (Miller, Hickson, & Wilson, 1996). A second approach defines decision making as the process of applying rules to problems. In this approach, matching rules with problems is the essence of decision making (March, 1997). A third approach views decision making as a political process in which groups exercise power to achieve their goals (Miller, Hickson, & Wilson, 1996).

This chapter aims to help students understand how decisions are made so they can better benefit from using the cases in this book. The cases following each chapter provide decision-making practice in a number of managerial areas. Effective practice occurs when a person understands the decision-making process. Because of the limited space in this chapter and the complexity of decision making, this chapter will emphasize decision making as a process divided into steps, although managers do not necessarily specify the steps they take as they make decisions.

Defining Decision Making

There are many definitions of decision making. For example, Simon (1960) wrote, "Decision-making comprises three principal phases: finding occasions for making decisions; finding possible courses of action; and choosing among the courses of action" (p. 1). Harrison (1987) defined a *decision* as,

> a moment, in an ongoing process of evaluating alternatives for meeting an objective, at which expectations about a particular course of action impel the decision maker to select the course of action most likely to result in obtaining the objective. (p. 2)

Many of the traditional decision-making definitions concentrate on the process as a rational one involving a person or group with common goals. However, Taylor (1984) emphasized the role of organizations' sociopolitical contexts and environments, suggesting that decisions are not as deliberate as often assumed, but occur from interaction among people and groups with sometimes conflicting goals.

The range of definitions for decision making suggests a somewhat arbitrary defining process. However, some concepts are common to most definitions. Decisions almost always involve resources, they usually address goals or objectives, they always involve people, and the environment in which these people work always affects decisions.

With these common concepts in mind, we define decision making as the allocation of scarce resources by individuals or groups to achieve goals under conditions of uncertainty and risk. This definition has six important terms. First, *allocation* means that things have been distributed among alternatives. Just as a family allocates its income for food, clothing, housing, transportation, and entertainment, media managers must decide how to distribute their resources.

A manager who has *scarce resources* has never had all of the resources he or she would like. Available resources are people's time and money. To a degree, these two resources are interchangeable. If you have money, but need time, you can hire others. If you have time, but need money, you can sell that time. Certainly, other forms of resources are available, but all are related to time and money. For example, technology can increase the effectiveness and efficiency of time and is acquired with money. Other forms of resources derive from time and money or improve the allocation of time and money.

The word *scarce* is equally important. If resources were not scarce, decision making would not be central to management. With a limitless supply of money and time, people simply could try every alternative until they found one that worked best. Scarce resources limit the time and money spent on a decision.

The third definition includes individuals and groups. One, two, or more people functioning as a unit can make a decision. All other things being equal, one person takes less time to decide than a group. However, ease of decision does not equate to effectiveness of decision. Groups make some decisions better than individuals.

Goal is the fourth term. *Goal* means a decision has a purpose. The nature of business goals is complex and the subject of much debate and research. The cases in this book may or may not state specific goals, but no decision can be adequately made without considering the goals of that decision and the overall goals of the organization.

In pursuing goals, managers can assume they act in a strictly rational way or they act with bounded rationality. Managers act in a strictly rational way when their goal is to maximize some aspect of business. Simon (1957) defined a *rational decision* as occurring when a decision maker confronted with alternatives selects the one with the highest return. This definition of rationality is the basis of classical economic theory and has resulted in the idea that business should maximize some goal, whether profits, revenues, or sales.

Acceptance of the assumption of rationality began to crumble after World War II, as scholars began to recognize the limits of the "rational man" approach. Cyert and March (1963) said the profit maximization assumption for businesses was not realistic because people within organizations do not have single-minded purposes; people pursue a variety of goals. Cyert and March added that firms do not have the perfect knowledge necessary to maximize profits. Maximizing profits occurs when the cost of an additional unit of a product equals the price a consumer pays. This maximizing point is hypothetical because such detailed price and cost data are impossible to collect.

In place of this rational assumption for decision making, Simon (1957) suggested the principle of *bounded rationality*. This principle recognizes that humans cannot be rational in the strict, traditional sense, but Simon was not willing to say people act randomly. Rather, he proposed that humans pursue goals in a purposeful manner, limited by the nature of people and their social environment. As a result, people seek goals and make decisions that work to satisfy instead of maximize their benefits from the decisions. This *satisficing* approach means people adopt goals and decision outcomes that are acceptable within the constraints faced by the organizations.

Not all scholars accept the idea of bounded rationality. Managers often take actions without evaluating the outcome. They apply what they see as appropriate rules to situations. This can succeed in a well-defined, unambiguous situation. However, in an ambiguous situation, applying rules can become problematic if the rules don't fit the situation (March, 1997). Other scholars note that organizational behavior can be political, and the result can be groups within the organization pursuing goals that may or may not promote the goals of the organization (Miller, Hickson, & Wilson, 1996).

Uncertainty is the fifth term of the definition in need of discussion. *Uncertainty* means all decisions are probabilistic, and no decision outcome is 100% certain. Reducing uncertainty starts with a subjective estimate of the probability that an outcome will occur. A graduating public relations major, for instance, might estimate that she has a 50% chance of finding a job within a month. Part of the estimate is figuring out the factors affecting outcomes. Once a person has made such an estimate, the reasons behind the estimate can be used to reduce uncertainty.

These estimates of probability may be as crude as saying that an outcome is more likely than not, or they may be as sophisticated as a derived mathematical statement of probability. For instance, a person might bet another person that Michigan State University will beat the University of Illinois in a football game. This is a statement with subjective probability, as is the statement that there is a 60% chance of rain tomorrow.

However, all such subjective estimates share two characteristics: (a) they are based on analysis of information, and (b) they are based on ssumptions about measurement and time that limit their objective nature. The accuracy of the information and quality of analysis determine how well the subjective statement of probability predicts rain or the football game winner.

Uncertainty then rests on a continuum from 0 to 100% uncertainty about a decision outcome, as shown in Fig. 1.1. Because perfect knowledge is impossible, 0% uncertain decisions do not exist, and a 100% uncertain decision would be a random solution. As Bass (1983) pointed out, in the absence of other information, people substitute their own experience or that of their acquaintances. As uncertainty increases, the difficulty of making an effective decision increases.

The word risk, the final term in the definition, is used differently here than in traditional decision-making research. *Risk* refers to the

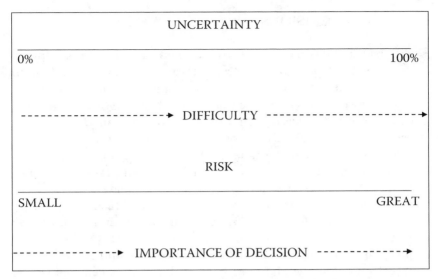

FIGURE 1.1. The relationship between uncertainty and risk.

amount of resources committed to accomplishing a goal and, therefore, the maximum amount of resources that might be lost. Risk also exists on a continuum, also shown in Fig. 1.1. The risk runs from small to great. Small means few resources are allocated, whereas great means a large number of resources is involved. As with uncertainty, organizations rarely operate at the ends of the risk continuum.

Few organizations allocate a large percentage of resources to a given project, much less a single decision, so risk is a relative term. Allocating $1 million would be a huge proportion of resources at most weekly newspapers, but a relatively small proportion of resources at a large media corporation such as CBS or Microsoft. The greater the risk, the more important the decision is for a company.

Figure 1.1 can illustrate the importance and difficulty of decisions to a media organization. A decision with a relatively great risk and a high level of uncertainty is important and difficult. In fact, such a venture might be suppressed. A decision with little risk and uncertainty would be relatively unimportant and easy to make.

Types of Decisions

Decisions fall into two types: (a) programmed and (b) nonprogrammed (Simon, 1960). A *programmed* decision sets up a rule stating that an action will take place once a certain condition has been reached. A *nonprogrammed* decision is one that cannot be made by referring to a rule. Programmed decisions tend to be highly structured with established goals and channels of information. Nonprogrammed decisions have poor structure, vague goals, and ambiguous information. Determining an employee's pay every month is an example of a programmed decision. Newspaper publishers do not have to decide how much money to pay their employees at the end of each month. They set the amount and form in advance, usually on an annual basis, and most organizations have computers that issue the checks. The concept of programmed-nonprogrammed decisions seems similar to the concept of decision by rules, but the two ideas differ. Management by rules concentrates on matching situations with rules rather than identifying decisions that can be made effectively with rules and decisions that cannot.

Nonprogrammed decisions occur at irregular intervals and require information and analysis specific to a particular set of options. A newspaper's decision to provide free Web-classified advertising would be a nonprogrammed decision if it irregularly occurred. Because nonprogrammed decisions—such as hiring a new news anchor on TV or starting a magazine—irregularly happen, an effective programmed policy is difficult or impossible to develop. Each time new information and analyses must be conducted to make an effective decision.

The distinction between programmed and nonprogrammed decisions is important. If a decision can be effectively programmed, it is wise to do so. The greater the number of programmed decisions, the more time a manager will have to spend on more difficult, nonprogrammed decisions. Whether a decision can be programmed depends on the uncertainty and risk involved. The lower the uncertainty and risk, the more likely a programmed decision will work.

The two types often occur in the same process. News selection, for instance, involves programmed and nonprogrammed decisions. News values are programmed decisions. If an automobile accident kills several people in a city, it will be on the evening TV news in that city. It has the news values of proximity (it is local) and impact (extreme consequences). Little debate occurs because applying the news values to such events has become programmed. The difficulty comes in deciding whether an event truly represents certain news values.

Proactive and Reactive Decisions

Another way to categorize decisions involves the impact of external events and trends on an organization. Managers tend to react to changes in the business environment with either proactive or reactive decisions (Ivancevich, Lorenzi, Skinner, & Crosby, 1994). *Proactive decisions* occur in anticipation of external changes, whereas *reactive decisions* happen as a result of external changes.

A newspaper company's reaction to Web sites that provide information about its community illustrates these two types of decisions. If the newspaper went online in 1995 with a Web site about its community, it is likely that managers made a proactive decision to establish a source of information before other companies did. If the newspaper managers waited until competitors had already established a community Web site, in 1998, for example, they made a reactive decision.

Proactive decisions can work well when they promote solutions to problems before they become particularly burdensome. Reactive decisions often occur after a company's competitor has gained a foothold in the market, which can limit the effectiveness of the reaction. However, a company can be proactive to an imagined problem and end up wasting money solving a problem that does not exist. Successful proactive decisions require accurate predictions of future external trends and events. Successful reactive decisions require that an organization not wait too long in responding to changes in the business environment. Timing is crucial.

The Decision Process

Despite variation in the names given to the steps in the decision process, most decision-making models are similar. For example, Drucker (1983) gave six steps: (a) classify the problem, (b) define the problem, (c) specify what the decision must do, (d) seek the right decision, (e) build in the action to carry out the decision, and (f) use feedback to test the decision's effectiveness. Griffin and Moorhead (1986) offered a model that incorporates the difference between programmed and nonprogrammed decisions and acknowledges the role of information at each step.

The model shown in Fig. 1.2 is called a *decision wheel* because it represents the cyclical nature of the decision process. It differs from the Griffin and Moorhead (1986) model in two ways. First, it does not include the idea of programmed versus nonprogrammed decisions. Programmed decisions, although important, are not the basis of the case-study approach. Although creating a policy may be the solution to a case, this solution results from a nonprogrammed decision process.

A second difference between the decision wheel and other models is the central placement of the collection and analysis of information. Just as decision making is the heart of management, the collection and appropriate analysis of information are the hubs of decision making. All steps of the decision-making process must involve the collection of information and its appropriate evaluation. Analysis, which breaks down the information and then examines and classifies it so that it can be used, is a key to effective decisions. Correct analysis with little information often is more useful than poor analysis with abundant information.

Defining the Problem

The first step is to define the problem. It involves the collection of information about some form of behavior (either inside or outside the

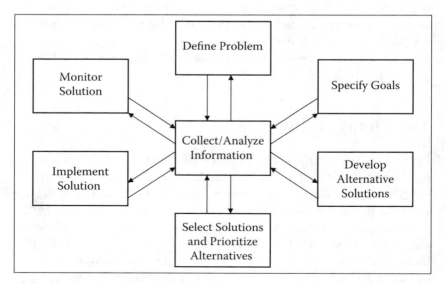

FIGURE 1.2. The decision wheel.

organization) that creates a problem for the media firm. The manager must analyze this information in a way that helps to frame the problem appropriately. For example, a TV news department losing audience has a problem. To define the problem behind this ratings decline, management must develop a list of possible causes and collect information about them. Then management must analyze the information about the potential causes to determine the cause. Perhaps the audience does not like the hard-news focus of the news shows or it does not like the anchors. Each problem holds several possible causes; in most cases, problems may have more than one cause. The effectiveness in reversing the sliding ratings, however, depends on management's ability to define the problem in a way that correctly identifies the causes.

Specifying Goals

After the problem is defined, the next step specifies the goals of the decision. The goals need to be concrete. Vague statements about reversing a trend do not allow for effective decision making. The goals should be as specific as the problem and available data allow. Usually, the decision process addresses multiple goals. All goals should have a time frame in which they will be accomplished.

In the free Web-classified ads decision mentioned earlier, the newspaper publisher decided the newspaper needed to draw more page views to its Web site, specifically to its classified ads page. The goal could be to generate an additional 1,000 page views a day within a month, generate 2,000 new page views a day within three months, and to retain at least 1,000 page views when the promotion ends after three months. These specific goals allow better monitoring and force managers to use detailed data analysis. Managers can set several goals at various times. For example, the publisher could have a goal of 1,000 more page views at one month, 1,500 at two months, and 2,000 at three months, and a permanent increase of 1,000 page views at six months, three months after the promotion ended. The crucial element of goal setting is degree of specificity and a time for meeting the goal.

Developing Solutions

The third step in the decision wheel develops alternative solutions. This step should yield as many viable alternatives as possible. Inadequate solutions can always be rejected, but a solution not considered can never be selected. A weeding-out process follows the listing of the solutions, and the obviously unsuitable solution can be dropped, leaving those items with some possibilities for accomplishing the goals.

As with all steps, the narrowing process requires acquiring information and its analysis. Two questions for developing this short list are (a) Will the solutions actually accomplish the goals? (b) Will the costs of the solution outweigh the gains to the organization? If the answer to the first question is "no," the solution should be dropped. If the answer to the second question is "yes," the solution should be dropped.

If a newspaper decided to increase page views at its Web site, managers might list the following options:

1. Partner with a local TV station and stream news video.
2. Hire a reporter to write just for the Web site.
3. Set up live Web cams around town to stream live video from popular community locations such as malls and parks.
4. Partner with local news/talk radio stations and stream news audio.
5. Give away free Web-classified advertisements for 3 months.
6. Acquire additional news services to load online.

These are just some of the possible solutions; only a few will get serious consideration, but examining all possible alternatives will help managers identify plausible ones.

The two-question test can be applied to eliminate some of the listed alternatives. For example, acquiring additional news services, such as *The New York Times* service, probably will not attract more page views because many sites already provide these news services. In addition, solutions 1 and 3 might require an investment in live video-streaming technology and employees to use the technology. The investment might exceed the increased revenue from additional Web-page views.

Selecting a Solution

With a short list of solutions, a manager moves to Step 4, which involves selecting a solution. The solution may combine more than one alternative solution, but the next step requires a decision to pursue a specific solution.

The collection and analysis of information becomes crucial at this point. Even though one solution is selected, the alternate solutions should not be forgotten. Often the original solution does not work as well as management would like. As a result, managers have to return to the problem and either generate new solutions or choose one or more of the solutions dropped in Step 4, in which case it is a good idea to prioritize them based on the information and analysis in Step 4. This may save time if the chosen solution fails.

Selecting solutions is a matter of costs and benefits. Often more than one solution will work, so the correct option involves balancing costs with the benefits. One solution may generate more page views than another, but the costs would be so high as to consume the entire increase in revenues from getting more page views. At the same time, a solution may be inexpensive, but the results will not reach the specified goals.

Returning to the problem/goal of increasing page views of the newspaper Web site, we find the managers considering three options not eliminated by the two-question test. They reject Option 4 because the newspaper exists in a medium-sized market without a commercial news/talk station.

The two remaining solutions involve either investing in new employees, which will increase expenses, or allowing free classified ads, which will reduce revenue because some of the people using the free ads would have paid for ads. Both solutions would reduce profits in the short run to increase profits in the long run. Over time, the goal of increasing page views will allow the newspaper to charge higher prices for online advertising, particularly for online classified ads.

Comparing the two options, the managers realize that hiring an online reporter may be a good idea, but it will require a permanent increase in the number of employees and a continuing increase in the budget. Giving away free ads for 3 months will reduce revenues only temporarily. The managers also realize giving free online classifieds will bring people who are looking at classified ads, and it will possibly bring the advertisers results that will encourage them to buy classified ads in the future. Such a double benefit might not derive from the exclusive online reporter.

Implementing the Solution

Once the solution is selected, it must be implemented. This is the fifth step in the decision wheel. The solution means nothing unless applied correctly, which requires a detailed plan of action with a timetable for specific actions, a budget, and a breakdown of who has responsibility for executing the changes. The details should be as specific as possible.

So, the decision to provide free online classified ads begins a string of decisions. To accomplish the goals, the free ads must be promoted, the process of taking ads must be planned, and the managers must decide how to measure the impact on page views. Promotion can occur through the print edition of the newspaper, on the Web site, and even through other media, such as radio ad spots. The promotion will most likely involve a variety of activities, but the cost will have to reflect what the managers think the return will be. The existing classified ads staff most likely will place the free ads, but the newspaper might have to hire temporary help. Finally, the managers must decide how to measure the impact, which would involve measuring a baseline of page views over several weeks before offering the free ads so that the managers can compare any change in number of page views with the baseline.

Monitoring the Solution

The final step monitors the implementation in light of the goals. This monitoring should provide feedback on a regular basis to judge progress toward the goals and be part of the implementation plan. For example, the newspaper Web manager would examine the data from Web-site page views weekly, with special attention to page views on the classified ad pages. Every 2 weeks or so, the managers would discuss the results to see if they need to change the promotion that draws people to the free ads. Of course, they might have to deal with problems from having more free ads than were anticipated. A rush for free ads could increase the expenses more than anticipated, generating new problems.

A timetable is crucial to the monitoring system. A solution that is not working should be given an adequate test, but a media organization should not remain committed to a solution once it becomes obvious that it will not accomplish the goal. Deadlines should be set for deciding to continue or end the plan.

This monitoring process makes the entire decision process cyclical. If the solution does not work, this becomes a problem that starts a new cycle of decision making. A new cycle requires the same steps, but some may take less time and effort because the previous decision process already provides relevant information. However, managers must always be careful not to assume that they have all the information they need. An effective manager continues to acquire information until the cost of additional information outweighs the probable benefit from having that information.

Constraints on the Decision Process

The decision wheel is an ideal. It is a blueprint that is seldom followed exactly because of practical constraints falling into two types: (a) who makes the decision, and (b) time available for the decision.

Decision Makers

Both individuals and groups make decisions. Whether a group or individual makes the decisions will influence the efficiency and effectiveness of the decision. In some cases, individuals may decide best. In other cases, group decisions work better. Huber (1980) listed three advantages and four disadvantages of group decisions, whereas Harrison (1987) gave nine strengths and four weaknesses. Griffin and Moorhead (1986) presented six advantages of group decision making and three advantages of individual decision making. Table 1.1 summarizes the advantages and disadvantages of group decision making and categorizes them under the headings of timing, uncertainty, and goals.

TABLE 1.1 Advantages and Disadvantages of Group Decision Making

Advantages	Disadvantages
Timing	
Slower decision process	Slower decision process
Division of labor for complex task	Disagreement over goals may result in no decisions
Uncertainty	
Larger amounts of information	Political behavior of group members and knowledge generated reduces acceptance of information from others
Fewer errors in analyzing information	Groupthink or the tendency of group members to think the group is infallible
More alternatives generated	
Goals	
Groups can clarify goal understanding	Groups sometimes act in ways inconsistent with goals
Participation increases acceptance	Groupthink of group goals

Interestingly, weaknesses of group decision making can also be strengths. For example, one of the advantages and disadvantages of group decision making is its slow process. Group decision making usually increases the time needed for a decision because of problems in organizing meetings and in the long process of forming consensus among people with conflicting positions. An individual decision maker does not have these timing problems. Whether the time element is an advantage or a disadvantage depends on the decision. If timing is crucial, individuals make quicker decisions. If timing is not crucial and risk and uncertainty are high, a slower process has advantages.

Deadlines exemplify the timing importance in news departments. News stories do not get used if they are not ready by the printing or broadcast deadlines. Therefore, individuals make most decisions about what stories will run. However, important stories are exceptions to this rule. An example of a group decision involving a news story is the case of the Pentagon Papers. The Pentagon Papers were a secret report about the history of the Vietnam War. They were prepared in the late 1960s for Secretary of Defense Robert S. McNamara, who served for President Lyndon Johnson. *The New York Times* got the report from Daniel Ellsberg, who helped prepare it. After four installments of the Papers ran in *The New York Times* in June 1971, a federal court issued a restraining order. Meanwhile *The Washington Post* had obtained a copy of the report. A group of 10 managers at the *Post* met for 12 hours to discuss whether they should publish parts of the report. They published (Witcover, 1971).

The inherent lack of speed in group decisions is not the only advantage or disadvantage of groups. In complex tasks, groups have the advantage of division of labor. Dividing tasks among group members can actually speed the process because no one person must learn the wide range of complex information required for complex decisions. For example, a new computer system for a newspaper often serves multiple departments; so it would make sense to include someone from each of these departments in the decision making. It is easier to have people from each department who know the departments' computer needs than to have one or two people learn about the computer needs of all the departments.

Advantages and disadvantages of group decisions also fall under the heading of uncertainty. Group decision making can reduce uncertainty in three ways. First, having more than one decision maker brings more information and knowledge to the process. Second, it can decrease the number of errors. The cliché that two heads are better than one applies here. Having more people also can reduce information errors because people can evaluate each other's information and analysis. Third, groups generate more alternative solutions. The ability to compare alternatives with each other can result in better solutions.

Although uncertainty will decline with some groups, it can increase with others. The probabilities that develop from the satisficing approach are subjective. The attitudes and perceptions of other group members influence this subjectivity. Political behavior among group members can create doubt as to appropriate goals and desirability of solutions. For instance, when a city editor and sports editor try to persuade other group members that each department is key to improving quality, the process of persuasion can cast doubt on either department's effectiveness at attracting readers, resulting in uncertainty of actions.

Just as dangerous as political behavior, which can divide, is *groupthink,* which occurs when group members are so set on sustaining unanimity that they fail to properly appraise the alternative solutions (Janis, 1982). Although the group feels it has reduced uncertainty because it agreed on the best alternative, it actually decreased the probability that any one solution will work. The solution does not get an adequate evaluation.

The final heading in Table 1.1 is goals. Because of the number of people involved, groups often develop a better understanding of the organization and decision group goals. Reading a statement of goals adopted by an organization does not automatically mean that the employees understand those goals. Hearing others discuss the goals can help clarify them.

Another advantage is that participation in group decision making will increase acceptance of the goals and solutions that are adopted. Increased acceptance can translate into increased effort in accomplishing the goals. People tend to accept more readily those decisions in which they participated.

A disadvantage of group decisions with respect to goals is the tendency of some groups to develop their own goals, which may be inconsistent with the organization goals. For example, a group set up within a media organization to develop ways to cut costs may decide that cost cutting is not a proper goal, resulting in a conflict of goals between management and the decision group. Resulting decisions are less likely to accomplish the aims of management. Many of the disadvantages of group decision making result from the political behavior that comes from managers delegating authority to others. However, not all decisions take the same form (Miller, Hickson, & Wilson, 1996), and some decisions could benefit from the political process if the process is fair, open, and builds consensus for a decision that has an outcome consistent with the overall organizational goals.

The many advantages and disadvantages of group decisions create problems for deciding when groups or individuals should make decisions. Vroom and Yetton (1973) said that individual managers are likely to make decisions when the problem is well structured, information is plentiful, a previously successful solution to a similar problem is available, and time constraints require a quick decision.

Individual Decision-Making Styles

As with all human skills, managers vary in the style of decision making they use. A decision-making style has to do with common patterns of reaching decisions. Most managers exhibit more than one style, but often a particular style emerges under pressure.

Driver, Brousseau, and Hunsaker (1993) identified decision style by the way managers use information and how they focus on solutions. *Use of information* involved either satisficing or maximizing. As mentioned earlier, satisficing requires collecting information to reach a satisfactory conclusion that may not result in as good a result as possible. Maximizing involves collecting information until a decision maker has enough to reach what he or she feels is the best decision. The difference is related to how long the decision makers will collect information before acting.

Solution focus concerns the use of data to identify possible solutions. *Unifocus* people collect information and identify one solution they think is best, whereas *multifocus* people collect information and provide a variety of solutions to a problem.

These two dimensions were combined to produce the following five decision styles:

Decisive style. This style involves people who are satisficers and are unifocus with respect to solutions. These people collect a limited amount of information and act quickly. Once they identify their solution, they are unwavering in their support of that solution.

Flexible style. Flexible decision makers are satisficers who have multifocus on solutions. They also act on limited information, but they show more flexibility in using solutions. If one solution fails to work, they turn to another.

Hierarchical style. This style involves maximizing and unifocus. These decision makers act slowly because they collect large amounts of information to select the one best solution among those being considered, which is pursued using a detailed plan.

Integrative style. People using this style are maximizers with multifocus solutions. They tend to take their time in collecting and evaluating information, but unlike the hierarchical style, these people do not believe the problem has one "best" solution.

Systemic style. This style incorporates both the integrative and hierarchical styles in a two-step process. The first step involves using the integrative style of evaluating large amounts of information and dealing with multiple solutions. The second step is more hierarchical in that the solutions are prioritized with one or more criteria being considered the best. This style is more contemplative than the hierarchical style, but involves more organized and active solutions than the integrative style.

These types of decision-maker classifications can be useful in understanding decision making, but care must be taken. Often managers exhibit a combination of these styles with individual decisions and in decisions across time. The usefulness of the classification is its emphasis on types of goals (satisficing and maximizing) and nature of focus (unifocus or multifocus).

Time and Decision Making

In addition to classifying decisions by type of decision-making style, decisions can be broken down based on time available. Three general timing patterns seem appropriate. Nonprogrammed decisions can be classified as (a) immediate, (b) short term, or (c) long term. Immediate decisions must be made quickly. The time available between Steps 1 and 5 in the decision wheel is measured in hours or even minutes. Story decisions on deadline are the prime examples in media.

As a result of deadlines, it is common to find individuals making content decisions at newspapers, magazines, and TV news departments. However, the deadline pressure hides the danger that individuals will begin making *all* decisions quickly and alone out of habit. In effect, managers generate informal and even unconscious rules rather than evaluate problems. No decision should be made before time requires it. If a decision does not need to be made immediately, participation of others should be sought.

Short-term decisions need not be made immediately, but they must be made within a reasonable time. At a newspaper, the plans for a breakdown of news and advertising space for the coming week would be short term.

Small groups usually make these decisions even if one person has responsibility. For example, the publisher, who has final authority for space in a newspaper, may meet with the advertising manager and editor to determine news holes for a week. Often the publisher has determined a breakdown for the year between news and advertising space. The meetings are monitoring sessions by which the three managers discuss news—editorial needs in light of the year's goal, previous use of space, and the newsroom space needs for the week.

Long-term decisions affect the organization over a period of years and, therefore, warrant a longer decision-making process. This type of decision includes selecting network news anchors and format changes at a magazine or newspaper. Because of their complexity, these decisions require participation by a large number of people in groups and as individuals. In effect, a long-term decision, such as what next year's budget should be, requires hundreds or thousands of smaller decisions.

Overall, time constrains the process shown in the decision wheel. Each step has a time limit that determines how much information can be collected, how much analysis can be conducted, and how many people can participate in the decision. Immediate decisions allow little time for each step and for information collection and analysis. Long-term decisions should include adequate time for each step.

The timing of various types of decisions places a premium on different types of managers. When an immediate decision is needed, a satisfactory solution is more important than an optimal solution. Therefore, the person with command of a great deal of information in an area and who can analyze quickly will perform best. This person need not be as good at working with people as a manager who deals with short- and long-term problems. Decisive and flexible decision styles work well here.

A manager faced with short-term decisions needs people skills and the ability to reach decisions within a reasonable time. In contrast, managers who must make long-term decisions are better served by skills that allow them to work with people and examine a problem from several angles. This person should be good at analysis, but an analysis with a different time frame. This manager must be good at developing many alternatives and evaluating them against each other. The variation of needed skills explains why some people make better upper-level managers, such as editor, than lower-level managers, such as assistant city editor. Long-term decisions that involve high risk and uncertainty work best with integrative or systemic styles for decision makers.

The key to effective decision making is to put people in positions where their abilities fit the job requirements and then train them in the areas where they are weakest. The ability to understand and handle time constraints is essential if a person is to be promoted within the media organization.

Tools of Management

Just as time constrains decision making, so does the quality of information and analysis, which relates directly to the skills of the decision maker. As with all skills, collecting and analyzing information can be improved through learning. This section briefly addresses the sources of information and some of the tools of analysis.

Sources of Information

Because information plays so important a role in all six steps, we should examine where we get information. Basically, information comes either from our own efforts or the efforts of others. The efforts can take various forms, however, and those forms can affect the quality of information. The two main types of efforts are (a) experience and (b) research. *Experience* involves participating in events or processes, and *research* is the application of generally accepted systematic methods of examining events or processes. Someone who works at a news magazine has experience in magazine journalism. Someone who conducts a survey of news magazine reporters researches magazine journalism. Experience differs from research in that it does not have accepted standards for analyzing data. Experience is inseparable from the person having the experience. Yet a researcher, if conducting research properly, should have a limited impact on the events or processes being studied.

Research should be more objective and systematic than experience. *Should be* are important words because quality of research depends on the researcher's skills, just as quality of experience depends on the wisdom of the person experiencing the event. A manager can analyze her or his experience systematically and somewhat objectively, just as a researcher inadvertently can alter the result of his research through poor use of methods.

Managers have roughly four sources of information: (a) their experiences, (b) the experiences of others, (c) their research, and the (d) research of others. Media managers often depend on their experiences and the experiences of trusted colleagues. Experience is specific to a particular situation—an advantage when a decision must be made about a situation similar to previous events. However, using your experience becomes a liability when you apply that experience to a problem that differs from the original experience. The result is often a poor decision.

Managers should know the value of all forms of information and seek many diverse sources of information, especially in the monitoring step. A successful manager analyzes past decisions so the next decision is more effective. The results of every decision should become information for future decisions, but the usefulness of this information depends on the ability to use tools of analysis.

Evaluating Information

As the decision wheel illustrates, information and its analysis lie at the center of effective decision making. The invention and development of computers, personal computers in particular, have generated a flood of information that can help or hurt managers in making decisions. Computers have created this information flood for two reasons. First, they allow for the faster collection and manipulation of data about all types of human behavior. From sales information to surfing on the Internet, computers collect data in minutes that would have taken days or months before computers. As computers have grown faster and smaller, more data can be processed more quickly. Second, computers allow the instantaneous distribution of large amounts of information anywhere in the world. Multiple employees of an organization can share the same information at the same time, so group decisions can be made in a more timely fashion. This allows decision makers to live in different parts of the world and still make group decisions.

Of course, computers also have reshaped the way media organizations distribute information to consumers, but this impact defines the type of decisions for media companies more than the decision process. Media companies experience the same impact of computers on the decision process as all organizations. Information is more accessible now than it has ever been, but accessibility does not guarantee accuracy. Accessibility concerns how easily a given piece of information is to obtain. The Internet and other information distribution systems have made information much more accessible. However, this availability may be a Trojan horse allowing information into the decision process that could lower the effectiveness of decisions.

Accuracy of information concerns whether the depiction of human behavior in numbers or words is a valid representation for that behavior. For example, if a readership survey supposedly represents what readers think about a magazine, the issue of accuracy addresses whether it truly does. Computers certainly make information more accessible, but whether information becomes more accurate depends on by whom and how the information was generated. Although an excellent researcher can use computers to generate even more accurate information, an incompetent one will provide only more inaccurate information.

Before using information for decisions, managers need to determine whether the accuracy of that information is sufficient to make effective decisions. The accuracy level of information involves probability. Little information used for making decisions is 100% accurate if for no other reason than decisions involve future actions and the future is always uncertain. However, some information is more accurate than other information, and managers need to evaluate information level of accuracy. Because the only true test of information accuracy is how well it can predict future behavior and events, accuracy can only be estimated. The following steps can be useful in evaluating information accuracy:

1. Decide whether the material under consideration is information or opinion. *Information* is a description of behavior or phenomena, whereas *opinion* is a person's belief about the behavior or phenomena. An example of information is the evaluation of accounting data that show publicly owned newspapers are more likely to have a smaller percentage of revenues devoted to the newsroom budget than do privately owned newspapers. An example of an opinion is a statement from a critic that publicly owned newspapers do not spend enough money on their newsroom budgets. The information is a statement about budgeting behavior, and the opinion concerns whether the budgeting behavior is good or bad. Opinion often masquerades as information. A person not trained in data analysis might interpret the accounting data incorrectly. Without proper training on how to analyze data, the conclusions from the data will be no better than opinions and can even lead to ineffective decisions because the manager mistook the opinion for information.

2. Know accepted procedure for creating information. The process of creating accurate information has certain procedures accepted as appropriate by scientists and scholars who use the scientific method or critical method to generate information. Whether the information is

considered valid depends on the procedure used. Journalists also have generally accepted rules for reporting and writing stories. However, the two processes differ because scholars must report their method as part of their scholarship, whereas journalists are not expected to do so.

3. Managers, who use information to make decisions, should understand research procedures considered appropriate by the community of scholars and scientists. Knowing the methods for creating information allows decision makers the ability to evaluate its accuracy. Media managers should understand how surveys and content analysis are conducted so they can evaluate the research methods and ask researchers intelligent questions if they doubt the accuracy of information they are supplied.

4. Know who created the information you use. Even if managers understand research methods, and especially if they do not, it is a good idea that the sources of information be identified and evaluated. As mentioned, not all researchers and journalists are equal in their ability to generate accurate information. When acquiring information for decisions, a manager should know the source of the information. This explains why companies often have their own research division; if they do not, they tend to use a research company proven to produce information that has resulted in effective decisions. One of the great problems of the Internet is that sources and method of information are often absent.

Cost-Benefit Analysis

A manager with few analytical skills or little knowledge and experience will end up depending on others to judge the reliability and validity of information. Managers who understand analysis are in a better position to select information appropriate for decisions. Analysis involves ways of processing information. Several different types of analysis, which vary in complexity, can be used.

Perhaps the most recognized analytical tool is cost-benefit analysis, which is an attempt to estimate the costs and benefits that would result from alternative actions. McKean (1975) listed five steps: (a) identifying benefits to be achieved, (b) identifying alternatives that will reach the goal, (c) identifying costs for the alternative methods, (d) developing a model or set of relationships that explain the impact of alternatives on the costs and benefits, and (e) a criterion involving both costs and benefits for selecting the preferred alternative. These steps sound familiar because they correspond to steps of the decision wheel and they involve evaluating information.

The traditional approach to cost-benefit analysis is to place a monetary value on all costs and benefits and compare the resulting differences (Huber, 1980). Because this is difficult to do with many types of costs, cost-benefit analysis may include the "dollar-equivalency technique" (Huber, 1980, p. 80), which is the development of money equivalents for costs that are difficult to measure in dollars. Obviously, this becomes problematic when costs and benefits involve human behavior.

Two concepts are useful in dealing with the nonmonetary aspects of cost-benefit analysis: (a) opportunity costs and (b) intangibles. *Opportunity costs* include the expenses that accrue from giving up alternative actions. It is equivalent to the old saying, "There is no free lunch." For every alternative selected, a person loses what he or she would have gained from another alternative. For example, a manager hiring a reporter must pick from two candidates. The first is stronger at writing and the second is stronger at reporting. If the first is hired, an opportunity cost is the reporting ability that will be lost from not hiring the second. If the second is hired, an opportunity cost is the writing skill that will be lost from not hiring the first.

Intangibles are the things that cannot be measured well. An intangible may be leadership in a manager or the ability of some people to raise morale in an organization. Whatever the attribute, a dollar amount cannot be adequately assigned. Intangibles are often ignored in formal tools of analysis because they cannot be measured well.

Opportunity costs and intangibles are the Achilles heel of cost-benefit analysis and most other types of formal analysis. These two concepts relate to all decisions, although sometimes they are more important than at other times. Despite these two problems, cost-benefit analysis can be useful even if it simply allows a manager to think more clearly. The following example demonstrates the potential use of cost-benefit analysis in a situation where quantification is difficult.

The *Times-Leader* recently conducted a readership survey in which 48% of the readers said they would like to have more in-depth local coverage. Managing Editor Jane Smith was assigned to come up with a plan for doing this. Her first observation was that it can be done either by hiring a new reporter or using existing staff. She came up with the benefits and advantages presented in Table 1.2.

The monetary benefits for either alternative are equal in Table 1.2 and amount to $54,000 per year. These benefits are based on retaining 250 readers a year and attracting 250 more readers annually as a result of increased in-depth coverage. Two main areas of monetary benefits are saving $4,000 from not having to replace the 250 readers and making

TABLE 1.2 Cost–Benefit Analysis of Increasing In-Depth Reporting at the *Times-Leader*

	Alternatives	
Costs	**Hiring a Reporter**	**Using Existing Staff**
Monetary	$30,000 a year salary	$10,000 a year additional overtime
	$5,000 a year expense for travel & research	$5,000 a year expenses for travel & research
	$13,000 for 26 additional pages at cost of $500 per page	$13,000 for 26 additional pages at cost of $500 per page
Opportunity	Dissatisfaction among existing staff because they will not be allowed to do in-depth work	Use of staff for in-depth reporting will reduce time for day-to-day reporting
	Editing time lost on day-to-day coverage due to increased editing needs of day-to-day coverage	Editing time lost on day-to-day coverage due to increased editing needs of day-to-day coverage
Intangible	Possible negative impact of new reporter in the newsroom	Added effort needed to balance in-depth reporting
Benefits		
Monetary	Save $4,000 needed to gain 250 lost readers	Save $4,000 needed to gain 250 lost readers
	Save $50,000 in advertising revenue that could be lost with decline of 500 readers	Save $50,000 in advertising revenue that could be lost with decline of 500 readers
Intangible	Increased morale among staff from increased quality of the newspaper	Increased morale among staff from increased quality of the newspaper
	Promotional value of expected recognition from in-depth coverage	Promotional value of expected recognition from in-depth coverage
		Increased staff morale for those who do in-depth reporting

Note: The goal is to increase the amount of in-depth coverage by one page every 2 weeks.

Benefits are based on an estimated retention of 250 readers and attracting 250 new readers resulting from increased in-depth coverage.

$50,000 in advertising revenue that would be lost if the 500 readers were not taking the newspaper.

Both approaches also have intangible benefits in the form of staff morale and the promotional advantage of having in-depth coverage that will generate recognition of the newspaper's journalistic efforts. The use of existing staff has an added advantage in that it will increase staff morale because reporters will be allowed to spend time on more lengthy projects.

Monetary costs of hiring an additional reporter are about $20,000 more a year because the new reporter would earn $30,000 a year, whereas overtime needed to use existing staff would only amount to $10,000. Both alternatives have opportunity costs. Each alternative would require about the same amount of additional editing, which would have to come from the time spent on editing of day-to-day stories.

Two opportunity costs and two intangible costs stand out as important factors. First, hiring a new reporter could create dissatisfaction among the existing staff who would like to pursue in-depth reporting. Reporters usually look on in-depth work as a kind of reward because it is more satisfying and interesting than most day-to-day coverage. However, taking time from day-to-day coverage has the opportunity cost of reducing the amount of space and effort spent on everyday reporting. This could negatively affect circulation.

The intangible costs also involve the staff reaction to a new plan. If a new reporter is hired, he or she may alter the chemistry among people in the newsroom. This impact, combined with the possible resentment, may have negative consequences. Yet a new reporter might add to the newsroom chemistry. Whether this becomes a cost would depend on who is hired as the new reporter. The use of existing staff means an added cost for the editors because they must ensure that the in-depth assignments are distributed fairly. Otherwise staff resentment could develop.

By examining Table 1.2, a manager could see that which approach to take comes down to whether the additional $20,000 cost of a new reporter and the potential newsroom disruption exceeds the impact of reducing the day-to-day coverage in the newspaper. This, in turn, is related to the adequacy of the current staff. If the newsroom already is understaffed, expanding the work required could be disastrous. More readers might drop the paper because of poor day-to-day coverage than would take the paper because of increased in-depth reporting. To make an appropriate selection, a manager needs to have an understanding of the nature of the reporters currently working and an awareness of the informal organizational setting in the newsroom.

This illustration demonstrates that many of the costs and benefits are not quantifiable, but this should not lead to these costs and benefits being ignored. A second point is that the analysis is only as good as the information that goes into it. The monetary costs and benefits should be accurate, but the knowledge of how the people in the newsroom will react needs to be just as reliable and valid.

Summary

Decision making is the heart of managing. The process can be depicted as a formal process based on bounded rationality, as a process of applying rules to situations, or as a political process by which groups within an organization exercise power to achieve goals. Under assumptions of bounded rationality, decisions are either *programmed*, which means the solutions take effect under prescribed conditions, or *nonprogrammed*, which requires attention to the individual problems that must be solved. Nonprogrammed decisions are more difficult to make. Programmed decisions were originally set up by nonprogrammed decisions.

Decisions can also be classified as proactive and reactive. *Proactive* decisions anticipate changes in the environment that will affect the organization, and *reactive* decisions are made as a result of environmental changes.

Reaching decisions has an abstract form presented here as a decision wheel. The steps in this wheel occur to some degree in all effective decisions, although the time and effort devoted to the individual steps vary with the conditions surrounding the individual problem.

Just as decision making is at the heart of management, analysis and information collection are the hubs of decisions. Both lack of information and poor analysis of information account for a high percentage of decisions that fail to achieve their goals. Several tools are available to improve analysis and information collecting, including social science theories and cost-benefit analysis.

As with the majority of human endeavors, management can be made better with thought and practice. The remainder of this book is designed to facilitate thought and provide practice through cases. Each chapter also presents background information to help explore the cases. The principles, theories, and research presented in the early part of the chapter should be used to analyze the information that is provided with the case or needs to be collected from outside sources. In all cases, the decision process applies.

Case 1.1 Looking at Past Decisions

People often make important decisions without properly preparing or fully examining the decision process. The purpose of this assignment is to have you think about your decision-making process by concentrating on a specific decision. Select an important decision (choosing a college or college major, moving in with someone, etc.) that you made during the past few years that has disappointed you. Think about how you made that decision and why you were disappointed. Using the decision wheel from this chapter, try to remember the actions you took that would have fit into the various steps in the wheel.

Assignment

Write a brief summary of the decision and then answer the following questions:

1. Did you take all of the steps in the decision wheel? If not, which ones were not taken and why?
2. Did you complete each step as thoroughly as you should have? If not, which ones were not completed thoroughly and why?
3. If you could make that decision over again, what would you do differently to improve your decision?

Case 1.2 Specifying Goals and Developing Solutions

KDLD-TV in Centerville was just bought by Big Corporation (BC), which currently owns the local daily newspaper and the local radio station with a news-talk format. BC bought the TV station in order to share the journalism of the three organizations across the three media. Members of the class all serve as managers at these three news organizations. The class should be divided into groups of three to five people and given the following assignments, which the entire class will share and discuss. Before breaking into groups, class members should ask questions about the assignment, so all groups will start with the same understanding of the assignment.

1. Specify at least three goals, in as much detail as possible, that should be pursued now that the same company owns these three news organizations. These goals should address the outcome of sharing the journalism created by the newspaper, radio station, and TV station.
2. Develop at least three alternative ways that could help achieve the goals that were specified in number 1. In what ways can the journalism be shared to accomplish the goals from number 1?

3. Each group should present their goals and solutions to the class, and the class should discuss the process by which the groups came up with different goals and solutions

Case 1.3 Improving the Web Site

Your newspaper, *The Daily Bugle,* currently places its staff-produced content on its Web site. In addition, it has recently added a reporter to produce daily copy just for the site. However, the publisher is still not convinced that these efforts will build the page views that are necessary to sell more online advertising. She knows that local businesses are skeptical that enough people visit the *Bugle* Web site to make advertising effective. Currently, the site is really just an electronic version of the print newspaper.

Assignment

Generate ideas for how to draw more users to the Web site and make them visit regularly. Develop additional methods of generating content for the site, prioritize them as to how likely they are to generate repeat users of the site, and provide information to support the priorities you assign.

Use the Web to identify particular elements of Web sites that might be attractive to people in a community and find research that explains how people currently use such elements. The research may be available online, in databases such as Lexis/Nexis or in newspapers and magazines found in the library.

Finally, develop your analysis as a cost-benefit analysis with two of your ideas.

2

LEADERSHIP AND THE WORKFORCE

At no time in the history of the modern media industry has leadership been more important than now. During most of the 20th century, newspapers, broadcast stations, and television networks were considered to have a "license to print money." Today, however, mushrooming competition, changing technologies, and impatient investors make the media management environment highly challenging. Success depends on the ability of a media manager to understand the issues facing the industry, develop a vision for meeting those challenges, and inspire colleagues to adopt that vision and realize it. In short, success depends on the media manager's leadership ability.

Able leadership is particularly critical in the media industry because media are *talent* products (Reca, 2005). A talent product's quality depends heavily on the producer's individual talent, knowledge, and experience. Not just anyone can replace talent such as Katie Couric, Christiane Amanpour, Jon Stewart, and Steven Spielberg. The same is true for top scriptwriters, photographers, producers, and other behind-the-scenes media professionals. This dependence on employees' talent makes the ability to find and retain good people critical for media companies. Finding and inspiring top people is the essence of leadership.

The Foundations of Leadership

If your actions inspire others to dream more, learn more, do more, and become more, you are a leader—John Quincy Adams

Eighty percent of what makes [you] successful is believing in yourself. A lot of people don't try because they're afraid to fail. Most people would rather follow than lead because it's safer.—Richard D. Parsons, CEO, Time Warner, (Quoted in Clark, 2005).

Early studies of leadership focused on leadership traits, raising the perennial question of whether leaders are born or made. Today, experts in leadership acknowledge that some people are "natural" leaders, gifted with confidence and charisma difficult for others to learn or imitate. However, whether natural leaders or not, most people have a natural leadership "style," an approach to leadership they tend to adopt when thrust into leadership positions.

Despite these "born" tendencies, people can develop or improve their leadership abilities if they understand leadership traits, skills, and styles. Furthermore, many leadership experts argue that success-ful leadership depends on combining the style and skills of the leader, the styles and skills of the followers, and the specific conditions of the working environment (Fiedler, 1967; Hersey & Blanchard, 1982; House & Dessler, 1974; Hughes, Ginnett, & Curphy, 1999). In other words, even the most gifted born leaders will fail miserably if their traits and styles do not match their followers or the circumstances. On the other hand, even the most unlikely leaders may succeed if they develop their leadership skills and understand their followers and situation.

Leadership Traits and Skills

Research has identified a long list of traits common to effective lead-ers As the word "trait" suggests, many of these characteristics come more naturally to some people than others, although most individu-als can probably improve at least somewhat in these areas with effort. Although individual lists of traits vary, common characteristics include intelligence, ambition, self-confidence, expertise, charisma, creativity, perseverance, flexibility, commitment, integrity, the ability to inspire and motivate others, and the ability to envision what the future ought to be. Students of leadership argue that of all of these characteristics, vision is most important.

It is not enough, of course, just to have vision. Successful leader-ship demands that leaders transform their visions into realities. It is in executing the plans that makes vision into reality that most leaders fail. Bridging that gap requires planning (see chapter 7) and leadership skills. *Skills* are abilities that can be developed with training and effort. Central among the required leadership skills are (a) communication and listening skills, (b) empowerment, (c) coaching, (d) delegation, (e) assertiveness, (f) decisiveness, (g) problem solving, (h) goal setting, (i) conflict management, and (j) negotiation.

Communication, which includes *listening skills*, is arguably the single most important skill a leader must have. Leaders must communicate their vision, goals, and instructions clearly and in terms that motivate and inspire. Some managers cling to the idea that information is power and, thus, communicate as little as possible with subordinates. Employees who constantly receive partial or misleading information quickly stop trusting the boss. Skilled leaders communicate effectively through formal channels, such as memos, e-mail, speeches, and meetings, and informally in casual conversation and social settings. Regardless of the channel, failure to communicate leads to misdirection, misunderstandings, inefficiency, and lost trust.

Nonverbal communication is another important element of leadership communication. How leaders dress, carry themselves, and interact with others communicates much about their power, self-confidence, and expectations for their employees' dress and behavior. Managers who sit behind their desks with arms folded when talking with subordinates communicate a lack of receptivity. The newspaper sales manager who gives full attention to male staff members but doesn't look up when female subordinates talk to him communicates loudly. Employees monitor their boss' every move and expression, looking for signs of trouble. The news director who comes into the office every morning wearing a scowl because of the bad commute soon will have the entire newsroom on edge.

Listening skills are no less important than verbal communication; skilled leaders are active listeners, giving the speaker full attention, ignoring cell phone, e-mail, or other interruptions. They ask questions, take notes, and rephrase back to the speaker what was said to make sure they understood correctly. More importantly, they act on advice and suggestions from employees. When managers tell employees, "My door is always open," or "I really want to hear what you think," but never act on their input, they tell subordinates that the boss' posture of openness is a sham.

Communication and listening skills play a role in other leadership skills such as empowering, coaching, and delegating. Leaders *empower* subordinates by seeking their input on important decisions, trusting them to succeed at critical tasks without constant supervision, and permitting them to find their own ways to accomplish goals as long as the goals are accomplished. A former executive editor of a Midwest newspaper loudly told newsroom visitors, "This newspaper is successful because I hire smart, terrific people, and then I get the hell out of their way and let them make me look like a hero!" His public declarations powerfully communicated to the staff his trust, empowerment, and high expectations.

With such trust, managers can delegate some of their responsibilities. *Delegation* allows them to focus on tasks that can't be shared, such as the development of vision and strategy. However, delegating requires having employees ready and able to take on additional responsibilities. The leader must develop those capabilities through coaching and mentoring.

Assertiveness and *decisiveness* also are key leadership skills. Leaders and managers must be comfortable confronting problems, advocating for their own, their organization's, and their employees' needs, and telling people when they don't meet expectations. Decisiveness is equally important: An editor who dithers in a breaking-news situation or a leader who can't quickly make tough decisions loses subordinates' confidence. However, decisiveness does not mean refusing to change course once the chosen course appears wrong; effective leaders constantly seek and evaluate new information and admit when they've made a mistake. Decisiveness does not equal blind stubbornness, the fear of admitting mistakes, or the illusion of personal infallibility; all can afflict people in leadership positions—often with disastrous consequences.

Assertiveness enters into conflict management, negotiation, and problem solving, which are all important leadership skills. *Conflict* is a natural part of any organization and can be a healthy and creative force. Fear of conflict creates a passive, change-averse environment that slows development and excellence. On the other hand, uncontrolled conflict is a destructive force, causing good people to leave a company and encouraging the survivors to focus on defeating their internal rivals rather than on achieving mutual success. A leader has to manage conflicts at organizational and individual levels, allowing differences to surface, be aired, and to contribute to change and development, but not allowing them to evolve into running feuds or disruptive outbursts. In the very public, high-pressure, ego-driven world of media professionals, conflict is inevitable. Assertiveness and conflict-management skills are particularly important for media leaders.

Conflict management requires negotiating skills. Skilled negotiators focus on win-win solutions allowing all parties to save face and gain something. Effective negotiations focus on the interests at stake, not the positions the parties take (Fisher, Ury, & Patton, 1991). Well-managed negotiations serve everyone's interests to some degree and leave relationships undamaged.

Finally, problem solving and goal setting are the core of a leader's responsibilities. Most of a leader's activities involve *problem solving* at some level, while *goal setting* is a necessary step in any effort to translate vision into reality. Setting goals is harder than it looks. Leaders often fail to do it effectively, if they do it at all. For example, most newspaper publishers in one study said their goal for their new online editions was for them to be "successful" (Saksena & Hollifield, 2002). Such fuzzy goals rarely materialize because there is no specific definition by which to measure "success." Well-defined goals are *SMART*: *Specific, Measurable, Attainable, Related to the organization's larger goal*, and *Time-bound* (Nelson & Economy, 1996). Chapter 1 in this book discusses decision making and chapter 7 discusses planning and problem solving. Both chapters discuss the processes of problem solving and goal attainment in detail.

Leadership Styles, Followership Styles, and Situations

Leadership style refers to the way a leader works with subordinates and superiors, including how much autonomy subordinates have, how much emphasis is placed on subordinates' personal goals and development, and whether the leader makes accomplishment of the task or the maintenance of collegial relationship most important. Leadership styles relate to the decision-making styles discussed in chapter 1 but involve more than just decisions.

Most leadership theories argue that there is no "best" style of leadership, despite the popular press' fondness for "humanistic" and "transformational" leadership. In reality, successful leadership requires leaders to respond to their followers and the situation. However, experts describe leadership styles in many ways. Some styles focus on the relationship between organizational culture and individual leadership. Others focus on individual leadership styles.

Theory X, Theory Y, and Theory Z

Theories X, Y, and Z pose one of the more common frameworks for understanding differences in leadership styles and explain the connection between organizational structure, culture, and leadership.

Theory X refers to a top-down, authoritarian style in which supervisors command and subordinates obey (McGregor, 1960/2006) Theory X leadership typically exists in highly structured, hierarchical organizations where members' status derives from their job title and lines of authority are clear. Subordinates may have some input in Theory X environments, but when a decision is made, compliance is expected. The military is the most obvious example of this style; other examples include police and fire departments and airline and ship crews. These types of organizations use Theory X because it is most effective when people work in changeable, potentially dangerous, or extremely time-pressured conditions—reasons the media-industry newsroom management often displays elements of Theory X.

Experts often describe *Theory Y* leadership as a "humanistic" or "human-needs-oriented" style (McGregor, 1960/2006). Theory Y leaders strive to create harmony between the organization's and employees' goals. Generally found in more decentralized, horizontally structured organizations, Theory Y leaders give workers some power and autonomy. The approach assumes most people are self-motivated and produce better results if they control their own work and if their work fits with their personal goals and values. Media also widely use Theory Y, particularly in the creative industries and new media.

Theory Z leadership (Ouichi 1981), often referred to as "Japanese-Style Management," first attracted attention in the 1980s when Japanese industry became a major global competitor. Theory Z combines elements of X and Y. Theory Z organizations tend to be hierarchically structured, with the opportunity and expectation that employees at the hierarchy's bottom will be consulted by senior management on issues within their expertise. In return, workers take personal responsibility for the quality of the product and the success of the organization.

Theory Z management requires a high level of trust, loyalty, and mutual respect across all levels of the company. It works well in organizations where managers and employees expect workers to stay with the company for most or all of their careers. However, today's competitive economy prohibits many organizations from making long-term commitments to workers. As workers' employment security erodes worldwide, Theory Z leadership is harder to find—even in Japan.

For those who might wonder why these approaches to leadership are called Theories X, Y, and Z, the terms don't have any special significance. The author of Theory X and Theory Y designated them as such simply to "avoid the complications introduced by a label" (McGregor, 1957, as cited in McGregor, 1960/2006, p. 341). Theory Z , which came later, was so named by its author (Ouichi, 1981), because it built on McGregor's earlier work.

Individual Leadership Styles

Leadership experts have identified many different individual leadership styles. Although different scholars use different names, the terms and phrases (a) authoritarian, (b) expert, (c) consensus building, (d) coaching, and (e) hands-off summarize the range of styles generally discussed.

Authoritarian leaders use Theory X style with subordinates. *Expert leaders* rely on their own expertise as their source of authority and tend to emphasize standards and rules. *Consensus builders* tend to work in groups, building consensus among members. *Coaches* focus on mentoring their staff, being directive when necessary and empowering when possible. *Hands-off leaders* generally don't involve themselves in daily tasks and functions, leaving front-line decisions to others.

Most people probably use more than one of these approaches, and individuals' styles often change with time and experience. However, at any given time, an individual is probably more comfortable with some of these styles than with others.

Another important element of leadership style is task-relationship orientation. Originally identified in the 1940s and 1950s (Hughes, Ginnett, & Curphy, 1999), leaders' orientation toward tasks and relationships has worked its way into many leadership theories. The *task-relationship orientation* basically argues that some leaders are more concerned about job-related tasks, while others focus on maintaining good relationships with colleagues. Whether one approach is more effective is debated among leadership scholars, but several theories suggested the answer depends on the combination of followers and the situation.

Leading Followers

Leaders do not operate in a vacuum. They accomplish their goals primarily through followers' activities. Effective leaders understand the strengths and weaknesses of the people working around them and adjust their leadership style accordingly.

Leading a staff of media professionals can be challenging; as a rule, media professionals are highly educated and self-motivated (Weaver, Beam, Brownlee, Voakes, & Wilhoit, 2003). Media production is a creative activity, so "artistic personalities" abound. On the news side, journalists make their living by asking tough questions, skeptically evaluating answers, and pointing out nonsense as publicly as possible. They are no more likely to swallow the "company line" from their boss than they are from the mayor. A rare publisher or general manager looks forward to meeting with the editorial department, and it has been said that managing media professionals of any kind is like trying to herd cats.

The *Situational Leadership Theory (SLT)* (Hersey & Blanchard, 1982) maintains that an effective leader challenges followers via understating their task and psychological maturity. *Task maturity* refers to an employee's education, experience, and technical ability relative to a task. *Psychological maturity* refers to the individual's task-related self-confidence, attitude, and motivation. Task and psychological maturity are not necessarily related. The newsroom intern may lack experience but have tremendous enthusiasm, while the senior reporter may be burned out and alienated.

SLT attempts to match leadership and "followership" styles. According to the theory, an authoritarian approach likely works best with followers without job skills and motivation. Consultative or inspirational leadership would better apply for those who, like the senior reporter, have the skills but lack motivation or confidence. Coaching would help develop the highly motivated but inexperienced intern, while leaders blessed with highly skilled and highly motivated followers should empower them through delegation.

A second theory of leadership, the *Path-Goal Theory* (Evans, 1970; House & Dessler, 1974), holds that a leader's primary job is to motivate followers and predict that followers' behaviors depend on whether they think their work will help them achieve their own goals. Two other factors shape followers' behaviors: (a) their perception of whether the leader's behavior will contribute to their personal satisfaction, and (b) their perception of their own self-efficacy. Followers who see themselves as powerful and in control of their own destiny prefer consensus leaders, while followers who see themselves as at the mercy of fate prefer more authoritarian leaders (Mitchell, Smyser, & Weed, 1975).

The task-relationship dichotomy also comes into play in leader-follower relations. Most people relate best to those most like themselves in task-relationship orientation, while differences can lead to tension. When relationship-oriented people spend time chatting with colleagues, their task-oriented coworkers are likely to see them as time wasters. When task-oriented people brush off efforts at small talk, their relationship-oriented colleagues may see them as cold, arrogant, and unfriendly.

In reality, good relationships among coworkers help organizations work more smoothly, and it requires time and nontask-focused communication. Conversely, a strong task focus gets things done. Managers need to recognize the valuable contributions both types of employees make to organizational effectiveness and take care not to try to force everyone into the same mold. Observing each coworker's task-relationship orientation and then matching it when interacting with that individual helps improve working relationships.

Leadership Styles for Different Situations

Many leadership theories also suggest that the organizational environment impacts leadership effectiveness. For example, unlike the Situational Theory of Leadership, which assumes the ability of leaders to adapt their style to their followers, the *Contingency Theory of Leadership* (Fiedler, 1967) holds that leadership effectiveness rests on choosing the leader whose style is appropriate to the situation. Fiedler identified several situational factors that predict leader success: (a) the quality of leader-follower relations, (b) the degree of task structure or uncertainty, and (c) the power of the leader in relationship to the followers. Tests of the Contingency Theory of Leadership suggest that task-oriented leaders are more likely to be successful when these factors are extremely favorable or extremely unfavorable, while relationship-oriented leaders are more likely to succeed when conditions are more moderate.

For example, in a start-up media company, such as a new weekly business newspaper or an online operation, the tasks will be fairly unstructured as everyone learns what needs to be done, the staff usually will be small, new to the organization, and enthusiastic about the opportunity and about working with each other. Individuals will have a high degree of professional autonomy since the organization will be making many things up as it goes along. In such circumstances, a task-oriented leader probably will be successful because that person will be more likely to focus on making sure that myriad of things that need to be done get done. Conversely, in an established organization going through change where established routines and relationships are being renegotiated, a people-oriented leader will probably be more successful because he or she will be more likely to pay attention to the human dynamics involved in the situation.

When leader-follower relations are either very good or very bad, relationship maintenance efforts are not likely to matter. Similarly, highly structured or highly unstructured tasks benefit from a strong task-focus, while very high or low power may be more important to task accomplishment than to relationship maintenance. Where conditions are not as clear cut, the relationship-oriented leader may have more success navigating the ambiguities.

The Effects of Structure on Leadership

Organizational structures also affect leadership styles and effectiveness, especially when it comes to centralization, unity of command, span of control, division of labor, and departmentalization.

Centralization refers to the number of people in the organization who control power. Highly centralized organizations tend to be more authoritarian, while decentralized organizations tend to be more participative. *Unity of command* refers to how clearly the lines in the chain of command are drawn. In media organizations, authority is often quite diffuse; journalists may work with several different editors on a story, while creative teams often oversee projects in entertainment industries.

Span of control refers to the number of people and projects managers supervise. A wider span of control makes it more difficult to keep track of individuals and details. For example, industry consolidation in the 1990s forced many radio-station managers to go from managing one or two stations to overseeing many more. Their new properties often ran wildly different programming and sometimes were scattered across several cities. A radio executive in the South used to say that when he left the driveway on Monday morning, he knew he was 1,000 miles away from the next weekend.

Division of labor measures how specialized staff members' roles are in the production process. Digital technologies have significantly reduced the divisions of labor in media industries. For example, smaller digital cameras and laptops make it possible for reporters in converged operations to create and edit video for broadcast, extract a still shot for the newspaper and Web, and rewrite the story for all three platforms. Generally, as divisions of labor blur, so do unity of command and centralization, while managers' spans of control increase.

Departmentalization refers to the internal structure of an organization and whether people with similar or complementary jobs work together and report to the same managers. Typically, highly departmentalized organizations also are more centralized. Convergence appears to be reducing the level of departmentalization in many media companies.

Leading Small Groups and Teams

In the media industry, teams or small groups commonly perform work. *Team* refers to a small group working toward a shared goal and has a high level of interdependence (Hughes, Ginnett, & Curphy, 19). *Groups* generally are less cohesive, and members may have differen reasons for belonging to the group and different objectives for the outcome. Media, film, television, newspaper, and music production, among others, require teamwork to produce the final product.

Leading teams and small groups is a complex process. Teams and groups develop their own internal identities and cultures and, like other organizations, are affected by size, task structure, and member relationships. As mentioned in chapter 1, teams and groups have the advantage of harnessing the ideas and efforts of multiple people, but they have the disadvantage of requiring more time and effort to manage because of the necessity of negotiating between members and developing consensus.

Many leadership issues can arise in teams or groups and affect their success. These include (a) domination by the leader, (b) poor relationships between members, and (c) the team's or group's perception of itself and its relationship to the outside world.

A dominant leader negates most of the advantages of teams and groups because generally only the leader's view is heard. Even if a leader does not actively dominate group interactions, if the person is powerful, group members may engage in self-censorship and offer only ideas they think will be acceptable, thus curtailing the group's range of action. Effective group leadership in such cases requires that the leader withdraw, appointing someone else to head the group.

Relationships between team members also can affect teamwork. If a group divides into factions or cliques, consensus may be impossible. If two members dislike each other, disruptive bickering, and even mutual sabotage can result. Many TV reporters have learned the hard way just how bad an angry videographer can make them look on air.

And almost every student knows first-hand the final relational issue in teams: the Free Rider—the team member who doesn't contribute. This occurs primarily in groups where rewards, such as grades, will be equally distributed. As long as at least one person works for the group's success, the rest can afford to free ride. Free riders demoralize productive members. They should be confronted and, if necessary, removed.

Identity and perception issues also can hinder team success. In their earliest stages, teams and small groups build a shared identity and understanding of the group's relationship to the organization and to other groups—a *fantasy theme* (Bormann & Bormann, 1992). It develops almost unconsciously during the social interactions in the first few meetings. Once the group's identity takes root, it is hard to change, and members who challenge it become outsiders.

can be positive or negative. For example, members
levision production team may decide that together
e an award-winning new series that will change
they may convince themselves that the networks
new and will only schedule rehashed concepts.
case, the group's fantasy theme is likely to become a self-fulfilling prophecy. Leaders should monitor the development of fantasy
themes during the group's formation stage, and actively counter negative themes that emerge.

Leading Creative Projects and People

Media are fundamentally creative businesses. Managing creative people—and managing people in a way that encourages creativity—are
important leadership responsibilities.

Creativity requires divergent thinking—i.e., thinking in unusual,
unconventional, unexpected ways. Creativity's nature makes it hard to
understand and predict, but some people clearly are more creative than
others. Even with an element of talent or genius to creativity, media
managers must do many things to enhance creativity in themselves and
in organizations.

Research suggests that the recipe for creativity includes a certain
amount of expertise mixed with a dose of naiveté (Kuhn, 1996), a
steady infusion of new ideas, adequate but not excessive resources, and
an organizational structure and culture that empowers individuals and
rewards risk taking (Küng, 2004).

Studies of scientific revolutions suggest that truly revolutionary
ideas tend to come from relative newcomers to a field—people who have
expertise in a subject, but whose ideas about how things work have not
yet become fixed (Kuhn, 1996).

Creativity also requires constant exposure to new ideas, images, and
information. Creativity-focused organizations often surround workers
with bright colors and creative visual spaces. They also seek diversity
in their employees because if coworkers are basically alike, little variety in the life experiences, knowledge, and perspectives that fuel new
ideas will exist. Most people can enhance their personal creativity with
simple exercises—going into a different neighborhood to shop, reading
books and magazines they normally wouldn't open, worshipping with
people of a different religion. The key is to constantly seek new experiences and information and to keep an open mind.

Studies of highly creative media companies such as Pixar Studios, BBC News Online, and HBO found that they shared some characteristics (Küng, 2004): teams handled creative activities; teams were given autonomy; members had appropriate expertise and they received adequate, but not excessive, resources to encourage inventiveness with the resources they had. Leadership also played a key role. Company leaders developed a vision for the company that represented a challenge to members' creativity, provided the resources to meet that challenge, and then got out of the way, having little direct involvement in daily activities.

In recent years, news organizations have tried a variety of approaches to broaden their perspectives and increase their creativity. *Civic journalism* encourages contributions of stories, photos, and video from members of the audience. *Blogs* give reporters a forum for voicing their opinions, which is normally forbidden in news content. Some organizations have even experimented with rotating the leadership of story-budget meetings as a way of increasing the likelihood that new story ideas will surface. Others have created teams of reporters, graphic artists, and photographers to work on stories so that the visualization of the story will affect the reporting and writing, and the reporting will influence the visualization.

These findings in media organizations parallel those in other studies of creativity. Fostering creativity requires an organization to develop a culture that gives employees a high-level of autonomy in their work, rewards risk taking, and permits failure. If managers constantly monitor, critique, and control creative work, or if employees believe they'll be penalized if something they try fails, workers will strive for risk-reducing conformity, not creativity.

Leading Change

It has become a cliché: The only constant in the media industry today is change. The cliché, however, is reality. As discussed in chapter 5, changing technologies are forcing media companies to constantly reorient themselves. Fragmenting audiences and changing industry structures also are forcing media organizations to rethink the way they do things. The next generation of media managers must be prepared to lead their organizations through constant change processes.

Leading change is difficult. Change creates tension and uncertainty in organizations and has been shown to reduce job satisfaction and organizational commitment and to increase the likelihood that staff will quit (Brockner, Grover, Reed, DeWitt, & O'Malley, 1987; Wanberg & Banas, 2000). In a talent-based industry, such losses can be costly.

Research on change management suggests that leaders can do certain things to help offset change's negative impact. These include involving employees in the process, clearly communicating how the changes will occur and what the future will look like, providing employees with continuous information, and making sure staff members understand how the changes relate to the company's long-term goals (Beckhard & Harris, 1987; Cummings & Worley, 1993; Miller & Monge, 1985).

However, even when led by people with extensive training in change management, change is hard on organizations. In a study of newspapers led by editors who had completed a change-management training program, Gade (2004) found that editors and newsroom employees had very different views of how newsroom changes had been handled. The differences in perception were so large that Gade said, "it was hard to understand the two groups as sharing the same experiences."

A study of change management at *CNN Headline News* in the late 1990s had similar findings (Daniels & Hollifield, 2002). Staff members generally viewed the organization's changes negatively. Older employees were more negative than younger employees, but they also were more likely to stay on the job. Staff members of all ages were most concerned about changes they thought might hurt the quality of their work. The majority of respondents said they had considered quitting at least once during the transition, but respondents who felt they had had input into the change process or who said they understood why the changes were being made were less likely to have considered quitting.

The study also suggested that change is a long-term problem for managers. While staff members' attitudes toward changes improved over time, they continued to believe they had been happier in their jobs before the changes were made. Moreover, the staff's view of management improved more slowly than did their view of the changes.

However, these experiences with managing change in news organizations suggest that there are things that effective leaders can do to make change easier. Leaders should seek employees' input on the changes and respond to that input as much as possible. Identifying staff members who are influential with their colleagues and involving those individuals in the change-management process often helps others become more accepting of the changes. Regular and open communication about the changes, paying special attention to older and long-term employees, and making sure everyone clearly understands why the changes are being made are particularly critical to smoothing the process.

Leading the Changing Media Workforce

Media managers can also expect to face change in the nature of the media workforce, the profile of which has changed tremendously since the 1970s. Although most research on the media workforce has focused on journalists, other media sectors appear to have somewhat similar trends. Chapter 3 discusses in detail the implications of the changing workforce for personnel management and motivation.

However, in general, studies of the U.S. journalism profession show a graying workforce: The average age of journalists is now 41, 5 years older than a decade ago (Weaver, Beam, Brownlee, Voakes, & Wilhoit, 2003). More journalists now have college degrees. Women make up a third of all professional journalists, a percentage that hasn't changed significantly since 1982. More telling, women make up the majority of students enrolled in journalism and mass communication programs nationwide and represent more than half of all working journalists with 5 or fewer years of professional experience. In other words, women enter the journalism profession in larger numbers than men, but don't remain in it as long.

Full-time journalists of color made up 9.5% of all professional journalists in the United States in 2002. While that percentage is up slightly from 10 years ago, it remains well below the level of minority representation in the U.S. population as a whole (30%) and among college graduates (24%). Television had the largest percentage of journalists of color, followed by daily newspapers.

In recent years, the percentage of journalism and mass communication graduates finding jobs in mass communication industries has been rising (Becker, Vlad, & Coffey, 2005). Starting salaries also have grown. In 2004, the median salary for a journalism and mass communication graduate was $27,800, a record high even when adjusted for inflation. Graduates taking jobs in online media had the highest starting salaries, while jobs in radio paid the least.

This profile of the journalism workforce raises serious issues for future newsroom managers—and managers in other sectors of the media—to the degree their workforces are similar. Although entry-level salaries in media are at an all-time high, they still seriously trail the entry-level salaries available in many other industries with similar educational requirements. Salaries, of course, respond to the law of supply and demand. The industry argues that there still are more people seeking jobs than they can hire, so there is little need for growth in starting salaries.

This begs some important questions that the next generation of media industry management must consider. In a talent-based industry that plays a critical role in society, it is not just a question of how many people you attract, but also how smart, educated, talented, and experienced those people are. It is critical to attract the best people and then retain them. If many top mass communication graduates opt out of the industry in favor of other professions that pay more, the industry and society suffers. The graying of the journalism workforce, the exodus of women out of the profession after a few years, and the continued under-representation of journalists of color in relationship to the number of minority college graduates suggest that the industry is losing many of the very people it needs most in this time of challenge and change.

Tomorrow's media leaders need to address these issues by raising starting salaries and benefits to levels comparable with other critical professions. Media leaders also need to examine and address the issues that are driving women out of the industry. Finally, industry executives must work harder to attract more people of color into the field and into positions of leadership. To accomplish these goals, media leaders will need to develop more thoughtful, focused long-term efforts at recruitment, competitive salaries and benefits, and working environments that value diversity of both cultures and perspectives.

Leading Ethically

American businesses, government, and media are in the midst of an ethical crisis. Scandal follows scandal: The Enron, WorldCom, and Imclone scandals have their media counterparts in the fraud convictions of Adelphia Cable executives, the Jayson Blair scandal at the *New York Times,* and similar incidents of plagiarism and fabrication in other news organizations including *USA Today* and the *Boston Globe.* Perhaps most troubling of all is that such scandals have become so pervasive, they are losing their ability to shock and outrage. A leading criminal psychologist and expert on psychopathy recently argued that corporations and corporate leaders who focus completely on investors' interests at the expense of their employees and society are showing the same of lack of empathy and conscience seen in criminal psychopaths (Deutschman, 2005).

Although ethics are discussed in great detail in chapter 6, it must be noted here that at their core, ethics are a leadership issue. Honesty and integrity have been considered necessary attributes of true leaders since at least the time of Aristotle. Only the leader can set the ethical tone for an organization, and the failure of ethics in an organization is the failure of leadership.

In recent years, the media industry has suffered from its own series of scandals, ethical issues, and questions. Among them the Janet Jackson wardrobe malfunction in the 2004 Super Bowl; the increased use of sex, violence, and profanity to attract ratings; the failure by some journalists to protect confidential sources; the identification of suspects in high-profile criminal cases before charges are filed. Some media executives have admitted taking ethically debatable actions because their competitors did it first. Such ethical reasoning can easily lead the industry into a race to the bottom, leaving even the pretense to integrity behind.

Ethical leadership in the media industry goes beyond content management. Leaders and managers also have a responsibility to deal honestly with regulators and the public, and fairly with their employees. Corporate leaders owe workers safe and reasonable working conditions, fair wages, and adequate resources to get the job done. In this age of pervasive connectivity, managers need to respect employees' right to have a life outside of work and their responsibilities to their families.

However, leaders of the media industry have ethical responsibilities beyond those of many industries. Media are a critical societal infrastructure. The media's performance in providing high-quality, responsible, professional journalism affects the integrity and transparency of government, the functioning of democracy, and the health of the economy. Media are the only industries given special protections by the U.S. Constitution. In their selection, production, and framing of news and entertainment content, media leaders shape our perceptions of our world. Few any longer dispute that media content affects society over the long term in a variety of ways.

It remains for the next generation of media leaders to meet the challenge of balancing the industry's need for reasonable financial returns with its responsibility to serve the public interest.

Summary

In the media industry, the need for talented, visionary leaders who can find and inspire talented professionals has never been greater. The critical changes the industry faces demand leadership from people who are students of their industry: knowledgeable, insightful, and visionary. The talent-based nature of media makes it critical that media leaders be able to manage not only tasks, but also people. Media leaders today must be insightful, adaptable, and strategic in their actions. Leaders succeed when they match their leadership style to their followers and to the dynamics of the situation in which they are working. Successful leaders work constantly to strengthen their natural leadership traits and development their leadership skills.

The rapidly changing structure and nature of the media industry makes the job of leading media organizations today exceptionally challenging—and exceptionally exciting. The next generation of media leaders will captain the industry into a new era, making their mark of the future of the industry no less than did the pioneers who led the development of early television. However, succeeding in today's uncertain industry conditions will require strong leadership traits, exceptional leadership skills, and the ability to manage change, foster creativity, and lead ethically.

Case 2.1 Leading in a New Direction

Mark Thompson has just taken the job of executive editor of *Main Street*, a paid-circulation weekly business newspaper in a major West Coast port city. Prior to this, he was the business editor for a daily in a small city in the Midwest. On his first day on the job, Mark held a meeting with the newsroom staff.

"You all are the heart of this operation," he told the editors and reporters. "This paper is successful because you're skilled, excellent professionals. I look forward to working with you and learning from you. You know this paper and this city better than I do, and I will draw upon your expertise. Working together, we'll take this newspaper to the next level of journalistic excellence."

Two weeks later, Mark met with Cynthia Johnson, the senior reporter at the paper. Johnson had been with the paper since its start and regularly wins state-wide awards for her investigative reporting. Mark called to her from inside his office where he remained behind his desk. "Cynthia, can you come in here?"

As Cynthia entered, Mark continued typing on his computer. After about three minutes, he turned his chair around to face her and leaned forward with his arms crossed on his desk.

"Cynthia, I've decided that we're going to do a special section each week on agriculture. This section was the most-read section at my old paper," Mark explained, "and *Main Street* hasn't done a single story on agriculture in the past year. You know, a lot of agricultural products ship out of this state through those ships out there in the harbor. Agriculture is big business in this state. I want you on this."

Cynthia hesitated, "Mark, agriculture is big business in this state, but it isn't big business in this city. Our city has almost no direct economic connections to the agricultural industry, and *Main Street* only circulates in the city. Your old paper was in a huge agricultural region with lots of readers in outlying counties. That's not true here. When we've done audience surveys of the topics people want us to cover, no one has ever listed agriculture."

"Look, Cynthia, everyone eats, so everyone has an interest in food and food industries. They may not know they want it yet, but when they have it, it will become an important part of why they read the paper. I know. It was a huge money maker for my old paper and it will be here, too." Mark handed her a sheet of paper. "Now here's a list of the stories I want you to write for the first section."

Cynthia looked at the list. "Mark, these are all soft feature stories. If you want us to start covering agriculture, okay. But let's at least cover it the way we cover everything else—as news. I'm sure that I can come up with some good hard stories with an agricultural angle."

Mark shook his head. "Those are the stories I want you to do. Get busy on them. And I want you to check back with me at the end of the day to report your progress. Now get going."

1. What did Mark communicate to his staff in his opening remarks at the first staff meeting? What kinds of expectations might they have had for his leadership style based upon what he said?
2. What did Mark communicate to Cynthia in his interaction with her about his leadership style? How did Mark communicate those things to Cynthia through what he did, what he said, and how he said it? Be specific in identifying the signals he was sending and how he was sending them.
3. Based on the information provided about Cynthia and her responses to Mark, how would you characterize Cynthia's followership style?
4. What do you think Cynthia's reaction to Mark would be? What effect might their interaction have on Cynthia's attitude and followership style in the future? As word of Mark's conversation with Cynthia spread through the paper, what impact might it have had on the rest of the staff?

5. Assuming that Mark was right and that *Main Street* should be cover-
    ing agriculture, how might he lead Cynthia and other staff members
    around to his point of view? Consider yourself Mark's leadership
    consultant. Advise him as to what specific steps he might take and
    the leadership styles and approaches he might adopt to convince
    Cynthia and other staff members that his proposed agriculture sec-
    tion is a project worth trying?

Case 2.2 A Case of Style

Select a dramatic film, television program, or documentary that
takes place in an organizational setting. Do not use a comedy for this
assignment.

Watch an episode or lengthy scene and use it as a case-study observation of leadership behavior. How is the leader's style portrayed? What
about the followers' styles? What environmental conditions are they
dealing with in the organization?

Include as many of the leadership elements discussed in this chapter,
as appropriate: verbal and nonverbal communication, conflict management, negotiation, change, creativity, organizational diversity, organizational structure, etc.

Position yourself as a management consultant to the organizational
leader portrayed in the program and write a detailed analysis of the
interactions that occurred in the episode and make recommendations
for improvement, as appropriate.

Case 2.3 Personal Observation

Contact a media or communication company in your area. Arrange to
spend several hours shadowing either the senior executive or a departmental manager.

During your visit, carefully observe the manager's leadership style
and staff members' "followership" styles. Note the environment and
situation and how the manager and staff work together. Look for indicators of task and psychological maturity, and task-relationship orientations. Observe small-group interactions, if you have the chance to sit
in on meetings.

Watch the manager's approach to encouraging or discouraging creativity, managing conflict, managing change processes, negotiating issues,

communicating and listening, and establishing or enforcing standards, rules, and ethics.

Are there points of conflict in the organization? Do there seem to be differences in how people are treated based on their age, race, or gender? Be sure to carefully observe nonverbal communication behaviors by the manager and staff. These include not only body language, but also dress, movement, vocal tones, and even how they decorate their workspaces.

Note: If you write a case study or description of your visit or discuss your experiences in class, it is important that you protect the privacy of your hosts. Be sure to change the names of the company you visited and of all the people you observed. Alter any descriptions of the company or its operations so that readers and listeners won't be able to identify the company or any of its employees.

3

MOTIVATION

You enter the room unnoticed. Everyone looks busy. No one looks up from their computer. When people do see you, it's as if they are looking right through you or have identified you as a stranger. Televisions hang from the ceiling, blaring various events and commercials, but no one is watching them. Phones ring intermittently, and life in the newsroom continues. Your desk, looking every bit its age, lies in the corner, next to two unfriendly looking older people. *This* is where you wanted to work? What were you *thinking*? How will you survive? *Do you want to*?

You don't know it, but across the room, behind a glass wall, someone eyes you. "New kid in town," she mutters to her boss sitting behind the desk.

"Fresh meat!" he growls.

"That's easy for you to say," she says, adding, "You don't have to figure out how to motivate them."

"Who says *you* have to?"

Two people, different jobs, same anxieties. The manager behind the glass wall wants to understand. A newsroom mainstay ever since college, she was the first female to win major reporting awards and when she finally got promoted to management, her bosses touted it as "a long time in coming" and said she was a role model for the other females in the newsroom. Yet she feels insecure in her new role, afraid to make a mistake, particularly on coverage issues that her predecessor used to decide in seconds. Talent can be rushed too much, she believes, but she can't show that she's a wimp, either. She would like to find a way to motivate others to improve. Motivation, she believes, is being able to manipulate an employee into doing what the manager wants.

At first glance, however, the new recruit isn't thinking motivation so much as survival. And yet survival and success themselves are motivating forces. The recruit fails to realize that motivation involves more than something you do. In fact, motivation may at times seem to constitute your whole being, even your life.

Media managing (and understanding media managing) requires knowing, comprehending, and appropriately analyzing complex human behavior. Motivation is complicated, and managers must understand it in context (Fink, 1993) if they are to successfully deal with employees. The media workplace with its rapid, cyclical nature of change and production often presents unusual, demanding, and sometimes chaotic circumstances for managing. The media manager needs an objective-based framework for viewing motivation and motivational opportunities.

This chapter emphasizes motivation in the sense of how a typical editor or news director thinks of it, with all the special circumstances of media workplaces. The chapter examines media employees' motivation from two perspectives: as individuals and as groups, while exploring the application of various theories. A discussion follows of common motivational concerns and current trends in the media workplace.

Motivating Individuals

Common Needs and Influences

Mass media require many tasks of their employees. For example, a TV newsroom requires anchors to write and report, think critically; be skeptical (even cynical), aggressive, and curious; know how to manage time, coordinate and collaborate, and develop a sense of community and civic duty—to name a few duties. Whatever the medium, employees, particularly those in creative jobs, must perform many different tasks. In doing so, they experience emotions that may range from humor or compassion to outright apathy. Therefore, *goals* are imposed on a recruit by the mere fact of being hired.

Often managers can simply look at motivation as a basic process of *needs* (in this example, job requirements) producing *drives* or *motives* that then lead to goals being achieved. Abraham Maslow (1954) classified needs into a five-tier hierarchy: (a) physiological (food and thirst, sleep, health), (b) safety (shelter, security), (c) social (acceptance, belonging, group membership, love), (d) esteem (recognition and prestige, success), and (e) self-actualization (self-fulfillment of potential). Depending on the individual, job mandates may affect one or all of these needs. However, Maslow theorized only one level of need motivates a person at any given time. Needs, according to Maslow, are satisfied in order, from lowest (physiological) to highest (self-actualization), as illustrated in Fig. 3.1.

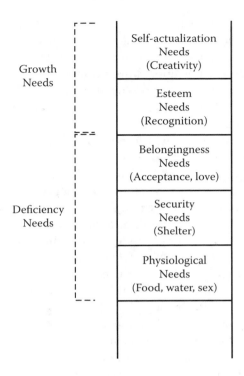

FIGURE 3.1 Maslow's hierarchy of needs.

Clayton Alderfer (1972) said an employee's needs may be partially but not completely met, or anyone may be motivated by two or more needs simultaneously. For example, the new recruit may be concerned about his salary (safety) and his need to grow as an investigative reporter (esteem). If higher-order needs are met, such as a reporter's need for journalistic prestige, then he may become frustrated and regress to being motivated by a lower-level need.

Alderfer would say that any manager would do well to analyze an employee's complaints about his or her salary. Yet if that is, indeed, a reporter's goal and it is not reached, it logically follows that maybe there was no drive or motive to stimulate action. The drive in this case could be manifested in a decision to excel in another area, perhaps in making deadlines. The manager must determine an employee's needs and goals. In addition to job mandates, other factors must be considered.

Some management experts (e.g., Straub, 1984) believe that effective employee selection is a prerequisite for successful motivation. In this chapter's opening scenario, the manager behind the glass wall needs to know whether the recruit is psychologically capable, capable of carrying out the tasks required of reporters, and whether the recruit's values and skills match the position. However, most media managers generally lack the time and tools to perform such an analysis and, instead, usually try to develop effective motivational techniques that appeal to most employees.

Motivating people requires forethought and strategy. Besides the previously mentioned need to achieve, most people want to influence others (*power*) and be liked (*affiliation*). Psychologist David McClelland (1961) developed this typology and suggested that one of these needs usually dominates. For example, to effectively motivate, managers must recognize all such needs and try to determine which is dominant for each employee. For example, a good editor knows many young reporters have a need for power (what beginning writer doesn't want to make an impact?). A reporter's need for affiliation probably is less clear, although his or her complaints of newsroom isolation could be evidence of concern for being liked. The manager probably also has a high need for power and achievement, which influences the assumptions made about a reporter's performance or lack of achievement. Yet knowing which need dominates or holds the key to reporter/employee motivation/performance is only part of the battle. The manager must then know what to do with that knowledge and what results to expect.

For example, people generally repeat behavior that is rewarded or reinforced and avoid behavior that is punished. Such conditioning falls into two general categories: (a) classical and (b) operant. Classical conditioning tries to generate involuntary, reflexive, or semi-instinctual actions through unconditioned stimuli. For example, when a reporter writing a story notices she has 10 minutes before deadline, she experiences an adrenalin rush, a quickened pulse, and other symptoms indicating heightened anxiety. Therefore, the repeated experience of an impending deadline results in the same physiological changes each time this type of stress is encountered.

With operant conditioning (Skinner, 1971), depicted in Fig. 3.2, reinforced behavior is repeated voluntarily and behavior not reinforced is less likely to be repeated. Reinforcement can be positive (as when the news director rewards the anchor for the desired behavior of producing high ratings by giving her a raise), negative (as when the news director rewards a quiet producer who keeps legitimate complaints about the newsroom's functioning to himself by increasing his pay), punishing (as when the news director rewards the assignment editor's undesired

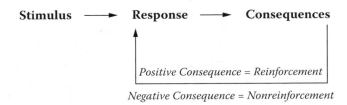

FIGURE 3.2 Operant conditioning.

complaining with the negative consequence of firing him), or extinctive (as when the news director eliminates the unwanted complaining by not rewarding it). Regardless of how the news director attempts to condition the employee, he or she should be aware of options and their consequences.

Of course, many times motivation relies on what an employee believes rather than on what is observable or true. The previously discussed theories mainly focus on how managers (and other factors) manipulate motives, suggesting an element of control. People influence their own drives via their beliefs of *personal efficacy* (Bandura, 1997, p. 2): unless people believe they can produce desired effects by their actions, they have little incentive to act. This refers to beliefs in your capability to plan and take action to produce a desired effect (not to be confused with self-esteem, which involves judgments of self-worth).

A reporter can believe in her abilities and still dislike herself, although reporters usually develop abilities or perform tasks that make them feel good about themselves. Self-efficacy beliefs regulate motivation by determining goals and the results a person expects for his or her efforts. For example, a reporter with fairly high self-efficacy probably would be more willing to try to meet a challenge to improve his or her skills. Such performance concerns are discussed in the next section.

Differences and Job Performance

Aside from job requirements and the needs they generate, managers also need to note the interaction between job and employee. Doing so will broaden the manager's perspective on employee behavior and thus provide another decision-making tool. First, managers should know the motivation process. Three theories—(a) equity theory, (b) expectancy theory, and (c) goal-setting theory—address this idea. In equity theory (Adams, 1963), the key assumption is that inequity is a motivator. When employees feel they have been unfairly treated, they will attempt to achieve a sense of equity. If a reporter's unhappiness stems from inequity (let's say she sees comparable reporters earning more), she could become happier by changing how much she works, attempting to increase her pay (or asking for a raise), reassessing how she compares herself, distorting the comparisons to make herself compare more favorably, or quitting.

Expectancy theory (Vroom, 1964) asserts that people will do what they can do when they want to. Figure 3.3 depicts how motivation is the product of the interaction among expectancy (a person's belief that working hard will enable various work goals to be achieved), instrumentality (a person's belief that various work-related outcomes will occur as a result of doing the job), and valence (the value the person assigns to those work-related outcomes). The motivational appeal of a reward (e.g., higher salary) is drastically reduced whenever expectancy, instrumentality, or valence together or alone nears zero. For example, a reporter's motivation to earn a pay raise will be low if she feels she cannot do the work needed to earn the raise, or if she's unsure that the extra work will result in the raise, or if she places little or no value on getting a raise.

Meanwhile, goal-setting theory says that employees behave the way they do because it helps them reach their goals (Locke, 1968), with goals' difficulty and specific nature particularly important. For example, planning to win an Emmy Award sufficiently motivates many TV writers to achieve excellence in writing. However, if a new writer sets such a goal in his first year of work, the goal can be too difficult and lead to frustration. If the writer modifies and specifies the goal (e.g., winning an Emmy in 5 years or attempting to have a certain number of ideas or scripts produced in 5 years and 1 year), then he enhances the chance for honest evaluation of the goal and proper assessment of his

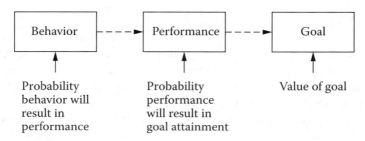

FIGURE 3.3 Expectancy theory.

writing. It is important for his manager to know what goals he has set and how that affects his behavior.

In the case of our new recruit, the recruit needs to know the editor's goals, assess their difficulty, and identify their realistic qualities. This helps the recruit know whether and how to help the editor meet those goals and develop strategies to do so. If the recruit believes the goals are set too high, it is appropriate to discuss them with the editor to help adjust the editor's expectations.

Managers, meanwhile, also may look at job-employee interaction through the lens of job satisfaction. For example, most managers assume that a satisfied employee is a productive one. Yet sometimes satisfaction does not cause performance—it may be the reverse. An employee who performs her job is a satisfied employee (Greene, 1972). So knowing how employee satisfaction works will help managers more completely understand motivation.

Alderfer (1972) stressed the role of frustration in terms of unmet needs. Recognizing the frustration factor implies that a manager can positively react to the frustrating item and help satisfy the employee. Frederick Herzberg and his colleagues (Herzberg, Mausner, & Snyderman, 1968) developed the two-factor theory, illustrated in Fig. 3.4, which suggests that satisfaction and dissatisfaction are not related, but rather affected by different needs and motives.

Herzberg contended that hygiene or preventive factors do not produce motivation, but can prevent motivation from occurring. Preventive

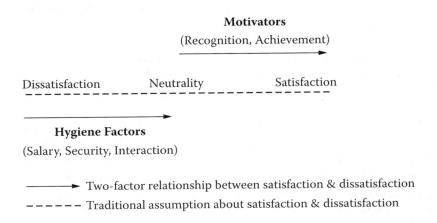

FIGURE 3.4 The two-factor theory of motivation.

factors, such as money, status, security, working conditions, work policies, supervision, and interpersonal relations are sometimes viewed as
environmental influences. If a manager attends to these items, she helps
keep employees from being highly dissatisfied. However, job-related
motivators such as achievement, challenging work, increased responsibility, recognition, advancement, and personal growth provide true
motivation when combined with hygiene factors. Herzberg's theory
has not always been supported (Griffin & Moorhead, 1986), so media
managers should note the important exceptions and nuances within
the satisfaction concept.

For example, Chang and Sylvie (1999) found that satisfaction and
dissatisfaction affected newspaper reporters differently. Wilhoit and
Weaver (1994) found in a major study that journalists differ by medium
as to what they consider the most important factor for job satisfaction.
Daily newspaper, wire service, and radio journalists cited job security,
whereas TV journalists said the importance of helping people is a primary factor. Although pay was likely to be at the bottom of most journalists' lists (regardless of their employer), wire service and broadcast
journalists were more likely to cite pay as an issue in job satisfaction.

Additional studies show the difficulty of managing for satisfaction.
For example, in the 1980s, how often a journalist received comments
from managers strongly predicted satisfaction for all journalists except
those at medium-size newspapers. The strongest predictor of job satisfaction at small newspapers was how well journalists believed their
newspaper informed the public (Bergen & Weaver, 1988). A decade later,
the size influence had disappeared. Perceptions about effectiveness in
informing the public and frequency of managerial comments about
work were significant predictors for journalists working at newspapers
of all sizes. In addition, older journalists in small- and medium-size
papers were most satisfied in the 1980s, but by the 1990s the older journalists in small and large papers were most satisfied (Kodrich & Beam,
1997). The point: Satisfaction sources change, as do people.

A case in point: Scholars also have linked satisfaction to autonomy
since the 1970s. Size and type of ownership also determined feelings of
autonomy. Journalists who worked for smaller, independently owned
media were more likely to report personal discretion at work. Still,
Weaver and Wilhoit (1996) concluded that these factors didn't fully
explain autonomy and noted that journalists' sense of autonomy had
eroded since the 1980s. An editor recognizing such feelings may better understand her reporters and would do well to examine employee
resources and how they deal with job satisfaction in general.

This is especially true in the face of the rapid corporatization of news media. For example, journalists working for organizations that they perceive as valuing good journalism are more satisfied (Beam, 2006). When news organizations emphasize making high profits, journalists—predictably, because of their natural suspicions of nonjournalistic operational motive— say they are less satisfied than they would be otherwise (p. 180). However, news supervisors probably don't see this issue as clearly, given the fact that they probably are more accustomed to dealing with profit orientations. This blindspot could then affect how they manage their more profit-dubious subordinates—particularly in newspapers, where editors believe that organizational integration (i.e., communicating the values of the rest of the organization to the newsroom, working in cross-departmental teams and being an "organizational team player" (Gade, 2005) is desirable. Such managers tend to perceive higher levels of organizational support and, as a result, tend to manage for change more confidently (p. 29), albeit in direct conflict to the way many of their newsroom subordinates view change (Sylvie & Witherspoon, 2002).

So managing, as we observed in the decision-making chapter, is a matter of how the manager uses this and other kinds of information. Individuals differ, national studies may obscure those differences, and sometimes other issues come into play. Typically, *different* has meant *difficult* or hard to handle. Media managers have traditionally grappled with how to treat *star* employees, whose work performance sets them apart, often resulting from a unique, talented job approach born out of their personalities. As a result, such employees tend not to respond to typical motivational methods. Therefore, their supervisors may have to seek alternatives (Moore, 2002) for myriad problems, such as fairness (less talented employees are watching), appropriate rewards (stars do not always respond to money or promotions), evaluation (what is an appropriate work standard?), as well as recruiting and retaining stars (see this chapter's discussion of common problems).

Another alternative or explanation lies in self-efficacy theory, which essentially states that believing in your capability to plan and take action to produce a desired effect correlates with your actual capabilities to do so (Bandura, 1997). In this context, *different* does not have to mean *difficult*. Instead, an editor would do well to understand that being different is a personal matter, one that requires an individually tailored solution or approach. High self-efficacy, viewed appropriately, becomes a goal or quality that an editor wants to groom in as many subordinates as possible. For example, many older employees (or those who've decided to remain in their jobs longer than most) present a challenge for managers because they often need to be engaged or presented with growth opportunities to remain motivated. Programs such as professional development, training, or job rotation may help—but it's up to the manager to ensure these opportunities exist. Unfortunately, not every manager adequately promotes such opportunities (Cleary, 2005).

However, as media industries evolve, *different* has increasingly translated to *diverse*. A growing body of research is beginning to illuminate the numerous factors that increasingly diverse workplaces introduce to the satisfaction equation. For example, one school of thought (Pease, 1992) suggests that newspaper journalists of color are less likely than most journalists to accept promises of career advancement. They are more likely to seek alternative career paths. Particularly at risk of newspaper switching are minority females. Bramlett-Solomon (1992, 1993) found African American and Latino journalists to be twice as likely than their White counterparts to be dissatisfied and to stress job advancement opportunities (over the generally cited "chance to help people") when judging job attractiveness. Another study (Woods, 2005) showed that media employing minorities ages 35 years of age or younger must be proactive and provide more feedback and training in order to retain such employees. This disconnect extends into management; minority news directors were less likely than nonminority news directors to say training was offered to their staff (Cleary, 2005), while there's evidence to suggest that women managers do not negotiate as persistently as male managers and, thus, need to change their styles (Arnold & Nesbitt, 2006). In short, motivating and understanding managers themselves is no easy task either.

Finally, technology also affects individual motivation. When management introduces a technology to employees, the consequences usually vary along three dimensions viewed as good or bad: (a) direct (changes that occur in immediate response) or indirect (changes resulting from immediate responses), (b) desirable (helps the employee or system function more effectively) or undesirable (dysfunctional), and (c) anticipated (changes recognized and intended by management) or unanticipated (changes neither recognized nor intended). Yet from a motivation standpoint, the manager needs to ensure a good technology-employee match. Managers should work to help employees see the technology is (a) better than its predecessor, (b) compatible and consistent with existing values, (c) compatible and consistent with past experiences and employee needs, (d) relatively easy to understand and use, (e) experimentally friendly, and (f) capable of an observable job impact

(Rogers, 1983). This is easier said than done, especially when values enter the equation; often an editor won't know which values come into play until after a technology is introduced. So how well a manager knows her subordinates may determine what approach she uses.

In addition, the move toward technological convergence, whereby media expect employees to use various formats (e.g., broadcast, online, and print), has accelerated the need for alternative motivational strategies. Convergence often means more work for the employee, requiring managers to learn to motivate employees to converge. For example, the local TV meteorologist must be persuaded to broadcast the weather report, write a daily column for the newspaper, intermittently appear throughout the day on a sister radio station, and habitually update the TV Web site. As employees experience new technologies, they learn new skills, develop new ways of thinking about their jobs, and thus require new methods of motivation (e.g., Covington, 1997) and management (Killebrew, 2001).

One study (Singer, 2004a) of four U.S. newsrooms suggested that, despite culture clashes and other issues of compatibility, journalists see clear advantages in new convergence policies—i.e., as a career booster, the enjoyment of working with colleagues whose strengths differ from their own, and subsequent respect for people in other parts of the news organization. However, the study also suggested convergence within the newsroom may be hindered by cultural and technological differences in approaches to newsgathering and dissemination, as well as by a lack of training to alleviate concerns about the perceived complexities of new media formats. For a detailed discussion of how a manager should approach this and other technologies, see chapter 5.

But what of our new recruit? "Managing up" as a new employee means knowing how to build a good relationship with your supervisor—this is true for managers as well (Marshall, 2005), and involves understanding motivation from the other side of the coin. You've heard the conventional wisdom: Want to be a good employee and be receptive to your supervisor? Know your supervisor's goal and do your best to deliver it. Don't be afraid to work in groups or ask questions if you're not clear on directions or goals. In short, motivate your supervisor to provide you with the things and resources that result in success for both of you. However, knowing the values and decision-making styles of your boss helps but can be a challenge. For example, one U.S. survey (Sylvie & Huang, 2006) of newspaper editors who choose, justify, edit, and publish the news found that mid-level editors' value systems correlated with their decision-making styles but that the editors did not rely on a single style. Male editors were more likely than female editors to use an avoidant style—i.e., trying to evade decision making—as well as a more spontaneous style (by usually trying to decide as soon as possible). Other differences center on length of job experience and how much they value occupational culture and journalism.

Therefore, good managers and savvy employees recognize that each individual brings different attributes and values to the job. Each person's perception is selective or each person emphasizes those aspects of a situation that reinforce or appear consistent with that person's beliefs, attitudes, and values. The situation evolves further in groups.

Groups

A media organization is composed of groups such as committees, task forces, cliques, and entities that help it accomplish its objectives. To effectively motivate, media managers must become familiar with groups and group influences. Media managers must especially acknowledge occupational groups: collections of people sharing values, standards, and views that apply to the workplace and beyond. These groups confer, vie, and compromise with each other, functioning as "major players" in organizational decisions. Therefore, although hiring individuals influences everything, when your boss places you in a group, you have an implicit obligation to learn the forces driving the group. Our manager behind the wall must not only view the new recruit as an individual affected by personal, task, performance, and technological issues, she also must view him within the context of his group memberships and vice versa.

Groups and Cultures

Group members often get their identities or self-images from their occupational group roles, take other members as their primary reference group, and often socialize with group peers (Van Maanen & Barley, 1984). Groups develop along two basic forms: (a) formal and (b) informal.

Managers create *formal groups* when authorizing two or more people to devote time and resources to a task. Such groups include committees, task forces, project teams, or departments. Organizations cannot function without these groups, which often may gain considerable clout and power. Managers directly control groups through selection of members (and, in some cases, leadership), definition of purpose, and performance oversight. Often the group's purpose and status determine its level of motivation. For example, selection to prestigious or powerful groups fulfills certain needs for some, whereas omission or removal from a nondesirable group is a positive motivator for others. Formal groups not only provide a way to get work done but a structure-based motivation tool as well.

Informal groups pose a more complex issue. As opposed to formal groups, *informal groups* develop indirectly from socialization encouraged by formal structure. Creative influences on informal groups range from physical proximity of employee workspaces to the common values their jobs (and backgrounds) instill in them. These groups also serve a function, albeit not necessarily one the manager intended or devised.

As mentioned earlier, groups provide an identity of sorts for their members. Television news anchors closely identify with each other based on shared experiences and visions of what it is to be a news anchor: a witty, acerbic at times, conversationalist with an eye for news and a sense of how to entertain and accommodate TV viewers on their way to dinner or bed. Anchors may become friends with other anchors at the station or in the community. They may wear similar clothes, speak the same job-related jargon, cut their hair similarly, and carry themselves the same way in public. Employees in all departments of media organizations are subject to such conforming behaviors. Chances are their jobs bring them (or many of them) together socially, so they may begin to closely identify with their jobs.

This is particularly true of journalists and editors: many see themselves as journalists first, human beings second. Journalism encourages a distinct pattern of beliefs, values, norms, and interpretations. Not only do journalists learn the values of news, they learn to be skeptical, cynical, critical, detached, and analytical. This requires—particularly for younger journalists—the adoption of a particular lifestyle. It is not uncommon for journalists to feel they are always *on*; they can never completely discard the journalistic lens on their environment. Journalists often speak with pride of dangerous, ordeal-like career experiences called *war stories*. Their passion for news also takes a toll on their leisure time and lifestyle, leaving little time for nonjournalistic pursuits and fostering close relationships with other journalists. Even journalists in the same organization differ, especially if their jobs differ markedly. For example, online journalists within a print organization behave differently because they have different ideas on news cycles, deadlines, and values than their newspaper counterparts (Amari, 2000).

Managers can guide the development of occupational groups by how they plan and structure work. Organizing work on a functional basis typically ensures that those performing the functions will form informal groups. Such is the case in most media organizations, although some companies organize or suborganize around certain products (e.g., an organization with a Web site needs to develop a staff to maintain it) or markets (such as when a TV station creates a regional bureau). The key for the manager is to recognize the byproducts of informal groups.

One such consequence involves the pressure groups place on their members (Kiesler & Kiesler, 1969). Group members acquire shared norms and values, become cohesive as a group, attract other members, and form allegiances. The greater the attraction and loyalty to the group, the more likely the members conform to group norms and values. A culture exists within many occupational groups when they share a set of basic assumptions about the world; these assumptions determine that group's perceptions, thoughts, feelings, and certain overt behaviors (Schein, 1985). Group members reach consensus on these basic assumptions because of recurring success in implementing certain beliefs and values (Schein, 2004). Some (Argyris & Schön, 1974) argue that employees avoid confronting or debating these "theories in use," making them hard to change. Any attempt to do so means that a group supervisor must overcome sizeable sums of anxiety within the group. Meanwhile, spoken beliefs, values, norms, and behavioral rules, which group members use to depict the culture, rest between the explicit signs (artifacts) and the previously mentioned assumptions.

Asking a group member, "Why are you doing what you're doing?" reveals these values. What the group learns usually reflects members' original beliefs and values that have to be reinforced by the group's shared social experiences in order to fully develop. A key event in the development process occurs when group members learn that a certain level of comfort and relatively low apprehension arise when they abide by these values (Schein, 2004). However, managers should distinguish between such values and "espoused" or spoken values (Argyris & Schön, 1978); the latter are not based on prior learning but predict what group members will *say* in certain situations, but not necessarily *do* in other situations.

The group attempts to dissuade members from violating group norms. The pressure to conform can be enormous depending on the stray member's will and attachment to the group. The group exerts such pressure to survive and further the group's self-interests. This pressure can be subtle, as when advertising sales staffers attempting to stifle superperformers in their group by jokingly deriding their extraordinary peers as *brownnosers*, or when journalists call their investigative brethren *hot shots*. In each case, the message is, "you're different," and the group has indicated limits for its members. The alert media manager has three decisions to make: (a) What is best for the group? (b) What is best for the threatened employee? (c) What is best for the company?

Sometimes the same action has positive ramifications for all concerned, albeit not immediately. For example, one newspaper editor, feeling overwhelmed by negative tensions in his newsroom, invited a motivational speaker to lead a workshop on changing workplace attitudes; more sensitive and honest communication was recommended, something that would take time (Straus, 2005). At other times, an individual is terminated, as Jayson Blair and Jack Kelley were by *The New York Times* and by *USA TODAY*, respectively, for plagiarism. And, sometimes the response is gray, as in the case of the Tampa Bay TV reporter Don Germaise who was "disciplined" for apparently agreeing to answer questions from a White separatist in exchange for the separatist's cooperation with his own story (Deggans, 2006). In each case, group pressure, however subtly, was used to produce the desired result.

Media settings also play host to another informal group phenomenon when innovation and creativity come into play. Media constantly generate new ideas; the journalistic media do so daily. Media managers facilitate creativity without thinking about it using incentives such as bylines (in print), video stand-ups and standard out cues (in broadcasting), and merit pay—in short, in creating content and in organizational administration. Creative media employees also naturally share the determination, eccentricity, curiosity, and experience required of ingenuity (Straub, 1984). Much innovation depends on the organizational or group culture in place and the degree to which employees feel involved with the organization. For example, one group of journalists took up a collection to help reunite a family because staffers felt it was in line with the company tradition of doing the right thing (Petersen, 1992).

Yet informal groups also need consistently shared meanings, adaptability to the external environment, and a shared vision (Denison, 1990). These shared items are not easily found when two informal groups suddenly merge, as often occurs in the ongoing age of technological and corporate convergence. For example, prior to the newsroom staff merger of the two competing Pittsburgh newspapers, one had a corporate management staff, whereas the other was described as "freewheeling, loose, and breezy." To facilitate the transition, the staff created several committees of reporters and editors from both organizations. Yet the lack of involvement with the new organization, the lack of a shared culture (inconsistency), and the initial absence of a clear mission (other than to produce a newspaper) led to conflicts in the new, combined newsroom (Jurczak, 1996).

In contrast, convergent environments require constant contact between and among groups to avoid conflicting viewpoints (Killebrew, 2001). For example, *The Peoria* (Ill.) *Journal Star* in 1994 started a major overhaul of its advertising production process; it created teams. This meant consolidating various departments (sales, billing, design, and production) and remodeling some offices to put team members in close proximity. Still, teammates had to learn to work as a team and overcome their anxieties (Martel, 2006).

Invariably groups inevitably generate conflict with other groups. As groups become more cohesive and members identify closely with each other, the potential for self-direction (and the desire for autonomy) grows as well (Sherif, 1962). Groups come to see their goals as different from those of other groups in the same organization (Deutsch, 1949). Various studies have shown that media are no different. For example, subdepartments in a TV production facility each brought its own agenda to the product (Elliott & Chaney, 1969). Departmental membership affects how broadcast station employees perceive goals and resolve conflicts (Allen, Seibert, Haas, & Zimmermann, 1988). The departmental affiliations of one state's newspaper managers affected how much cooperation they believed was needed in their individual newspapers (Sylvie, 1996). And in small newspapers, editors place less value on the role of copy editors than on other newsroom positions (Crable, Morelock, & Willard, 2005).

Part of the problem lies in the increasing complexity of modern organizations. As a company becomes more complex, it adds more tiers to its hierarchy and lengthens its chain of command. The chances for communication distortion (and thus conflict) increase. This increasing complexity convinces groups of their controlling expertise in the company and thus their discretion to lead it (Van Maanen & Barley, 1984). As a result, productive media managers need to understand groups and cultures, especially ingroup communication networks (Collins & Guetzkow, 1964). By doing so, managers gain a grasp on information flow and the group's decision-making dynamics, ultimately allowing a better understanding of the group's motivational needs.

Common Problems

Labor-intensive organizations, such as media firms, inevitably run into motivation-related struggles. The following section deals with a few of the more common complications, followed by a discussion of some of the strategies a manager can use.

Retention

The ultimate motivational problem is *turnover*, when an employee quits. Reasons vary, but usually dissatisfaction carries much of the blame. Turnover rates vary by company, but in media can range as high as 50%, so in a year's time, half of a company's employees will leave. Managers must then recruit, select, and train replacements while some remaining employees may become concerned as to their own status.

Turnover is an inconsistent foe of media managers because not everyone quits at the same time. Yet turnover represents a major problem with minorities and women, who make up a disproportionate share of departures and who are often expected to help news organizations diversify their content. In some years, certain departments have higher turnover rates than others. For example, newspaper circulation departments lost slightly more than a third of their workforce despite having only a fifth of all newspaper employees in the early 1990s. Yet even within departments, minority employees are more likely than nonminorities to leave. This should not surprise the media manager, who only has to look at studies showing that African American and Latino journalists are twice as likely than White journalists to be dissatisfied (Bramlett-Solomon, 1993) or that women newspaper sportswriters—despite 75% of them being satisfied with their jobs—say they receive more sexist language from their newspaper colleagues than did women in news departments (Miller & Miller, 1995).

Now consider that journalists at the beginning of their careers are more likely to defect than veteran journalists (Weaver & Wilhoit, 1996). Recruits fresh out of college often think of newspapers and TV as media their parents consume that are out of touch with younger people. Much of the problem may center on the race, gender, and age differences between managers and those they supervise. Also, managers may have little time to interact with employees on an informal basis, may fear the general 1990s backlash against diversity, or see diversity as weakening operations. Finally, some experts concede that they lack the proper methods to evaluate minority employees (Phillips, 1991).

Retaining quality employees in newsrooms and other media work environments remains probably the greatest challenge for media managers. Much of the solution resides in discovering the unmet needs of the employee considering leaving. In regards to diversity, countless surveys have determined that minority groups differ in what would keep them on the job (e.g., McGill, 2000). Minority broadcast producers, for example, say they are not as aware of training opportunities as Whites are; and minority news directors are more likely to say the availability of professional-development training is a deciding factor in considering whether to stay in the job.

Managers must not be quick to overgeneralize, however. This does not mean that minorities do not care about factors such as pay and supervisory relationships And it's not only minorities who present a retention issue; women represent a much smaller percentage of the journalism workforce than they do of the U.S. national workforce.

Stress

With the bombing of the World Trade Center, its subsequent coverage, and the beginning of hostilities in Iraq, journalists seemed to rediscover that media life is stressful. It wasn't exactly news that many ex-journalists left the field because of frustration, low pay, poor management, and bad hours (Fedler, Buhr, & Taylor, 1988). Nor was it surprising newspaper copy editors reported a higher level of emotional exhaustion and depersonalization than reporters (Cook, Banks, & Turner, 1993), or that nearly two fifths of editors also said they have a job-related health problem (Giles, 1983). Public-relations practitioners said that stress is a constant factor (Butler, Broussard, & Adams, 1987). Newsroom managers were even more aware that stress is an inherent perception and reality for employees.

Stress is a matter of perspective. Noting that earlier research (Giles, 1983) reported editors find disagreements with subordinates challenging and stimulating, Endres (1988) also reported that reporters think such incidents are stressful. Second, expectations play a role. McQuarrie (1999) discovered that professional mystique or "the expectations built up through training and through the early stages of on-the-job socialization" (p. 21) affects how journalists see their supervisor. Professional mystique creates an expectation of how supervisors behave and essentially makes journalists dissatisfied. Finally, journalism students are no more or less stress prone than professional journalists nor is their stress manifested differently. Common symptoms include depression, daydreaming, less concern about work quality, and considering a change in major/career (Endres, 1992).

Stress effects vary depending on employee reaction to job demands. The media manager must be vigilant in sensing stress signals, but stress can take so many forms as to render it relatively invisible. Generally, these signals tend to stand out by their frequency, intensity, or abnormality. If an employee misses too many deadlines or reacts emotionally or out of character, the manager should make a mental note of the incident. For example, stress can be expected when major changes such as layoffs, new rules, technology, or increased expectations occur, as often happens in change-intensive media workplaces.

Some jobs or environments inherently create stress by design (Aldag & Brief, 1978). In media, such design flaws usually include deadline pressures, the need for creative content and packaging, and the need for continuous production. Feinstein and Owen (2002)—evaluating signs of psychological distress for 140 journalists who had reported on at least one war and for 107 journalists who had not covered a war—found that, war journalists reported higher weekly alcohol consumption and higher levels of depression and post-traumatic stress disorder (PTSD).

A new source of stress is the emerging pattern of misalignment between the goals of journalists and those of the media owners and managers. Many of the latter, infrequently educated in journalism, scorn in-depth, intricate stories in favor of more marketable content, which upsets or discourages journalists (Gardner, Csikszentmihalyi, & Damon, 2001). For instance, rank-and-file journalists psychologically connect a stronger profit orientation with weaker journalism (Beam, 2006). These major stressors may not be totally within the media manager's control, but awareness helps the manager understand and prepare for employee reaction.

Missing Inspiration, Creativity, or Challenge

Media employees crave their ability to create, react constructively, or see the meaning of their work. Since the Baby Boom generation began entering the news, entertainment, advertising, distribution, or production workforce, nothing has related more to an employee's role and corporate or occupational identity than the ability to innovate or create something or overcome an obstacle in producing a quality product. A happy journalist or one contemplating leaving the profession can both be interested in a new challenge (Weaver & Wilhoit, 1996).

However, a media manager's capability finds limits here. For example, a survey of newspaper and magazine designers (Coleman & Colbert, 1999) found that the innate personality characteristics that most predict creativity—e.g., daydreaming, having crazy ideas, and intrinsic motivation—can only be influenced indirectly by managers who encourage designers to express this side of their personalities (p. 7):

> Successful managers know that what looks like employees wasting time by staring out windows or at posters on walls could actually be the incubation of original and creative solutions to design problems. Thus, managers who avoid punishing or discouraging this behavior, either overtly or subtly, tend to work better with creative employees. Likewise, apparently crazy ideas are encouraged rather than ridiculed. As long as all involved realize that these ideas need to be refined into workable design solutions, the freedom to put forth wild ideas can motivate designers to do better, more creative things that still meet the standards of good visual communication.

As a media organization's lifeblood, when creativity is strangled, reduced, or obstructed, the media manager has a difficult task helping the employee relocate his or her inspiration. Much of the problem stems from insufficient resources, staffing, and space. Other factors include long hours, inadequate supervision, an improperly designed job, and burnout. Perhaps the primary cause is the increasing need for self-determination on the job (Braus, 1992), particularly in younger employees. Two of the strongest predictors for job satisfaction in younger journalists are autonomy and interest or challenge.

The case for managerial scrutiny of employee autonomy cannot be emphasized enough. Autonomy is cited throughout this chapter as a crucial factor in motivation. In a study of Texas daily newspaper reporters, the predictors of job satisfaction included a sense of achievement, personal growth, newsroom policy, impact on community, and autonomy (Chang & Sylvie, 1999). Older, more experienced workers often have a different view than younger employees of the day-to-day problems that seem to threaten autonomy. Veteran employees take a longer view of job pressure, changes, and stress. The opponent, the tedium, and seeming-oppression that at times can characterize media work, is simply outlasted by the smarter, more patient, wiser, long-range-viewing, older employee. Media managers must be creative and innovative in battling any or all three of these typical motivational maladies, but especially when it comes to autonomy.

A study of newspaper change suggests that variables such as fear and structural politics deter change (Sylvie & Witherspoon, 2002). Re-examine, for instance, the Pittsburgh newspapers' merger. One paper bought the other, whose reporters so feared the new management that they created tension and conflict in the transition (Jurczak, 1996). Reporters also have cited concerns for traditional autonomy in rebuffing civic or public journalism as a ploy of increasingly powerful corporate interests to erode autonomy. They believe it takes the news-making process out of the reporters' hands and places it in the hands of local communities by letting communities define news through public forums on issues of concern. This endangers the journalistic autonomy that supposedly protects reporters from outside influence and bias (Gade, Perry, & Colyle, 1997; Sylvie & Witherspoon, 2002). Notions of autonomy develop early in student journalists' campus newspaper careers, seemingly implanting a feeling of autonomy that lessens the acceptance of civic journalism (McDevitt, Gassaway, & Perez, 2002). Obviously, autonomy deserves singular managerial scrutiny.

The wisest course involves planning for these contingencies. Wiser still is organizing and structuring policies, procedures, and programs that prevent morale problems from arising and foster a healthy corporate culture. For example, turnover problems might be approached at various points in the employment process.

Even if a manager examines the peculiarities of the job and the idiosyncrasies of the employee in respect to motivation, the combination of the job and the person brings with it a completely new set of issues for the manager to consider. The manager behind the glass wall in the introduction should carefully reconsider the interviewing process when new employees are hired. Interviews are not just negotiations for salary, benefits, and production expectations. They should reveal how the job fits the person seeking employment.

In the case of creativity and autonomy, media managers often complain that managing creative employees is difficult because these employees want more autonomy than other perhaps lesser-talented peers. It becomes an issue of whether the manager or employee has control. This is not uncommon in media organizations where employees become stars of some kind. Managers must balance pleasing employees and their adoring public, behaving fairly (to stars and nonstars), maintaining the indirect revenue stream the star may help generate, maintaining credibility, and perhaps maintaining self-respect.

Managers must be patient and realize their job requires pursuing and choosing the best options. One such option is to establish strong loyalty within stars because loyalty can stem turnover, which is caused by lack of challenge or autonomy. Many creative employees lack an initial strong commitment to an organization because their creativity and confidence in that creativity allows them mobility, making job security less of a need. Therefore, the media manager needs to establish trust in star performers (after all, as stars they could argue they merit stronger consideration than most employees). Many news directors and editors have found that the participative management style constitutes a good way to do so.

This is especially evident in the growth of teams, team building, and formal work groups. However, whereas some teams develop into the basic unit of design for organizing work (Kolodny & Stjernberg, 1993), news media adoption of teams has struggled for acceptance because of the media's long dependence on individual innovation and creativity. To suggest teamwork in some media settings is viewed as another managerial attempt at stifling creativity and autonomy. Some particularly resistant employees view it as co-opting employees. Management appears to share power, but the team actually is a ruse to squelch complaints and get employees to buy into management's agenda.

Despite such concerns, teams are beginning to blossom in media. Now it is not uncommon for newspaper reporters to work together on stories (Russial, 1997). Media managers facing change or distinct technological challenges instill a sense of *we-ness* in their staffs depending on the technology's relative advantage and compatibility with existing methods of operation (Sylvie & Danielson, 1989). More proactive managers see teams as a collective way to manage the uncertainties of change that beset media. Still, teams garner mixed reactions in that some "teammates" feel that teams reduce individual autonomy (Endres, Schierhorn, & Schierhorn, 1999; Sylvie & Witherspoon, 2002) and thus require innovative approaches.

Whatever the approach, a media manager's leadership style is crucial to how a staff is motivated depending on the workplace and situation (McQuarrie, 1992). In TV, a gradual switch in managerial style (from authoritarian to participative) increased job satisfaction and productivity (Adams & Fish, 1987), whereas for some newspaper journalists, a manager's style did not affect his or her relationships with editors (Gaziano & Coulson, 1988).

Summary

As the workforce continues to change and the economy becomes more global, motivation is even more crucial to successful media management. Media organizations are too complex and unique for any manager to hope to get by without some understanding of human needs and desires.

An effective first step is to gain first-hand knowledge of the work context, such as what employees bring to the job, what the job requires, and how the two interact. That implies not just familiarity with motivation theories and concepts, but also sensitivity for how those theories factor in the workplace. In other words, for the new recruits of the world, the reluctant supervisors need to know that for each action the recruit takes there is a reason; second-guessing is unacceptable.

This approach requires a deep appreciation for diversity, not just demographically speaking, but also for the idiosyncrasies and unique traits of each potential employee. Women and people of color bring experiences that White male media managers do not understand and perhaps fear. Yet, proper motivation must be a fearless duty. Social wallflowers should not become managers because dealing with people constitutes the bulk of managing.

Finally, the media are filled with potential psychiatric bombshells in the guise of their workforce. Most people do their jobs and need no external motivation; they are self-driven. However, the efficiency orientation of the increasingly corporate and converging workplace mandates that managers know how to solve problems and act immediately to do so.

The media manager should view this information not just as motivation to become a better manager, but as an incentive to help plan and structure systems that properly and adequately recognize and reward media employees. Motivation can be understood, managed, and planned. The manager has to decide how to structure such a plan according to the needs of the workplace and the people who potentially work there. Without that perspective, managers will see motivation as a problem to be solved rather than an opportunity to manage effectively.

Case 3.1 Charles and Mae

After covering everything from the courthouse to city hall to local schools, Mae Tyler, the 38-year-old, 16-year veteran of the newsroom took the 5 P.M. (solo anchor) and 6 P.M. (co-anchor) slots 18 months ago. She says she is happy, but Charles Gaines, the news director and her immediate boss, thinks Mae is dissatisfied. He never sees her smile in the newsroom. He has noted that she has been frequently ill lately, causing her to miss deadlines. She complains her salary (about $75,000) trails that of 6 P.M. coanchor Mark Vigar, who is younger and has less experience. Her 5 P.M. ratings were down 15% from the last ratings period, and the show is ranked second only by a half-share ahead of the third-place competitor.

Charles wants to understand. Mae has been a station mainstay ever since she graduated from college. She was the first female to win major reporting awards at the station; when she finally got promoted to anchor, station General Manager Anthony Llorens touted it as "a long time in coming" and said she was a role model for other females at the station and across the city. Mae prides herself on being a good wife and mother as well as a professional, although she has always struggled to find balance among them. Lately Mae's attitude, like a yawn, is contagious; her younger colleagues in the newsroom often take their cue from her on various matters, particularly on coverage issues such as story angles and source selection as it pertains to gender and race. Mae thinks Charles is sexist and, perhaps, unintentionally racist. She has seen how he treats Mark (they joke around a lot) and how differently he criticizes the anchors: He is direct and blunt with her and almost apologetic with Mark.

Mae is the only African American on the city staff. There have been other African Americans on the staff over the years, but none in Charles' 10-year tenure as news director. Mae feels as if she also is being singled out because of her race. Her evaluations for the last 6 months have noted her inconsistency in meeting deadlines and an apparent lack of team spirit. Yet Mae feels these complaints are race-based and sexist primarily because, when she started to change her hairstyle, Charles told her he did not like it. He is also critical of her wardrobe choices (he tells her, "You looked good today," about once every couple of weeks) as well as her package selections ("too many talking heads," he tells her) for 5 P.M. Charles, who said there were more pressing deadline pieces, ignored her ideas for news features about schools and health and more hard news on how city policy impacts the African American community.

Mae asked Charles for a meeting. She wants to challenge her evaluation and find out whether Charles has a problem with women and African Americans and stories about them. She thinks the problem extends to a salary inequity, too. In preparation for the following questions, review the chapter guidelines.

Assignment

1. If you were Charles, and using the decision wheel from chapter 1, show how you would you prepare for the meeting with Mae.
2. Which factor, job mandates or employee potential, seems to be most influential in this case? Is autonomy a factor at all? Which idea or concept in the chapter most influences your opinion and why?
3. Assign one student to play Charles' role, another to play Mae's. Have the two conduct their meeting. Afterward, (a) analyze the discussion to determine which psychological theory—equity, expectancy, or goal-setting—plays a major role in each person's approach to the conversation; and (b) determine Charles' next most logical course of action.
4. In relation to number 3, how big a factor do the race and gender of each participant play in the meeting? Conduct some research in your library (especially on media and minority retention) to show whether Charles should consider Mae's race or gender in how he approaches the meeting and in how he devises a solution. Be prepared to defend your answer.

Case 3.2 New Kid in Town

Put yourself in the shoes of the new recruit mentioned at the beginning of this chapter. Aside from internships, assume it's your first real journalism job.

Deona Laurent, the manager who's been eyeing you behind the glass wall, has been working in the newsroom for 5 years. She is the go-between between you and the metro editor. She was a local government reporter prior to her current position, which she has held for 5 years and 9 months.

You were an editor at your college paper, so you think you understand how she feels, but you have your own worries concerning this place.

Assignment

1. What kind of preparation should you have done before entering the newsroom?
2. What kinds of things should you know about Deona's role in the newsroom? How does her role affect her approach toward motivation, and how would that approach differ from the metro editor's approach?

3. What are your prime motivators as a new reporter? In what ways do those motivators conflict with your perception of Deona's approach to motivation?

4. Go to the Poynter Institute's Web site (and at least one other respected industry source) to find additional information about motivation. Report to the class your formal advice about motivation tailored to the needs of a new recruit fresh out of college.

5. Go to the same two sites you used in number 4 and evaluate motivational tools. Report to the class at least three motivational tools that Deona can use to help her discover the recruit's concerns without having to talk to the recruit.

Case 3.3 Motivating Convergence

"Convergence" is coming to your KRUM-TV newsroom, and you've been asked by your boss to prepare your staff. These are the issues you face:

1. As part of the convergence process, your TV newsroom is partnered with the local newspaper. You have always felt like the paper had an objectivity problem, and you've made it no secret among your reporting staff.

2. Another component of convergence will incorporate the station's online staff into the newsroom. Your bread and butter is immediacy, breaking news, delivering content as it happens, but you've got to figure how to make the assignment desk, the producers, and the "Webbers" work together, and how it will trickle down to the reporters.

3. People—how are they going to adapt to the new structures that numbers 1 and 2 above will require? There's Jamie Morris, your star veteran known for his investigative work. Jamie detests blogs for the way they blur news and opinion, but—he doesn't know it yet—the boss wants him to do one. Then there's Katrina Flood, KRUM online news director, who constantly worries about quality control on the site (stories go through only one edit) combined with the station's breaking news brand. Katrina's worries are warranted, especially considering newspapers typically edit stories at least three to five times before publication. But your reporting staff thinks that Katrina's timid and—thanks to the fact that she's the only woman on the online staff—a "wuss" when it comes to making decisions. Then there's training. No one on the reporting staff has a clue about newspapers or the Web or how each works. They've heard talk about

"forgetting old boundaries" in an even greater push to marketing stories that people want, rather than what they need.

Assignment

1. What should you do to make things better between your staff and the online staff? And, what should you do to make things better between your staff and the newspaper staff?
2. Assign students to role-play the respective heads of the three converging groups. Set up a meeting to discuss organizational concerns.
3. Describe the needs the following theorists would identify in this situation: Maslow, Alderfer, McClelland, Skinner, and Bandura. Whose theory would be most appropriate to your job as convergence motivator and why?
4. What group cultural concerns are at play in this situation? How will you use them to your advantage to motivate employees to converge successfully?

4

MANAGEMENT OF GLOBAL MEDIA ORGANIZATIONS

One of the most dramatic changes in the media over the past 25 years has been the rapid expansion of media companies into global markets. Today, many young media professionals will find themselves working for global media companies in their first jobs after graduation, and even more will find themselves part of global corporations as they advance through their careers. Some may even be assigned to one of their employers' overseas offices. Media are an increasingly important global industry.

Managing a global media corporation offers unique opportunities and special challenges. Companies operating across national borders must serve audiences and advertisers with widely different needs and tastes. When media companies expand overseas, organizational structures become more complicated, workforces become more diverse in language and culture, and managers must become sensitive to the complexities of international politics, economics, and business practices.

All of the management skills that have been discussed in this book apply to managing international operations However, in the global media corporation, the management situation is much more complex. If such problems seem a distant concern for many media students, be assured that they are not. Major media companies such as News Corp., Viacom, Bertlesmann, and Disney generate significant portions of their revenues from foreign markets, while nearly all of them say that continued global expansion is a key part of their future strategic management plans.

In addition to global expansion, media companies also are engaged in a brisk international trade in cultural and creative products. The value of that trade more than doubled between 1994 and 2003 to a conservatively estimated U.S. $60 billion (UNESCO, 2005), and the United States has long been one of the biggest players in that market.

There are excellent career opportunities in media sectors, such as television syndication and film distribution, heavily involved in the global sales, marketing, and export and import of media products. Finally, in an increasingly interconnected world, most national and regional news organizations have journalists on location in hot spots around the globe, which means that even companies that don't own subsidiaries overseas often have employees working overseas.

This international expansion has many practical implications for today's media managers. It has become important for media managers to understand global media markets and the risks and advantages of international expansion; to be able to work in a multicultural environment; and to understand how to manage content development and distribution for international audiences. This chapter will explore the practical challenges of media management in an increasingly international environment.

Why Globalization? Why Now?

Although the globalization of the media has become a widely discussed topic in recent years, it is not new. What *is* new is the rapid move of almost all types of media companies, including television and radio, into international markets. Also new is the increase in the international trade in media products and the implications of that trade for both the development of media content and the financing of media production.

When you look at how quickly media companies have moved to expand their operations globally in recent years, there are two obvious questions: (a) Why globalize? and (b) Why now?

The answers are important because they relate directly to the strategic management of media companies, whether domestic or international. They also relate to the ability of the next generation of media managers to develop successful media products and run successful companies.

To understand those answers, you must first understand that media companies—and media managers—operate at the intersection of three forces: (a) markets, (b) technologies, and (c) policies (Fig. 1). In other words, media managers are constantly responding to changes that occur in the market for media products, the technologies used to produce and distribute media products, and the national and international policies that regulate media industries. Making the job of media management even more complicated is the fact that a change in one of these

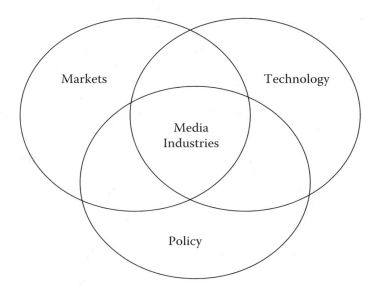

FIGURE 4.1. The relationship between media industries, markets, technology, and policy.

three areas often causes changes in either or both of the other two areas. In the case of the rapid globalization of media in recent years, each of the three forces played an important role.

Markets

Markets refer to the economics of media: the resources needed for production, the demand for media products, and the business models media companies use to ensure that they can stay in business. Media products—whether news or entertainment or physical or electronic in nature—are *information products*. As such, they are subject to the same basic economic processes as any other type of product, but they also have some unique economic characteristics most other products do not share (Priest, 1994). Several of those unique characteristics make it advantageous for media companies to expand their markets as widely as possible, or in other words, to globalize.

- *There is a high level of risk and uncertainty in media production.* Media producers have to decide how much they will invest to produce content without being able to predict audience and advertiser demand for that content. It also is almost impossible to test market media products. You cannot produce only a few minutes of a film or one chapter of a book and ask people how they like it before you decide whether to invest in the full cost of production. The inability to test market greatly increases the risks and uncertainties of media production.
- The greater the financial risks of production, the more important it is for producers to distribute the final product to as many people as possible. If producers can offer a product to enough people, eventually enough people will probably buy it, and the producer will make a profit. The global market is, of course, the largest market available.
- *Media have high "first-copy" costs.* In other words, almost all of the costs of producing media products are incurred producing the very first copy. Reproducing that copy for wider distribution is much less expensive. Because of high first-copy costs, the more people the media company can reach with the product, the more likely it becomes that the producer eventually will recover the production costs. That makes having access to audiences around the globe desirable. In fact, for media products with high production costs, such as feature films, having a global market is almost a requirement. Only about 2 out of 10 U.S. films recover their investment costs through domestic ticket sales (Valenti, 2002). In 2004, for the first time, more than 50% of the film industry's revenue came from box-office sales outside of North America (Pfanner, 2006).
- *Media products vary in their relevance to audience members.* Demand for media products is hard to predict because what appeals to one person may not appeal to another. Two people reading the same book or viewing the same TV program may value the experience differently. Media also are language-based products, so any media product produced in a language that a person does not speak is inaccessible and, therefore, irrelevant to that individual. All of these factors make it hard to predict the demand for a media product. That encourages producers to distribute the product as widely as possible in order to increase the chances that enough people will buy it for the producer to make a profit.

The issue of relevance is even more of a challenge in global media markets. Media are cultural products in that they carry messages that both shape and reflect cultures. Research has shown that audiences prefer media content that is culturally relevant to them (Straubhaar, 1991), which makes demand for media products in overseas markets very hard to predict, even while the variability of relevance makes global distribution desirable. The greater the distance between the culture reflected in a book, film, or other media product and the culture of the potential audience, the lower both the demand and the price for that media product will be. Comedies, for example, usually sell for less than action or drama programs in foreign television markets because humor tends to be very culturally specific. Similarly, few newspapers have expanded successfully into global markets because newspaper content tends to be primarily of local or regional relevance. Newspapers with successful international editions tend to be business papers, such as the *Wall Street Journal* and *Financial Times,* which capitalize on the global business community's need for information about the global economy.

- *Media products have "time-constrained consumption."* This refers to the fact that media require time, as well as money, to consume. In order to make buying a book worthwhile, you have to know that you'll have the time to read it. The time constraints on media consumption also refer to the fact that many information products, such as news, have a short shelf life. A news organization will not find many people willing to pay to get yesterday's news. Producers of media products with this characteristic have only one chance to sell to consumers, so it becomes important to reach as many audience members as possible while the product is still valuable. Again, this encourages development of global distribution networks.

- *The externality value of media.* Media content has "ripple" effects on society going beyond the direct value of a particular media product. For example, books are used in education. Education itself produces value in society through encouraging innovation, creating a more productive workforce, encouraging healthier lifestyles, etc. Therefore, a school textbook's true value includes the value of all of those positive ripple effects, although the author and publisher of the book cannot capture that value through price. On the other hand, the public suspects that violent content has negative externalities, such as encouraging violence or the toleration of violence in society.

The externality value of information also both encourages and discourages the globalization of media products. It encourages globalization in that people and governments want to make sure their countries have immediate access to the latest information, particularly in the areas of education, science, and innovation. They welcome companies that produce and distribute such information. But news and information products also carry culturally laden messages, and media experts have long been concerned about the impact such messages may have on policy, public opinion, and culture when the messages are produced by foreign media corporations. For this reason, until the last quarter-century, most countries had strict regulations prohibiting or limiting the foreign ownership of television and radio stations, telephone companies and, in some cases, newspapers.

Even today, many countries and economic blocs, such as Canada and the European Union, have strict quotas on the import of foreign media products. Indeed, because of their cultural content, media are among the few products for which the World Trade Organization (WTO) allows member states to maintain protectionist-trading policies.

In summary, because of the economic characteristics of information products, media producers are more likely to succeed if they can sell their content to as many people as possible. That encourages media companies to expand into global markets. Unlike most goods such as clothes, appliances, or automobiles, which have to be shipped overseas by plane or cargo ship, most media content can be sent electronically Therefore, for media companies, global distribution can greatly reduce risks while costing relatively little.

Technology

Technology opened new channels for content distribution and made it easier and less expensive for media companies to distribute their products worldwide. However, the new channels also fragmented audiences, leading to lost share in media companies' existing markets, which pushed them to expand into new markets.

In the 1970s, most countries had only two or three broadcast television channels, because the broadcast spectrum could carry only so many signals without having them interfere with one another. Particularly in regions such as Europe, where countries are small, not every country could have multiple channels; in 1971, five countries in Western Europe had only one television channel, and only two had more than two channels (*Screen Digest*, 2001, November 1). As a result, most European nations and many countries in other parts of the world operated only public service broadcast channels similar to the Public Broadcasting System (PBS) in the United States. Privately owned commercial broadcasting did not exist in many places.

In the 1980s, improvements in cable and satellite technologies made possible delivery of large numbers of television channels to audiences without signal interference. Many nations began allowing privately owned commercial broadcasting to develop. By the mid-1990s, at least 700 different channels were available on satellites that reached Europe

(European Audiovisual Observatory, 1997) and nearly 3,000 television networks were on the air in European Union countries, counting the channels available in each country separately (UNESCO, 2005). In the same period, the average U.S. cable system carried 61 channels (Newspaper Association of America, 2004). This growth created a chance for media companies to expand internationally and many did, creating foreign subsidiaries and exporting content and programming ideas.

While new technologies such as cable, satellite, VCRs, DVDs, digital music, and the Internet provided new global opportunities, they also brought new competition and an incentive for globalization. In a clear example of technology and markets affecting each other, the growth in the number of media channels resulted in audience fragmentation, and media companies lost market share in their home markets. They saw overseas expansion as a way to offset those losses.

Finally, digital technology's emergence further reduced the cost of reproducing and distributing media content. The cost decline made it potentially even more profitable for media companies to globally expand.

Policy

National and international policies also played a major role in the rapid media globalization; obviously, they made it legal to do so. Historically, most countries, including the United States, prohibited or limited foreign ownership of communication companies, particularly telephone and broadcast companies. Telephone infrastructure is critical to government and military operations, so foreign ownership was restricted on national security grounds, while broadcast ownership was limited to prevent foreign propaganda.

However, the 1980s saw three events contribute to major changes in world communication policies. The 1983 breakup of the AT&T telephone monopoly and subsequent deregulation of the telecommunication industry in the United States dramatically lowered the cost of long-distance U.S. telephone calls by introducing competition into the long-distance market. Since AT&T no longer had the power to decide what technologies could and could not be connected to the telephone network, it also brought a flood of new telecommunications technologies onto the American market.

As a result, U.S. businesses could significantly lower their communication-related production costs and gain a competitive advantage in the global marketplace. Those advantages became ever more apparent as computer networking grew in importance and, by the late 1980s, other nations began deregulating their telecommunications industries to help their industries gain similar advantages. To encourage competition and innovation, many countries began allowing foreign companies into their telephone markets; such liberalization and privatization of communication industries quickly extended to the electronic media, particularly as digital and wireless technologies eroded lines between telephone, data, and multichannel information and entertainment services.

The second major 1980s event involved the collapse of the Eastern Bloc in 1989. Literally, within hours of the fall of the Berlin Wall, Western European media companies set up offices in East Germany. Similar scenarios occurred across Central Europe as Communist governments fell. Western media companies often moved in before the new governments had a chance to formulate new media ownership policies. By 2004, a study by the European Federation of Journalists showed that foreign companies dominated media ownership in many, perhaps even most, Central European countries (European Federation of Journalists, 2004). Most of the owners were Western European media companies, although some U.S. companies also had investments.

The final key 1980s policy shift was the change in international trade rules, first through the General Agreements on Trade and Tariffs (GATT Agreements) and later through the World Trade Organization (WTO). But even as trade barriers on other types of goods lifted, many nations insisted—over U.S. objections—that they be allowed to limit media imports because of the culturally laden nature of media content. As a result, international joint ventures between media companies in film and television production increased. Most nations' trading rules hold that if one of the partners in the production is a domestic company, the film or program qualifies as domestic content and is exempt from import quotas.

In summary, the answers to the questions, "Why Globalization?" and "Why now?" are simply that market, technology, and policy forces have converged over the past 30 years to make global media expansion easier than ever before. It has always been economically desirable for media producers to reach the largest audiences possible. However, in the computer age, the global economy has become dependent on information and on the communication industries that provide it. As a result, governments have moved to deregulate communication industries to encourage the development of new information technologies. Those technologies have created new channels for media distribution and made global distribution of media products faster, easier, and cheaper.

The Structure of Global Media Companies

A media corporation expanding into international markets soon faces the question of how to structure its foreign investments. Decisions about structure affect the level of risk the company takes in its new venture, the human and financial resources it needs to support them, and the financial returns it can expect. A media company usually must consider at least three key structural elements: (a) the effect of overseas investments on a media company's overall corporate structure; (b) the ownership structures used for foreign investments; and (d) the managerial structures used to govern relationships between domestic and overseas operations.

Effects on Corporate Structures

A media firm investing overseas should decide what type of investment to make. A common reason for foreign investment is to expand a company's core business into new geographic areas. Newspaper companies such as Germany's Westdeutsche Allgemeine Zeitung group (WAZ) may buy additional newspapers in countries such as Hungary, Romania, and Serbia. News Corp. may distribute the Fox broadcasting network through joint ventures in Bulgaria and Serbia. The term used in business for creating or acquiring additional companies in the same industry sector is *horizontal integration*. With horizontal integration, a company expands the breadth of its operations within an industry sector in order to grasp more of the total market share.

However, some companies also see an opportunity to vertically or laterally integrate. *Vertical integration* occurs when a company buys subsidiaries that produce products that fit into its supply or distribution chain. An example is a newspaper that owns a paper mill that produces newsprint or a cable system operator that sets up a cable network. News Corp.'s investments in Sky Italia and BSkyB direct broadcast satellite television companies also are examples of vertical integration because with them, News Corp. owns content-production companies, such as film and television studios, and distribution companies that deliver such content directly to audiences. Vertical integration helps companies control the costs and uncertainties of supply and distribution.

Lateral integration occurs when a company invests in companies that operate in different but related industries, such as when a media corporation owns television stations and newspapers. In theory, lateral integration provides a competitive advantage by reducing cross-media competition and allowing the company to bundle its products and services for customers. It also helps companies estimate revenue streams by providing income from different industry sectors. When demand in one sector, such as the film industry, falls, the downturn may be offset by increases in another sector such as television.

Such opportunities prompt a savvy media manager to ask how a foreign investment will fit into the company's existing corporate structure and stable of products. Given the high costs and slow returns of foreign investment, media companies in recent years have tended to globalize using existing products or lines of business. However, a few take the somewhat riskier approach of using global expansion to move into new industry sectors.

Ownership Structures

Overseas operations require some thought about their ownership structure. The simplest approach sets up the overseas operation as a wholly owned subsidiary, a company that the parent company owns and operates itself. This makes some operational aspects easier, simplifying decision making and leaving little room for misunderstandings among partners from different countries.

However, running a wholly owned subsidiary also means that the parent company cannot learn about the new market from a local partner or another company with expertise in that market. It also means that the parent company must shoulder all the financial burden of the foreign investment.

Therefore, many companies use a *joint venture structure*, in which two or more companies own part of the operating company. Some nations require foreign companies wanting to enter their media markets to do so through joint ventures with domestic partners. In 2006, for example, Serbia issued licenses for five national television networks. Foreign applicants were required to prove that they were applying for the license through a joint venture with a Serbian partner who would own at least 50% of the proposed network.

Joint ventures help companies share the risks of market entry or product development by sharing the costs of the project with a partner. Joint ventures also allow companies to draw on the technical or local expertise of their partners, their contacts with government, industry, and clients, and their knowledge of the local market and culture. Cultural knowledge particularly helps media companies concerned about the relevance of products varying widely across audiences and the content's cultural proximity to the audience. For this reason, newspaper companies investing overseas often use joint ventures, leaving day-to-day editorial control to the domestic partner because of the fundamentally local nature of newspaper content. International joint ventures also have become common in film and television production as a way to avoid national and regional import quotas on foreign films and programs.

Such joint ventures have downsides, however. Risks are shared, but so are profits. Managing costs frequently are high because key strategic decisions must be negotiated with the partner. International joint ventures often suffer from friction between the partners over differences in national and professional cultures, expectations, and business methods. As a result, research on joint ventures across all industries shows that most have a relatively short lifespan (Kogut, 1989).

A third strategy for foreign market entry involves *licensing,* in which a company develops a product and then sells the rights to produce and sell a version of that product to someone else in the local market. Generally, licensing agreements restrict what the person buying the license can do, requiring them to produce a product faithful to the original along specified lines including structure, design, and quality.

Licensing has become common in many media industry sectors; many magazine titles produced and distributed in multiple languages and markets are actually licensed to publishers in those markets. In Serbia, for example, a Serbian-language edition of the German car magazine *Autobild* is produced under license by a daily newspaper company that is owned by a German-Serbian joint venture. Generally, the original owner who sells the license provides the majority of the content, with the licensee hiring local writers to translate that copy into the appropriate language and produce enough local copy to give the magazine a domestic flavor.

In television, licensing or *format programming* (as it's called in the industry), has become increasingly important as cable and broadcast networks seek proven program concepts as a strategy for combating audience fragmentation and falling ratings. There are local versions of *American Idol* broadcast in at least a dozen countries under different names, while programs such as *Sesame Street, Wheel of Fortune, Survivor, Who Wants to Be A Millionaire,* and even various soap operas have multiple localized versions playing in countries around the world.

In format programming, usually the structure, characters, and storylines are similar to the original, although hosts or actors are domestic and some adjustments may be made to the original concept to increase cultural relevance. In the South African licensed version of *Sesame Street*, for example, an HIV-positive character was introduced in 2003 to increase AIDS awareness and education among children in that country, while versions of the program that air in Israel, Palestine, and Northern Ireland feature Muppets that teach tolerance of religious and cultural differences.

Licensing is a low-risk market-entry strategy allowing owners of a media concept to generate revenues from overseas markets with minimal investment. The local licensee makes most of the investment and takes on most of the risk. On the other hand, the licensee gains the benefit of buying an established product already known to be successful with audiences, thereby reducing the risks of original media production. Additionally, for some licensed products such as magazines, the original owner produces most of the content and ships it to its licensees around the world, reducing first-copy production costs.

However, neither the original owner nor the licensee generates as much revenue from a market as they would if they owned the product outright. The original owner has the additional risk that licensees may do something that harms the original brand. For example, if the licensee does a bad job of producing or marketing the product, local audiences may reject it, costing the original owner future revenues from that country. Even more problematic, because audiences rarely know a product is licensed, irresponsible or unethical behavior by the licensee may harm the reputation of the original product and the company that owns it.

Managerial Structures for Foreign Investments

Once a company decides what type of foreign investment to make, it can choose from four basic management models to oversee the operation: (a) international, (b) multinational, (c) global, and (d) transnational.

In the *international* model, a media company focuses on its domestic market and creates content with those audiences in mind. It later exports the product to overseas markets to generate additional sales, perhaps making a few minor changes in order to appeal to foreign audiences. Television series such as *Law and Order* or *Dallas*, created for the U.S. market and then sold in syndication overseas, illustrate the use of this model for global expansion.

In the *multinational model*, the parent media corporation establishes subsidiaries in foreign countries but allows those subsidiaries generous autonomy in product development and decision making. The primary responsibility of each subsidiary is to serve the domestic market in which it's located, despite being owned by a global company. For example, Viacom's MTV subsidiaries total 120 locally programmed MTV channels in 165 territories and 25 languages. Most feature local hosts and focus primarily on local music artists.

In the *global* model, a company develops products that it believes will have global appeal, knowing in advance that they will be distributed globally. Disney Corporation uses this model for many of its products, developing products, stories, and characters that will appeal to audiences worldwide.

In the past two decades, the U.S. film industry also has moved to the global model. Historically, Hollywood primarily produced films based on their appeal to U.S. audiences, because the U.S. market provided the bulk of box office sales. Films were released first in the United States, premiering in foreign markets about 6 weeks later. Today, the potential appeal of a film to foreign audiences has become a significant factor in studios' decisions to approve projects. Films, such as comedies, that may be less relevant to foreign audiences generally get much smaller production budgets. Major films are now released simultaneously in theaters worldwide since the global market is on the verge of becoming more important to Hollywood than the domestic market.

The *transnational* model is a network approach to global expansion. Companies charge their overseas subsidiaries with developing products that serve their surrounding markets, while sending their best ideas back to the parent company for global development and distribution. Conversely, the subsidiaries are expected to take ideas from the company's headquarters or other subsidiaries and adapt them for sale in the country or region that the subsidiary serves. The transnational model is based on a fluid exchange of ideas, knowledge, and products across the company's subsidiaries and markets.

The German media company Bertelsmann may be the best example in the media industry of the transnational model. Bertelsmann, which has operations in 63 countries and generates more than 70% of its revenue in countries other than its home market of Germany, is a major producer of magazines and music, among other types of media content. Both magazines and music are ideally suited for production through a transnational structure. Major magazine titles are frequently produced in multiple languages and countries. Often in such publications, the bulk of the content is shared across its international editions, while a small portion in each magazine is generated by the local in-country staff to appeal to local interests and conditions. Similarly, 68% of all music sales worldwide are generated by local artists with little appeal outside of their immediate market. However, only a few of those artists go on to become international superstars with a global market for their work.

Management Issues in Global Media Companies

When a media company owns overseas subsidiaries, all of the management functions and challenges discussed throughout this book take on additional complexity. Market analysis and planning, regulation, leadership, motivation and personnel management, product development and marketing, finance, and other management functions become more difficult because of the variety of market conditions, regulations, and cultures that media managers encounter when they cross borders. This section will consider some of the key issues media managers face in this increasingly global industry.

Analyzing Foreign Markets

When planning overseas investments, media managers often encounter more complex and uncertain market conditions than in domestic markets. Thus, they have to pay particular attention to legal and regulatory structures, competition levels, and demographic factors.

Since about 1980, much of the foreign direct investment by large major media corporations has gone to operations in less-developed countries undergoing major political and economic changes. The reason is simple: Media markets in developed countries are saturated with well-established companies, and market shares among existing competitors are declining. Consequently, media companies seeking growth target places where the media market is in flux, population demographics are changing, and the economy appears likely to grow in the near future. Central Europe, Russia, India, and China are markets that have been of particular interest to media investors in recent years.

Such countries offer an excellent investing opportunity. In many, if not most, countries going through economic or political liberalization, media move from state control (and often state ownership) to a system largely made of privately owned, advertising-supported media. The media market, as the country itself, is in transition. Media investors often move into the market before the transitional government can write new laws and regulations governing media ownership and operations. While affording entrepreneurs a chance to establish an early market foothold, it also raises the risk that regulations and broadcast licensing procedures eventually may force out some companies in the market.

Additionally, during major political transitions, new governments often are unstable. Following the end of a particular regime or system of government, the new government may initially adopt liberal media policies. Later, leaders may seek to reassert government ownership or control, particularly in countries with no tradition of an independent media. In recent years, for example, the Russian government moved to reassert more control over the media after a period of relative independence following the breakup of the Soviet Union in the early 1990s. Similar experiences in other countries have led at least a few savvy media entrepreneurs to set up off-site back-up operations in neighboring countries from which they can produce and distribute their products in the event of a government crackdown. The goal is to keep their foot in the market until media regulatory conditions stabilize.

Another significant consideration in overseas investments is the level of competition in the target market. In recent years, regime change and liberalization of media policies in many countries have been followed by a virtual land rush of media investors and entrepreneurs into the market. As a consequence, media competition has mushroomed. For example, Serbia has 10 million people and more than 755 television and radio stations/networks competing for their attention. Estimates of total advertising spending in Serbia across all markets and media vary but range up to U.S. $100 million for 2005 ("Media Management and Economics," 2006).

By comparison, New York City has 8 million people and around 50 radio and television stations located in the city, not counting digital television channels (Broadcasting & Cable, 2003–2004). According to the National Association of Broadcasters (2004), the top 25% of stations in the 10 largest U.S. television markets in 2003 averaged $100 million *per station* in advertising revenue—about the annual estimated advertising revenues for all of Serbia.

Traditional economic theory holds that too many competitors in a market will result in a lack of profits that will cause some to fail, and the market will quickly stabilize until supply meets demand. However, growing evidence suggests that media markets do not always operate this way because of the externality value of media products. Owning a media company gives the owners a public voice in society and a tool for protecting or pursuing other interests, such as political or business interests. Consequently, in transitional countries where the level of competition in media markets is so high that almost all media lose money, media corporations, individual owners, and nongovernmental organizations (NGOs) continue to subsidize unprofitable media companies, keeping competition levels far above economically viable levels. As a result, media companies looking to make overseas investments in transitional nations must be prepared to invest money for years with little, if any, return.

Differing demographic characteristics of audiences around the world also requires careful consideration. The populations of many nations fall into significant language, ethnic, and religious subgroupings, and literacy rates and the distribution of wealth across populations vary widely. Such factors may make the actual size of the available audience smaller than it appears.

For example, in some countries, the population falls into two or more language groups. The actual market for any media product in that country is limited to the speakers of the language in which a media product is produced. Plus, often speakers of one particular language control the economic power in the country, making audiences that speak other languages less desirable targets for advertisers, even if they actually outnumber the dominant economic group. Even where language is not an issue, in countries where a small percentage of the population controls the wealth, the actual audience of interest to advertisers is much smaller than the size of the population. For print and Web-based media products, the potential market is limited to the literate audience. Such factors must be carefully considered when analyzing the market for overseas investments.

Product Development for Foreign Market

As already noted, a key characteristic of media products is that their relevance to individual audience members varies widely; this is especially apparent in international markets. Research shows that when things such as production values are equal, audiences will favor the media products closest to reflecting their own cultures and values (Straubhaar, 1991).

Some types of content, such as comedy, are particularly difficult to export even between countries sharing languages and cultural traditions such as the United States and Great Britain. Such content sells at deeply discounted prices in international markets.

Often the differences between cultures are so subtle they may be difficult for a non-native manager to recognize—but they still can spell the difference between success and failure. For example, magazines featuring recipes may have problems as they expand globally because of differences in tastes, cultural acceptance of foods, or availability of ingredients. Lifestyles, such as apartment living as opposed to suburban living, will affect readers' interests and needs. Even accepted medical and scientific beliefs vary across countries.

Similarly, advertisements and layouts must be screened to avoid offending local readers and viewers. In Western Europe, for example, newspapers and magazines often illustrate advertisements and editorial copy with pictures of topless women in order to appeal to male readers. United States audiences would consider such publications risqué, which would make obtaining distribution in grocery and mass merchandise retail stores difficult. Editors must even carefully evaluate the colors used in publications and productions as color can signal different things in different countries.

The promotion process also may change. Promotional slogans and even the name of a publication or program may not translate well into other languages. Common United States promotional strategies such as event sponsorship, live broadcasts, and other techniques for increasing audiences may be impossible or unacceptable. Similarly, in many less-developed and transitional countries, it is difficult if not impossible to collect ratings and readership data, which makes it hard to sell advertising or do audience analysis and target marketing.

Finally, copyright compliance poses a major concern in the international media environment, whether media companies invest overseas or export existing products. Some countries have not signed international copyright treaties, whereas others do not enforce international copyright laws. If a media company does business in a country with weak or no international copyright compliance, then the company's products will be particularly vulnerable to illegal copying and distribution, known as *piracy*. Piracy is, of course, already widespread in the film, recording, and software industries. Given the high first-copy costs of media production and the fact that consumers generally buy a media product only once, losses to piracy can quickly offset the potential advantages of international investment.

Human Resource Management

One of the greatest challenges in global media management is managing people. Media products are *talent products,* meaning that the quality of individual media products almost wholly depends on the knowledge, experience, and talent of its creators. Consequently, successfully hiring, retaining, and managing people is critical in media companies, no matter the company's locale.

Managing people in an international company is challenging, however. National cultures—including values, ethics, communication styles, standards for courtesy, work practices and standards, humor, dress, and religions, to name just a few things—differ tremendously, even in apparently similar countries. These differences can create unexpected challenges for managers working across borders and cultures.

Among the key differences media managers can expect to encounter are differences in communication style and work practices. International management and cross-cultural communication theorists have identified a number of elements in which cultures differ and which affect communication styles: for example, *power distance*, the degree of interpersonal power between supervisors and employees. Power distance affects the level of formality expected in communication (Hofstede, 1980). Another dimension is *individualism,* which focuses on the degree to which society values the individual good over the collective good. Cultures that value individualism, such as the United States, will be more likely to accept confrontational communication styles than will those in collectivist cultures such as found in many Asian countries (Triandis & Albert, 1987).

There also can be differences in nonverbal communication and behavioral norms. Nonverbal behaviors such as personal-space norms, touching behaviors, eye contact, table manners, and dress can differ greatly and create misunderstandings between colleagues. In many countries, comments and behaviors that would constitute sexual harassment in the United States are common in the office environment. In countries with strong divisions between genders, ethnic groups, political parties, or religions, intolerance can be an issue in the workplace affecting working relationships, job assignments, and the ability of management to hire and promote strictly on the basis of merit.

Such challenges are not limited to interpersonal behaviors. Professional cultures, which include professional ethics, routines, and expectations, also differ greatly across countries. For example, journalists in many countries view journalists' role in media and society differently than do journalists in the United States. Consequently, their professional ethics, standards, and expectations differ. In countries where media are changing from a state-controlled to an independent system, journalists' professional culture and values also usually change, and professionals may agree little about the new standards. Without accepted professional standards, establishing organizational ethics and standards becomes critical.

Finally, expectations and regulations about such things as employee productivity, salary and benefits, and work hours can vary widely across countries. France's official work week is 35 hours, for example, while the average employee in Germany puts in 37.5 hours. Media companies in less-developed countries often are significantly overstaffed when compared to commercial media operations in developed countries, and expectations for the productivity of individual employees can be considerably lower. In many nations, regulations restrict the ability of managers to layoff, fire, or reassign staff, and some countries require companies to have employee councils that have review and veto power over even routine management decisions about such things as hiring, promotions, and work schedules.

Leadership of global media companies is thus complex and challenging, and selecting the senior leadership for overseas subsidiaries is a crucial decision. At least two possibilities exist: (a) hiring or promoting someone from within the overseas market, or (b) sending an expatriate manager from the parent company to run the overseas operation.

Companies that send out a manager often find tensions arising between the "foreign" manager and the local staff. However, because the manager is familiar with the parent company, its expectations, and its operational procedures, relationships between corporate headquarters and the subsidiary tend to be smoother. Conversely, when senior management is hired from within the overseas market, relationships with the local staff may be better, but frequently operational and strategic problems arise between the parent company and the subsidiary. Some global media corporations, such as West Germany's WAZ, split the difference, sending expatriate managers overseas to run the business side of their media operations, while hiring the senior editorial staff from within the country to direct the content side.

Nor are the difficulties of multicultural leadership found only in overseas media operations. As the producers of talent products, global media companies seek to hire the best and most gifted people wherever they may found, transferring them between subsidiaries and countries as needed. Consequently, people from all over the world can be found working side by side in the offices of such global media giants as CNN and News Corp. Foreign language fluency and knowledge of—and sensitivity to—differences between nations and cultures will be increasingly important job requirements for future media managers, whatever their location.

Financial Management

Prior to making overseas investments, corporations undertake detailed cost-benefit analyses and develop projections for earning financial returns (see chapter 1). The financial plan must include higher operational costs associated with international travel to, and communication with, the overseas subsidiary. Experienced media managers know that international investments may take years to turn a profit, particularly in less-developed countries or countries going through transitions where the media markets tend to be oversaturated, advertising markets are often underdeveloped, and consumers have limited discretionary income with which to buy media.

Detailing how to capitalize an international investment until it becomes profitable is key to the success of international expansion plans, as is setting goals that include periodic progress reviews. If an overseas market does not develop, it may be wiser to sell or close the operation, rather than to keep funding it. Media managers should establish guides to determine that stop-loss point *before* they invest.

Even after operations are established, financial management remains complex. Media managers in transitional countries report having problems finding experienced financial managers capable of helping their companies survive (Hollifield, Becker, & Vlad, 2006; Hollifield, Vlad, & Becker, 2004). Accounting rules and tax laws often differ greatly between countries, sometimes making it difficult to reconcile the subsidiary's approach to financial reporting with the one the parent company must use. In countries where foreign media companies are required to set up a joint venture with local partners, the local partner is often undercapitalized, meaning the foreign investor must invest a disproportionate amount of the capital to keep the operation afloat relative to its ownership share in the joint venture.

Risks associated with different nations' monetary policies and fluctuating foreign exchange rates further complicate things. If a country suddenly experiences rapid inflation or if its currency's value falls on foreign exchange markets, then any subsidiaries a media company may own in that country immediately lose value for accounting purposes. That can affect the parent company's finances and stock price, and the resources available to subsidiaries.

Of course, specialists do the technical work of international financial management. But in global media companies, problems with international operations and fluctuations in world financial markets can impact the parent corporation's performance and resources. Therefore, in the global media environment, even middle managers in domestic operations need to understand and monitor international financial markets and trends.

Summary

Globalization of media companies is not a passing trend. The economic characteristics of information products make it advantageous for many media companies to expand markets as widely as possible. Changes in technology and policy over the past few decades have made such expansion easier to do.

Moving into international markets carries many risks, however. Well-established companies already saturate the media markets in developed countries. Media markets in transitional countries may appear to provide more opportunities for new entrants, but they also tend to have more media companies than the market can sustain given the sizes of the local population and advertising market. Surviving, then, requires substantial capital resources and the patience and willingness to sustain losses for many years.

Even so, media companies from many countries demonstrate a willingness to take risks. As they cross borders, they face increasingly complex management challenges at all organizational levels: Organizational structures change, and distant lines of responsibility and reporting must be established. Cultural differences and the varying relevance of media content to audiences complicate product development and promotion. Differences in customs, cultures, communication styles, and professional standards require leadership and personnel management properly attuned and especially sensitive to the talent-based nature of media products. The constantly changing international economic environment and financial market fluctuations affect profit potential and available resources for subsidiaries. Nor are these issues faced only by media professionals working overseas. Media managers at all levels need to develop their understanding of the global media market and their ability to work with colleagues from diverse national, ethnic, political, religious, and cultural backgrounds.

Finally, future media managers must sense the growing international concern about media globalization and its potential negative effects. Media companies seeking larger markets may reduce the resources they invest in their existing markets, undercutting those media's ability to serve as local watchdogs of government and business. In trying to develop globally appealing products, critics charge that global media companies homogenize and dumb-down content, only producing books, films, publications, music, and programs with broad appeal. This may result in an excessive sameness of lower-quality, lower-risk content.

Many world leaders and citizens also fear that global media have become a cultural fifth column, exporting American and Western values, culture and language, and effectively eroding or even supplanting other nations' cultures and values. As Lippmann (1922) noted in the classic *Public Opinion,* media provide most of the pictures in people's heads. Media help people learn what they think they know about the places, countries, and peoples with whom they have no direct personal experience. Many critics believe that the distorted and stereotypical portrayals of nations, people, and cultures so often found in films, news, and books help inflame international hostilities and misunderstandings.

Such concerns cannot be simply dismissed or ignored. Media content has externality value. Its importance to society goes far beyond the value of profits. As media managers expand their reach into global markets, they must be sensitive to the broader effects they may have.

Case 4.1 Sizing Up the Newsroom

Mark had looked forward to the challenges of his first international assignment. He was confident that his years of experience as the general manager of major-market TV stations in the United States would be valuable in his new job as director general of a station in the capital city of a newly independent Eastern European country. He had excellent working relationships with the executive team at corporate headquarters, and they trusted him enough to give him absolute decision authority over daily operations at their new station.

One of Mark's first decisions was to replace the station's news director. The former news director had strong personal and professional ties to the previous political regime, which had been run by a brutal but charismatic and still widely popular strongman. Mark believed that the former news director's widely known affiliation with the fallen dictator would undercut the station's and the parent company's credibility, both journalistically and organizationally. Sensitive to the need to leave control of news decisions in the hands of local journalists, he brought in Sergei, a senior editor from a former opposition newspaper, to be the new news director.

Despite the new hire, in Mark's view, the station's news operation was in complete shambles. The newsroom was severely overstaffed with 150 reporters, who collectively produce 3 hours of news per day—much of it by rerunning the same stories. He observed that most of the news staff wandered in and out as they pleased, with few people on the job more than 5 hours a day. The average journalist on staff produced about two regular-length stories a week and most of the staff spent the majority of their time in the office drinking coffee, smoking, and socializing.

The station's news coverage focused on accidents, scandals, and sports. The staff invested little time and effort in covering the difficult, complex stories about the incredible changes and challenges the country was experiencing. The policy stories the station did produce usually openly attacked the new government on almost everything it did, constantly comparing it unfavorably to the previous regime. By any measure, the station's political coverage lacked balance and perspective. To compound matters, Mark suspected that at least some of the journalists in the newsroom took bribes from officials and business owners to either run or slant stories—a common practice among journalists in the country.

When Mark raised these issues with Sergei, his new news director threw up his hands.

"What do you want me to do!?" Sergei asked. "The senior producers and reporters are all supporters of the former news director and the former political regime. They see you as a foreign capitalist and imperialist and me as a traitorous troublemaker who helped bring down their president at the cost of their personal and professional connections."

He continued, "This operation has always been overstaffed, so no one has ever had to produce much. Plus, they came up through a system in which all journalists acted on behalf of the government. Some of the younger reporters are eager to adopt a more Western-European approach to journalism—but the senior producers and reporters make their lives miserable, give them lousy assignments, or kill their stories whenever they try. For the senior employees, independent, balanced, watchdog journalism is not something they even believe in. Since the law won't let us fire any of them, I'll take any suggestions you have for getting them to change, because nothing *I've* tried has made a bit of difference!"

What should Mark advise Sergei to do? Develop a specific and detailed plan of action for Sergei to implement that will change the organizational and professional culture in the newsroom.

Case 4.2 Global Marketing

Sharon was the research director of a global media corporation that owned a wide range of media properties, including television networks, radio networks, and magazines. The vice president of international business asked her to develop a long-term plan for distributing four specific media products to overseas markets: (a) *Gorgeous*, a cable network that featured fashion and beauty tips for women and aired all of the big United States and European haute couture runway fashion shows; (b) *Hot 'N Cool*, a magazine that targeted 14–18-year-olds and focused on international youth music and culture; (c) *Small Business and Development*, a magazine for business people and small business owners; and (d) *Soaring*, a cable network that targeted 18–49-year-old Muslim women and focused on faith, values, and personal, and professional development.

Sharon developed the following country profiles. Examine the table she put together (Table 4.1) . For each of the four media products Sharon's company wanted to start selling overseas, rank order all of the countries in the table as potential markets. Use 1 for the country you think would be the best potential market for a particular product, and 7 for the worst. Explain your evaluations. Which factors in that country would make it more likely for that product to succeed and which factors would increase the risks?

The data below are only a start. You are encouraged to do additional research on these countries to enhance your analysis. Visit the CIA World Factbook and the World Bank Web sites to learn more about each of the markets below. Read the European Federation of Journalists' report on foreign media ownership in Central and Eastern Europe. Use reports from the Freedom House organization and other media monitoring organizations such as the Open Society Institute and IREX to learn more about media market conditions in nations around the world. Use the International Intellectual Property Institute Web site to learn about copyright protections in these countries. Find additional sources of information for your market analysis.

Assignment

If none of the markets listed in the table seems ideal for these media products, do one of two things: (a) develop your own list of potential new national markets for each product; or (b) pick a country from the World CIA Factbook list and develop an idea for a media product you think might be successful there. Use the sources suggested in the table to gain additional information.

TABLE 4.1 Potential Markets for Overseas Investment

	Armenia	Ethiopia	Indonesia	Macedonia	Moldova	Nigeria	Tajikstan
Population (millions)	2.9	74.7	245.5	2.1	4.5	131.9	7.3
Population growth rate	−.19%	2.3%	1.41%	0.26%	0.28%	2.4%	2.19%
Languages	Armenian, 97.9%; Yezidi (Kurdish), 1.3%; Russian, 0.9%	Amharic, Tigrinya, Oromigna, Guaragigna, Somali, Arabic, other local languages;	Bahasa Indonesia (official), English, Dutch, Local dialects	Macedonian 66.5%; Albanian, 25.2%; Turkish, 3.9%; 3 others, 6.7%	Moldovan Russian, Gagauz (Turkish dialect)	English (official); Hausa, Yoruba, Igbo, Fulani	Tajik (official); Russian widely used
GDP Per Capita	$4,500	$900	$3,600	$7,800	$1,800	$1,400	$1,200
Pop. In Poverty	43%	50%	16.7%	29.6%	80%	60%	64%
Median Age	30.4	17.8	26.8	34.1	32.3	18.7	20
Literacy Rate	98.6%	42.7%	87.9%	96.5%	99.1%	68%	99.4%
Religions	Armenian Apostolic, 97.9%; other, 4.3%	Muslim, 40–50%; Ethiopian Orthodox, 35–40%; Animist, 12%; other, 3–8%	Muslim, 88%; Christian, 8%; other, 3%	Macedonian Orthodox, 64.7%; other Christian, 0.37%, Muslim, 33.3%;	Eastern Orthodox, 98%; Jewish, 1.5%; other, 0.5%	Muslim, 50%; Christian, 40%; other, 10%	Muslim, 90%; other, 10%
Media Landscape	15 radio stations; 3 TV stations; Internet Users: 150,000	8 radio stations; 1 TV station; Internet Users: 113,000	721 radio stations; 11 TV networks; 54 TV stations; Internet: 18 million	49 radio stations; 31 television stations; Internet Users: 392,671	Radio stations, 57; 1 TV station; Internet Users: 406,000	119 radio stations; 3 (2 are gov't); Internet Users: 1.8 million	18 radio stations; 13 television stations; Internet Users: 5,000
Media Freedom* Gov't.	Not Free 64 Republic	Not Free 68 Federal Republic	Partly Free, 58 Republic	Partly Free 51 Parliamentary Democracy	Not Free 65 Republic	Partly Free, 52 Federal Republic	Not Free 74 Republic

Source: CIA World Factbooks, 2006.
Source: Freedom House, 2005. Higher scores indicate less freedom and independence.

5

INNOVATION AND THE FUTURE

Innovation generally is an idea with a purpose—a means to an end. It is the job of managers to determine how well that tool or technology serves its purpose and what effect it has on the people who use it.

This is especially true in a media company. Knowing the innovation's limitations eases the burden of managing. Understanding the limitations of the photo equipment helps a newspaper photo editor determine what situations call for which cameras and which photographers. Similarly, innovation determines internal structure. A TV station manager knows that producing the 6 o'clock news requires the work be divided into journalistic and video-graphic components, each with its own department and internal procedures. So innovation also determines employee behavior and task efficiency. For instance, as Internet usage increases, computerized research may replace newsroom librarians and free them for other tasks.

As technology advances increase, media managers must understand the strategic ramifications. Media firms, with their time-sensitive products, must grasp the market significance of rapidly developing and converging technologies (such as the Internet and broadband) and adapt. Doing so could mean the difference between new, growing revenue streams and a stagnant, noncompetitive future, particularly as media enlarged by mergers and acquisitions of other media become more organizationally complex and slower in their decision making. Remember the VCR? Broadcasters once regarded it as a fad with little potential for widespread adoption (Napoli, 1997). DVDs were viewed as a fad, too. Technologically driven change is the norm, so media managers must overcome organizational culture, routines, and biases (see chapter 3) to adequately deal with that change.

This is a roundabout way of saying a media manager's job is to turn the innovation to the company's advantage. To do so, the manager must analyze the organizational role and impact of innovation. This chapter examines how a company adopts innovation and how innovation impacts media organizations internally and externally. First, a manager needs a strategy.

Approaches

"Approach" is another way of saying a manager needs to think about what he or she wants before doing it. A news director sets the tone for how well her staff uses editing bays; if she constantly complains about the equipment's shortcomings, she undermines staff trust in the bays. If she consistently praises the computers and helps staffers master their capabilities and intricacies, she enhances the staff's ability to edit and design pages effectively, thus enhancing productivity.

Of course, any innovation itself may dictate what approach the director takes. If a machine is simple to operate and consistent in its performance, the director is likely to see it as dependable. But if a machine is cranky and inconsistent, the manager will view it with a wary and cautious attitude. Expectations determine part of this as well; if the director expects the computer to do little more than simple editing, and if that is its designed purpose, then the director most likely will react positively. If the director expects much more complex and sophisticated functions not within the computer's capabilities, a different, more negative reaction occurs (Sylvie, 1995).

Strategy.   A manager considers the intended use of the innovation and how it fits with the company's overall strategy to avoid overreacting to it or using the innovation to produce unintended results. Different media tend to adopt technologies for a variety of internal (e.g., market-based) and external reasons (Picard, 2002; see Fig. 5.1). For example, cable television companies might look to adopt new technology to decrease its high cost of operation or increase its low audience (e.g., satellite broadcast). Staying competitive is always a challenge, but staying competitive in a constantly changing market is even more challenging. For media managers, this necessitates planning. Gershon (2001) said that such strategy included environmental scanning and strategy formulation.

Environment scanning means searching for significant marketplace events such as a corporate merger, an improvement in the technology (e.g., new software or enhanced capabilities), swings in consumer behavior, or some noteworthy social change (e.g., war). The manager also routinely surveys the external environment—competition, political

Media Type	Internal	External
Online	More value needed Low marketing appeal	Younger markets Lower entry barriers More direct competition Less-proven audience preferences
Multimedia	More value needed Low marketing appeal	Younger markets Lower entry barriers More direct competition Less-proven audience preferences
Television	High cost of operation Low audience base	Higher entry barriers Moderate competition
Cable TV	High capital cost of operation Very low audience base	High entry barriers Dueling market revenue streams
Radio	More value needed	More direct competition Mid-range entry barriers Elastic advertising demand
Newspapers	High capital cost of operation & distribution dual market	Mature, limited market New technology threats dueling market revenue streams
Magazines	High cost of distribution	
Books	High cost of distribution	
Motion Pictures	High cost of operation	Global market Growing secondary market

FIGURE 5.1 Factors influencing innovation adoption.

landscape, regulatory structure, economy, technological development, and whatever affects customer behavior. Managers must continually monitor internal environmental factors ranging from operational procedures, work culture, relationships with other units within the company, to decision-making ability and everything in between.

Once the manager gathers this information, he begins to build, implement, and refine strategy. For telecommunications leaders, this is an ongoing process to make their products competitive (e.g., Time Warner's AOL division must keep pace with MSN to maintain its Internet service market dominance). In practice, this means providing Internet customers with the latest in ever-more convenient services plus maintaining the capacity to forecast, plan, and develop such services while anticipating what the competition may do. Such companies continually manipulate the technology product into a positive position.

Strategy and planning, although useful tools, can be overdone. Because of rapidly evolving technologies, shifting customer wants, and nimble competitors, planning is often useless. Sometimes success is a matter of timing, and some plans may not be timely. For example, recall the Internet's early 1980s forerunner, videotext—essentially the Internet without the Web and the audience. Few people had computers (too expensive, with limited capabilities) and fewer had modems (too bulky and unreliable). Even fewer media companies tried to put their products online (too expensive and time consuming because of the lack of standardized, cheap software). The few newspapers having videotext operations were curiosities planning for a future they could not define rather than pioneers (Sylvie & Danielson, 1989). So strategy alone is not enough.

As a result, managers must beware of market and internal organizational influences (such as the adoption process to be discussed later in this chapter) accompanying technology. Unaccustomed to thinking like marketers, many managers have previously concentrated on internal operations and concerns. For example, in-depth interviews with 14 newspaper online executives showed they had difficulty defining their market, not to mention their primary competitor (Chyi & Sylvie, 2000).

A manager needs to adopt a broad approach, relying on as much information as possible, when considering a new product. Open-system theory (Katz & Kahn, 1978) is a good tool for considering new products because it recognizes and charts the recurring organizational sequences of input/effort, change, output/production, and renewed input/effort. In other words, organizations bring in energy or materials from the environment, transform that energy/matter into some product, export that product into the environment, and then reenergize the organization from environmental sources. This allows the manager to see an organization (and thus its resulting product) as a collection of interrelated parts working in unison toward a common goal. The manager realizes that the system (organization) constantly interacts with its environment. That interaction yields a vast reservoir of relevant information with which to successfully manage. There are several implications for media managers looking to adopt an innovation.

Resourcefulness.   Anyone can develop a strategy, but it takes a readily able manager to effectively implement it. A planned program of implementation (adequate staffing, budgeting, goals, and work environment) is needed. Plus, the media manager must create procedures and policies to support implementation (Gershon, 2001). This managerial skill is especially vital in the current convergent atmosphere transforming the media industry. Structural and technological boundaries that historically separated markets and industries were erased (Albarran, 1998), requiring managers to develop new options.

For example, where there was once fierce competition between local broadcast stations and newspapers for certain news, there is now cooperation and mutual promotion. Newspaper reporters appear on TV, TV news gets promoted in the newspaper, or both are promoted via a joint online venture. Editors and producers must be flexible in managing their staff's time, train reporters unfamiliar with print, broadcast, or online styles, and coax journalists leery of convergence. Much energy is needed to maintain and nurture the partnership (e.g., Strupp, 2000).

This resourcefulness also extends to the willingness to honestly and openly examine core values and beliefs. TV station news selection is often based on ratings appeal and time allotments. Newspaper journalists operate under a sense of timeliness and urgency in selecting news. If TV station management views the relationship as a form of *scoop insurance* while dismissing in-depth, time-consuming investigative newspaper stories, this endangers the relationship. Editors and producers must recognize and deal with these different, conflicting values if convergence efforts are to succeed (Weaver, 2000).

Convergence also occurs within a medium. For example, TV stations traditionally broadcast a single signal to their viewing areas, and newspapers print their products for a local, geographically concentrated readership. Now multiple distribution is replacing single distribution due to the development of computers, digital and wireless technology, fiber optics, and the Internet (Albarran, 1998). To succeed, media managers must be resourceful and open to new ideas about process, people, and the product.

Sylvie and Witherspoon (2002) investigated how newspapers adapt to such change. When introduced, *USA TODAY* emphasized reader wants, color graphics, and maps, shorter-than-normal stories, and detailed sports coverage. This represented a departure from central, traditional journalistic values and assumptions such as (a) journalists know news/ content better than readers, (b) news is largely conveyed via text and an occasional photo, (c) the best news is detailed, and (d) other types of content (entertainment and sports) are lesser versions of news. Putting together this new type of newspaper was an adventure, because it required a large group of journalists to change their thinking, work habits, and the end result. In essence, it required an uncommon type of journalist—one willing to risk change and view innovation as an opportunity and not a threat. Such vision, with the aid of other factors, helps change agents/managers complete their task. Sylvie and Witherspoon (2002) suggested journalists and other newspaper employees must evaluate resistance to create a longer term, more meaningful or strategic change (see Fig. 5.2) and to avoid change that is reactive, control-oriented, or based on inappropriate models. The issue then becomes, Sylvie and Witherspoon argued, how to create, properly communicate, and strategically implement the vision that enables successful change.

Vision. Technologically driven products cannot be managed without forethought. Media visionaries continually maintain and update their understanding of business/product objectives and "define their business' identity within whatever future comes" (Brown & Eisenhardt, 1998, p. 148). This is not the same as strategy or the visionary's tool or plan for executing the vision. Nor is it the same as seeing the future; even the media operations that used videotext in the 1980s were probably unaware they were working on the forerunner of the Internet. In a sense, then, vision is being able to articulate an organization's role and identity *prior* to developing a strategy.

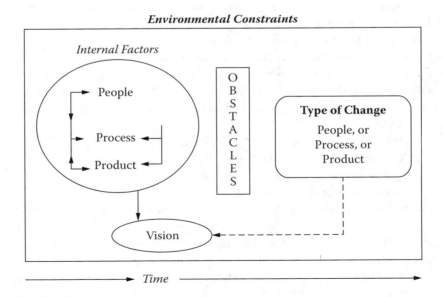

FIGURE 5.2 How newspaper change occurs.

Managers create visions not out of thin air, but through methodically thinking about the future and evaluating the wants and needs of the organization's client groups (Nanus, 1992). Managers must acquire or develop structures and processes to initiate and foster vision (Sylvie & Witherspoon, 2002). Recall the example of *The New York Times* online operation. Requiring users to electronically register allowed the organization to create a continuous flow of information about user habits, interests, and wants, creating an instant research-and-development (R&D) tool (Newman, 2002). This tool enabled *Times* managers to generate data and served as a dynamic source of constant feedback, which most open systems have in common (Katz & Kahn, 1978). The *Times* online management team used the feedback to brainstorm product possibilities and continually explore the online medium's potential to serve reader and advertiser interests. Vision became a natural, integral part of managing, enabling managers to "win tomorrow today" (Brown & Eisenhardt, 1998, pp. 127–129). The ability to constantly assess and evaluate the product permitted the online managers to take strategic, corrective action.

Another point of view (Chan-Olmsted, 2006) suggests additional, more complex reasons for adoption, include characteristics of the firm, traits of the innovation, the perceived overall strategic value of adoption, available alternatives to the innovation, available strategic networks, the intensity and timing of the innovation's adoption, and market conditions. Once the manager understands these factors, he or she should have a better idea of how to implement the innovation.

Structural Approach

The structural approach focuses on the impact of formal devices such as rules and organizational hierarchy. This approach uses technology as a planned, controlled instrument of management, which makes conscious, intentional decisions concerning the implications of the innovation. In this case, structure means considering innovation as a tool for improved production or for managing people (Leavitt, 1965).

A structuralist approach preaches change not by changing employees but by changing the organization's structure. The structuralist uses devices such as rules, role prescriptions, and reward structures, of which innovation is a part. For example, a news director adopts the latest in satellite trucks not because she thinks the reporter and videographer are doing a bad job, but because it adds more immediacy to the 6 P.M. broadcast. Senior managers often use new technology to attain strategic and operating objectives, indicating factors in addition to technology help determine choices of work organization (Buchanan, 1985).

Still, knowing what prompts technology adoption doesn't necessarily make it easy for media managers to exactly calculate the impact on organizational structure. Management often relies heavily on employees' skills, talents, and judgment at all phases of production. It may be impractical to view the innovation without including the employee/user in the picture to a limited degree—another reason many managers try the next approach.

Technological-Task Approach

The technological-task approach complements the structural approach, albeit via emphasis on a particular innovation's obvious, direct impact on the procedures and tasks. The technological-task manager sees innovation as being controlled and having a measurable response in the organization. The manager chooses a technology, hoping that it increases productivity by enhancing the processes and routine tasks of work.

Such substitution of one innovation for another happens, for example, when most reporters—no longer having to physically bring a story back to the newsroom for editing—use laptop computers to record notes and images, making editing portable, within the reporter's control, and rendering telephone dictation unnecessary. Similarly, TV newscasters upgrade how they package their product and deliver it more quickly by using digitized graphic systems.

Yet substituting technologies carries potential problems or trade-offs. In adopting news-editing software, one newspaper editor sought to substitute the journalists' (e.g., copy editors') expertise in design and editing for that of the nonjournalists (e.g., composing-room personnel). In doing so, the editor made the copy editors feel resentful, because they felt they were no longer doing journalistic work, but composing-room work as well (Sylvie, 1995). These unanticipated consequences often lead managers to consider the final approach.

Sociotechnical Approach

The sociotechnical approach lies somewhere between the structural and technological-task approaches. Here the manager stresses the needs and actions of the innovation's users and examines the innovation's attributes and characteristics. Sociotechnical managers see person and machine interacting to the organization's benefit (or detriment). They view innovation's purpose as dynamic and changing and to be used according to its perceived utility (Argyris, 1962).

Acceptance of the sociotechnical approach seems to be growing. Many managers are sensitive to employee needs and growth; they often recognize that formal organizational values may infringe on an employee's personal values or skills. These managers realize that psychological and social planning play an important part in new technology introduction. They evaluate innovation not just according to objectives, but also according to the process of change the innovation introduces and its impact on employees' motivations, skills, and organizational competence (Blackler & Brown, 1985). For example, as more newsrooms begin to converge, they will require revisiting the occupational cultures of the employee groups they want to mix and match.

These three approaches illustrate that management has to have a basic orientation in dealing with innovation. They emphasize the element of control, although some research shows managers also view innovation in terms of cost and market (Noon, 1994). Still, as mentioned at the start, managers need a basic objective when adopting innovation because adoption does not occur in a vacuum. Having an objective in large part determines how well the adoption (or rejection) process occurs and how well a manager can predict the innovation's impact on management as well as employee and market behavior. To do so, the adoption process must be examined and placed in context.

Internal Impacts

Innovation may have several types of effects: (a) desirable/undesirable, (b) direct/indirect, and (c) anticipated/unanticipated (Rogers, 1986) and possibly (d) disruptive/nondisruptive (Day and Schoemaker, 2000). These effects are approached from internal and external viewpoints.

Adoption Process

Internally, managers focus on the adoption process and its effects. When an organization decides to adopt a technology or innovation, several steps (Rogers, 1983) precede and follow the decision.

Agenda setting. Akin to strategy mentioned earlier, and somewhat similar to approach, agenda setting occurs when management identifies a need for a technology. The manager surveys the industry, related publications, and technological experts for potential solutions. In the media, technologies often seem to set their own agenda. For example, interest in the Internet burgeoned to the point where many media companies created Web sites to keep pace with the market for Web-based information. However, just as often, media managers respond to particular needs that employees identify in the work process.

Matching.   Here, the manager matches the agenda with a technology that befits it. For example, if a Web 'zine has marketing problems, particularly attracting older readers, it can hire a variety of consultants over several months to increase readership. Or if an independent filmmaker/producer cannot afford quality film, he may decide to use a video or digital camera. Now he must implement the decision, which brings us to the next step.

Redefining/restructuring.   Redefining occurs when a manager changes or reinvents the technology or idea to fit her particular agenda, objective, or situation. She asks herself, for example, whether the reorganization of her news team's work process is suitable for convergence purposes; in short: in what ways, if any, has the initial concept of the tool or idea changed as it was implemented? Then she introduces the idea to pertinent staff, who interact with it in various ways. Their interaction results in the effects types mentioned earlier: (a) direct (changes that occur in immediate response) or indirect (changes resulting from immediate responses), (b) desirable (helps the user or system function more effectively) or undesirable (dysfunctional), (c) anticipated (changes recognized and intended by management) or unanticipated (changes neither recognized nor intended), or (d) nondisruptive (procedures continue with minimum difficulty) or disruptive (tasks persist with much trouble).

Continuing a previous example, a digital camera sounds just right for our independent film producer, but after a week's worth of shooting she recognizes she really can't get the depth and shading on her video that she would like. She has to decide whether to continue as is (and risk criticism of the film's visual quality when it's finally shown) or figure out a way to pay for quality film and use the standard camera. However, she realizes that it's never that simple: She starts questioning her initial objectives for making the film and how visual quality impacts (if at all) the film's message. What does she want to say? Does the "how" of set lighting really matter? Would video seem a more "authentic" medium to the intended audience?

These individual-hardware/idea/process interactions can be mental or physical, pleasant or unpleasant, work or play, and positive or negative. Media firms often experience interactions fairly quickly due to the product's changing nature and the work's sequential and routinized nature. Therefore, a magazine journalist asked for the first time to write for both print and online likely will quickly report to his editor the differences in writing for both along with any suggestions for changes. And the editor likely will mull the viabililty of the idea for this particular employee and what changes, if any, need implementation. Yet the process still is incomplete.

Clarifying.   Three months pass, and our reporter's productivity is up 60%—good but not great considering he's been asked to write for both Web and print; theoretically his productivity should double (e.g., go up 100%). The editor confirms that the reporter followed her plan correctly. The problem is that the reporter is not keeping pace and often misses online deadlines. She talks separately with the online managing editor and the reporter, emphasizing the copy desk's role in the process, and urging the reporter to look at the task as reaching different readers—not only are they new, but they also read looking for different kinds of information and emphases in a story. The editor must ensure that the reporter, the online managing editor, and the editing process properly align in function and timing so that the reporter's stories make it to the Web.

In clarifying stages, the manager must review how adopters, such as the reporter or the managing editor, perceive an idea or new technology. Usually, they understand it and recognize it as useful. Such perceptions usually are reported in terms of (a) *relative advantage* (the degree to which employees perceive a technology as better than the idea it replaces), (b) *compatibility* (the degree to which employees perceive a technology as consistent with existing values, past experiences, and needs of potential adopters), (c) *complexibility* (the degree to which employees perceive a technology as relatively difficult to understand and use), (d) *trialability* (the degree to which employees perceive a technology may be experimented with before adoption is confirmed), and (e) *observability* (the degree to which nonadopters can see a technology's impact). Each perception or attribute can lead to good or bad consequences depending on the organization (Rogers, 1983).

Routinizing.   In this final step, the innovation is firmly in place and is part of work. At the magazine, our reporter learns how to write so he either automatically downloads the print-version of his story to the Web site, or, "tweaks" it slightly so it is online appropriate. In this example, our editor selected a technology or idea that controls work routines and dictates somewhat predictable outcomes.

The resulting interaction between employees and technology influence management's perceptions of the usefulness and adaptability of the technology or idea. Employees gain experience that leads them to new and updated uses of the new technology. This, in turn, leads the organization to modify the desired level of use of the innovation. Such a learning mechanism is self-adjusted by employees at a fairly slow pace. The innovation loses its newness and becomes embedded in company operations. In our example, multimedia writing becomes part of the furniture, instead of some new experiment, and an accepted or preferred way of doing business, rather than a change in the work routine.

Rules, new job descriptions, or rewards of some kind help bring about these changes. For example, one newspaper newsroom switched its structure to topic-team reporting, because analyses showed that topics such as science, health, and medicine received inadequate coverage. Teams helped solve the problem, increasing such coverage, but the policy changes in coverage and news display led to adoption of a new set of news values (Russial, 1997). Such adjustments are typical and fairly constant because managing is by nature adjustment. Typical managerial functions include planning, staffing, organizing, controlling, and motivating. Introducing innovation requires the use of one or all of these functions at some time in the adoption process. The key is when to perform which function and knowing when—in the adoption process—to adjust. Nowhere is timing more important than when the adopted innovation is the organizational product.

Convergence and Innovation as Product

Innovation also is adopted as an end in itself or as the resultant product. Technology becomes more routine for managers who work in a constantly and rapidly evolving swirl of computer-driven innovations. Fierce competition in the media industry (Compaine & Gomery, 2000) leaves managers no alternative but to adopt technological products out of necessity. This necessity for constant technological change and its consequences creates uncertainty, making many media managers cautious and conservative in approach. For example, the Internet changes so quickly that authoritative-sounding advice should be taken with caution. Reckless managers risk losing face and profits quickly because the changing technology enables competitors to bring new products to market much faster than before. Savvy managers know there is a difference between the mechanically possible and the profitable.

Therefore, this section looks at this interplay of innovation-as-product (primarily via the growing media trend toward technological convergence) and managerial impact. Media management texts and studies normally look at convergence as driven by the technology; but we will explore it as the product of individuals—especially media managers—who "follow diverging paths as a result of various combinations of technological, local and environmental factors" (Boczkowski, 2004, p. 210).

Brand awareness and strategy. Enhanced, technologically driven products require media managers to understand they have a niche and an identity to maintain and expand. This works in several ways. For example, local broadcasters have limited resources with which to cover and generate news. Whereas a typical small-city newspaper has one journalist per every 1,000 subscribers, a corresponding local TV station might have one fifth that number. As a result, TV news directors constantly search for ways to supplement local reporting. One source is the station's affiliated network, which daily provides several hundred stories to local affiliates via satellite technology. A local station can expand its newscast, appearing to have its own regional, national, and international correspondents (Barkin, 2001), thus extending its brand.

Future media managers (or at least those driven by technology-sensitive products) must learn and gain advantage from the previous experience and current branding of the traditional product. For example, when video-rental stores started replacing VHS-format videotaped films with films on digital video discs (DVDs), the stores were not simply trying to catch up to increasing sales of DVD players. They were learning from their experience with video customers as to what constitutes a comfortable viewing experience (Emling, 2002). In summary, a brand-conscious media manager makes the future happen through a new technologically driven product, thus energizing the existing business (Brown & Eisenhardt, 1998).

When it comes to convergence, the Internet allowed all traditional mass media to implement this brand extension. Most Web sites of local newspapers, radio, and TV stations emphasize certain distinctive types of content (Lin & Jeffres, 2001). Radio focuses on station/branding promotion; TV sites emphasize the same, and also feature e-mail, feedback, and search devices, making themselves into multisource repositories. Newspaper sites highlight community service, advertising, and news services.

As a result, the media manager is now concerned with an additional medium/market and its attending traits, such as how the medium is valued and how to take advantage of existing strengths within the medium's new format. For example, a newspaper online manager may—in constructing a real-estate section—want to partner with the local board of realtors and offer searchable listings. Similarly, the head of a network that sells mobile cell phone versions of the network's programs now has to ponder fashion-friendly ways to brand those programs such as ring tones, wallpaper, and news alerts. Or, when the local TV news station gets a "hot" news tip, it covers the story and "plugs" or promotes how the story will be covered in the next day's newspaper, with which it has a partnership.

Superior supervision. Technology as product forces changes in the way managers handle employees, especially in the era of convergence (and experimentation). Cooperation is required when media converge to produce a collaborative, cross-promotional product. A national study of photo editors and Web directors of newspapers that publish online and paper editions found virtually no communication or coordinated coverage plan (Zavoina & Reichert, 2000). Managers like to talk about synergy, but *Chicago Tribune* editor Howard Tyner (Dedinsky, 2000, p. 45) noted it is easier said than done:

> You have to be hard-nosed about it. You'll run into a situation where the print people come up with an idea for a cable show, and they'll get their noses out of joint when the cable guys come back and say, "That's a really dumb idea and will never work." But the print guys will say, "How can they tell me?" Print people are not TV people and vice versa, and each looks at it in a different way.

Chapter 3 also notes the implementation of innovation is closely tied to employee motivation, especially as convergence typically translates into "more work for the convergee." How does a news director persuade her reporters to switch from the normal news cycle to a day of habitual online updating, several cable news appearances, sharing story information with print reporters, and producing their own stories for the last broadcast—especially when each 2-minute segment on the local TV news takes a newspaper reporter away from his or her regular work 2 to 5 hours a week (Rabasca, 2001)?

The answer is complex. Covington (1997) studied four TV stations operating in a technologically challenging market. Successful managers noted their subordinates' experiences with the product and found that what subordinates learned transformed them and helped the product. For example, experienced reporters and anchors were given increased responsibility, so they did not feel caught in a dead-end job. Supervising and rewarding them required managers to use innovative approaches to motivation and evaluation. In a separate study, Powers (2006) surveyed print and broadcast journalists in convergent partnerships about their managers; not surprisingly, relationship-oriented management behavior predicted job satisfaction. However, it also predicted a positive level of convergence. Such behavior was more prevalent in newspaper newsrooms than in their broadcast counterparts, however. Therefore, management techniques sensitive to motivation appear likely to pay dividends.

Journalists may see clear advantages in new convergence policies— e.g., as a career booster, the enjoyment of working with colleagues whose strengths differ from their own, and subsequent respect for people in other parts of the news organization. Yet, convergence within the newsroom may be hindered by cultural and technological differences in approaches to newsgathering and dissemination, as well as by a lack of training to alleviate concerns about the perceived complexities of new media formats (Singer, 2004b). For example, a group of Swedish journalists merged with some of their newspaper's advertising sales staff to create the paper's Web site. The groups came to respect each other; close working conditions meant old-group identities were renegotiated and reformed. Oddly enough, while the print newsroom journalists began to accept the online journalists' view of the Web as a necessity, the print advertising staff created a new barrier between themselves and the online ad staff. They saw the online staff (which was hired solely for the Web edition) as competition for customers (Fagerling & Norbäck, 2005a). Therefore, groups working shoulder to shoulder helps smooth convergence but doesn't guarantee total integration, nor—as another study (Bressers & Meeds, 2005) illustrated—that some resentment by one group won't linger.

Additional research has shed light on why this happens. For example, even student journalists in a converged newsroom couldn't get along when put in close proximity. Print reporters said broadcast reporters didn't keep them informed of breaking news while the broadcast reporters said print reporters kept the best stories for themselves (Hammond, Petersen, & Thomsen, 2000). Simply put, a group comparing itself to another group with similar goals is more likely to show favoritism to its own group and be negative toward the other group. A study of broadcast and print journalists showed them more positive toward change "when it appeared to come from people they saw as more like them" (Filak, 2004, p. 229).

One suggestion advocates implementing "an organizational value shift" using a strong action plan that emphasizes a "next step" rather than a new change or end to an era (Killebrew, 2001, p. 45). Managers can show more concern for their reporters' satisfaction (Killebrew, 2001) by using communication, commitment, cooperation, compensation, cultural change, competition, and customer (Lawson-Borders, 2003). This approach is sensible because print journalists exposed to convergence aren't really concerned with convergence itself but, rather, with the way managers implement it (Singer, 2004b). Most of this can be viewed within Sylvie and Witherspoon's (2002) suggestions for newspaper leaders in facilitating change (see Fig. 5.3):

External Impact

Many of the suggestions in Fig. 5.3 go a long way, as well, in managing external impact—another way of saying that managing change or innovation directly implies dealing with elements of market structure. The following discussion highlights some of the more basic market elements.

Competition and market boundaries. A brand, by definition, is unique compared to its competitors. Therefore, a brand-conscious manager has to be aware of competition. Technology often allows some unique entry into a market that most would have thought closed. For example, digitization has allowed satellite-dish providers to set their product apart from typical cable programming because it allows the customer to manipulate (record, stop, pause, etc.) the content. Now some cable operators have gained the technology to digitize cable programming as well while also offering Internet broadband service. Each innovation becomes unique to the market in some way, just as the Internet changed market conceptions for electronic newspapers. No longer does a newspaper in San Jose, California, have the safe, relative monopoly of its print edition when it starts an online version. The electronic edition allows Taiwanese newspapers to compete with the

Skill	Skill Attributes
Sharing Control	Follow subordinates' lead; establish feedback mechanisms; allow employees to devise new methods of work; overcome fear of lack of control; gain more confidence.
Continuous Communication	Communicate vision of change clearly and often and through as many means and channels as possible.
Institutionalize Commitment to Change	Pay employees enough to make them want to stay; train employees for now and for the future.
Teaching Continuous Improvement	Tear down or breach departmental walls; foster synergy; frame cooperation as a positive; challenge employees to create new markets; add emotional component to the newspaper.
Cultivating Decision-Making Resources	Approach decision-making with "big picture" in mind; define problems carefully and within a larger framework; actively set aside time for thinking; make decisions proactively.

FIGURE 5.3 Media leadership skills to enhance change

San Jose paper in the advertising and information markets for the large Chinese and Chinese-American audience (Chyi & Sylvie, 1998).

As noted earlier, this requires a strategy for how to manage the technology and the competition itself. Because consumers rely on brands for regular delivery of goods or services, the manager simultaneously wants to encourage that reliance (so that it becomes a habit) and discourage the likelihood of ending that reliance. Your product must meet or exceed whatever product or service your competitor offers or introduces. Therefore, if radio stations are more likely to switch to new formats after radio stations *in other markets* have done so (Greve, 1998), it's a safe bet the competition is watching. Magazines also mimic a competitor if they're not the first to the Web and have no internal sources of information about it (Simon, 2006). Much of what a manager does in this area involves marketing and promotion, with which our later chapters on marketing and research, planning and market analysis extensively deal. Rarely can a manager eliminate competition, but technological convergence often occurs as a means of combining elements (whether they be formats [e.g., TV and print] or distribution channels [e.g., online and TV] or whatever) to produce something competitors can't yet offer.

To see how technology can diminish competition, compare two competing local TV stations in a market. Assume the leading station enhances its product (and market share) by investing several million dollars in capital improvements, such as a new and renovated studio, new cameras, new sound equipment, and a satellite newsgathering mobile van. The result is a clearer, crisper picture with better video footage, more colorful background graphics, and better facilities for producing high-quality local commercials. That leads to more viewers, which in turn reaps more advertisers, higher advertising rates, and more prestige. Unless the competing station has a large reserve fund or a good line of credit with local banks, it may never recover.

However, unique products and services can also confuse or strongly challenge a manager's ability to succeed. As media technologies converge, companies enter markets with greater ease and their products provide adequate substitutes for each other. This encourages market blurring, just as the development of radio and film increased competition for entertainment and the rise of cable and low-power TV stations delivered the same product as broadcast stations (Powers, 1990). Only by differentiating their products can these media create more distinct markets, but the question then becomes "What is the market *now?*"

For example, when a newspaper or TV station creates an online version, it has to investigate how that version is used, by whom, when, and why. Again, these are marketing questions, but the media manager has to then translate the answers to those questions into internal tasks and procedures that will satisfy that market. Think in terms of journalists learning to write for online audiences for the first time and asking themselves these questions: (a) Do standard news leads work? (b) Should I link part of the story to another Web site? (c) How will I obtain the video that would complement this story? (d) Am I betraying my training by writing like a TV (or print) journalist? Boundary-blurring convergence forces the media manager to adjust or develop new management techniques—as well as business models—suitable for satisfying a new market.

Revenue alternatives.   Companies trying to weather economic downturns often attempt to diversify; new technologies (or those embodied by other companies) make the decision somewhat easier and more attractive (e.g., Kanter, 2001). These diversification efforts may take the form of a partnership with, merger with, or acquisition of another company, but in any case they require rethinking of the business model to keep revenues flowing.

As a result, media companies try to shelter themselves by enhancing their existing products and approaching new markets. Let's say your TV network is losing audience share, and thus, advertising. In addition, new technologies allow consumers to skip commercials. You can tap into a new market and put your successful serialized programs on DVD to generate new revenue. Or, during sweeps months, you can generate additional audience members by distributing those programs (or exclusive previews) to cell phone makers. Or you can buy a cable network that specializes in programming for children and young adults, creating a whole new market for your company. Or you can build new, more lucrative relationships with audiences by adding a current, state-of-the art Web site. Or you can partner with a software maker who can provide TV programs on demand using Internet Protocol TV. Or you can reduce costs.

In short, the limit on revenue potential of new technologies primarily depends on the innovation and branding awareness of the manager. For example, the cable TV industry has had to think creatively when doing battle with the digital-video recording and the video on demand that satellite and other competitors offer. Without getting too technical, one possibility is to reengineer video servers to allow customers to record a week's worth of all cable offerings and then to pick and choose programs when they have the time.

While the message may seem to be "technology enhances profit," or "buy yourself an audience," the real message is that technology and innovation present opportunities to grow audiences when strategically managed; note how Amazon.com has helped book sales. However, the distributive prowess of an Amazon.com wouldn't work without a comprehensive plan for being able to decide what the consumer will tolerate or value and how it will translate into revenue. That's why "free newspapers" aren't really free; they're paid for through revenue from advertising, because managers know they've got to organize to provide those ads and, more importantly, that people read the advertisements the papers include.

Consumer behavior.   Consumers use media to survey the environment, to help make decisions, for entertainment, to help them socially, or to help them learn about themselves (Lacy & Simon, 1993). Not only do innovation and technology help improve the measurement of those audiences, as mentioned earlier, but they also encourage media consumption habits and behaviors.

More recently, innovation has transformed the consumer from a passive listener/viewer/reader of information to an active participant in the production process. Now consumers do not have to wait until the evening newscast for the current weather or short-term forecast. They need only find the local weather map on the Web or watch cable TV's Weather Channel. Cable and satellite technology provide more viewing choices so viewers become more selective in what they watch and—due to digital-video recording—when they watch it. The result is evident in the types of channels available: HBO, Cinemax, and Showtime (feature films); ESPN (sports); VH-1, TNN, and MTV (music); Lifetime (women's interests); Disney and Nickelodeon (children's programming); and Pay-TV (special events), to name a few.

As a consequence, audiences have become more complex and narrower. For example, the decline of newspaper readership prompted some publishers to target more affluent populations, to the exclusion of some audiences, particularly poor minorities. Editors have had to be careful not to ignore diversity of coverage. As an acknowledgement to Internet-related communication, virtually all newspaper Web sites provide either reporters' or editors' e-mail addresses; some provide online chat forums, where readers discuss news and issues (Gubman & Greer, 1997). Such devices are working: a survey found Internet use increased over time among the same group of respondents (Lindstrom, 1997).

Perhaps more than any other phenomenon, blogging has shown the complexity of predicting consumer behavior. Who could predict someone's online opinion could lead to revenue for news Web sites? But that's exactly what blogs do when they include links to their information sources. Even sites that simply aggregate (but do not produce original) news items and blogs can sell advertisements; such is the appeal of media products and the amazing variety of consumer behavior. Another example is the digital-video recording phenomenon so widely predicted to be the death of TV commercials; instead, viewers chose to watch what they want (including commercials) when *they* want. Some skip certain program parts, some watch over the weekend, and some watch large numbers of programs in one sitting—and these approaches may vary according to the type of program available.

Advertising and promotion strategies, method, and content.   Remember the VCR? Viewers could fast forward past commercials in recorded programs, in effect losing the ad's audience. This led some advertisers to switch to shorter, more creative commercials to attract viewers' attention before they decided to fast forward. DVDs have enhanced this feature.

New technologies force advertisers' hands, but also allow them to be more selective about their audiences. Advertisers constantly search for new ways to target specific audiences using specific messages. Many technologies make this easier. For instance, push technology sends Web content to users' computers, rather than users' typing in Web addresses themselves, giving users what they want, when they want it. Similarly, digital-video recording is altering the current advertising model in the broadcast industry. The device allows viewers to record programming as well as search and find the kind of broadcast programs they like. This may diminish the networks' capability to ensure a new program's success by placing it in a prime-time period. Such scheduling created artifices like *sweeps months*, when particularly attractive programs are broadcast to attract large audiences, increasing viewership and allowing networks to set advertising rates. The super VCR threatens that entire traditional approach (Lewis, 2000).

Advertising on the Web proved problematic for many media. Some question whether Web ads are as recognizable and memorable as print advertising (Sundar et al., 1997). Web audience measurement lacks standardization, making audience measurement and—thus attracting advertisers—more difficult.

On the positive side, because of the Internet's inherent targeting efficiencies, producers of some specialized sites tried to create classified advertising niches (e.g., in car buying and selling, real-estate listings or employment services, or to use existing brands and spin them off into sites of their own; Newman, 2002). The regional Bell operating companies also have or plan similar vehicles to siphon off part of the local advertising market. A key driving force is the intent of national advertisers to reach geographically targeted audiences using technology filters that compensate for the lack of focused content to buy (Chyi & Sylvie, 1998).

Summary

This chapter examined managerial approaches to technology, the process of how a company uses or adopts technology, and how technology may affect media organizations and their markets. To summarize, technology has internal and external impacts. Managers have to understand that technology demands adjustment. They must be sensitive as to how and when to manage. A media manager's job is to turn the technology to the company's advantage by using the correct approach.

Before the approach is taken, however, the media manager must have a strategy, resourcefulness, and vision. Strategy—including environmental scanning—helps avoid overreacting or unintended results. However, strategizing is incomplete without the ability to skillfully implement the strategy, using the right assets, people, and tools. Vision precedes these two elements, however, because strategy is but a tool or vehicle for obtaining the vision, which is a succinct characterization of the role and identity of where and what the organization wants to be.

The next step involves choosing from among the structural, technological-task, and sociotechnical approaches, all rooted in a slightly different managerial orientation and each with advantages and disadvantages. Most modern-day managers use some form of the sociotechnical approach. A media company adopts a technology for its own particular reasons. Then it introduces the technology to employees, who interact in various ways with the technology depending on the employee and nature of the task involved. Then management perceptions and employee reactions prompt a period of adjustment, ultimately leading to adoption or rejection of the technology. This adoption process includes the stages of agenda-setting, matching, redefining/restructuring, clarifying, and either routinizing or rejection of the technology or idea.

As a result, the technology or idea affects managerial functions, including planning, organizing, staffing, motivating, and controlling operations (see Fig. 5.4). Overall, technology causes a media manager to manage in an atmosphere of constant change and adjustment—and demanding attention to branding, market competition, boundaries, business models, consumer behavior, marketing, advertising, and content. How and when a manager takes action with regard to technology and innovation greatly impacts the company's future.

Case 5.1 Planning Convergence, Part I

You are asked to design a converged newsroom operation, capable of producing content for print, broadcast, and online media for your medium-sized market. It must introduce broadcast reporters to a print newsroom and vice versa. Before you start, however, the boss has

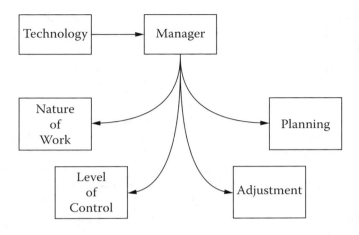

FIGURE 5.4 How technology affects media managers.

given you some questions to answer for her. They're in the following assignment.

Assignment

1. How will the space basically be organized within the newsroom? How would you place the news editors, sports editors, features editors, etc.? How would subject matter fit into space allocation? How would you place reporters and why? Where would print, broadcast, and online staffs go? Would you segregate them?
2. What, in your opinion, is the most important design element and why?
3. What software would you put on which workstations? How would it facilitate work flow?
4. What about lighting and sound? Ceiling height? Floor quality? Why?
5. Can you draw me a sketch so I can get the "lay of the land"?

Case 5.2 Planning Convergence, Part II

With visions of dollar signs dancing in his head, your boss, the station's general manager, has taken to the idea of convergence as another way of cutting costs and increasing profits. As the news director, you've been asked to call a meeting with the local newspaper editor to discuss the feasibility of the idea. However, first the general manager wants you to sell the idea to your staff—"No sense in going off half-cocked without the support of the ground troops," he huffed after your last meeting with him. You narrowly escaped having to implement another idea of his to merge the videography and reporting staffs as a cost-saving move. ("We can train reporters, videographers and even editors to shoot, edit, and report stories. We'll call 'em "video-journalists," he laughed.)

You rose through the ranks, dreaming of producing stories for television. You majored in broadcast at State University, and grew up hating newspapers for the way the print majors looked down on broadcast majors in college. Of course, you know the newspaper folks probably feel the same way about your staff (you've heard plenty of "hairspray and makeup" stories).

Back to your staff, where you have to sell the idea. Your assignments editor says that the newsroom has already started talking. Here's a list of comments he's overheard just today: "We don't have time to do what we have to do now, much less do anything new," said the crime reporter. "It's just a fad," from the education reporter. Your veteran anchor has chimed in with, "Sounds good. You first." And then, from the weekend producer, "This is about cutting jobs, isn't it?" Finally, this from the station meteorologist, a native Texan: "I ain't breakin' bread with those ink-stained wretches!"

Assignment

1. What sort of cultural maneuvering will you need to do to get the staff to buy into the idea? How would you overcome the competitive animosity? What would be the first thing you would do?
2. How would you prepare for your meeting with the local newspaper editor? Would you be frank and admit the concerns of your staff, or would you be more cautious and pick your words more carefully? Why or why not?
3. Do a cost-benefits analysis as to whether a station in this situation, in a medium-sized market, should enter into a convergent partnership? Is the newspaper the best choice of partner?
4. What convergence skills would you seek to cultivate in your staff? What would you be able to offer the newspaper editor?
5. Let's say you disagree with your general manager's plan. Write a memo telling him as much. Have a three-classmate panel read the memo and then take a vote as to whether you should be (a) fired, (b) directed to implement the partnership regardless, (c) given a chance to implement

a modified version of the partnership, or (d) patted on the back and taken to lunch.

Case 5.3 Spanning the Market

You are John Smith, the White publisher of the first Black weekly newspaper published by your national newspaper company, the *Beacon*. The paper is located in the small southern city of Conway—and you've already upset nearby competing publication *The Conway Times*.

The Beacon Company owns the *Morning Press-Herald*, among several other newspapers in the South, and you've just finished plans to start *The Conway Beacon*, a weekly newspaper specifically targeted to the Black community in East Conway. The newspaper, which could start printing as early as two months from now, expects to have a steady circulation of about 10,000.

Such papers usually are very much neighborhood- and community-oriented, and the *Beacon* will serve the news needs of East Conway, where the Conway daily paper the *Record* has the lowest concentration of readers. Despite the impending launch, you feel further research is needed on models of good weekly newspapers.

Conway Times Publisher and Editor-In-Chief Edie Jones has said she would be more supportive of the *Journal* if a Black company owned it. "We really have Black news," she said, adding that her newspaper, based in the state capital 60 miles away, already reaches the Conway market. *The Times* is one of more than 10 Black newspapers in the state that are members of the National Newspaper Publishers Association, a Black news service with more than 200 member papers, according to its Web site.

You know focus groups suggested there was no newspaper serving East Conway, so the parent company decided to bring out the paper in an era of rising niche-market news publications (other newspaper companies in the country have created Hispanic-targeted papers to reach the growing Hispanic community in the Southwest, Southeast, and large urban areas).

Information gathered from the latest U.S. Census Bureau report estimated that of Conway's 86,846 residents, 20,365 residents, or more than 23%, were Black. Almost 15% of the state's 7 million residents are Black.

Jones' remarks illustrate views of other Black Conway residents, who said *The Times* was a much-needed alternative to years of undercoverage by the city's dominant mainstream newspaper, the 47,000-circulation

Conway Record. In a city dominated by a branch of State University, they say, it is easy to overlook poor Black residents across town.

You've been hesitant, however, to admit the *Beacon* is a Black newspaper, insisting it all depends on how a Black newspaper is defined. Does it start out with some point of view or advocacy? You don't think so. You wanted to have a very good newspaper covering the community of East Conway.

However, experts on Black media say it takes more than stories on Black people to make a Black newspaper and that if the Beacon Company could leverage relationships with major advertisers to support *The Times*—accessing advertising dollars traditionally earmarked for ethnic media—it wouldn't matter if the new publication lived up to the classic mission of a Black newspaper. Black publishers insist that for years they've gone to major advertisers and been denied advertising. They feel that if the *Beacon* comes into Black media and brings all these advertisers with them, how can they compete?

All this negative attention surprises you. The criticism intensified when you fired your choice for editor, Black journalist Shanda Higgins for reasons known only to you. It heightened suspicions the paper's management might not be comfortable with editorial stands expected of Black newspapers, which have a history of diehard advocacy for Black people. "Having a Black newspaper without the advocacy won't work," Jones has said.

You admit that the *Beacon* is a hybrid of sorts between a traditional neighborhood newspaper and a Black-focused publication. If this seems phony to East Conway residents, they won't buy it, you believe.

Assignment

1. At the moment, what is your most pressing problem as publisher of the *Beacon?*
2. Of the external impacts listed in this chapter, which is your greatest weakness in this situation and how would you resolve it?
3. Should the *Beacon* be classified as a "Black newspaper"? Why or why not? Should you rehire Higgins?
4. Where is the town of Conway in the adoption process regarding the *Beacon?*
5. Should the *Beacon* help *The Times* with local advertisers? Should you be concerned at all—and if so, to what degree—with the *Record?*
6. How does the model of starting a Hispanic paper differ from the one of starting a Black paper? Did the Beacon Company, err in any way?

Case 5.4 The Case of the E-Newspaper

You are the corporate research director for *The Globe*, a media conglomerate owning 50 newspapers in states, as well as network affiliate TV stations in six of the top 10 U.S. markets. You have a good working relationship with Einstein Swenson, a notable futurist and electronic newspaper proponent. Swenson has been tinkering with e-paper technology for the last 15 years.

Last week, he insisted on meeting with you to discuss his latest invention, a small, pad-sized tablet that produces screens of news using various technologies, including electrophoreses, dipolar rotation, and something called "electrowetting." He thinks he can test and then mass produce the tablet so that it can be market ready in 5 years. You're skeptical, so you've put your staff to work on several questions:

1. What are the ownership issues surrounding this device? Who would own content? Distribution? If ownership is split, which party would take on customer relations? Should it be a joint venture?
2. What business model should be used? Will there be new competition arising from adoption?
3. What organizational concerns would arise? Does this mean 24/7 platforms? Deadlines? Multimedia journalism?
4. How would the product be designed? Is there the possibility for several editions? Sections? What about in-depth stories—are they possible? How compatible would mobile channels be with this product?
5. What would be the disposition of advertising in such a vehicle? Could it, too, change on demand?

Assignment

1. Pick one of the questions above, research it, and report back to the class.
2. Which is the greater concern or unknown with this product now—technology, audience, branding, strategy, competition, or consumer behavior—and why?
3. What would it cost to finance testing and development of this technology?
4. Is this technology more likely to be developed by a journalistic-oriented organization (e.g., *The Globe*), or by a telecommunications-based group? Which would have the most trouble managing the product once it's developed?

6

LAW, REGULATION, AND ETHICS

Managers make decisions for a variety of legitimate reasons, most falling into three categories: (a) to advance the organization's goals, (b) to meet legal requirements, and occasionally, (c) to do something just because it is the right thing to do. The other chapters in this text deal with the first reason, and this one addresses the last two.

Learning about law and ethics is crucial for managers because ignoring them can affect an organization's ability to achieve its goals. Law, regulations, and ethics act as constraints on the managers' decisions. This chapter will provide an overview of these constraints, but more in-depth examinations of media law and ethics are left to other texts.

Defining Law, Regulation, and Ethics

Law refers to rules created by legitimate authority, such as federal, state, county, and city governments. This includes a country's constitution, laws passed by legislative bodies, and common law that comes from the collective body of court interpretations. *Regulation* is administrative law, which includes laws and rules created by agencies set up through statute by legislative bodies. At the federal level, this includes the rules made by agencies such as the Federal Communication Commission (FCC) and Federal Trade Commission (FTC). *Ethics* refers to standards of conduct and moral principles or to a process of reaching morally acceptable decisions. Such standards are usually called *codes of ethics*, and the process of reaching decisions is called a *moral reasoning process* (Folkerts & Lacy, 2004, pp. 341–365). This chapter will address a subset of law, regulations, and ethics of specific interest to managers in organizations that produce and distribute content.

Types of media laws and regulations are not equal and have an order of precedence. That order in the United States is federal Constitution, federal statutory law passed by the federal legislative body (Congress), federal regulations (administrative law) created by administrative bodies, state constitutions, state statutory law created by state legislatures, and state administrative law (Folkerts & Lacy, 2004, p. 375).

Whereas laws and regulations exist through formal actions by governing bodies, ethics develop informally through social interactions and individual reflections. Although social activities affect ethics, they reside in individuals' minds, and these individuals demonstrate their ethics through behavior. A newspaper reporter's observations and discussions with others in the newsroom obviously affects her perception of fairness, but ultimately the reporter must decide how to produce a fair story.

Because individuals contribute to the development of their ethics, great differences exist among managers' and media workers' definition of ethical. Individual news companies and professionals groups have codified ethics in the form of lists of dos and don'ts, but media employees may or may not accept those lists. In addition, the lists themselves can vary as to what is and is not acceptable behavior. These variations can contribute to the difficulty of managing media workers. Usually, variations between an organization's ethical codes and an individual employee's ethics are not great enough to create dysfunctional behavior. Employees who do not accept their company's standards tend to move on. However, an organization imposing standards of behavior conflicting with the ethics of a large number of employees inhibits its ability to meet its goals effectively and efficiently.

Law, regulation, and ethics all deal with what should and shouldn't occur. Law and regulation have the force of government authority and ethics does not. A defining question facing managers is whether they should do something that is legal but what their customers may consider unethical. For example, some states have outlawed using the names of rape victims, but others do not. Journalists who can publish rape victim's names must decide whether they should, given the feelings among many people that this is not appropriate.

Decisions about legal but ethically questionable policies can have business repercussions. If the public perceives a media company as unethical, consumers and advertisers might decide not to use that particular media product. Conversely, customers also might punish a company valuing money more than taking ethical stances. If a television station runs advertising for a dangerous or worthless product, viewers might choose to watch other stations. This loss of goodwill can reduce the effectiveness of the station's advertising time.

Media Law

Law affecting media organizations falls into several categories. We are particularly interested in prior restraint, libel, privacy, information access, political versus commercial speech, indecency, obscenity, and business law, all of which vary in how much First Amendment protection they receive, but no type of speech is absolutely protected.

Prior Restraint

Prior restraint concerns government's ability to prevent publication of information. Over the years, courts have created a high standard for prior restraint. To prevent information from being distributed, government must show a "clear and present danger" from that publication, e.g., that the danger is not vague and is immediate. For this reason, prior restraint of commercial media is unusual.

The classic case of prior restraint involved the Pentagon Papers, a secret history of the United States' involvement in the Vietnam War. Secretary of Defense Robert McNamara commissioned the study, which was classified as top secret. Former CIA employee-turned-antiwar-advocate Daniel Ellsberg leaked copies of the Pentagon Papers to the press. The Nixon Administration received a restraining order to stop publication at several newspapers. However, the Supreme Court ruled that publication did not present a clear and present danger and ruled for the press. Even though newspapers such as the *Washington Post* and *The New York Times* eventually won the case, the companies took a big risk taking on the administration. Not only did the case have legal costs, but if the administration had won, it would have significantly reduced the ability of the press to get information about the government.

Although court rulings have made prior restraint difficult, that difficulty could decline with future court rulings. This possibility has grown with the "war on terrorism" and the Iraq War. Throughout history, wars lead to governmental efforts to allow censorship and information control that could affect media coverage. Managers should monitor the political landscape to see how it can affect their organization.

Libel

Prior restraint involved preventing publication, but libel law involves punishing organizations and individuals who injure individuals through published information. *Libel* occurs when publication results in false defamation of a person that causes damages. *Defamation* makes others think less of a person's character, but the defamation must cause some actual loss for the plaintiff to win the libel case.

Libel involves information that will likely be perceived as fact. Opinion cannot be libel. For example, someone could safely express the opinion that Mac's Hamburgers taste terrible. However, if the same person falsely said the hamburgers are made with uninspected camel meat, he or she likely would lose a libel suit. Courts also have exempted satire from libel laws.

Libel laws do not apply to all people equally. Statements about *public officials* (elected or appointed government agents) and *public figures* (people such as actors who have put themselves in the public eye) must meet a more stringent definition to be libelous. The higher standard for public figures and officials, called "reckless disregard for the truth," occurs when someone publishes a defamatory lie while knowing it was a lie (*actual malice*) or the person publishes a lie because of inadequately fact checking (*gross negligence*). The higher standard was established in 1964 in *New York Times versus Sullivan*. The Supreme Court ruled that some issues were so important to society that errors in truth had to be tolerated in order to promote vigorous public debate.

Defamation is part of journalism. Sometimes people who violate the public trust or commit crimes need to be exposed. In doing so, news organizations risk that they might make a mistake and wrongly defame someone. The result can be a lost libel suit, which costs a news organization the damages awarded by the court and the loss of goodwill in the community. However, a news organization that does not pursue risky stories fails to serve its community and can be shown up by competitors.

Privacy

Privacy laws apply to the reporting of information that people would prefer not be known by the public. Privacy is not found specifically in the U.S. Constitution, but is a derivative of the Fourth Amendment. Courts have ruled that people have the right to keep confidential some facts about themselves. Three areas of privacy law merit closer inspection: (a) disclosure of embarrassing facts, (b) intrusion upon seclusion or solitude, and (c) false light.

Disclosure of embarrassing facts covers a range of events. A television station broadcasting photographs of someone's facelift without permission could be considered an invasion of privacy. A Web site posting nude photographs of a person without permission also could be an invasion of privacy. As with libel, organizations and individuals sued for invasion of privacy have several defenses. One important defense is that the particular person is newsworthy and coverage of the private facts serves the public. As with libel, public official and public figures have less protection than do private citizens because they are of interest to the public by definition. An additional defense is the fact that a supposed private act occurred in public view. If someone behaves in an embarrassing way in public, the action is not private. Consent also is a strong defense. If an actor performs in a pornographic film and signs a consent form, that actor is not likely to successfully sue if the film is placed online at some future point. Unlike libel, where truth is an absolute defense, truth only makes the damage of privacy invasion worse. If the fact is false, then privacy law does not apply. The fact has to be true before it becomes embarrassing.

Another type of privacy law involves intrusion upon seclusion or solitude. This area concerns reporting rather than the publishing, posting, or broadcasting of information. Media workers have no right to go into private areas such as homes or automobiles and take information. The key centers on what is a private or public place. A person's home is private, but garbage placed on the street for pick up is not. A strong defense would show the area intruded upon was not private.

Some of the same management issues associated with libel relate to invasion of privacy. If someone sues a media organization for invasion of privacy, the managers must decide whether the organization settles or fights the suit. Either would cost money and could have an impact on how people perceive the news organization. As in all management decisions, financial costs and benefits need to be considered before a decision is made

Making people think less of someone, *defamation*, plays an integral part of investigative journalism; invading privacy does not. Investigative reporting often works best when reporters use publicly available information to discover wrongdoing. However, publishing embarrassing facts often falls within the realm of sensationalism. Ethical concerns about stories that could lead to both libel and privacy suits should be evaluated before the stories are run. What are the repercussions of a controversial story? How would the repercussions serve the community, and how might they hurt the community? Were ethical standards followed when the information was collected and published or broadcast?

Information Access

Prior restraint, libel, and privacy law relate to the presentation of information and news. They either apply to preventing the broadcast, publication, and posting of content, or they punish organizations after the fact. Because the First Amendment makes it difficult to restrain or punish ethical political communication, government agencies that want to control what the public knows are more likely to try to control the flow of information. Media companies cannot report what they do not know. As a result, some government agencies will limit media access and try to withhold information as much as the law will allow.

Because the First Amendment protects journalism as a government watchdog, the press often conflicts with politicians and bureaucrats. Controlling information can help politicians and bureaucrats hide mistakes and criminal activities. To promote the flow of information and improve the democratic process, federal and state governments passed freedom of information acts (FOIA) that specify the process by which media organizations can obtain information from certain government agencies. The process and applicable agencies vary by state and much government information remains secret. For example, the federal FOIA applies only to portions of the executive branch, such as cabinet departments and regulatory agencies. The law does not apply to U.S. Congress, the U.S. Supreme Court, and the president's staff.

FOIAs can be useful for journalists investigating government activities, but using a FOIA may not be easy. Agencies can charge for providing information, and the laws have loopholes that can be used sometimes to circumvent the spirit of the laws. However, the laws provide some support for the dissemination of information to citizens.

Equally important to journalists is access to government meetings where laws are discussed and passed. Access to federal and state government meetings tends not to be a serious problem because of the large number of news organizations that monitor these levels of government. However, at local levels, where news coverage is limited, city councils and county commissions do not always discuss issues and actions in public settings. To help insure public and journalistic access to local governments, states have passed open meetings laws. These laws define what local government units can do in private and what must be done in public.

Because most news organizations cover local governments, open meetings acts are valuable tools for learning about government activities and conveying that information to news consumers. To that end, editors and journalists need to know about applicable open meeting laws, and must, on occasion, be willing to go to court to make sure the meeting laws are followed. Unlike libel and privacy laws, which apply to individual reputations, pursuing the enforcement of opening meetings is unlikely to hurt a news organization's goodwill. Most people support open meetings so much that suing to force a city council to be open to the public actually can improve community goodwill.

Political versus Commercial Speech

Political speech, dissemination of information related to the operation of democratic government, is the type of communication addressed by the First Amendment. The protection stems from the need for vigorous open debate about issues and people of concern to citizens. In 1942, a distinction was made between political and commercial speech in *Valentine v. Chrestensen* when the U.S. Supreme Court ruled the First Amendment did not protect "purely commercial advertising." The ruling said governments under some conditions could regulate the distribution of commercial speech.

Distinguishing between commercial and political speech can be confusing because political candidates and organizations supporting political change often buy advertising. The famous libel case *New York Times v. Sullivan* (1964) involved an advertisement that ran in the *Times*. The court characterized the ad as an "editorial advertisement" (Moore, 1999, p. 191). In their *Central Hudson Gas & Electric v. Public Service Commission of New York* (1980) ruling, the U.S. Supreme Court created a four-part test for whether speech can be regulated by governments. The parts are (a) the speech must concern illegal activity and mislead; (b) the asserted government interest must be substantial; (c) the regulation must advance government interest; (d) the regulation must not be more extensive than necessary (Moore, 1999, p. 202).

Because news organizations participate in political and commercial speech, media managers need to have an understanding of the legal issues related to both. They need to decide when to accept and reject advertising and when the First Amendment protects advertising.

Indecency and Obscenity Laws

Media content that large portions of society consider offensive falls into two categories: (a) indecency and (b) obscenity. Indecent material is not as offensive as obscene material. As Kovarik (2003) wrote, "If a work is legally obscene, it may be censored and its producers may be punished. If a work is not legally obscene, it is protected by the First Amendment and cannot be censored" (http://www.runet.edu/~wkovarik/class/law/1.12obscenity.html). The problem is that courts have long struggled with what material is and is not obscene.

Both indecent and obscene materials are offensive, but they differ in one way: Obscenity involves content that appeals to prurient interest (obsessive interest in sex), but indecency may not. For example, the FCC can restrict the use of certain words, only some of which involve sexual activity. Because indecent material has First Amendment protection in print media, most issues regarding indecency involve broadcast television and radio.

The key case in modern obscenity law is *Roth v. U.S.* (1957). In this case, the U.S. Supreme Court confirmed that the First Amendment did not protect obscene material, the portrayal of sex is not necessarily obscene, and that obscenity is without redeeming social importance. In *Miller v. California* (1973), the court set up a three-part test for obscenity. To be obscene, an average person, applying contemporary community standards, would find that the work as a whole appeals to prurient interests; the work depicts offensive sexual conduct specifically defined by state law; and the work, as a whole, lacks serious literary, artistic, political, or scientific value. All three parts of the test must be met before a work can be declared legally obscene (Moore, 1999, p. 592). Of course, it is not always clear what does and does not appeal to prurient interests. The term "serious literary, artistic, political, or scientific value" has a variety of interpretations, as does the term "patently offensive." A further difficulty is that "community standards" vary. What would be considered obscene in Alabama may not be in California.

Most media organizations do not provide obscene content. However, the Internet, with thousands of sites devoted to sexual material, has raised concerns about easy access to material that is certainly offensive if not obscene. In *Reno v. ACLU* (1997), the U.S. Supreme Court ruled as unconstitutional elements of the Communication Decency Act that dealt with indecent and patently offensive Internet communication. The ruling gave the Internet a higher level of First Amendment protection than that enjoyed by broadcast media.

Although obscenity laws have become more liberal over the years, changing federal, state, and local political environments can alter what is legal. Media managers who deal with entertainment content must be aware of what constitutes indecent and obscene material because it can affect a variety of business decisions. The issue of indecency will be dealt with in the regulation section.

Business Law

Business laws apply to most businesses, and media companies are no exception. This section will briefly address some of the many business laws applicable to media organizations and how media managers can avoid violating these laws.

Antitrust

In *Associated Press v. U.S.* (1945), the U.S. Supreme Court said the First Amendment did not prevent the federal government from applying antitrust laws to newspapers, which antitrust date to the late 1800s in the United States. The Sherman Act of 1890 and the Clayton Act of 1914 outlawed contracts, combinations, and trusts that restrain trade and outlawed monopolies and efforts to monopolize (Lacy & Simon, 1993, p. 188). Antitrust action can take the form of a criminal case if a government agency brings suit, but it also can take the form of a civil suit if a company sues a competitor.

As media markets become more concentrated, mergers and sales of individual and media properties increasingly must receive antitrust approval to take place. For example, when media corporation McClatchy Co., bought newspapers from Knight Ridder, it received clearance from the Justice Department in June 2006 to sell some newspapers, but the department asked for additional information before it could sell two California dailies (Associated Press, 2006).

Antitrust laws are based on the assumption that competition among media outlets serves customers and advertisers. The assumption has support in research. Studies indicate that competition increases the amount of money spent on newspaper and television newsrooms, reduces the cost per thousand for advertising, increases the number of viewpoints available about public issues, and results in more stories about more topics (Lacy & Martin, 2005).

Media managers whose companies consider the acquisition of or merging with other companies need to consider the antitrust implications of their plans, including the possibility of criminal and civil actions. Clearance by the Justice Department may or may not prevent competitors from filing a civil antitrust case. If a case goes to court, the plaintiff must show that the merger or acquisition will lessen competition and have a negative impact on the company filing the lawsuit. Media companies should discuss possible lawsuits with lawyers specializing in antitrust law.

Antitrust concerns create a conflict for managers at news organizations. Reducing competition would improve a media company's financial performance, but competition better serves a community. The conflict occurs because, as discussed in the ethics section, many journalists assume that the First Amendment carries an implicit responsibility to serve society.

Copyright Laws

Because media companies produce information as content, intellectual property laws affect managers' decisions. The laws dictate who owns and uses content and information. Intellectual property covers several areas of law such as copyright, patents, and trademarks (Moore, 1999). Copyright law applies to most media companies.

Copyright law protects the creative endeavors of people and organizations and includes music, literature, photographs, graphics, movies, journalism, recordings, television programs, and radio broadcasts. These were designed to encourage creativity and the production of creative works. Without copyright laws, anyone could take anyone else's content and resell it. This would make it difficult for creative people to make a living.

Copyright law covers the presentation of ideas and facts and not the ideas and facts themselves (Moore, 1999, pp. 497–498). If a Web site publishes a story about illegal activities by a governor's office, the Website story is copyrighted, but that will not prevent other news outlets from covering the same story. However, the other new outlets cannot simply copy the story and other material from the Web site. The distinction between an idea and its presentation is important. Copyright does not allow one company to control an idea, because the free flow of ideas is crucial to the working of a democracy. For example, the inability of the *Washington Post* to copyright the idea that President Nixon committed crimes during his presidency allowed *The New York Times* and other news organizations to compete in developing this story. This allowed the story of the president's crimes to come out more quickly than it would have if only one news organization had pursued the story.

The need for information to flow freely in a democracy versus the need for companies to own the information they produce creates conflict between allowing people to use content and allowing organizations to control content. The solution has been to create limits on how long a person or company owns the information and the conditions under which a person can use content. Currently, the creator of a work holds the copyright for 70 years after the creator's death. If an organization holds the copyright or the work, the copyright lasts for 95 years (Keyt Law, 2006). All works before 1923 first published in the United States are in the public domain, which means no one holds the copyright and people can use the material as they want.

Even though a person or organization owns a copyright, he or she cannot exclude people entirely from using the copyrighted content without permission. The ability to use content without permission is called "fair use" and results from the need of society to have access to information. Middleton, Trager, and Chamberlin (2001) explained fair use as follows:

> The factors to be considered when a court is determining if copying constitutes fair use are,
>
> 1. The purpose and character of the use, including whether such use is of commercial nature or is for nonprofit educational purposes.
> 2. The nature of the copyrighted work.
> 3. The amount and substantiality of the portion used in relation to the copyrighted work as a whole.
> 4. The effect of the use on the potential market for, or value of, the copyrighted work. Most important in fair-use decisions is the commercial damage copying might cause to the copyrighted work (pp. 235–236).

Issues related to copyright protection have grown in importance as the information economy has expanded. Entertainment corporations such as Disney and Fox are particularly concerned about protecting their copyrights. Control of the material is crucial to the financial success of these corporations.

As media organizations increasingly become international in marketing and ownership, copyright in other countries becomes more important. There is no international copyright that protects content in every country, but many countries have their own laws and respect U.S. copyrights to some degree. The relationship among country copyright laws is defined by international conventions. The most important ones are the Universal Copyright Convention and the Berne Convention (Moore, 1999). The Berne Convention, which the United States joined in 1989, requires the signatories to extend the same copyright protection to citizens in other countries as they give their own citizens (Moore, 1999). Despite such conventions, the theft of intellectual property is widespread in some areas of the world. U.S. businesses lost about $4 billion in 2005 due to copyright theft in China and Russia (The Congressional International Anti-piracy Caucus, 2006).

Wage and Contract Law

Just how much any individual is paid reflects laws and market dynamics. Highly skilled, creative, and well-known employees can bargain with management for their salaries. In news media companies, these employees include television anchors and reporters, newspaper columnists, and managers. In entertainment companies, this would include radio personalities, actors, writers, directors, and managers. Of course, not all employees in these categories can bargain for higher than minimal pay. The ability to ask and receive a premium salary reflects supply and demand for particular skills and the "brand" that an individual has built for him- or herself. Highly paid broadcasters and columnists, such as Katie Couric and Mitch Albom, have a following among viewers and readers that can be compared to a product brand. Being an employee with a brand can apply at a national level as with Couric and Albom, or it apply at a local level where a TV news anchor has a strong following.

People who develop themselves as brands are unusual, and their incomes reflect how much media consumers value them and what they do. Other types of skilled labor can demand higher-than-average pay because the supply of their skills is low relative to the demand. Highly trained investigative reporters with experience in computer assisted reporting (CAR) are far scarcer than are general assignment reporters. As a result, CAR reporters normally receive higher pay than general assignment reporters and are in greater demand.

A number of state and federal laws affect how much media employees are paid. At the low end of employee pay, state and federal laws dictate the minimum wage an employee can make, and at the high end, contract law defines the wage relationship in a negotiated wage. Laws also affect who receives what and how much is received by employees in overtime pay.

State and federal minimum-wage laws affect employees, and the legal minimum varies greatly around the United States and throughout the world. Minimum-wage standards are mostly found in developed Western countries. In addition to the United States, New Zealand, Canada, and Australia, 18 of the 26 European countries had a minimum-wage standard in 2005 (Funk & Lesch, 2005). Latin American, Asian, and African countries mostly lack such laws, which explains why many Western companies have moved to these continents during the past 50 years. The absence of a minimum-wage law allows companies to drastically lower their payrolls. Critics have accused these companies of exploitation.

The federal minimum wage in 2006 was $5.15, the level since 1997. An effort to increase the wage failed in 2006. However, managers need to be aware of state variations. For example, in 2006, 18 states had minimum-wage standards that exceeded the federal level. Connecticut had the highest level, which reached $7.65 beginning in 2007 (U.S. Department of Labor, 2006). In many cases, such as Kansas' $2.65 minimum wage, the standard does not apply to companies that are subject to the Federal Fair Labor Standards Act (FLSA). The federal minimum-wage law covers employees who qualify under the FLSA. This includes employees of companies that have an annual minimum revenue of $500,000, engage in interstate commerce, use mails or telephones for interstate communication, or who work for federal, state, or local governments.

Managers should remember that these are legal minimum wages. Companies can pay higher wages and may be forced to do so by their labor markets. The geographic nature of labor markets varies with the type of employment. Journalists, for instance, work in a national labor market and often move for jobs. An advertising salesperson might move, but local connections with business would make a person more valuable.

If employees qualify for minimum wage under the FLSA, they also are subject to the federal overtime rules. Companies subject to minimum-wage laws also must pay wage earners at least time-and-a-half pay for any work past 40 hours. This rule does not apply to employees who work on sales commission, executives (management), and some professionals. Some journalists qualify for overtime pay and some do not. General-assignment and beat reporters typically qualify, but journalists who conduct investigative journalism, analysis, or commentary are considered professionals and are paid salaries (Lucan, 2004). The overtime law can be important at news organizations because breaking news creates erratic schedules for journalists and results in their working more than 40 hours per week. Violation of wage laws is more likely to happen at small news organizations with correspondingly small staffs and newsroom budgets.

Courts typically interpret the basic relationship between a company and employee as "employment at will," which assumes that employees and employers freely enter into an employment relationship and that the both can leave it freely (Gillmor, Barron, Simon, & Terry, 1990, p. 577). However, most television news employees now have contracts that specify their relationship with their employers. Such contracts also are common for syndicated columnists and cartoonists.

Despite contracts defining the relationship between employees and their employers, conflict can arise over contract interpretations. For example, a TV anchor in Louisiana sued when he was removed as anchor and claimed the removal violated his contract. The court ruled that as long as the anchor was paid, the station did not have to put him on air (Gillmor et al., 1990, p. 577).

Managers need to understand wage and contract law because a company's payroll makes up a large portion of its total budget. The budget, in turn, affects the company's profit. How managers deal with wage and contract also can affect employees' morale. Employees who feel valued and appreciated are more likely to invest their own efforts and time in the company.

Dealing with Employees and Preventing Legal Problems

The relationship between companies and employees without contracts is not an entirely "at-will" situation. A variety of federal and state laws, including antidiscrimination law, define what employers can and cannot do regarding their employees. Media managers can institute general principles and procedures to minimize legal problems. Generally, all communications and agreements among supervisors, employees, and those outside the organization should be documented. The following section on performance evaluation provides documentation guidelines that can be adapted and applied to other areas. These guidelines come from numerous situations and are the "best practices" that will protect the organization.

Performance Management and Evaluation

Regular, formal communication from supervisors with their employees about performance is simply good business practice. Documenting performance problems using factual information supports a firm's legitimate, nondiscriminatory reasons for rewarding, disciplining, or firing an employee. Try to standardize performance criteria and measurement across the organization, if possible, to enable comparisons between employees in various departments and to demonstrate that standards and procedures are applied consistently (Fentin, 2002; How to Align, 2002; How to Remake, 2002; Two Ways, 2002; Zachary, 2000). Standardization helps to create a fair process for all employees and reduces the idiosyncratic influences of individual managers.

Notify employees and educate them about how to prepare for evaluations long before they occur. Develop organizational goals, allowing managers, supervisors, and employees to participate in setting them. Meet with employees to discuss the written goals, performance measurements, and deadlines of evaluations. Explain what rewards may be given for exceptional performance and the penalties for unsatisfactory performance. (How to Align, 2002). People perform better when they have a clear understanding of what is expected.

Managers should provide specific written comments and examples in performance reviews. State performance accurately, clearly, and concisely, because it is in everyone's best interest to do so (Fentin, 2002; Skoler, Abbott, & Presser, 2002). Managers might decide on a central message for the evaluation and then support that appraisal when completing the evaluation form (How to Remake, 2002; Two Tools, 2002). If an evaluation reveals that an employee lacks necessary job skills, provide and document training in those skills. Document and offer continuous feedback to every employee who performs below expectations. Also consider how employees achieve results; for example, if an account executive surpasses sales goals using unethical, inappropriate, or counterproductive methods, do not reward the behavior (How to Align, 2002).

Follow all written performance evaluations, especially unfavorable ones, with face-to-face conversations with the employee. Two managers should be present. Require the employee to acknowledge in writing that she or he received the written performance evaluation and the meeting was held to discuss it. Allow employees who disagree with an evaluation to make written comments and appeal within an appropriate time period (Fentin, 2002; Skoler et al., 2002; Two Ways, 2002). These steps promote a communication and record of the performance process, which reduces the chances of any misunderstandings.

Treat performance problems consistently across evaluations to avoid discrimination claims. For example, if two employees are often tardy, document and address tardiness the same way in their evaluations. Consistency in evaluation helps protect a firm from wrongful discharge actions (Hinkle, Hensley, Shanor, & Martin, 2002; How to Align, 2002; How to Remake, 2002; Skoler et al., 2002; Two Tools, 2002).

Ideally, a performance evaluation enables a manager to set goals for the employee to accomplish before the next review. These goals could include problems, or below-par performance to eliminate, as well as accomplishments to achieve. Include a written acknowledgment signed by the employee and supervisor to work toward those goals. Allow the employee to sign a different form acknowledging disagreement with the evaluation and/or goals. Give the dissatisfied employee an opportunity to respond (Hinkle et al., 2002; Skoler et al., 2002).

Train all managers on the proper way to conduct evaluations and common errors to avoid. For example, instruct managers to avoid rating employees who resemble them or who they like more highly than other employees. Resist the tendency to rate all employees in the middle of the scale, especially when performance clearly deserves a lower or higher rating. Be careful not to rate an employee against peers rather than objective job standards. Resist the tendency to give recent minor events more importance than major events that occurred months earlier. Instead, continually keep notes in a file of employee performance throughout the evaluation period to refer back to when conducting the evaluation (Hinkle et al., 2002; How to Remake, 2002; Skoler et al., 2002; Two Tools, 2002; Zachary, 2000).

When done properly, employee evaluations will allow employees to perform better and protect the organization against suits from disgruntled employees. These goals require an evaluation process that is standardized, clear, consistent, and fair and promotes communication between managers and employees.

Progressive Discipline

Managers must be familiar with appropriate procedures for disciplining and, if necessary, firing employees when unsatisfactory evaluations occur. Using progressive discipline (or using an oral warning, written warning, and then dismissal) gives employees a fair chance to correct performance before termination and provides documentation for employers who must fire employees for legitimate, nondiscriminatory reasons (Fentin, 2002). Wrongful-termination lawsuits may result from a failure to document progressive discipline. A progressive discipline system should begin with recruitment and continue through orientation, training, performance evaluation, and supervision (Falcone, 1997).

Fentin (2002) and Falcone (1997) provided documentation guidelines for implementing progressive discipline. Begin with private, informal counseling about the unsatisfactory performance or behavior. The manager should document the conversation, including when it occurred and what was discussed, and place a memo in the employee's personnel file.

A verbal warning typically follows. Two managers (e.g., the employee's direct supervisor and the head of that department) meet in private with the employee, discuss the performance problems, provide specific steps for correcting them, and give goals and deadlines to complete the corrections. The two supervisors and the employee sign a notice documenting that the employee received the verbal warning. Only other employees who need to know about the warning to conduct their jobs are informed, but directed to keep it private. That protects the employee's privacy and the company does not risk defamation charges.

If the verbal warning fails, give the employee a written warning based on objective performance criteria that include specific examples about the problem or apparent inability to perform at minimum standards. The document should explain why the performance was unsatisfactory, suggest a way to improve, establish a disciplinary time period for improvement, and outline the consequences of failing to improve. Give the employee the opportunity to respond verbally and in writing.

If the employee does not respond, Fentin (2002) said that several supervisors (e.g., the direct supervisor of the employee, the head of that supervisor's department, the supervisor of all departments, and/or the head of the firm) should meet before firing an employee to establish whether progressive discipline was followed fairly and correctly. This protects the employee from being fired unfairly by a biased or incompetent manager and protects the firm against a wrongful termination suit.

Managers might ask the following questions in the meeting to ensure that a termination is fair (Baxter, 1983): (a) What is the employee's overall record? (b) Are there any mitigating factors that might explain or excuse the employee's misconduct or unsatisfactory performance? (c) Are any statutory problems involved (e.g., regarding race, age, gender, etc.)? (d) Were any job security representations made to the employee? If yes, is the termination consistent with those representations? (e) Are there any public-policy concerns? (f) Has the employee received progressive discipline? (g) Is the termination justified? (h) Does it fit the offense?

Have two managers present to document the entire conversation when terminating an employee. Require the employee to conduct an exit interview with an ombudsman or independent manager not involved in the termination. Exit interviews provide an early warning of potential harassment or discrimination claims and/or management problems that need to be addressed (Fentin, 2002).

Although it is difficult to fire someone without due process, on-the-spot firings are warranted when an employee breaks the law, engages in substance abuse on company property, or engages in illegal conduct, gross insubordination, or negligence. If there is any doubt, a manager can suspend an employee until an investigation of the conduct is completed. This allows time to speak to an attorney versed in labor law. Previous disciplinary actions may also be examined to ensure disciplinary actions are fair (Falcone, 1997).

Understanding and Preventing Discrimination

Title VII of the amended Civil Rights Act of 1964 proscribes employment discrimination (or treating an employee unfairly or unfavorably) based on race, religion, gender, or national origin. Prohibited actions include refusing to hire employees based on race or gender, providing unequal conditions of employment, and providing unequal pay for the same job (Lacy & Simon, 1993).

McGill (2002) reported that in 2000, persons of color made up 11.64% of employees in U.S. newspaper newsrooms. In 2006, the percentage had increased only to 13.87%. The annual report in which this figure was reported stated, "Though newspapers are increasing their hiring and retention of minority journalists, newsroom diversity is falling behind the nation's rapidly changing demographics. A third of the U.S. population is now minority, according to the latest estimates from the U.S. Census Bureau" (American Society of Newspaper Editors, 2006). What does the inability to attract and retain sufficient numbers of people of color say about an industry that reports on discrimination in other firms?

Persons of color and their coworkers have strongly differing views on employment issues. Seventy-three percent of African American journalists felt that African Americans were not as likely to be considered for career opportunities, yet only 2% of newsroom managers felt that way. Perhaps this is why 78% of African American journalists felt managers had unrealistic perceptions of them, whereas only 24% of managers felt that way (McGill, 2002). These beliefs of journalists of color demonstrate why it is so important to implement fair and consistent performance evaluations.

McGill (2002) said such perceptual discrepancies indicate that separate cultures have evolved in newsrooms. In one culture, White managers and journalists think opportunities for advancement are equal. In another culture, managers and journalists of color perceive that different standards are being applied to different types of people. Such perceptions are reinforced when people within the White-male-management culture talk mostly to others in that same culture, neglecting interaction with people in other cultures. People from different cultures must be able to communicate their differing perceptions with each other in a supportive environment.

The primary reasons journalists of color give for leaving the profession have been consistent over time: lack of professional challenge and lack of advancement opportunities. Although pay, quality of the work environment, interpersonal relationships, and other factors are important, advancement and challenges must be equally available to journalists of color to retain them. Promotions bring the new duties and challenges that journalists of color desire, yet feel they must work harder and longer than White employees to get. Unfortunately, most journalists of color leave the newspaper profession feeling disillusioned and disappointed—a far cry from the high ideals they held at the beginning of their careers (McGill, 2002).

McGill (2002) said managers must find ways to promote more journalists of color into professionally challenging positions. Such promotions signal an organizational culture change to other employees of color who perceive the same advancement opportunities for themselves. Managers must communicate more effectively with people of color and be open to their different perceptions.

Many of the same types of issues also apply to female employees (see the "Leadership Traits and Skills" section in chapter 2). For example, women make less money than men for the same jobs and receive fewer management opportunities. Managers must acknowledge these discrepancies and create a positive climate conducive to open communications, fair and equitable promotions, productive work environment and job satisfaction for employees of all colors and genders. Not only is this the right thing to do, it will also encourage women and employees of color to remain in media industries and prevent incidents of discrimination.

Diversifying a media organization involves more than just law. It also involves business and ethics. A company that produces cultural goods such as journalism and entertainment needs to understand the diversity of its audience. This occurs best when the workforce and management includes members of the various cultural groups in that audience. A 1992 study concluded that media managers were more likely to support diversity because of business reasons rather than because it is socially responsible to do so (Smith, 1992). Simply put, diversity also is good business. However, the issue also involves ethics in that representing the range of groups in a society has been identified as the right thing to do by the media professional groups. With the increasing diversification of the U.S. population, this issue will remain important during the rest of the 21st century.

Regulation

Not all media are created equal before the U.S. Constitution. The FCC has been given regulatory power over broadcast communication. This power includes the assignment of broadcast licenses for radio and television stations, the establishment of rules of ownership, the punishment of indecent content, and rules for political communication on broadcast media. Justification for such regulation rests on the physical scarcity of the broadcast spectrum. To maintain order, the FCC assigns licenses and, therefore, can require that the stations act in the public interest (Middleton et al., 2001, p. 518). As technology developed, Congress extended regulatory power over cable distribution, although the regulation remains at a lower level than with broadcast TV and radio. During the last two decades of the 20th century, the federal government began to deregulate the telecommunication industries, although debate continues about the appropriate degree of deregulation. States also have rules governing electronic communication, but federal rules supersede state regulations.

Broadcast Television, Cable, and Radio Regulation

The Communication Act of 1934 established the FCC and was the primary regulatory act until the Telecommunications Act of 1996. During the 62 years between, regulations changed periodically as technology developed. Three important areas of regulation are (a) ownership, (b) political communication, and (c) indecency.

Ownership rules.   Ownership rules have undergone extensive change since 1981. The most recent effort to change the rules occurred in 2002 and 2003 (Shields, 2003). The FCC wanted to let television networks own stations that reach up to 45% of U.S. TV households, up from 35%, and own up to three stations in the same market. The FCC also wanted to overturn the rule that keeps a newspaper from owning a TV station in the same market, which would apply to most markets except those that had cross-ownership situations when the rule was first created (those markets were allowed to keep cross-ownership). A federal appellate court stayed these changes, preventing them from taking place. In 2006, the FCC again voted to again reconsider ownership rules.

The radio industry became more concentrated than television as a result of changes of ownership regulation during the past 25 years. Currently, there are no caps on the number of radio stations a company can own nationally. In local markets, the rules specify that (a) in a market with 45 or more commercial stations, a company may own up to eight commercial radio stations, but no more than five AM or FM stations; (b) in a market with 30 to 44 commercial stations, a company may own up to seven commercial radio stations, not no more than four AM or FM stations; (c) in a market with 15 to 29 commercial stations, a company may own up to six commercial stations, but no more than four AM or FM stations; and (d) in a market with 14 or fewer commercial stations, a company may own up to five commercial stations, but no more than three AM or FM stations. Overall, a company cannot own more than 50% of the stations in a market (Federal Communication Commission, 2005).

Changes in ownership rules reflect growing media competition and efforts of broadcast radio and television companies to reclaim lost market share and revenues that have shrunk due to competition. The changes have resulted in the rapid growth of some companies. More than 3,300 TV and radio stations were sold between 2003 and 2006, and this has alarmed FCC ownership rules critics concerned (Holland, 2006) that concentration will reduce the station's local emphasis and service.

Political communication.   From the early years of broadcast regulation, the federal government has monitored the role of television and radio in the political process. Until 1987, broadcast stations were subject to the Fairness Doctrine, which required that stations provide fair and balanced coverage of controversial issues. Some journalists said the Fairness Doctrine violated journalists' First Amendment rights. In

1987, the FCC removed the doctrine as part of the deregulation process. Congress tried to reinstate it, but President Reagan vetoed the bill (Limburg, 2005).

Although the Fairness Doctrine no longer exists, the FCC continues to oversee some elements of broadcast political communication. The Equal Time Rule requires that broadcast stations give or sell time on an equal basis to political candidates. More recently, it requires that it offer political candidates the same advertising rates given its most "favored advertisers" (Klieman, 2005).

The role of regulation of political communication in TV and radio continues to provoke debate. Even though stations must give political candidates favorable advertising rates, political advertising continues to generate hundreds of millions of dollars in revenues for broadcast stations and networks during a presidential election year. Critics argue that the need for large amounts of advertising expenditures to win elections excludes independent and third-party candidates from participating in governance at all levels. They also point out that the income generated from political advertising is a deterrent for broadcasters to give free time to political candidates. As with all regulations, the debate over broadcasting's role in the political process will continue. Media managers need to keep abreast of the debate and to consider the impact of regulation on both information and advertising.

Indecent content. The FCC has always monitored indecent material broadcast over the airwaves. The concern varies in intensity depending on the political leaning of the majority of FCC commissioners (appointed by the president), and changes in cultural norms. For most of the past 25 years, the majority leaning has been conservative. This leaning, combined with a conservative leaning in Congress, has created a growing concern with indecency, resulting in a new structure for indecency fines. Pop singer Janet Jackson's "wardrobe malfunction" during the 2004 Super Bowl half-time performance created a stir and a record fine for indecency. The total fine came to $550,000 ($27,000 for each station owned by CBS).

The increase in sexual content on broadcast TV and radio has led to two important FCC regulation changes. First, Congress increased the fines to $375,000 per incident, which means a company owning multiple stations must pay the fine for each station that ran the indecent material. The second important change concerns who carries the burden of proof when someone files an indecency complaint against a station with the FCC. Traditionally, the complainant had to demonstrate that the station aired indecent content. However, more recently, the FCC has indicated a desire to shift the burden of proof to the broadcasters (McConnell, 2002). The result could be that stations will become more conservative in their approach to content.

Indecency issues affect entertainment content more than journalism because entertainment increasingly contains sexual content. The regulation of sexual content on broadcast television puts broadcast TV networks at a disadvantage in competing with cable and satellite channels, whose content is not regulated by the FCC.

Because indecent content can lead to fines, broadcast TV and radio managers need to be aware of how their programming decisions affect the budget. However, the impact of running indecent material may be even greater. The FCC could tighten indecency regulation even more. The fines could increase, and the FCC might punish networks and stations by not renewing station licenses when they expire. The need for TV and radio companies to attract younger viewers, who have come to expect a certain level of sexual content, has created a difficult situation for the managers who have to deal with more conservative regulators.

Advertising Regulation

Managers may need to train employees to clear or review advertising to determine whether it offends the audience. Sections 5 and 12 of the Federal Trade Commission (FTC) Act of 1914 give the FTC the power to regulate deceptive advertising and other unfair acts or practices. An advertiser injured by a competitor's misleading ad may sue under Section 43(1) of the Lanham Act, which provides protection for trademarks. *Deception* under the Lanham Act is defined as any false or misleading description or representation of fact (Gillmor, Barron, & Simon, 1998; Preston, 1994, 1996).

The FTC definition of deception is (a) There must be a representation, omission, or practice that is likely to mislead the consumer; (b) the representation, omission, or practice is examined from the perspective of a consumer acting reasonably in the circumstances to the consumer's detriment; and (c) the representation, omission, or practice must be a material one (Policy Statement of Deception, 1983). Richards (1990) said, "regulable" deceptiveness results only if purchase behavior of a substantial number of people is likely to be affected" (p. 24).

Deceptive claims or practices include false verbal or written statements, misleading price claims, selling dangerous or defective products without adequate disclosures, not delivering promised services, and failing to meet warranty obligations. The FTC considers whether the entire ad is likely to mislead reasonable consumers, meaning that even if all of an ad's claims are true, if the general impression of the ad is false, it still may be deceptive (Policy Statement on Deception, 1983; Preston, 1994).

The FTC said certain practices are not likely to deceive reasonable consumers. For example, misrepresentations about inexpensive products that are evaluated easily and purchased frequently by consumers are of less concern because these advertisers depend on repeat sales for survival. The FTC usually does not pursue cases based on puffery or correctly stated and honestly held opinions about a product or obvious exaggerations about the product or its qualities (e.g., the "best" or "greatest") (Policy Statement on Deception, 1983; Preston, 1996). Newspapers, magazines, broadcast stations, cable channels, Internet sites, and so on can screen ads prior to public dissemination to ensure they are not deceptive or offensive.

The Changing Nature of Laws and Media Management

As earlier chapters have suggested, media managers must expect that media industries will dramatically change in the future. They will face decisions pitting the business interests of their owners against the public interest. Recent events demonstrate how laws, rules, and regulations affecting the media often change.

For example, the Telecommunications Act of 1996 changed the broadcast, cable, and telephone industries by eliminating or changing radio and TV station ownership limits, extending broadcast license terms, simplifying the license renewal process, deregulating cable rates, and increasing fines for obscenity. Section 202(h) of the Telecommunications Act of 1996 requires the FCC to review its media ownership rules every 2 years. Ownership rules are a major industry concern because relaxing them would allow media companies to buy a variety of media outlets and gain economies of scale in news operations, for example. Yet having a limited number of media owners could result in too few companies controlling the flow of information, including news and entertainment, thus hampering the robust marketplace of ideas (Hickey, 2002).

The U.S. Supreme Court ruled in *Associated Press v. U.S.* (1945) that the widest possible dissemination of information from diverse and opposing sources was central to public welfare. Hickey (2002) said if media ownership rules are eliminated or relaxed further, fewer companies could control the content of news and entertainment programming. He also identified potential problems with joint ownership of newspapers and TV stations in the same market. The number of independent newspaper owners would likely decrease, reducing the number of diverse news voices. These jointly owned newspapers and stations might be unlikely to investigate each other, self-censoring themselves to protect their owners' interests.

Owners, publishers, and general or station managers, as well as editors, news directors, and reporters, must expect to face thorny decisions regarding ownership issues. Managerial decisions that support a diversified information marketplace could result in difficult, potentially job-threatening, and legally complex consequences. Yet the future of a strong, independent, and free press is at stake.

Ethics

Thirty-five years ago when one of the authors studied in business school, the curriculum required business law but not business ethics. Business schools seemed to consider ethics and law equivalent. If it was legal, it was ethical. However, this idea seemed to dissipate during the 1990s and early 2000s as business scandals such as that at Enron grabbed headlines. Managers who cared nothing about right and wrong pushed the boundaries of legality. Even after they were convicted on criminal charges, many of the managers argued that they did nothing wrong.

Today, ethics and law are interrelated. Laws and regulations define what a manager must do, and ethics defines what he or she should do. Laws prevent a manager from stealing trade secrets from a competitor, but laws may not prevent him or her from lying to gain an advantage. Courts settle disputes over just what a law means, but no formal authority settles disputes about ethics. Some journalists believe that reporting should be fair, balanced, and complete, but others believe that journalists should express their opinions in what they write. Regardless of what they believe, managers of news organizations need to understand that the individual citizens who use media pass judgment on what they feel is ethical journalism. This judgment by the court of public opinion does not require that news organizations do everything their readers, viewers, and listeners want. Not only is it impossible to suit all potential media users in a market, sometimes doing as the audience wants can violate professional ethics. For instance, some readers expect newspapers to run the names of people arrested for crimes. However, many newspapers have a rule that the names of arrested people run after the people are officially charged by the prosecutor.

Just as there are disagreements as to what are appropriate ethical standards, managers, journalists, and ethicists also disagree on the best way to establish ethics. Most news organizations and professional journalism associations have codes of ethics. Other media organizations, such as those in the information and entertainment business, are less likely to have codes. Such codes, however, do not guarantee ethical behavior. In most cases, enforcement is voluntary (Goodwin, 1987, pp. 16–19). In other cases, the codes are so general and vague as to be impossible to follow (Goodwin, 1987, pp. 15–16). Merrill (1974, p. 164) argued that journalists must decide whether to be ethical. By extension, a code will not cause a journalist, or a manager, to behave according to standards if the individual has not already decided to be ethical. The argument about the relationship between codes and behavior explains the two approaches taken to media ethics. Those who doubt the effectiveness of codes argue that ethics must be established through a rational process that applies general principles to each ethical situation. This "moral-reasoning" process makes ethical decision making more flexible than just adhering to a list of rules.

Ethics Codes

Codes of ethics exist in many media industries. The American Society of Newspaper Editors wrote a code in 1923 (Goodwin, 1987, p. 14). In the early 1930s, the motion-picture industry adopted a code of conduct called the Hays Code. It was abandoned in 1968 and replaced by a ratings system because few moviemakers adhered. The National Association of Broadcasters has codes for television and radio, although the courts ruled in 1983 (Rivers & Mathews, 1988, p. 203) that they were illegal.

Codes represent behavior acceptable to employees of a media organization, such as the *Washington Post*, or to members of a professional organization, such as Public Relations Society of America. The codes can take a negative tone by listing behaviors that are unacceptable, or a positive tone by listing behaviors that are encouraged. An example of a positive listing would be this statement from the Society of Professional Journalists Code of Ethics: "Test the accuracy of information from all sources and exercise care to avoid inadvertent error" (Society of Professional Journalists Code of Ethics, 1996). A negative standard from the same document is, "Never distort the content of news photos or video."

Most codes represent the position of the organization that created the code. Although it wasn't a code of ethics, the Commission on Freedom of the Press, also called the Hutchins Commission after Chairman Robert Hutchins, undertook an effort in the 1940s to define standards of behavior for a responsible press (Commission on Freedom of the Press, 1947). Reacting to a growing economic concentration of media, the Commission listed five requirements of a press that was responsible to society (Commission on Freedom of the Press, pp. 20–29):

- A truthful, comprehensive, and intelligent account of the day's events in a context which gives them meaning;
- A forum for the exchange of comment and criticism;
- The projection of a representative picture of the constituent groups in the society;
- The presentation and clarification of the goals and values of society;
- Full access to the day's intelligence.

This was not a code of ethics, because it prescribed requirements for the entire media system, not individual organizations. However, the underlying assumption is that individual media organizations should be responsive to the needs of their communities and not just pursue their own self-interest. This assumption, called *social responsibility*, differs from that of the libertarian approach, which assumes that if news organizations each pursue their own interest, then the system as a whole will supply the diversity of voices and positions a democratic system requires. Most codes of ethics are based either on the social responsibility or libertarian approaches toward journalism.

Codes of ethics have drawbacks. They can be overly general and vague and they can be difficult to enforce. A media organization's code will only be as strong as the individuals in the organization are ethical. However, codes also have the advantage of explicitly communicating to employees what is expected of them. In effect, codes can be a form of programmed decisions that tell employees what can and cannot be done. They force the people within the organization to think about and discuss values of the organization and the behaviors that promote those values.

Managers need to understand the advantages and disadvantages of codes of ethics. If an organization has an ethics code, management should examine it periodically and include employees in that examination. The assessment should evaluate how well the organization's code fits with professional standards and social norms, how well employees follow the code, and how well the code fits the goals of the organization. If an organization does not have a code, management should consider whether it wants to add one, and if so, what form it would take.

Moral Reasoning

Moral reasoning concerns how individuals use logic to solve moral and ethic problems (Jaksa & Pritchard, 1988). A consistent process of reasoning allows people to solve problems without relying just on their emotions. The role of reasoning in ethics is central, according to Merrill. He said (1974),

> If there is not a large dose of reason in one's ethical determinations, there can really be little or no consistency and predictability to ethical actions. And, of course, one of the main purposes of ethics is to serve as a reliable and helpful guide to right actions. Such a guide cannot be provided simply by whim or instinct; otherwise we could talk of dogs and cats as being ethically motivated. (p. 185)

Moral reasoning can be thought of as a process, or a series of processes, by which people evaluate and solve ethical problems. A variety of processes are available to help individuals analyze a problem (Bok, 1989; Goodwin, 1987), but most of these involve a manager or employee asking a series of questions about the impact and benefits of the ethical decision. The following questions are consistent with the various questions used to promote reasoning:

1. What is the goal of the action?
2. Is this the only or best way of accomplishing the goal?
3. Who is harmed by the action?
4. Is the harm justified?
5. Who benefits from the action?
6. Do the benefits outweigh the harm?
7. Will the action be consistent with generally accepted standards in the business?
8. If not, do the benefits demand that the action be taken?

An example for applying these questions would be the decision of a newspaper to use the name of a rape victim in a story in an effort to reduce the stigma attached to rape. Rape is a violent assault, but some people continue to assume that the victims somehow "asked for it." Because of this stigma, news organizations hesitate to run rape victims' names. The counter argument is that the withholding of rape victims' names when other victims are named contributes to the continuation of the stigma.

With regard to the eight questions, the goal would be to reduce the stigma of rape. However, this is not the only way to do so because a variety of educational programs could help. It may not even be the best way, but if the action is explained, running the name will begin a conversation about the practice. Of course, the fact that a stigma exists means a victim whose name is used could suffer psychological harm. The degree of harm would vary with the way the victim perceives the stigma. If a victim volunteers to have her name used and does not accept the stigma, the benefit may outweigh the harm.

The community in general and future rape victims will benefit if the stigma is removed. The question that cannot be answered is whether the harm to the individual who volunteered outweighs the gain to the community and future victims. This cannot be predicted or measured, and the inability to do so explains the continuing disagreement on this issue.

Running a rape victim's name is not consistent with generally accepted practice, so a decision to do so would rest on a positive answer to the eighth question. Some editors would argue that the benefits demand that the action be taken. Although the reasoning process did not use these eight questions, the *Des Moines Register* won the 1991 Pulitzer Prize for Public Service after the editor, Geneva Overholser, decided to run a series of articles about Nancy Ziegenmeyer, a rape victim who volunteered to have her name used in the series. The reasoning was that the practice of not running the rape victim's name was contributing to the stigmatizing of the victims (Overholser, 2003).

The moral reasoning process is similar to the decision wheel discussed in chapter 1. In both cases, the success of the process revolves around collecting sufficient information about the decision. This is especially true of the potential harms and benefits. Rather than speculating, managers should collect hard data. Another similarity to the decision process is that some ethical decisions can be programmed through ethics codes. For example, at large commercial news organizations, truthful, balanced, fair, and complete reporting should be required regardless of the news story. These types of generally accepted professional behaviors need not be discussed with editors in making individual story decisions. The time managers save can be devoted to solving more controversial ethical issues.

Dealing with ethical problems is central to the management of any business that expects to serve the public. This is particularly true of media organizations. Ethics codes and moral reasoning can help managers cope. The two are not mutually exclusive. Both require that management and employees commit to the idea that businesses have responsibilities beyond what is legal. Such commitment cannot be assumed. Managers should create an environment in which ethics are discussed, encouraged, and used on a daily basis.

Summary

Understanding U.S. and international law, regulations, and ethics remains central to a media manager's ability to achieve the organization's goals. Laws and regulations constrain an organization's goals and manager's decisions. They are dynamic, changing with political, social, and economic shifts. Ethics also change, but because they carry no formal enforcement process, they constrain decisions less than that of laws and regulations. Ethics concerns whether decisions met standards of right and wrong. This chapter provides only a surface introduction to the issues related to these areas. Students should access online material and the various sources cited here.

Case 6.1 The Aggressive Legal Expert

You are the news director at Fair & Balanced News (FBN), a new news network distributed over cable. In order to gain audience from the existing network (CNN, Fox and MSNBC), you have taken an aggressive approach toward your reporting. Some might call it sensational, but you prefer the term "muckraking." One of your stars is Susan Allen, who looks for criminal cases from throughout the country and interviews people connected with the cases. The promotional phrase of the program, called the *Allen Report*, is "Searching for Justice."

The program has been on air for about 6 months and has seen a fairly rapid increase in viewers. It is a close second to Fox for the timeslot and does well with the 18–45 demographic. This morning you received a letter from a reporter at *The Daily Tribune* in a medium-sized Midwest city. The letter addresses a program from last month about a criminal case covered by the reporter.

The letter includes the following information about the case. Six months ago, John Smith pleaded guilty to aggravated sexual assault of a child and indecency with a child by contact and received a 10-year suspended sentence. Any violation of the conditions in the sentence would result in Smith going to jail for up to 99 years. He has to undergo counseling for sex offenders and, as a registered sex offender, cannot come within 1,500 feet of locations where children congregate. In addition, Smith can never be around the child in the case. As part of the sentence, Smith must complete 500 hours of community service, but because of health problems, the service will be working in a library.

The child is Smith's 8-year-old stepdaughter and the daughter of Smith's former wife. The accusation came to the attention of the prosecutor during the divorce proceedings. The mother had contacted the Child Protection Agency six times before the divorce, accusing Smith of sexually abusing her daughter. In each case, doctors examined the child and found no physical evidence of sexual abuse.

The reporter's letter went on to criticize Allen for the program about this case. Allen had the prosecutor on her show as a guest, but constantly cut him off when he tried to make a point that conflicted with Allen's position. At end of the interview, Allen made a statement that implied the prosecutor had physical evidence of assault, and before the prosecutor could disagree, she closed the interview. At the close of the segment about this case, she accused the judge in the case as being too liberal and called for the removal of the judge.

The letter disagreed with this assessment and explained that the judge is known in the county as a fair and hard-working judge. It also points out that if the case had gone to a jury rather than being plea-bargained, it was unlikely that a conviction would have resulted because there was no confession and no physical evidence of abuse.

The reporter writes that she talked with a producer on the Allen program and was told that the statement about physical evidence was a misunderstanding between the writers and Allen. However, the producer said Allen would not retract the call for the judge's recall.

The reporter's letter ends with, "Susan Allen's call for the judge's resignation was uncalled for and inconsistent with the facts of the case, as was her insinuation that the prosecutor had physical evidence of abuse. The behavior was unethical, and the viewers of the Allen Report should know about the story."

Assignment

As news director of FBN, you need to react to the letter and to discuss the case with Allen and her staff. In doing so, you should think about these questions.

1. Did the story violate journalism ethics? Explain your answer.
2. What should the news director do about this particular story? How will your solution help the network? How might it harm the network?
3. Should the network run these types of programs in the future? Why or why not?
4. Would you change policy in the newsroom? If yes, how? If not, why?

Case 6.2 Expanding the Web Site

You and a friend started a commercial Web site in a small college town in Ohio. You are both graduates of the college and enjoy living in the area. After 2 years, your gross revenues reached $400,000 and you have three part-time employees. The Web site, YourTown.com, carries news and features about the college and community. In addition to you, your friend and the part-time employees, many residents contribute information at no cost.

The publisher and editor of the town's weekly newspaper approaches and offers to sell you the newspaper because she is planning on retiring. The weekly is the only other news organization in the town, except for a weekly college newspaper. In addition to the publisher/editor, the weekly staff includes two full-time and two part-time employees. The weekly, which is distributed for free in the central portion of the county, has gross income of $450,000 a year.

You and your partner are interested in acquiring the newspaper, but you are not sure how this might affect the way in which business laws apply to your new media company. The acquisition would double your revenues and number of employees, as well as affecting competition in the town.

Assignment

Using the information in this chapter and that gathered from the Internet, identify the laws that might affect the creation and running of the company that would be created by combining your Web site and the weekly newspaper. Discuss the impact of the laws and how that might affect your decision to buy the weekly. What information do you need to better evaluate the impact, and why? Would some of the laws have a greater impact than others? Which ones and why?

Case 6.3 The Banker and Laundering Drug Money

A reporter at KCCR-TV in Muleshoe, Texas, recently received an anonymous message in the mail claiming that the president of the Fifth National Bank is laundering money for illegal drug dealers from Mexico.

According to the note, the banker, James Wilson, has created several fake companies. The dealers send money to the banker, who deposits the money in the account of one of the companies. This company then buys goods from another one, and that from another one, until the money has gone through several companies. Of course, no goods ever change hands. In the end, the money is deposited into an account that belongs to the drug dealers, minus a service charge for the banker. The note said he makes four trips a year to Mexico to meet with the drug dealers.

The reporter talks with his news director, who said she has met the banker on a few occasions at the Rotary Club lunch. However, Wilson is not active in community politics or any other sort of public activities. He lives on a large ranch in a very big house, but that would be expected of a bank president.

The reporter and news director discuss what they can do and identify the following actions:

1. They simply ignore the note because they don't have the resources to investigate this type of story.
2. They send a copy of the note to the Texas Rangers to see if the Rangers would like to investigate. If there is any truth to the note, the station can run the story after the Rangers arrest the banker.
3. They begin discreet inquiries into the banker's background and behavior without mentioning the note to anyone. They would start with finding out whether the banker travels to Mexico on a regular basis.
4. They confront the banker with the note and see how he reacts.

Assignment

Put yourself in the place of the news director. Using the material in the chapter and any other material, answer the following questions.

1. Can you think of any other options? What?
2. Discuss the legal and ethical implications of each option. Could the option violate the law? How? Is the option unethical? Why?
3. Which option would you pursue and why?

Case 6.4 The Case of the Poorly Performing Salesperson

Ed Markham, the African American sales manager at WCTV, is considering how to handle a problem with one of his salespersons, Jane Folsom, who is White. Ed was promoted to sales manager three months ago after working at WCTV for 2 years. He earned his promotion by exceeding sales goals every month after his first on the job. He developed a research report using secondary data like MRI and the Lifestyle Market Analyst to analyze the market. His former boss praised the report, gave a copy to all salespersons, and included a summary of it in the rate card. When his former boss left for a new job in a larger market, he recommended Ed as his replacement.

Jane has been a salesperson at WCTV for 2 years. For most of that time, she has exceeded sales quotas about as much as Ed had. For the past 3 months, she has not met sales quotas. After his second month as sales manager, Ed talked to Jane about her performance. She attributed her below-average performance to the closing of a major advertiser, Anthony's Fashions. This local clothing store closed because several major retailers, including JC Penney and Dillard's, had opened at the local mall.

Ed listened to Jane's explanation and then suggested ways to obtain new clients. He asked Jane whether she had set personal sales goals, set up a prospect file of new and inactive advertisers as well as existing businesses that were potential clients, come up with research and data on the market to use in presentations and reports to clients, come up with new ideas or opportunities to advertise for clients, or asked her clients about their needs and goals (Shaver, 1995). Jane said no, she simply telephoned or visited her clients regularly to see if they wanted to run ads.

Ed also asked Jane why several of her clients had not paid their bills. He explained that a salesperson must check out a client's ability to pay before running a schedule. Jane replied that she was not aware of that fact and that no one had ever trained her to sell. She had sold time for a radio station before, but that was all the training she had. Ed's predecessor had just hired her and cut her loose.

Ed gave Jane a memo after their first meeting a month ago asking her to focus on sales training for the next month. First, she should read Shaver's (1995) *Making the Sale! How to Sell Media With Marketing*. He gave her a copy, told her to read it, and asked her to contact him if she had any questions. After reading the book, he told her that she should establish written personal sales goals, begin to develop a prospect file (with two new and two inactive clients), and develop three ideas for new advertising opportunities for existing clients. In the memo, Ed told Jane that he would not hold her to sales performance standards that month. He wanted Jane to focus on doing the background work he assigned to help her improve her future sales performance.

At the meeting a month later, Ed discovered Jane had made only a halfhearted attempt at training. For example, she had not developed a prospect file; she told him she had no idea how to do it. Ed asked her why she had not contacted him to set up a meeting to discuss questions she had about the book or completing the assignments, as noted in his memo. She said she had forgotten. Asked specific questions about Shaver's (1995) sales book, she was unable to respond, suggesting she had not read it.

Ed asked Jane to read the book again, and scheduled a meeting with her to discuss the book. He instructed Jane to have a written memo ready for the next meeting that identified the assistance or training she needed to accomplish the tasks he had set for her the previous month. "Base your needs assessment memo on the Shaver book and be prepared to discuss the book fully," he told her. Ed said he would send her a memo about their meeting, outlining what he had verbally asked her to do during the next month as well as the consequences of not completing these tasks. Ed told her, "Jane, if you don't start to make a serious effort in participating in your training, and ultimately improving your sales performance, your job here could be in jeopardy." He followed through and sent the memo, keeping a copy for his files.

Ed's gut feeling was that something else was bothering Jane. He wondered why she had gone from exceeding sales quotas to below-average sales performance. He was surprised an employee would respond half-heartedly to a written notice of unsatisfactory job performance. He wondered if there was another reason she was not responding to his attempts to help her. Ed wanted Jane to succeed because he thought she was a good salesperson despite her apparent lack of formal training and her poor recent performance. He wanted to give her a fair chance to improve, but knew he would have to fire her if she did not take her training seriously and improve her performance. He wondered how to be fair to her while protecting the station. He had never faced this kind of problem before. "Welcome to management," he told himself.

Assignment

Using information from this and previous chapters, answer the following questions:

1. Have Ed's actions in working with Jane been fair and appropriate thus far? Why or why not?
2. Are there any other steps Ed should take now in dealing with Jane and this situation? If yes, explain them in detail.
3. What do you think may be the reason for Jane's sudden poor performance?
4. How can Ed discover whether there is another reason for Jane's apparent unresponsiveness to his efforts to help her improve her performance without incurring any legal liability? Should he take steps to find out? Why or why not?
5. What steps should Ed take to identify the training Jane may need? Why?
6. How can Ed determine fairly whether Jane simply lacks adequate sales training without opening his station to a wrongful termination or other lawsuit? Explain your answer and provide examples of what Ed should do.
7. How should Ed document the steps he takes to train or, if necessary, discipline Jane? Why?
8. How should Ed respond to today's meeting with Jane? To answer this question, write a sample memo from Ed to Jane about today's meeting.
9. Write a sample memo for Ed assuming that Jane does not respond satisfactorily to the meeting scheduled for 1 month from now.
10. Write a sample memo for Ed, assuming Jane does respond satisfactorily to the meeting 1 month from now.
11. What other present or future steps or actions would you recommend to Ed? Why?

Case 6.5 Reviewing and Analyzing FOIA Resources and Issues

Select a state of interest and review online and other available sources to discover its information access laws, if any. Conduct a database search in ABI In-form/ProQuest or Lexis-Nexis Academic Universe to find recent cases or issues regarding access to information in your state of interest, or any state or national freedom of information legislation, issues, cases, or debates. For example, see if any access issues or cases involving national security have arisen. Have there been any abuses of access in the name of protecting national security? Have any other cases involving celebrities or public figures, such as the Dale Earnhardt case, arisen? Is there a new category of access issue that has emerged recently?

Visit the nearest law library to review copies of the access laws in your state of interest. Contact the appropriate government agency or office for more information about access in your area. (If your research into state access to information becomes too difficult, research access at the federal government level. Access most federal agencies at the Federal Web Navigator [http://lawdbase.law.villanova.edu/fedweb/] and examine their online postings and instructions regarding access and freedom of information requests.)

Then conduct an online review of FOIA sites. Check out the SPJ's FOIA Resource Center (http://www.spj.org/foi.asp/) and The Internet Law Library (www.lawguru.com/ilawlib/). Review other sources that may have articles and information on access. For example, try searching the Reporters Committee for Freedom of the Press site (www.rcfp.org) for information on your state of interest. *Editor & Publisher* (www.editorandpublisher.com), the NAA's Web site (www.naa.org), and the RTNDA's (http://www.rtnda.org) Freedom of Information link with information on access (www.rtnda.org/foi/atp.shtml) are good sites to explore. Also try Cornell University's Legal Information Institute (www.law.cornell.edu), A Journalist's Guide to the Internet (reporter.umd.edu/), including the Records and FOIA link (reporter.umd.edu/records.htm), and any other FOIA resources or links you find.

Assignment

Develop a report, including but not limited to, the following questions, which could be used by reporters or others as a guide to understanding the FOIA and the major issues surrounding it and for requesting government documents.

1. What laws, if any, are applicable in the state you selected?
2. What are the major contemporary issues regarding access to government information in your state and nationally? Identify and describe each type of issue, both national and state, and provide a description and example of each.
3. What are the general techniques for obtaining documents from the appropriate state government or federal entities?
4. What are common problems or pitfalls to avoid when attempting to gain access to government documents?
5. What other important information or advice did you find in your research? Identify and explain each factor here.

7

PLANNING

As prior chapters have noted, managers are dealing with *change*—some observers even claim we are in a revolutionary phase. Regardless, nowhere is this more clear than in the design of planning strategies that preserve the best of traditional practices while preparing their companies for exciting new ways to consider opportunities. Planning is a management tool for maintaining practices that are successful and should continue. It is also a management tool for restructuring and adapting to opportunities that require transition or major restructuring. Media managers start with a vision that considers resources, policies, and schedules as well as attitudes, beliefs, and values in forming strategic documents.

Planning and Change Management

While the concept of change has not been well documented in systematic longitudinal studies of media companies, much can be learned from Hall and Hord's (2006) 35-year international research examining the change process in schools, colleges, businesses and government agencies. Their report focuses on managers at the front lines of change, and they found that the best managers understand there are at least two phases to the planning process: (a) development and (b) implementation. Hall and Hord said able development-phase managers generally are visible and dynamic and plan for all steps and actions necessary for creating, testing, and packaging an innovation. Outstanding implementation-phase managers demonstrate patience and make plans for the steps and actions necessary to learn how to use innovation. Media managers must plan and lead through *both* the development and implementation phases since media companies definitely deal with technological innovation and change (see chapter 5 for an in-depth discussion of technology).

Leadership issues are covered more thoroughly in chapter 2, but planning must take into account the time and resources necessary for staff members as well as an organization to absorb the implications of innovation and change. Hall and Hord (2006) reported that staff members often experience sadness, because they lose a favorite or comfortable way of acting when innovation and change are introduced. While some managers may misdiagnose this as *resistance* to change, it is actually a predictable reaction. In addition, managers need to plan for some staff members to have serious questions about the need for change and be concerned that the changes planned will not result in improvements to products or services they currently offer. Intervention through systematic training and constant reinforcement can mediate this.

The research also indicates that even brief, informal conversations between a manager and target individuals or departments/groups can have positive effects. This has implications for human resources and effective organizational communication (see chapter 2 for more discussion) as well as strategic planning, which should include resources for formal training, onsite coaching, and multiyear development and implementation support of innovations (see chapter 5 for an in-depth discussion of innovation related to emerging media technology).

Probably one of the most important variables for supporting change is appropriate planning for the daily support systems and infrastructure needed to successfully integrate innovation into the media company. Therefore, although change may be carried out at a lower operational level, its support must clearly come from top levels of management where budgets are approved and resources allocated. Top-level managerial mandates can sometimes be helpful, but only if accompanied by resources supporting staff members' efforts.

Tying Vision to Planning

Today's media manager uses planning to move from dreams to achievements by tying the company's mission to specific objectives supported by resources. The manager, in designing a plan, identifies obstacles as well as opportunities, factors unexpected difficulties into the plan, and controls and adjusts through inclusion of key feedback mechanisms. Without adequate planning, managers find themselves reacting rather than leading on a daily basis.

This chapter introduces a case that requires not only a review of topics explored in this chapter but in other chapters as well. This is because planning is not a separate task of media managers but an integrated dynamic process requiring managers to continuously scan their environment, adjust their thinking, and use all the management tools provided in this book. The introduction to the chapter case follows. Readers will return to this case several times throughout the chapter with questions posed at the end of the chapter. Key words or terms are underlined in each case snippet.

Introduction to Chapter 7.1 Case

Red Star Media Corporation has been in business for 20 years and <u>is known as a reliable traditional supplier</u> *of programming for six different radio stations. However, its new owner (Mary Grantsman) is concerned that it is* <u>not focused on its greatest potential audiences</u> *and is* <u>not positioned to take advantage of emerging technological opportunities.</u> *She thinks Tomas Carmona, her 40-year-old marketing director, might be able to provide insights that will* <u>move her company from traditional to the one she visualizes: niche-oriented, innovative, and profit producing.</u>

Before joining Red Star Media 2 years ago, Carmona worked for several large successful marketing firms servicing media in major markets. However, what Grantsman likes best about Carmona is his ability to think creatively and his willingness to take calculated risks (two characteristics she identifies with success), so she tells Carmona she wants him to take a leave from his current job for the next 2 years in order to focus on "special projects." Grantsman announces Carmona's new assignment to the other managers and employees, making it clear Carmona will be reporting directly to Granstman and will have <u>unlimited top-level support.</u>

Most of the company managers admire Carmona because he has a collaborative style of communication and is considered experienced and trustworthy. He also is quick-witted and practical, having suggested successful changes over the past 2 years that have increased audiences and profits. Nonmanagement employees do not know Carmona and are curious about him and what changes he might suggest. Carmona begins by studying Red Star's forecasting documents.

Steps in Planning

In planning, effective media managers identify documents, business opportunities, unique resources, current or future strengths and provide a careful analysis of assets and liabilities. Planning is forecasting that focuses on resources, opportunities and strategies for predicting challenges a company will face to facilitate maximum positioning of policies and plans that will make the best use of available data.

Forecasting

Traditionally, forecasting has timeframes connected to three planning formats: (a) strategic, (b) intermediate, and (c) short-run planning.

Strategic planning involves allocating resources to achieve the firm's long-term goals. These plans can cover 1 to 10 years, but usually span a 3- to 5-year period. They represent the ways a company expects to fulfill its mission. Strategic management builds in contingency planning for unfavorable events as well as unforeseen opportunities. Media company contingency plans consider the introduction or withdrawal of major media competitors, unexpected profit losses or gains, unusual demand or lack of demand for particular products or services, responses to natural or man-made disasters and, of course, technological changes that might make products obsolete. Such planning provides the company with quick-response options that are proactive, somewhat predictive and alert to triggers that signal a management adjustment is advisable.

Intermediate plans generally cover 6 months to 2 years and provide reinforcement or correction data for long-term goals. Because of current economic uncertainties, many media companies find it challenging to remain proactive rather than reactive to market fluctuations affecting customers and product demands. Successful companies adjust nimbly to environmental changes, avoiding distractions from their strategic planning goals due to temporary fluctuations.

Short-run planning involves a few weeks up to a year. This type of plan allocates resources on a day-to-day or month-to-month basis. Figure 7.1 shows how the three plans fit together. The strategic plan fulfills the firm's mission and overall general goals. The intermediate plan involves the general way in which the strategic plan is pursued, and the short-run plan is how the strategic plan works on a day-to-day basis.

Case 7.1 Red Star's Forecasts

When marketing head Carmona looks at the <u>strategic plan</u> *for Red Star, he finds that* <u>the goals call for the company to develop and focus on niche programming popular with 50-year-olds,</u> *who are seen as loyal*

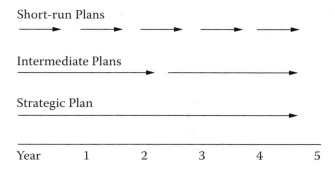

FIGURE 7.1 Relationship among strategic, intermediate, and short-run planning.

and lucrative listeners. The plan calls for the <u>major percentage of programming (more than 60%) to be directed to this demographic by 2009.</u>

Most of the strategic plan is directed at steps the marketing department *will take to implement the goals, which are attached to* timed phases outlined each year from 2006–2009. *He finds no other* departments mentioned in the strategic plan and only vague references to engineering updates related to Internet delivery *of programming over the Red Star Web site.*

In addition, he finds that the intermediate plan calls for regular systematic testing *to provide data for reinforcement and correction of programming from 2006–2009. He can find* no evidence that resources *have* been allocated to any kind of testing or examination *of how well the programming is meeting the strategic goals.*

Carmona also is disappointed to learn the corporation does not have a short-run plan. *Carmona realizes the* strategic plan really has not been driving decision making *at Red Star for quite some time. Because he has read about the importance of planning, he decides to explore how he might restructure the planning process to better meet the challenges and opportunities facing Red Star.*

Issue Versus Unit Planning

While the above schema sounds familiar to most managers, recent research by Mankins and Steele (2006) suggested that forecasting may fail to result in good decisions if (a) the planning process is segregated into departments or units in a company rather than the company as a whole or (b) it is an annual calendar-driven exercise. This is not good for managers—and certainly not advisable for companies—wishing to nimbly respond to environmental or financial changes in the market place.

Planning that does not drive decisions has no impact or use. Managers obviously make decisions several times a year, and they rarely make a decision affecting only one unit (generally several departments or units need to act in collaboration to meet changes, challenges, and opportunities).

Media managers must prepare to make decisions when competitors or consumers change in some way or when technology forces a response.

Good planning provides a template for decision making that moves beyond predictable calendar dates and individual departmental responsibilities. If newspaper readers are not happy with unpredictable delivery of the newspaper, strategic planning should suggest several responses addressing the issue beyond pointing the finger at the circulation department. If predictable home-delivery service is a goal in the strategic plan, then there must be involvement by all units in this issue and cooperative discussion and analysis of how to meet that goal. For instance, if newspaper delivery is hampered by slow production turnaround, which is sometimes disrupted or even stalled by unrealistic advertising or news department deadlines, then the "issue" is not really delivery but, rather, poor coordination between and among departments or perhaps noncoordinated work routines.

Experts recommend today's managers apply planning principles to a realistic framework unconstrained by the calendar or segregated into disconnected departmental responses. Managers tend to implement planning *based on issues,* rather than on individual departments or units, so it makes sense for planning to be issue based, rather than unit/department based. Researchers (Mankins & Steele 2006) have found a department/unit focus can needlessly build division and sometimes even foster antagonism between managers, so there is ample reason to adopt an issue-focused planning process.

Common Characteristics of Planning

All types of planning have commonalities, although the time period, responsible parties, and actual steps vary. Media companies have general organizational goals stating objectives tied to specific performance expectations. These goals stem from the media firm's vision and mission statements, which reflect their business domain and may include statements about their role(s) outside their primary business markets.

The vision and mission statements for public-media companies are written for legal and business clarity. Most managers could not recite them word for word but do have a pragmatic understanding of how the statements guide decision making and resource allocations. The statements do not have to be overly complicated or laden with descriptors.

For example, both the vision and mission statements for Gannett are short and easy to remember. Gannett's vision statement says, "Consumers will choose Gannett media for their news and information needs, anytime, anywhere, in any form." A vision statement is meant to be consistent no matter how the environment or business climate might change. Gannett's vision statement clearly gives priority to consumers and their news and information choices. It challenges managers in all departments to respond to consumer-driven timeframes (not just organizational timeframes), delivery preferences, and packaging formats. There also is an implied challenge to managers to not only consider consumer needs/wants, but also to do a better job of anticipating their needs than competitors.

A mission statement flows from the company's vision, and it can change and adjust as business environments and markets change. Gannett's mission is, "to successfully transform Gannett to the new environment. We will provide must-have news and information on demand across all media, ever mindful of our journalistic responsibilities" (http://www.gannett.com/about/visionmission.htm, June 29, 2006). The mission statement implies that in order to meet the company's vision, managers must facilitate transitions and provide ways for the company to transform to "new" environments that enhance Gannett's goal to provide timely, useful, news and information through all media that are faithful to journalistic standards. The vision and mission statements guide planning for all units that must work together to meet the goals.

To assess progress, an organization must set goals related to the vision and mission statements with specific, measurable operational definitions. For example, a company with a goal of increasing viewership among long-term residents of a community could operationalize its goal as increasing ratings by two points during the next 6 months among audience members who have lived in the area of dominant influence (ADI) for more than 10 years. The operational definition must specify in measurable terms the group to be affected (people who have lived in the ADI or market area for more than 10 years), a time period during which the change is expected (next 6 months), and a measurable level of performance being sought (two ratings points).

Planning without well-defined goals is like attending a potluck dinner where the diner may enjoy the meal, but by chance rather than culinary design. Every plan involves preparation. The better the preparation, the greater the chances of reaching the goals. Preparation is simply the collection of information about the goals and possible alternatives for achieving them. The goals that fit the mission and can be operationally achieved are the ones followed by the organization.

All planning includes procedures for executing the plan. The procedures outline mechanisms for analysis, information collection, and monitoring that assist in developing and executing plans. Of course, knowing what tools are available for planning is not the same as knowing how to apply those tools. Application is perfected through experience, practice, and reflection.

Finally, all planning involves assessment to provide tangible evidence of the process. The steps for achieving goals and the timeframe and resources necessary for carrying out the plan are identified. Results are compared against goals for assessment purposes. The next section covers the three major planning documents in detail.

Case 7.1 Red Star's Vision and Mission Statements

Red Star's vision statement is, "Red Star will program its stations, so that a <u>deep loyal niche audience</u> in their 50s will choose it as their <u>primary station</u>." The mission statement is, "Red Star will introduce <u>innovations</u> into its programming that will continue to <u>draw and increase the support</u> of its major target audience thus <u>improving profits</u>."

Strategic Planning

As mentioned previously, strategic planning is the long-term process by which an organization pursues its mission and tries to reach its goals. If an organization participates in two or more of the three traditional media markets—(a) information, (b) advertising, and (c) intellectual—the strategic plan must explicitly address these markets and explain the relationship among them. A TV station cannot make plans for the advertising market without including the information market that attracts viewers. A newspaper cannot plan for the information market without examining the role it plays in the intellectual market.

Smith, Arnold, and Bizell (1985) used the term *strategic management* in lieu of *strategic planning* because the traditional concept of strategic planning did not include control of the plan as it was implemented. They said strategic management includes (a) analyzing the environment, (b) determining objectives, (c) analyzing strategic alternatives, (d) selecting strategy alternatives, (e) implementing the strategies, and (f) evaluating and controlling performance.

Combining these approaches plus adding control to planning results in a more refined approach to strategic thinking, which includes the following steps (see Fig. 7.2):

1. Examine the business environment and past performance.
2. Evaluate available resources.
3. Identify, select, prioritize, and operationalize planning goals.
4. Identify alternative approaches for obtaining goals.
5. Select from among the alternative approaches.
6. Implement the plan.
7. Monitor implementation.
8. Evaluate the plan's progress and adjust the plan.

Collection and analysis of information are part of the eight steps in strategic planning outlined in Fig. 7.2. Plans for the future must be grounded in experience and an understanding of current market conditions. Environmental factors affect how media companies approach their planning. Economic downturns have forced companies to adjust the timeframe for strategic planning.

Market analysis is the primary method of evaluating the business environment. The internal examination involves how well the firm accomplished its goals in the past and why. Failure to reach goals can result from any number of problems inside the firm, including inappropriate goals, goals set too high, poor analysis of data, inadequate resources, or poor performance.

Examining Business Environments

Technology in the last 5 years provided a dynamic way for managers to be closer to customers (whether they are advertisers or subscribers). For example, turnaround time has been greatly reduced for solving and

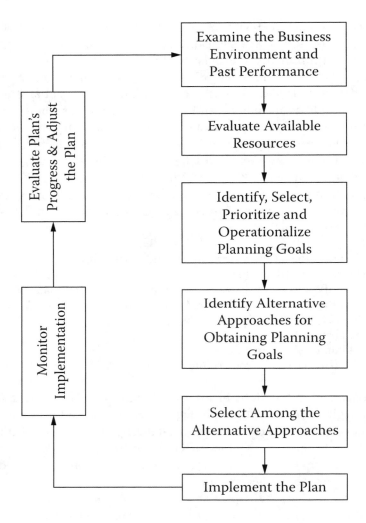

FIGURE 7.2 Steps in strategic planning.

responding to problems. Building technology options into the planning process is essential for media companies.

Many traditional media companies consider the Internet and online services as complementary products and plan accordingly. They cross-sell advertising, readers, viewers, and listeners. They sort regular subscribers so that sports enthusiasts receive e-mail alerts about special sales on sports equipment or offer additional discounts to customers who respond to cross-promotions on the Web. Managers see the Internet as a way to draw in and grow the customer base as well as a way to facilitate customer service. For example, subscribers can be sorted into regularly contacted groups. Within 2 weeks of subscribing, a new customer might receive an electronic welcome packet with coupons, special offers, and notices of presales at the retailers they identified as favorites. The next e-mail contact might thank the customer for being loyal and invite comments on the quality of service. The third contact might announce a special payment option for quality customers. Later on in the relationship, the subscriber might be identified as a preferred customer who has won two free tickets to a concert the media company is sponsoring.

Such timed, consistent, and planned targeting is attractive, allowing customers to be sorted and contacts adjusted according to demographics, lifestyle variables, geography, or customer longevity. Advertisers are easily built into the plan. The media company thus facilitates dynamic and multidimensional relationships among the medium, subscribers, and advertisers. Media business environments include convergence (sharing content across media platforms—a standard strategy for media companies seeking cost savings), enhanced ability to reach audiences through multiple channels, and better diversity and wider coverage for a community's media. In fact, the American Press Institute (API) convergence tracker page lists 107 convergence relationships in 2006. Of these, the majority are news relationships with advertising and promotion the second and third most common relationship (The Media Center, 2006). Lowrey (2005) reported that in a study of more than 200 converged relationships most partnerships are initiated because of specific goals related to the arrangement rather than just following fads/current trends or beating competition. However, one third of the respondents in the survey had no idea why their organizations were partnering and could not articulate specific benefits their company was expecting from the arrangement.

Media managers understand that convergence requires new skills and training as well as the ability to perceive and understand cultural differences between departments that may have been organizationally separate previously. However, even more importantly, the goals for emerging and converging must not be ambiguous and must be part of the strategic plan with training, conversation, and reference to the role partnerships and convergence play in meeting goals.

Evaluate Available Resources

A manager must evaluate at-hand resources to ensure that goals can be met. At-hand resources include the company's name and reputation, personnel, plant and equipment, and finances. *At hand* means the resources are held currently by the firm or can be easily borrowed. Thus, financial resources also include an organization's credit.

Evaluating available resources is important because resources determine whether goals can be achieved. Although resources can be changed from one form to another, the process does not always occur as quickly as management would like. If a large metropolitan TV station needs an experienced award-winning anchor, it will take time to recruit such an anchor. The uncertainty of time necessitates good resource planning based on accurate evaluation of which anchors are good prospects.

As the strategic plan develops, evaluation reveals whether the resources needed to achieve the plan's goals are currently available in the form necessary. When the organization lacks the resources in the appropriate form needed by the plan, the plan must include ways to acquire new or convert current resources. If the needed resources are not and cannot be made available, the goals associated with those resources should be reconsidered or abandoned.

Setting Goals

No guidelines exist for the number of goals a firm needs to identify or select. However, all of the selected goals should be obtainable and consistent with the firm's general vision and mission. Each goal requires resources that are relatively fixed. The more goals a firm pursues, the more competition there is inside the organization for resources. For example, a small Ohio newspaper group might select the following goals:

1. Add daily newspapers until the group has papers in markets that make up 20% of the circulation in Ohio (information market goal).
2. Increase by 3% the penetration of existing markets (information market goal).
3. Increase by 2% revenue from national advertising (advertising market goal).
4. Increase by 5% the column inches of display advertising that run in the papers (advertising market goal).
5. Increase by 10% the column inches and percentage of the news hole devoted to letters to the editor and guest columns (information market goal).

The goals listed for the information and advertising markets conceivably could compete for resources. For instance goal number 4 calls for more space to be devoted to display advertising, and goal number 5 calls for more space to be devoted to letters and columns. If the company does not have many advertising sales people or designers and would need to hire more staff to meet goal number 4, media managers might be faced with deciding whether to hire additional advertising staff to cover goal number 4 *or* investing in editors to oversee more opinion pieces to expand the news hole to meet goal number 5. Obviously, choices and balances will have to be discussed before any changes in personnel occur since personnel costs are among the highest expenses facing managers.

While more advertising will provide more news space, the acquisition of newspapers costs money, as will efforts to increase penetration. The penetration goal involves additional spending for the circulation and news departments, as well as to promote the changes from the increased spending.

All five goals would consume resources and initially compete. However, as the plan goes into effect, achieving some goals will generate revenue, which can then be applied to meeting other goals. Timing is important to consider because not all goals have to be reached at the same time. Some are set for the second or third year of the plan, and some are contingent on reaching others.

Alternative Approaches

Almost all long-term goals are reached with more than one approach and often require multiple approaches. For example, a radio station that wants to increase its share of listeners can alter its music format and promote itself in a number of ways. The aim is to select the most efficient and effective ways to reach or surpass the goals. The ability to select the best approach depends on how exhaustive the analysis procedure is. Often management settles for a less-than-optimal plan to achieve a goal because all ideas were not identified in the decision-making stage.

Brainstorming is a commonly used technique for generating ideas. It applies two basic principles of creative thinking: (a) a positive attitude is established, which means criticism is withheld until after ideas are developed, and (b) unusual ideas are encouraged even if they seem impractical (Whiting, 1995).

Assessing alternatives includes eliminating impractical or improbable ones. Improbability and impracticality are based on any number of characteristics, including approaches with high-risk, high-environmental uncertainty, and high-resource needs. The list of approaches is then pared to a manageable number of three to six good alternatives for achieving the goals. Comparison of alternative plans can be as formal or informal as management likes. From these comparisons, efficiency and effectiveness are determined. Efficiency is measured by the amount of resources needed to reach a goal, and the most efficient approach achieves the goal with the smallest expenditure of resources. *Effectiveness* is the probability that the approaches achieve the goals of the plan. (Readers can review chapter 1 for an excellent discussion of the sources and information key to developing multiple approaches to sound planning).

Implement/Monitor and Adjust Plan

The plan must indicate exactly what will be implemented in what timeframe as well as how monitoring and adjustments will occur. For instance, if a radio station is changing its format to better serve its identified preferred audience, then regular assessments of who is listening and how this audience likes the format must be built into the plan. The radio station needs to identify how long it can "test" the new format before it moves into a contingency plan. The length of the trial period will depend upon resources and advertising revenue the radio station has at its disposal.

Case 7.1 Red Star's Strategic Thinking

Carmona examines the business environment for Red Star against Fig. 7.2 and notes <u>no major competitors</u> show interest in Red Star's market. Past performances show the station has a <u>modest profit</u> margin, which has allowed the company to distribute steady performance raises to outstanding employees. He sees available resources are adequate.

Carmona next decides to collect information from the field and makes immediate plans to visit all six stations over the next 2 months. However, before doing that he talks with new owner Grantsman and the other corporate officers familiar with the vision and mission statements. However, he finds his corporate marketing manager, <u>Keesha Skelling, is the only manager with any specific plans for reaching goals</u> in the mission statement. Keesha openly ridicules the other departments for being lazy and confides to Carmona she sees no way for Red Star to improve unless this changes. She says she is pondering leaving because she is so frustrated by top management's disregard for planning. Other corporate managers tell

Carmona that Keesha and her "attitude" are resented and describe her as overly ambitious and brash.

In his first day in the field, Carmona learns that station managers think of Red Star as all things to all people and <u>are not effectively connecting either the vision or mission statements to planning or goal setting</u>. Carmona shadows the traffic directors, the news managers, the production and engineering staffs and learns the employees are loyal and talk highly of their products and services and many tell him they love working for Red Star.

However, Carmona notes some common challenges: <u>formats vary radically</u> between the six stations; <u>marketing plans are somewhat tied to corporate mission and vision statements,</u> but station <u>formats do not match the marketing strategies;</u> news managers worry about their lack of consistent training given what they are hearing about <u>robotic advancements</u> in the field. One manager confides he is worried about his lack of solid training in Web design since pod-casting and the Web site are very important to his station. He confides that sometimes he lies awake at night worrying that a live package will need to be put on the Web site after the Web staff has left for the day. "I don't know how to do that, and when or if that moment comes, I'll be in big, big trouble," he tells Carmona.

When Carmona returns to the corporate office, he has a number of interesting ideas to present to Grantsman. They include (a) <u>what the mission statement says and what the field managers are doing that is not related;</u> (b) his study of research on the target market shows that <u>50-year-olds are an appropriate market</u> for Red Star, and they can be segmented into two groups he nicknames <u>Woodstock Grads and Mall Rats.</u> The Woodstock market is irreverent, enjoys listening to jazz, has disposable income, and loves innovations like pod-casts and Web sites. The mall market is older than the woodstockers, has less money to spend, enjoys jazz, and is not comfortable with change or innovation. Carmona sees <u>both groups as large and viable markets</u> for Red Star if the corporation can format its music, develop innovations that appeal and provide an acceptable format. He also notes that no other competitors are vying for this audience; (c) change is occurring in the profession but <u>training and technology at Red Star are behind</u> the competition; (d) staff <u>morale is good</u> and overall <u>respect for Red Star is high in the communities it serves.</u>

Intermediate Planning

Intermediate planning requires a marketing plan, a financial plan, and a human resources plan. The three must be coordinated with each other as well as with the overall strategic plan. The marketing plan provides managers with a realistic scan of opportunities for the product or service being considered. Who needs this and why are common questions answered by a marketing plan. The financial plan plots not only expenses but potential expected revenues that will support the product or service being considered and predict how long it might take for the product or service to be self supporting or even profitable. And the human resources plan outlines what kind of expertise will be needed to meet the goals. The human resources plan evaluates who might need training and predicts if and when new employees might need to be recruited to meet the planning goals.

Marketing Plan

A marketing plan deals with the marketing mix, which includes product, place, price, and promotion (the four Ps). The marketing mix is applicable to the information, advertising, and intellectual markets. Although they are interrelated, each should have a marketing plan of its own. The *product* is simply what is sold or given to a consumer in exchange for time or money. In the information and intellectual markets, the product is information and ideas. In the third market, it is the potential attention of consumers to advertising information. The value of the advertising exposure depends on the number of viewers, readers, or listeners as well as the types of people paying the attention.

In most organizations, the product decision is based on the location of older products in their life cycle. Buzzell and Cook (1969) discussed the five stages of a product's life cycle:

1. Infancy is when a product enters the market. Sales are low.
2. Growth occurs when the product matures as to whom and where it will sell. Sales grow rapidly if the product finds its niche in the marketplace.
3. Approaching maturity is when the established product begins to battle competitors over market share. Sales continue to grow, but at a slower rate.
4. Maturity occurs when a product finds its place in its category. Competition continues and sales grow much more slowly than earlier stages.
5. Decline is the final stage when consumers lose interest in the product and sales begin to decline.

With most media products, *place* is an important consideration. News commodities such as newspapers and newscasts are aimed at specific geographic areas. The content reflects this aim. A society's size, geography, social aspects, cultural characteristic, and political nature affect the places for which news products are designed. Place also is related to price in the United States. Some parts of the country have higher and lower standards of living than others. The same book would face a lower demand due to price in one region than in another.

Place also affects the process and cost of distributing the media product. The cost of delivering a newspaper increases as one moves away from the production site. The cost of distributing a broadcast TV program is basically the same within the signal's range. If the station wants to distribute the program elsewhere, satellite transmission would increase costs.

While place remains an important variable in managerial decision making, it is also worth noting that as Internet products and services expand, niche rather than place may become a more critical issue. Media managers using the Web to sell information, products, and services have found that place has in some cases been replaced by the need to more thoroughly study the target market, which can be international rather than local or regional. Distribution of media content over the Internet does not require the same kind of economic consideration that traditional media do.

Price affects demand and determines how much revenue the firm takes in. Pricing is a difficult process because the joint nature of most media commodities creates extreme uncertainty. Managers are afraid to overprice in one type of market because it reduces demand in another. Increasing a magazine's subscription price might reduce circulation, which could affect the price charged to advertisers.

The traditional way to price existing products is to look at inflation, examine competitors' prices, add on additional expenses that have developed, estimate the impact of price on demand, and state the price with a profit goal in mind. The traditional way to price new products is to calculate production and distribution costs and add a desired profit margin.

The final *P* in the marketing mix is *promotion*. Promotion involves persuading people to use the product. Promotion includes advertising, public relations, and promotional activities.

Financial Plan

Budgets are the yearly plan of the organization. However, they are tied to a larger overall planning process that may cover several years identifying expected sources of money and predicted expenses. Budgets are dynamic documents that are continuously examined and readjusted in long-term, intermediate and short-run planning processes. The budget must reflect the priorities of the strategic plan or the mission of the organization will not be accomplished.

The strategic plan includes general budgetary priorities, whereas the intermediate plan reflects details for acquisitions as well as distribution of assets. Intermediate plans generally include documentation for all anticipated expenditures so that company accountants can anticipate and predict losses and gains connected to the intermediate plan. Likewise, the short-run plan must demonstrate that annual and even daily financial decisions support both the intermediate and long-term planning documents. If there is an extraordinary inconsistency in anticipated annual expense or revenues, this can be a strong indicator that media managers have failed to calculate costs/benefits accurately, the environment and business climate are changing in unanticipated ways or some uncontrolled factor is causing fluctuations. Media managers follow budgets carefully because many times budgets signal first that planning documents need reevaluation.

Human Resources Plan

Employee planning involves the development of the talents, skills, and aspirations of people within an organization. The well-designed human resources plan analyzes the talents and skills a firm currently has compared with future needs. The key areas for manipulation and adjustment in human resources plans include (a) work flows (which are connected to efficiency, control, and job-description issues), (b) staff choices, (c) staff sizes (including how hiring freezes, terminations, and early retirements will be handled), (d) performance appraisals, (e) training and development, (f) compensation, (g) employee relations (including top-down/bottom-up communication, feedback, etc.), (h) employee rights (including ethical codes/enforcement as well as discipline), and (i) international management (including the use of expatriates, country nationals, or other staffing needs).

If a newspaper plans to move most classified sales to its online product to update ads in a more timely fashion and offer links to customers, managers have to assess whether to make the transition with current advertising staff (who are skilled in writing and selling advertising, but not in technology) or hire technologically skilled workers (who need training in advertising sales and copy writing). A third possibility is to hire recent college graduates from advertising programs (who have both sets of skills, but little experience).

All the choices are rational, but there are different costs and benefits associated with each alternative. Even more important, the decision should connect to a clear technology priority in the company's mission. That way training programs, recruiting efforts, and employee assessment procedures are proactive and suggestive of an appropriate decision connected to decisions managers are making in other departments.

Short-run Planning

Just as intermediate plans serve as maps for the strategic plan, short-run plans are ways to meet the goals of the intermediate plans. However, short-run planning is vulnerable to becoming reactive, and this is what sometimes happens when media companies go public to gain access to capital to upgrade or expand their operations. One of the negative aspects to being a public company is that it makes the media corporation more vulnerable to short-term thinking in order to appease analysts and investors. If managers don't make their predicted figures, company stocks may go down causing the company to announce another round of layoffs, or managers may consider quick ways to raise a dividend share for the next quarter. These strategies may not match long-term or intermediate planning documents and may even be counter-productive to the overall vision of the company.

Managers responding to temporary environmental or business fluctuations must assess how long the effects of the changes will be a factor and whether those changes can be ignored until stability returns. A firm with an inflexible strategic plan has the most difficulty in responding to change. Such a firm is most vulnerable to following a fatal path that drains resources, fails to address immediate opportunities, and is overcome by more alert competitors.

However, a firm with an ambiguous mission may invest too early in a new product or service, or it may prematurely abandon an idea that just needs time and effort to succeed. Constant and consistent assessment is critical with short-run planning.

Summary

Planning is the essence of good management. Because the media create, test, and package innovations and are driven by technological changes, media managers must be prepared to not only oversee development but implementation of plans. The planning process always begins with a strong vision supported by a mission statement connected to measurable goals. Outcomes are constantly monitored and evaluated with contingency plans included in the process.

Planning should involve people from all organizational levels, since the success of the planning depends on the media company working as one business, not several separate departmental divisions. Planning takes three basic forms: (a) strategic, (b) intermediate, and (c) short run. Strategic is long-range planning, usually involving 3 to 5 years. Intermediate planning often involves 6 months to 2 years. Short-run planning involves a week to a year.

Case 7.1 Red Star: A Company in Search of a Plan

Red Star is a company seeking to change and respond to opportunities identified in its vision and mission statements. However, there are several challenges for Carmona to bring to Grantsman's attention. Write answers to the following and then prepare an executive summary that folds in the answers and suggests ways for Red Star to become more successful in meeting its mission. Refer to appropriate chapters in the book as needed to respond to the following:

1. Write down all the facts you know about Red Star.
2. What strategic measurable goals should Red Star consider in order to meet its vision and mission statements?
3. What music formats should be considered?
4. Identify the resources (both physical and human) that will be required to carry out the goals set above.
5. Is Keesha an asset or liability and how could she be used effectively in the future?
6. What training will be required before Red Star can meet its goals?

Case 7.2 Connecting Online and Traditional Media: Not Always an Easy Planning Task

Sheila was promoted 3 months ago to vice president of interactive media at a medium-size newspaper in the West. Her new responsibilities include coordinating strategic planning for the entire organization. Next month she is scheduled to present a 3- to 5-year strategic plan for integrating online classified advertising with traditional newspaper classified advertising to the newspaper's executive board.

Sheila was promoted primarily because she used technology to open new markets for her company. Ten years ago, she started at the newspaper in part-time classified advertising sales taking orders over the phone. Within a year, she convinced the advertising director to experiment with online ads, and after a few years built up a small department. In 1997, she was named director of new media. Her primary goal then was to have the largest possible database of classified ad listings. She started her campaign with car dealers and real estate firms. "We knew the vast majority of car dealers and real estate companies only ran a portion of their listings in the printed newspaper. We began to offer packages to run *all* their listings online," she said.

Next, Sheila created a Web site for each advertiser and then merged their listings into the newspaper's search program. At first, she did all the work herself, but then added a programmer, two production people, and one salesperson. Today she has 18 full-time employees, including four salespeople, three sales support staff to help with ad creation, and two programmers. The rest are producers who function as news journalists. They manage two Web sites. One is a regional portal with partnerships that serves as a repository for all the newspaper's classified ads. The other site is devoted to a news product that contains most of the daily newspaper's contents plus four or five local stories updated throughout the day. The online news product has increased overall readership as well as the number of times the same people visit the company's server.

Marketing Potential

The goal for the classified advertising Web site is to have the largest number of listings possible. "If people want to see a full inventory of local jobs, cars or houses available in the region, we want them to think of us and our Web site as the place to come," Sheila says. Recently, she focused her attention on increasing online job advertisements. Hiring is down because of economic factors. However, Sheila knows local employers still have jobs to advertise because she assigned most of her staff to interview local businesses.

From the staff research, she learned there were businesses wanting to advertise jobs, but not the traditional way. In the past, businesses with jobs to fill hired a recruiting firm to place ads in the newspaper for a fee, sort through applicants, and schedule interviews with the most qualified applicants. The recruiting firm also received a commission from the newspaper for every ad it placed. The relationship between the newspaper and recruiting firms was closer than the one between the newspaper and businesses. Sheila learned the newspaper advertising staff did not contact businesses directly, but relied totally on recruiting firms to bring classified job ads to the paper. Several local recruiting firms folded in the past year, and the newspaper's classified job listings dropped 10%. During this same period, the online job listing service, Monster.com, drew over 14% of local adults to its Web site. The newspaper's advertising manager said recruiting firms claimed online services like Monster.com were unpopular with local businesses because they draw too many resumes and unqualified applicants.

Sheila would not stake her company's competitive advantage on providing fewer resumes and applicants than online services. While acknowledging that online services can draw resumes from people who are clearly not qualified, she knew electronic formats allow easy and almost instantaneous sorting. She could offer job listings at about a tenth of the cost of recruiting firms. She sees Monster.com and similar services as strong competitors for local job listings. She had 10 staff members make personal contact with local employers to find out how they recruit using the Internet. She found that businesses do not care how many resumes or unqualified applicants they receive because their human resources software filters and then matches qualified people with job openings. They even archive applicants who are perfect for jobs opening soon. They do not want the newspaper or a recruiting firm to screen for them.

Competitive Advantages

Sheila thinks her online service offers local employers at least three unique advantages. The first is the combined distribution channels of the newspaper and Web site. Half of the 200,000 people who visit her Web site never check the newspaper for employment ads. Other people only read the newspaper and never do an Internet job search. Unlike online sources, she offers high visibility in two media.

Second, she offers local customer service—something the newspaper had turned over to recruiting firms. She admits it is old fashioned, but such personal attention worked well in the automotive and real-estate classified markets. It is a service that national online providers cannot duplicate. If there is a problem, the local businessperson "can march right down here and talk to me about it."

Third, a local online service delivers better-quality applicants. She is testing to confirm this. Early findings show applicants who use a newspaper Web site have higher demographics than random responders from a larger area.

Financial Concerns

Whereas the newspaper uses a rigid rate card, Sheila printed an online rate card once in 1995 that cost $5,000 for a nice design and folder, but it was outdated in a month so she never printed another. In general, Sheila does better by tailoring and customizing to the advertiser, especially for banner ads and sponsorships. Job posting rates and packages are published online and the online rates are nominal (compared with the newspaper). An interesting Internet dynamic is there are no marginal costs when adding one ad or job posting online versus adding 20 or 100. "There's no difference to us," Sheila says.

Sheila's online operation is similar to TV and radio stations that provide clients with a list of things they can do or the overall value of an ad. Selling online banner advertising space is like buying time on radio stations. If you call a month in advance, when much radio time is available, it costs one price, but if you call at the last minute, the price goes up because there is little time left. Sheila tracks how much banner space is available on both Web sites (the classified ad site and news site) and prices according to availability when customers inquire.

In addition to job, car, and real estate ads, Sheila's online site caters to small independent companies like Nosey Neighbor, which offers public records searches (for criminal checks, financial backgrounds, employment histories, etc.). Sheila's online classified ad site also attracts smaller advertisers who find the traditional newspaper too expensive. Sheila is certain online classified advertising can be a major contributor to the company's profits. First, she must develop a flexible plan that can handle the dynamics of an online medium without losing the traditional revenue generated by newspaper classified advertising.

Human Resources Issues

Sheila is excited about the prospects of online advertising, but concerned about the conflict between her online salespeople and the newspaper salespeople. Until recently, the online and newspaper salespeople were not even in the same building. About 8 months ago, Sheila moved two online salespeople into the same building as the newspaper's advertising staff. There were mixed results from the forced interaction. The newspaper sales staff said the online advertising people are cannibalizing their revenue. "That's in spite of the fact that we're just one drop in the bucket," said Sheila, pointing out that if the newspaper Web site was not capturing the online advertising revenue, a competitor would be stealing the business from the company.

Incentives are also an issue because they are higher for newspaper salespeople than online salespeople. It is hard for Sheila to develop a competitive incentive package for her sales staff because the revenue overall is smaller (than for the newspaper). She wants to keep a decent online profit margin.

In addition, there are serious job-skill differences between Sheila's staff and the newspaper's staff. Some newspaper salespeople are unfamiliar with online ads and do not even use the Internet. Because they do not use it, they are skeptical about how many customers use it, even though her Web site gets significantly more traffic than readership figures show for the entire newspaper.

> Sheila said, "We have trouble conversing. Even in the simplest ways—it's so easy to have misunderstandings in terms of terminology and things. I have actively encouraged our print counterparts to hire people with Internet experience. We will not make progress if the technology-savvy people are in some small department off to the side and don't have any chance at career advancement. They'll leave and go some place other than newspapers. I think it's really important for us to take the skills they have and integrate them and the technology into the heart of the newspaper. There will come a time when the vice president of advertising will be somebody who started off in the Internet."

Staffing is a major concern. How do we train people? How do we plan for future hiring and integration of the two staffs (online and printed newspaper)? These are questions Sheila must answer in her strategic plan. Sheila was an English major who taught herself to use the Internet. Early media technology staff were generalists and company entrepreneurs. They would sell ads, make callbacks, work on the Web site—do it all. However, to achieve real excellence, we need people who specialize, Sheila says.

Connecting Mission to Action

Sheila's biggest challenge is figuring out how to integrate the online business into the established functional organizational setting where separations among the newsroom, advertising department, circulation department, and production exist. Online products are much more cross-functional. Sheila says that they must be flexible and able to change rapidly. Fitting the online business into the traditional top-down organizational structure of a newspaper is difficult.

Sheila knows her strategic plan must be tied to the company's mission statement: "It is the mission of this newspaper to provide a timely, convenient, ethical, and accurate product of excellence and public service designed to inform, entertain, and enlighten readers living in our community and region."

Assignment

Using the information in the chapter and the case, write Sheila's 3- to 5-year strategic plan for integrating online and newspaper classified advertising. She will present it to the company's executive committee in 1 month.

1. Be sure to clarify how the mission statement guides the strategic plan. The strategic plan should include an analysis of (a) the business environment, (b) past business performance, (c) available resources, (d) identification of goals, (e) preferred as well as alternative ways to meet the goals, (f) implementation plans, and (g) evaluation/assessment tools.
2. Prepare an intermediate plan including marketing, financial, and human resources components designed to support the strategic plan.
3. Design a short-run plan that outlines the steps to take and how resources are allocated during the first few weeks of the plan's initiation.

8
MARKET ANALYSIS

The current environment of constant change—as it does with other elements that this text addresses—makes monitoring and analyzing national and local markets a daily requirement for media managers. Today they must constantly study their industries, continually gathering information about audience trends, advertiser preferences, and competitors' strategic movements. To not actively analyze the media environment will mean rapidly falling behind the competition.

Simply defined, *market analysis* identifies the opportunities and risks in a particular market or for a particular product. Market analysis plays a critical role in strategic media management and goes hand in hand with planning and marketing research.

You can think about market analysis in three ways. First, as part of the daily routine for media managers at all levels of an organization. Effective managers, whether top executives, department heads, or lower-level line managers, constantly scan the competitive environment, looking for changes in the structure of their markets, demand for their products, and the nature of their competition. Every manager should identify unseized opportunities or emerging competitive threats.

Second, market analysis also can be a formal project conducted before a company makes a major new investment, develops a new product, or changes its overall business strategy. In the past decade, media companies have launched Web sites, started distributing news and information across new platforms such as Personal Digital Assistants (PDAs) and cell phones, and expanded into new lines of business by buying out their competitors. Ideally, companies conduct detailed market analyses before making such investments, creating cross-departmental teams that examine the risks and opportunities and manage the project. Research suggests, however, that a surprising number of media companies leap into major investments without looking very closely, at least in part because many in the current generation of media managers lack training and experience in market analysis and new product-development processes (Saksena & Hollifield, 2002). However, rapid change in the media industry suggests that media managers should quickly learn to develop their market analysis skills.

Finally, think of market analysis as a strategic career-management process—at the project and professional levels. Analyzing the market for a project idea before pitching it to a supervisor can only help reporters, authors, and producers succeed in getting approval to go forward. Editors, news directors, or agents likely will show more interest in a project if the author can identify the project's market niche, the production cost in time and money, how it compares to the competition's effort, and its return in terms of circulation, ratings, prestige, and revenue. All market analyses are designed to answer such basic issues.

Similarly, savvy media professionals constantly survey the market for their own skills, quickly learning new technologies and techniques that emerge and adapting their work methods and processes to changes in the industry. Sophisticated professionals also continuously monitor the health of the media sector in which they work, looking for indications that there will be more or fewer opportunities for advancement or employment in the future and responding accordingly. Analyzing the market for your own professional skill set is essentially the same process as analyzing the market for your company's product.

Defining the "Market" in a Market Analysis

As to how to conduct a market analysis, the first step defines the market that needs analysis. A *market* usually is defined by two elements: (a) geography and (b) product. *Geography* refers to where the product is sold or bought. For example, a newspaper's geographic market includes the area in which it distributes its papers, either through home delivery or newsstand sales. A television or radio station's geographic market is the area reached by its broadcast signal. While newspapers and broadcast stations may have carefully defined local geographic markets, other types of media companies, such as film, television, music, and online producers see the entire world as their geographic market.

Product refers to the type of product a company sells. A market analysis for a product would include demand for that product and the number of competitors selling that product or substitutes for it in the company's geographic market. For example, how many community households subscribe to a local newspaper? How many local newspapers are in the market, including dailies and weeklies? Are regional or national papers such as the *Chicago Tribune* or *The New York Times* locally available as potential substitutes for the local paper? If people in the community don't read a newspaper, what news sources do they use instead?

For media companies, analyzing the product aspect of their markets is more complicated than for most industries because media products are *joint commodities*: Media companies simultaneously sell the same product into two different markets. They sell content to audiences and, at the same time, they sell advertisers time or space around that content for advertising targeted to the audiences the content is expected to attract. Consequently, in media, analyzing the product market requires that managers examine demand and competition in the audience and advertiser markets.

In recent years, media economists identified a third element defining media markets: the investment market for media companies themselves (Albarran, 1996). This third element grows in importance as media managers compete with other media companies and industries to attract investors. Decisions often are based on how managers believe an investment or project will affect the company's stock price or overall value. Consequently, a media company may not invest in or develop a product that might help its competitive position in the long-term if management thinks the move might harm its position in the investment markets in the short term.

Conducting a Market Analysis

The market analysis process carefully examines three types of factors: (a) external conditions, (b) internal conditions, and (c) financial conditions (Stevens, Sherwood, & Dunn, 1993) (Table 8.1).

Most discussions of the market-analysis process focus on external conditions because more external than internal factors exist, and managers have less control over them. The specific external conditions that a manager will want to examine will vary by situation. However, in general, external conditions include such things as long-term trends in market growth and new technologies, factors affecting demand for the specific product, political/regulatory conditions, and relevant market conditions such as structure, level of competition, and sociological and economic conditions.

TABLE 8.1 The Market Analysis Process

The Market Analysis Process
External Conditions
   Forecasting
      Trends in technologies
      Trends in audience demand
      Trends in demographics and lifestyles
      Trends in advertiser demand
   Demand Factors
      Price
      Price of substitutes and complements
      Consumer income
      Consumer uses and gratifications for
     Trends in political/regulatory conditions
     Technology forecasting
  Specific market factors
   Market structure
      Seller concentration
      Buyer concentration
      Barriers to entry
      Product differentiation
      Cost structures
      Vertical integration
     Access to distribution channels
     Target market
     Economic and sociological conditions
Internal Conditions
   Company mission and objectives
   Organizational structure and culture
   Expertise and product mix
   Resources
   Strengths
   Weaknesses
   Opportunities
   Threats
Financial Conditions
  Revenues
  Costs
  Return on investment
  Availability of capital
  Intangible returns

Internal conditions include the company's mission, objectives, capabilities, current products, resources, and strengths, weaknesses, opportunities, and threats. Financial conditions include revenue estimates, cost estimates, return on investment, and intangible benefits.

In practice, these factors overlap and mutually influence one another. However, the categories provide a useful framework for trying to make sense out of a complex process.

External Conditions

Forecasting long-term industry trends. The first questions to ask in a market analysis are fairly general: (a) What are the overall trends in the market? (b) Are there new technologies or other factors on the horizon that may change the market?

Unfortunately, long-term forecasts are increasingly difficult to make. They require examining a number of factors, including trends in new technologies, trends in audience demand for media products, demographic and lifestyle trends in society, and trends in advertiser demand in the various media sectors.

Trends in new technologies. Since 2000, the flurry of new digital-media technologies emerging on the market has made life difficult for media forecasters. For example, the video-game industry has emerged as a new competitor to existing media for audiences and advertisers. On the audience side, the gaming industry has become larger than the film industry in terms of annual sales, and data suggest that—as gamers spend more time and money on games—they spend less time with other media, such as television. At the same time, because of the gaming audience's size and of makeup and new software development that allows insertion of ads or products into (and deleted from) games, advertiser demand for space in games has risen sharply.

More predictably, interactive media continue to rise, as does their potential future effects on demand in traditional media markets. In recent years, the size of the Web "Blogosphere" has exponentially risen, doubling every 5 months (Kluth, 2006). In a national survey, 57% of U.S. teenagers reported they were creating Web content (Lenhart & Madden, 2005), while demand for some Wiki-media, e.g. content created by user communities, also has mushroomed. The Wiki newspaper *Omy News* in South Korea averaged 700,000 daily visitors in mid-decade, comparable to the circulation of a large major daily newspaper, while *Wikipedia*, the Wiki-produced online encyclopedia, had more than 3 million user-contributed articles and received more hits than the Web pages of mainstream news media (Kluth, 2006).

Younger audience members in particular create and use interactive media in ever greater numbers. Their willingness to trust community-

created content makes predicting their future demand for more traditional mediated content difficult and greatly complicates long-term
media trends forecasting. As new media innovations constantly beget
other new media innovations, predicting the "Next Big Thing" and
its appearance on the market also will become more difficult. Indeed,
the media industry has been identified as one of the industries most
affected by emerging technologies in recent decades (Day & Schoemaker, 2000).

Trends in audience demand for media products.   Research shows
that consumer demand for media products, in general, has risen steadily
in recent decades. However, increased competition, audience fragmentation, and changing consumer tastes slowed demand for specific types
of media products. For example, from 1998 to 2005, the national average number of Persons Using Radio (PURs) dropped 2%, continuing
the steady downward trend in radio usage seen throughout the 1990s
(Arbitron, 2006; U.S. Census Bureau, 2000). Similarly, from 1960 to
2004, total daily newspaper circulation in America dropped 7%, even
as the U.S. population rose more than 57% (Newspaper Association of
America, 2006; U.S. Census Bureau, 1994, 2000). Television networks
also suffered; the average number of hours that Americans spent watching television rose in the 1990s, but because the number of available
channels increased even more, the average audience size per channel,
per network and per program sharply fell (Adams & Eastman, 2002).

Demographic trends.   The 2000 census showed that fewer than 70%
of the U.S. population identified itself "White only, non-Hispanic."
Just as importantly, the economic power of minority communities has
grown significantly in recent decades. In the early 21st century, the
United States underwent the largest wave of immigration in its history,
creating large populations for whom English was a second language. In
general, this meant that U.S. mass-media audience had become much
less of a mass, and demanded more diversity in content.

Lifestyle changes also affect the media's product markets. Since
the 1970s, women entered the U.S. workforce in large numbers, with
at least 60% working outside the home (U.S. Census Bureau, 2001).
As a result, many major trends emerged in media markets since then:
Demand for daytime television programming declined. Drive time and
workplace listening increased in importance for radio as the in-home
daytime audience declined. As the average number of hours Americans
spent working outside the home increased over the past few decades,

demand for newspapers shifted from evening deliveries to morning. By 2000, the same trend showed in television news. Ratings for early evening television newscasts declined steadily, and retirees and women who don't work outside the home dominated that daypart audience. By the new millennium, much local TV news competition shifted to the early morning daypart (5 A.M.–7 A.M.), when more people are home and preparing for the workday, illustrating the importance of considering demographic and lifestyle trends in media market analyses.

Trends in advertiser demand for media products. As traditional media audiences fragment and new technologies create new vehicles for advertising, many advertisers are rethinking traditional approaches to advertising and marketing. Throughout the last half of the 20th century, national advertisers built the core of their advertising strategy around television and newspapers. Today, more advertisers are broadening their approaches to marketing, allocating more funds to placements such as banner ads on the Web, event sponsorship, direct mail and e-mail, theaters, video games, product placements in films and at sporting and entertainment events, and even Webcasting and pod-casting.

The long-term effects of these shifts on the advertising revenue picture for traditional media still are unclear, but some indicators emerge. U.S. Internet advertising totaled $12.5 billion in 2005, up 30% over 2004 levels (Interactive Advertising Bureau & PricewaterhouseCoopers, 2006). While the total spent on Web advertising in 2005 was lower than the $21.5 billion spent on radio, the $46 billion spent on television, and the $49.4 billion spent on print newspaper ads in 2005, Web advertising was gaining quickly. Perhaps more importantly, the pace of growth in Web advertising was dizzying compared to the 2% increase in ad revenues posted by newspapers in 2004–2005, the flat growth in radio, and the 2% decline broadcast television experienced for the same period.

Estimating Demand for a Product

Demand is a measure of the quantity of a product that people will buy at a particular cost. It is a function of the cost of the product, the cost of substitutes and complements for the product, the ability of consumers to pay the costs of consumption, and consumers' tastes and utilities (Stigler, 1952).

Product costs. For most products, the cost of consumption is measured strictly by the price of the product. With media products, however, costs are measured in time and money because audiences have to invest significant time to consume media; e.g., you have to invest at least 2 hours to go to the theater to see a movie, and reading a book takes a great deal more time than that. Indeed, in many developed countries, media managers worry more about the competition for audiences' time and attention than they do about the competition for the audience's money.

In predicting demand for media products, most media managers calculate that demand will fall as the time required for consumption rises—although obvious exceptions exist. Editors have shortened news stories in newspapers and television because research shows audiences are more likely to change the channel or turn the page after a certain point. Television networks now produce fewer new episodes in prime-time series and play more reruns because research has shown that only a small percentage of even the most loyal viewers watch a program 2 weeks in a row.

In the competition for audiences' and advertisers' money, price negatively relates to demand for most products and services: As prices go up, demand goes down and vice versa. The relationship between the change in price and the change in demand is called *elasticity of demand* and the sensitivity of demand to price varies by product. When the price of a product increases 1%, if demand decreases more than 1%, demand for the product is said to be *elastic*. If demand decreases less than 1% when the price rises 1%, demand for the product is *inelastic*. If price and demand change at the same rate, the product is said to have *unit elasticity*.

Media managers need to understand the nature of the demand for their products because it directly affects their ability to set prices. For example, if demand for a product is inelastic, increasing the price likely will result in higher revenues because demand will fall more slowly than the price rises. However, if demand for a product is elastic, then an increase in the price can actually cost the company money as demand falls faster than revenue rises.

For example, look at the case of a city magazine entitled *Downtown*, which has a circulation of 100,000 per month (Table 8.2). If the subscription price is $1 per copy, *Downtown* will generate $100,000 per month in revenue from circulation. If demand for the magazine is inelastic, when management increases the cover price 25% to $1.25, the company will actually increase its monthly circulation revenue to $112,500, even if the number of subscribers falls 10% to 90,000. The gain in revenue from the price increase will exceed the loss in revenue from the drop in

TABLE 8.2 The Effects of Elasticity of Demand and Price Increases on Revenue

	Current	Inelastic	Elastic
Price	$1.00	$1.25 (+25%)	$1.25 (+25%)
Circulation	100,000	90,000 (−10%)	74,000 (−26%)
Circ. Revenue	**$100,000**	**$112,500**	**$92,500**
Ad Rate (CPM):	$10	$10	$10
Number of ads per issue	100	100	100
Ad Revenue	**$100,000**	**$90,000**	**$74,000**
Total Revenue	**$200,000**	**$202,500**	**$166,500**

circulation. However, if demand were elastic so that a 25% increase in cover price produced a 26% decrease in circulation, circulation revenue would actually fall.

The fact that most media are joint commodities complicates the process of setting prices even more because the market analyst also has to consider the potential impact on advertising revenue. Advertisers buy ads on the basis of circulation size or ratings, usually on a cost-per-thousand basis. Thus, in the case *Downtown,* advertising revenue may fall when circulation drops.

If demand had unit elasticity and a 10% decline in circulation for *Downtown* caused a 10% drop in advertising revenue, the magazine would still enjoy an increase in total revenues. However, the increase would be small because the loss in advertising revenue would almost offset the growth in circulation revenue. If reader demand for the magazine were elastic, however, following a cover-price increase, the publication would wind up with much lower revenues, even if ad rates and the volume of advertising sold stayed the same. The potential effects of price increases on sales to readers and advertisers must be considered when a media company thinks about raising its prices.

Elasticity of demand also refers to the effects that changes in the health of the overall economy may have on consumer demand for a particular product. The money an advertiser spends on advertising is somewhat flexible, and companies often cut those funds first in economic downturns. As a result, demand for advertising can be elastic, and the media industry is highly vulnerable to swings in the national or local economy.

On the consumer side, demand for media products tends to be relatively inelastic, although it varies from product to product. Free over-the-air radio and television demand is largely immune to changes in price and the economy because consumers pay nothing to receive them. Sales of expensive premium cable channels and tickets to movies are much more sensitive to price and economic swings.

Substitutes and complements.   Price elasticity also relates to the number and prices of substitute and complement products available to consumers. A *substitute* is a product that can be used in place of another product. A *complement* is a product purchased to use with another product. DVDs complement DVD players, which are useless without them.

If the price of a substitute product is significantly lower and the substitute's *utility* or usefulness is comparable, then the elasticity of demand for both products will increase. Similarly, if the prices of complementary products are too high, then demand for the product will fall. If the average cost of a DVD rental were $25 a day, there would be little demand for DVD players.

Consumer income.   A person's demand for products is related to his or her income. As individual income rises, audiences have more discretionary money to spend on optional goods and services such as information and entertainment, so media consumption usually rises.

Because most media products are joint commodities, consumer income also has an impact on the advertising side of the media market. Advertisers generally prefer to reach audience members with higher incomes because those individuals will have greater discretionary income available to spend on products—necessities and luxuries. Thus, populations with higher average incomes are more attractive to advertisers than those with lower incomes, and advertisers often are willing to pay more to reach high-income audiences.

Consumer tastes and utilities.   *Consumer taste* refers to the question of why audiences select the products they do. Few theories predict changes in consumer taste but, from an economic view, consumers must find *utility* in a product in order to be willing to buy it. Utility is the usefulness or satisfaction that a consumer derives from using something. Many products media companies thought were sure hits have failed because consumers didn't find them useful. In the 1980s and early 1990s, for example, ordering pizza online was promoted as a reason for subscribing to online services. Consumers, however, found it easier to use the phone.

While consumer tastes change and often elude prediction, research on information use (Lacy & Simon, 1993), uses and gratifications (Severin & Tankard, 1992), and dependency theory have identified some general ways people use media. These uses include surveillance, decision making, diversion, social-cultural interactions, self-understanding, and psychological needs.

Surveillance includes monitoring the environment to identify new, useful, or interesting information. *Decision making* involves conscious information-seeking behaviors with the goal of deciding on a course of action. *Diversion* includes using media products for entertainment. *Social-cultural interaction* includes the use of information or media to establish common ground with those with whom one interacts. Discussing a news or sports story at the office or, for teenagers, being well informed about the current hot pop star, can help establish bonds with other people and may even be a source of power within a social or professional group. *Self-understanding* is the use of media or information to develop personal value systems or philosophies or to improve the ability to manage life. *Psychological needs* refers to the use of media for emotional gratification or release, such as watching a comedy to lift your spirits or reading a favorite political commentator, who reconfirms the correctness of your convictions about a particular issue.

Predicting consumer demand for media is always difficult. However, paying attention to utility and to what is known about how and why people use media plays an important part in market analysis. The media manager needs to understand how and why audiences might find a particular media product useful.

Political/Regulatory Conditions

Changes in laws, policies, and regulations affect all media companies. Laws regulating wages, benefits, labor relations, working conditions, taxes, employee health and safety, and the environment apply to all businesses. Because regulatory policies change over time, market analyses must consider the current state of regulation in product and geographic markets and any changes that might happen.

Within the media industry, some industry sectors, such as broadcasting and cable, are more subject to government regulation than others.

For example, broadcasters must get a license from the federal government in order to go on the air, and they operate under federal rules governing decency and obscenity in content. Local governments must grant access to local public rights of way to cable companies if the companies are to deliver services.

Print media such as newspapers, magazines, and newsletters are not subject to government licensing or content regulation. However, an increase in the price of postage can dramatically raise distribution costs and reduce profits. Additionally, all media are subject to limits on ownership consolidation through federal antitrust laws and, in the case of broadcast companies, direct regulation that sets limits on the number of stations one company can own in a market.

Media companies also are increasingly subject to international regulations as they expand into foreign markets. Cable networks, for example, frequently distribute channels by satellite and local cable systems in countries around the world. For media products with global market potential, a market analysis must examine laws and trade regulations that may govern media companies or products crossing borders. Additionally, in a market analysis conducted prior to a potential international investment, management would examine regulations that might affect business conditions in a local market, such as wage and hour laws, tax laws, business restrictions, etc.

Specific Market Factors

In addition to long-term forecasting, a market analysis includes a careful examination of the specific conditions that will affect success in a given product or geographic market. Among the conditions to consider are market structure, the nature of the target market, and the market's economic and sociological environments.

Market structure.   One of the most important considerations in a market analysis, market structure analysis is conducted for product and geographic markets. When examining the structure of a market, a manager considers several things, including seller concentration, buyer concentration, vertical integration, product differentiation, cost structures, and barriers to entry.

The first of these, *seller concentration,* measures the number of companies competing in the market. Too much or too little seller concentration in a market makes it hard for newcomers to survive.

If there are too many competitors in a market, it will be hard for most companies to make money, since each one will have only a small share of the available audience or advertisers, as online media companies have discovered. The literally billions of Web sites and the fact that many sell advertising make it hard for all but a few to sell enough to make a profit. On the other hand, in a highly concentrated market—e.g., one with only a few sellers—the established companies generally have enough market share to capture economies of scale. That gives them production-cost advantages that they can then pass on to consumers through lower prices. That makes it harder for newcomers to the market to compete on price. The optimal level of seller concentration in a market depends on the size of the market and the demand for the product.

Analyzing seller concentration is complicated in media markets because different types of media products substitute for one another for both consumers and advertisers. Someone analyzing the market for radio, for example, needs to look not just at the number of other radio stations in the market, but also the number of newspapers, magazines, television stations, cable providers, satellite radio and television channels, movie theaters, and the level of online use in the community. All those media compete for the local audience's time and attention and, perhaps even more importantly, for the revenue provided by local advertisers.

Buyer concentration is the opposite of seller concentration in that it measures the number of buyers in the marketplace for a given product. Again, media managers examine this for audiences and advertisers. With audiences, the question is whether enough people in the market fall into the target-audience group to make it worthwhile to distribute a particular product. For example, if a community had only one household in which the primary language spoken was Russian, there would not be enough buyer concentration to justify having an entire channel on the local cable system devoted to Russian-language programming. However, if 10% of the households in the community spoke Russian as their first language, there would be.

Estimating buyer concentration among advertisers is particularly important because, in the advertising market, having either too much or too little buyer concentration is a problem. Having too little buyer concentration means there are a lot of advertisers, but most buy only small amounts of time or space. In such cases, locating and negotiating with many small customers may cost more than it's worth—another problem facing online media businesses.

The opposite problem is having too much buyer concentration. Not all businesses are potential advertisers. Most companies that advertise through the mass media sell products or services directly to consumers, such as automobile dealers, fast-food restaurants, banks, and insurers. In some media markets such as in rural areas, there are not very many such clients available, and the local media may depend on one or two major advertisers for the majority of their revenue. That gives the large advertiser tremendous power in negotiating advertising rates and other benefits, such as positive news coverage because the media company can't afford to risk losing the client. Similarly, a video-production house with a large client that provides most of its business faces the same issues. If the client leaves, the business may fail. Because of these risks, analysis of a media market should include consideration of the number and quality of potential buyers in the market relative to the number of sellers in the market.

Another element of market structure is *vertical integration,* where a company also owns the companies from which it buys supplies or, on the other end, to which it sells its final products. When analyzing markets, media managers measure their competitors' vertical integration as one way to determine market power. It is difficult to compete in a market where other sellers are highly vertically integrated. Nonintegrated companies may have trouble getting access to production supplies or distribution channels at the same prices their integrated competitors receive.

For example, prior to 1995, the Financial Syndication (Fin-Syn) rules prevented U.S. broadcast networks from vertically integrating to own the production studios that created primetime television programming. That ensured that the networks had to buy prime-time programs from independent producers. In 1995, the Fin-Syn rules were eliminated and today, network-owned studios create the majority of primetime U.S. programs airing, making it difficult for independent television production studios to survive; several have announced they are leaving the market.

Product differentiation, another factor in market structure, measures the difference between the various products competing in the market. Media companies often are accused of failing to offer consumers much product variety; when *Law and Order* became a hit, NBC spun off multiple versions of the same concept. CBS did the same thing with *CSI.* The success of the reality show *Survivor* produced dozens of variations on the theme in countries around the world.

For the market analyst, the question is whether a proposed product differs too much or too little from available products. In the latter, consumers will have little reason to choose it over the original version. In the former, media companies take a greater risk because it will be hard to estimate consumer demand before making the investment.

Information product economics make investing in product differentiation a serious problem for media companies. In most industries, producers can manage investment risks in a completely new idea by producing and test marketing a prototype. For media companies, test marketing is difficult (Priest, 1994). A book publisher has to buy the rights to a book and go through the editing and printing process before it can judge how well it will sell. A film studio has to make a film before it can test it with audiences. By the time the audience sees a media product, the producer has incurred most of the cost of production, and there are few options for change.

The media industry's typical response produces an endless stream of sequels and spin-offs. If the first film or television series was successful, the sequel probably will have a built-in fan base. An entirely new product may have no audience at all. Using writers, directors, and performers already popular with audiences also helps reduce risk because their names alone will create a certain level of demand. These factors make media managers reluctant to invest in new talent, new storylines, and avant-garde approaches to production, which reduces the product differentiation, or choice, available to consumers. It also makes it harder for new talent to break into the industry.

However, when media companies offer too little product differentiation, failure follows. Following the incredible success of *Who Wants to Be a Millionaire?* in the summer of 1999, almost every U.S. network created a game show for their fall primetime lineup. The spin-offs all failed. Audiences may have loved *Millionaire,* but apparently one such game show was enough to satisfy audience demand.

Therefore, media market analysts must maximize product differentiation and minimize risk. This is always difficult, but one strategy looks for products or concepts successful in limited geographic markets elsewhere, and then introduces versions of them into new areas. In the early 1980s, a local weekly business newspaper was launched in Kansas City, Missouri, providing the local business community with in-depth coverage of their markets and competitors. The concept was immediately successful and by the end of the decade, similar papers were found in cities across the United States and around the world. Similarly, *Millionaire, American Idol, Survivor,* and *Wheel of Fortune* all originated in Europe but by 2006, local versions of them could be found on the air in dozens of countries.

Managers also consider a market's *cost structures,* which refers to production costs and includes fixed and variable costs. *Fixed costs* are costs over which managers have little control because they are incurred in producing the first unit of the product. In other words, they are the basic costs of being in a particular line of business. High fixed costs in a market are a barrier to entry because they mean that a tremendous amount of investment capital is needed to begin operations and stay in business until the company begins generating profits. For example, the cost of the presses required to start a new major metropolitan daily newspaper is an almost insurmountable barrier to urban newspaper startups.

Variable costs are costs over which a manager has some control, such as travel and entertainment budgets and, to a more limited degree, personnel, advertising, and marketing expenses. For media companies, personnel costs generally are one of the largest budget lines. In television, personnel expenses makes up about 43% of all expenses for stations in the United States (National Association of Broadcasters, 2004).

Finally, media market analysts look at *barriers to entry,* in general. A *barrier to entry* is anything that makes it difficult for a new competitor to enter the market. If a media manager already is in a market, having barriers to entry against new competitors is an advantage because they limit competition. For those trying to enter a new market, barriers to entry are disadvantages.

All the elements of market structure discussed are barriers to entry, but there are others, as well. For example, a shortage of people with the right skills in the local labor force can become a barrier to entry. For broadcasters, the geography surrounding a town in the mountains may be a barrier to entry since the hills may block broadcast signal transmission. For graduating broadcasting and film students, the entertainment industry's tendency to depend on proven talent is a barrier to entry in the job market. Media managers constantly scan their current and proposed markets for barriers to entry—the obvious ones, and those that are more subtle.

The target market.   A market analysis necessarily includes an analysis of the target market. From the standpoint of media companies, not all audiences are created equal. Some audiences are more desirable to advertisers than others, which makes those audiences more desirable as target markets for media companies.

As a general rule, women 18–49 years old are the most desirable target market because they tend to make most of the household buying decisions and, therefore, are the most valuable to advertisers. Advertisers also believe that people 18–49 still have flexible brand preferences and are more likely than older viewers to be influenced by advertising.

Despite the general preference for women, in recent years men 18–49 have become an increasingly desirable target market for media content. Historically, young men have watched less television than women and, therefore, have been harder for advertisers to reach. In recent years, their TV viewing has been dropping off even more. As young men have become harder for advertisers to reach, advertisers have become more interested in reaching them.

Finally, as mentioned previously, the income level of audiences also affects their desirability as target markets. Affluent audiences of both genders are more desirable to both advertisers and media-product retailers than less-affluent audiences.

While media companies worry about the growing fragmentation of the mass audience across narrowly targeted media channels, advertisers seek niche media as an advantage. Media targeted to only a narrow demographic allows advertisers to know exactly who they reach, and they can be confident that more of the audience members are likely to buy their product. Consequently, advertisers may pay higher advertising rates for comparatively smaller—but higher quality—audiences. When a media outlet targets a mass audience, as a daily newspaper or the broadcast networks do, advertisers may reach more people, but only a small percentage of the people they're paying to reach are potential customers.

Specialized media also may be able to attract advertisers that mass media cannot. Business newspapers sell space to business-to-business advertisers such as office supplies, equipment and furniture companies, who would be unlikely to buy much space in the mass media. Trade publications, which focus on serving a single industry, can sell space to companies that supply that industry. Targeted consumer magazines, such as city magazines or society magazines, sell ads to interior decorators, exclusive luxury spas, and other high-end service providers that would find mass-audience buys inefficient.

On the downside, the move toward narrowly targeted niche media leaves large segments of the population—those groups that are less attractive to advertisers—unserved by content appropriate to their information and entertainment needs. People older than 49 find few television programs with storylines built around their interests, issues, or lives. Similarly, radio stations that program music from the 1950s and 1960s for the baby boomer generation have had problems with advertisers in recent years. As more of those terrestrial stations changed formats to appeal to younger listeners, the over-49 age group became one of the major earlier adopters of subscriber-supported satellite radio.

Historically, media companies also have ignored ethnic minorities because relatively few advertisers specifically targeted minorities as potential customers. In recent years, that has started to change. Numerous cable networks designed for specific ethnic and language audiences have been launched, and Spanish-language television and radio is one of the fastest-growing formats in the United States.

These concerns not withstanding, in the increasingly fragmented media market, identifying the target audience for media products plays a critical part in any market analysis. Media managers must understand the nature and limits of the audience segment most likely to want their product. Having identified a potential target market, the manager must then be sure either that that group has enough income to buy the product, or that advertisers are interested in reaching that audience segment.

Analyzing the target audience in a market analysis means identifying the audience and advertisers existing media companies are going after. However, it also requires looking at other available audiences in the market—particularly those who are underserved—and considering whether any advertisers might want to reach those groups. Finally, a careful target-market analysis will examine the potential advertisers in the market who would *not* be likely to buy space or time in a mass-audience medium. The existence of such advertisers might suggest an untapped business opportunity.

Economic and sociological conditions.   The final element to include in an analysis of the external conditions in a market is an examination of the economic and sociological conditions in the geographic area of interest. These include such things as the unemployment rate, how it compares to state and national averages, the long-term growth trends in the area, and the diversity of business and industry in the economy.

A market with higher-than-average unemployment should concern a market analyst, particularly if the unemployment rate represents a long-term trend and not just a temporary increase. High unemployment means that people in the market will have less disposable income. Similarly, a city or region not growing is less desirable than one that does grow; for the media analyst, lack of local economic growth will make it harder to increase the media company's revenues and value. An area heavily dominated by a single industry is less desirable than one with a diverse economy because a downturn in that industry can lead to a sharp economic decline in the market. Of even greater concern is a community with a single company providing most jobs; losing that company would devastate the community.

Demographics and psychographics are the sociological elements that a media market analyst examines. *Demographics* describe what people are in terms of factors that they generally can't change, such as age, race, gender, education level, and income. *Psychographics* describe lifestyle, culture, and values. The importance of demographics already has been outlined, but media managers also need to understand the audience's psychographics. A community dominated by a politically conservative population is fundamentally different from a town that is politically liberal. A community where most people have strong religious affiliations is different from one where they don't. And a market with a large, affluent population of corporate executives would be expected to differ in its media needs and tastes than a community of farm families or factory workers. For media executives, understanding such differences is critical to making successful decisions about content. Content that might succeed in Berkeley, California, would not necessarily be popular in Albany, Georgia.

Internal Conditions

Analyzing internal conditions in the course of a market analysis is a process of self-examination. At issue is whether the company has the internal resources it needs to succeed with a new product or in a new market.

SWOT analysis. One technique for analyzing internal conditions is the SWOT analysis (Pearce & Robinson, 1997). SWOT stands for Strengths, Weaknesses, Opportunities, and Threats. A SWOT analysis will include an examination of the company's mission statements, goals, organizational structure, market position, leadership, personnel, financial resources, organizational and professional cultures, and existing product mix and markets. In each case, market analysts ask themselves what the company's strengths and weaknesses are in that area, and what opportunities and threats exist.

Company mission and objectives. Whether you conduct a formal SWOT analysis, you should always ask whether the proposed investment or project is consistent with the company's mission statement and goals. If not, then it probably should not be undertaken.

rganizational structure and culture.   Another immediate question is how the new project or investment will affect the company's structure and culture. For example, is the new market geographically near the company's current operations, or will the company be incurring additional costs because it will now be managing distant operations. Does the company have the physical infrastructure to undertake the project, or will it need new office space or a new communication infrastructure? Less obvious is how the new project will fit with the company's organizational and professional cultures. Different organizations and professions have different cultures. Clashes between these cultures are a major source of organizational tension and often are implicated in the failure of corporate mergers.

Following the merger of AOL and Time Warner, for example, there was open conflict between the executives of AOL, who were used to a centralized, fast-moving, interactive culture, and the leaders of Time Warner, who worked autonomously from one another with little input from the others (Munk, 2002). Cultural clashes also can occur between two companies in the same business but with slightly different products. Television news operations have a very different professional culture from television entertainment operations. In the early days of convergence, reporters working for newspapers' print operations had slightly different professional cultures than reporters working on the same newspapers' online editions (Singer, 2003). These differences need to be examined, understood, and managed.

Expertise and product mix.   Another series of questions to address involve the available expertise and existing product mix. Can the company's leadership assume the added responsibilities of a new project, or are they managing as much as they can handle? Do they have the expertise to handle the new product or market? If no one in the company has the expertise needed, is it possible to hire that expertise?

How does the new product fit into the existing product mix? Successfully running a newspaper does not necessarily mean that a company also will succeed in running a radio station—or a retail sales operation, which many media companies are launching through their Web sites. Indeed, in recent years, major media corporations have invested widely in different media sectors as they have tried to diversify their positions in the industry. Research suggests that, in most cases, diversification reduced media companies' financial performance in the years immediately following the investments (Jung, 2003; Kolo & Vogt, 2003).

Company resources. When examining internal conditions the company's position in its existing markets should also be considered. Is it in a strong position? Is it a market leader? Or does it face serious competitive threats or an eroding market? Many companies make the strategic decision to exit markets in which they are not one of the top two or three players, rather than tying up resources that could be used more efficiently in other ventures. If the internal analysis shows the company in a strong position, it probably will be a good time to make new investments. New projects may be harder to launch if the company faces serious competitive threats in its existing markets. Even so, if the company's business is eroding, it may be difficult, but advantageous, to begin moving into new lines of business with a better long-term future.

An obvious question is whether the company has the financial resources to make the investment. Can it afford to support the new project for as long as it takes to become profitable or absorb the losses if profitability never happens? Does it have the credit rating and financial stability necessary to take out loans or attract investors?

The media market analyst uses the information about internal conditions to gauge the company's strengths and weaknesses relative to the proposed project. A company's strength in one set of circumstances may become a weakness if conditions change—and vice versa. A sophisticated analysis of internal conditions will consider how the company would be likely to perform under different scenarios were the project to go forward.

Similarly, media managers examine what the new opportunities offer the company. However, they also ask how it might threaten the company. Most projects will provide both opportunities and threats, and they need to be carefully—and honestly—examined.

Finally, as noted at the chapter's beginning, the analysis of internal conditions needs to account for how the proposed project may affect the third market in which media companies operate: the investment market (Aaker, 1995). Company leaders need to understand how investments or new products likely may affect the company's short- and long-term financial performance because that will have a direct effect on the company's value in the eyes of owners and investors. A drop in the stock price of a publicly held company will bring its top executive under fire from major stockholders and financial analysts. And even in private companies, owners expect to see the value of their holdings grow over the long term.

Financial conditions. Finally, a market analysis should estimate the financial costs and returns that will result from the project. This involves forecasting the revenues that the new investment or project will generate, the costs involved, what long-term return on investment (ROI) to expect, the availability of capital to finance the project or investment, and the possibility of intangible benefits that the company might gain. If a company purchases an existing property, information will be available to help estimate revenues and costs based upon previous performance. However, if a media company is considering something such as a format change, a new business start-up, or a change of network affiliation, then revenue and cost data might not be available or might not be a good guide to the future. Similarly, if the new owner will gain or lose economies of scale through the buyout of another company as compared to the previous owner, previous cost estimates may or may not be valid.

In examining financial conditions, you must forecast how long it will be before revenues exceed costs so that the company will make a profit off the investment. The analyst must examine current and future costs including planned operational changes and the investment those changes might require, and current and future economic conditions in the market. You will need these data to help estimate when the break-even point is likely to be reached. Executives must be sure the company can sustain losses for as long it takes for the new operation to establish itself. All too often, companies are forced to give up on promising projects because they don't have the financial resources to sustain the investment until the market develops.

Return on investment (ROI) measures how much profit the owner will make relative to the investment required. Companies try to seek the highest ROI possible. Therefore, when a company compares competing investment options, it usually will invest in the one with the highest ROI potential. A good investment decision requires an estimate of the likely ROI.

If the project will require a substantial investment, you also should examine the availability and cost of financing. Companies usually finance investments in one of three ways: (a) revenue, (b) borrowing, or (c) expanding ownership. All three methods have risks.

When a company uses *revenue,* it pays for the project out of the money it generates from its existing business, reducing profits at least temporarily and possibly pressuring the stock price of publicly held companies. *Borrowing* involves taking on debt, usually long-term investments. Borrowed money must be repaid with interest, the cost of financing. Taking out a loan requires careful attention to the interest rate because revenues pay that cost. If the combination of operating costs and debt service exceed the company's revenues over a long time, the company will fail.

Expanding ownership can also help finance a company, but it risks diluting the company's ownership. Multiple investors can increase the costs and complexity of corporate decisions by requiring negotiation with more people. In some instances, it can lead to battles for corporate control. Expanding ownership by selling stock publicly means the company faces additional state and federal securities regulations, and compliance with those regulations will increase operating costs. Management also will face new pressures to continuously maximize shareholder value through the stock price, which will affect the range of future options for the company.

Even more difficult to evaluate are the intangible elements of a financial analysis. In addition to revenues and profits, new projects also can return value in the form of public relations, reputation, and prestige. The value of these intangibles is difficult to calculate, but over the long term, enhanced reputation may generate additional business and thus return revenues and profits. However, there is no guarantee that actual financial benefit will result and such returns are difficult, if not impossible, to measure. Nevertheless, they often are used to justify major investments and should be considered.

Summary

A market analysis carefully, critically considers the factors that may affect a company's success in a geographic or product market. Undertaken as a formal project, it generally is done to evaluate the potential for a new investment or a new product. However, effective media executives constantly scan the competitive environment in which they work, searching for unrealized opportunities and emerging threats. Understanding the process also can help authors, producers, reporters, and other content creators by making them more likely to get support for projects via fostering the ability to explain the market for the idea to supervisors or investors and to estimate the likelihood of positive returns.

Finally, conducting an ongoing analysis of the labor market in the media industry is absolutely crucial for ambitious professionals. Successful professionals are constantly estimating demand in their industry for their skills and experience, evaluating their abilities against those of colleagues and competitors, and forecasting future trends in the industry, so they can gain stay one step ahead in gaining required skills.

Although the specific issues in a market analysis will vary from project to project, generally, the process includes an examination of external conditions, internal conditions, and financial conditions. This entails careful evaluation of long-term trends and developments in the market, the actual conditions in the product or geographic market being considered, the compatibility of the proposed project with the company's mission, objectives, capabilities, and current business, and the impact that the project will have on the company's long-term financial performance.

A market analysis serves several critical functions. It helps managers effectively monitor the competitive environment in which they are operating so that they can take advantage of new opportunities or deal with emerging threats, and it helps them make better short and long-term decisions about their business. In the media industry, the ability to effectively evaluate the market is a critical skill for managers, whether they are low-level line managers, such as producers in the newsroom, or top-level corporate executives.

Case 8.1 Making a Choice

You and your colleagues are senior analysts with RCR Media Consulting and Brokerage Co. Sarah McLaren, owner of a small television station group called McLaren Communications, has contacted RCR. Ms. McLaren is aware of two TV stations in two different, but comparably sized markets going up for sale. She only has the capital to buy one of the two. She has hired RCR to conduct a market analysis of the two stations and make a recommendation as to which of the two—if either— she should buy (See Tables 8.3, 8.4, 8.5, and 8.6).

McLaren Communications currently owns three TV stations in three small markets, all size 150+. All three of the company's current holdings are in the Midwest plains states. Two of the stations are Fox affiliates stations. The other one is a CBS affiliate.

McLaren Communications' company mission statement says, "McLaren Communications is a strong, positive commercial enterprise that succeeds through serving its communities with high-quality information and entertainment programming that reflects strong community values."

TABLE 8.3 Community Profiles

	Midtown	Areaville
Market Size		
Television market rank	177	188
Population		
Total population	173,987	145,291
Total households	66,248	53,942
Population change 1990–2000	−.03	+.04
Households by income		
Median household income	$49,688	$56,522
Percent of households in poverty	9%	11%
Age	%	%
Under 18	25	19
18–34	24	26
35–44	15	22
45–64	21	20
65+	15	13
Ethnic population	%	%
Caucasian	92.5	75.4
African American	2.4	8.3
Hispanic	4.5	11.1
Asian	0.6	3.0
Native American	0	2.2
Education	%	%
College 1–3 years	23.3	31.8
College 4 + years	27.6	34.9
Occupation	%	%
Manufacturing	10.3	5.5
Wholesale/Retail	10.7	8.3
Finance/Professional Services	7.3	9.5
Health	4.3	7.0
Public Administration	1.9	4.3
Retail Sales Data	$	$
Total retail sales	1,953,000,000	1,435,000,000
Retail expenditure per household	22,738	25,424
Grocery, food, & beverage	878,118	850,351
Restaurants & bars	320,581	310,586
General retail & clothing	800,037	795,222
Motor vehicles and parts	783,146	765,543
Building supplies	319,548	294,456
Health & personal care	153,247	150,672
Furniture, appliances, & electronics	119,309	105,428

TABLE 8.4 Station Finances

	WCRZ-TV	KRVW-TV
Range of Estimated Annual Revenue	$6.7 million–8 million	$5.6 million–$6.0 million
Range of Estimated Annual Growth in Revenues	3.1%–8%	3.4%–6.5%
Estimated profit margin based on station affiliation	28.7%	24.5%

McLaren Communications has done its own analysis of internal and financial conditions and determined that it has the financial resources to buy either one of the two stations. It has the management expertise to run an additional station, if acquired. Specific financial data for the two stations will not be available until McLaren Communications opens negotiations with the owners, but some general estimates are available.

The preliminary market analysis that Ms. McLaren is hiring RCR to conduct should provide some insight into what types of short- and long-term revenue and profitability she might expect from the proper-

TABLE 8.5 Midtown Television

Rank (Evening News)	Call Letters	Channel	Network Affiliation	Owner
1	WCRZ-TV	2	Fox	Ligon Communications[a]
2	WRDV-TV[b]	11	CBS	Parker Television[a]
3	WQQT-TV[b]	6	Fox	Byers Media
4	WNBB-TV[b]	4	ABC	Claude Communications[a]
7	WJJZ-TV[c]	7	NBC	Smythn Television
8	WYQY-TV[c]	9	CBS	Jonsie Television[a]

[a]Denotes a major media group: More than 150 radio stations nationwide; 15% or more of the total TV viewing audience nationwide; 10% or more of the local cable systems nationwide; 15+ daily newspapers nationwide.
[b]Denotes a station located outside of Midtown in a city 50 miles from Midtown but that broadcasts into Midtown and sells advertising to Midtown businesses.
[c]Denotes a station located outside of Midtown in a city 150 miles from Midtown but that broadcasts into Midtown.

TABLE 8.6 Television in Areaville

Rank (Evening News)	Call Letters	Channel	Network	Owner
1	KSTJ-TV	2	CBS	Big Group Television[a]
2	KDCR-TV	11	ABC	Terrell Family Media[a]
3	KRVW-TV	6	CW	RMR Television[a]
4	KBZA-TV	4	Fox	Pictures Communications[a]
6	KJQW-TV	13	NBC	Jones Communications[a]
7	KGRN-TV	8	PBS	University of Areaville

[a]Denotes a major media group: More than 150 radio stations nationwide; 15% or more of the total TV viewing audience nationwide; 10% or more of the local cable systems nationwide; 15+ daily newspapers nationwide.

ties based upon the markets they are in, the competition they face, and the prospects for growth. She has told RCR that she does not expect specific financial figures, but rather a general description of which one of the two properties is likely to generate the best ROI in the short and long term based upon the information that is publicly available.

The two stations up for sale are WCRZ-TV in Midtown and KRVW-TV in Areaville.

The president of RCR assigns you to conduct the market analysis of the proposed acquisitions for McLaren Communication. Your job is to write a thorough, detailed market analysis that concludes with a firm recommendation to McLaren Communications as to which of the radio stations she should buy and why, provided you decide to recommend that she buy one at all. Your report should include,

- a step-by-step discussion of the critical factors that a market analysis includes;
- a comparison of those factors between the two markets under consideration;
- an analysis of what you think those factors will mean in terms of the stations' short and long-term performances and why;
- a final recommendation as to which station McLaren Communications should buy, if either one, and *why* you are making that recommendation based upon the factors you identified in your market analysis.

Midtown*

Midtown is a small community in a rural Midwest state east of the Mississippi River. It lies in hills and forests one hour from two different major metropolitan areas. Signals from some of the media based in those cities reach Midtown.

Historically, the community has had a strong manufacturing and agricultural base of family farms that have provided a solid middle-class lifestyle to its population. However, most of the most affluent members of the community are in the health and financial services industries, which provide only a comparatively small percentage of the jobs in the community.

In recent years, two major manufacturing plants in town have closed as their owners have moved their manufacturing operations overseas, leaving only three still in operation: a chemical manufacturing plant, a textile mill, and a paper mill. Additionally, the consolidation of the agricultural industry has forced a number of local farmers out of business. As a result, the unemployment and poverty rates in the community have risen, and the population has fallen as people have left to look for employment elsewhere. However, the community also is home to a branch campus of the state's flagship university, and it is in a popular recreation area, with numerous state parks, hiking trails, lakes, and rivers.

From a geographic standpoint, Midtown is a small valley bordered on one side by a river and on the other by steep hilly terrain, limiting its ability to grow. The community is connected to each of the two nearby cities by a two-lane highway.

Lifestyle scales have identified the population of Midtown as being dominated by a combination of "Working Towns"—that is "older families, lower-income blue collars" and "Ex-Urban Blues," somewhat younger middle-class blue-collar families in mid-sized towns. Politically, the community is moderately conservative, but not particularly religious.

In terms of media, WCRZ-TV is the only television station in town, although signals reach Midtown from the stations in both of the nearby cities. The community has 15 radio stations, about half of which are owned by major international media corporations. It has one local cable system operator, also the subsidiary of a national company. The cable

---

* All persons, stations, communities, media companies, and data in this case study are completely fictitious. Any similarity to actual individuals or companies is purely coincidental.

system has 80 channels and sells local advertising. Finally, the town has one locally owned daily newspaper, which has been losing circulation and has a household penetration rate below the national average.

Areaville

Areaville is a mid-sized community in the Pacific Northwest that is rapidly transforming itself from a farming town into a small city. It is located 3 hours from the nearest major urban area, and a range of hills between the two communities blocks most of the city's radio and television signals from reaching Areaville. However, some of the TV signals are carried on the Areaville cable system. The community is 3 hours from the sea in a valley dotted with orchards, farms, and small lakes.

Historically, the community has been solidly middle class. It is a university town and has the state's only medical school. Consequently, a large percentage of the town's population works in health care and other professional services. Additionally, in recent years, Areaville has benefited from an ex-urban migration by young professionals, who are moving their families out of the city because they are able to use the community's excellent broadband infrastructure to connect to their clients. Additionally, the pastoral lifestyle and excellent medical care in the area have started attracting media and entertainment professionals from Southern California. The result has been an increase in both the size and affluence of the local population.

The picture is not entirely rosy, however. Despite the recent growth, there are major income disparities in Areaville and its surrounding areas. The rural counties around Areaville have suffered for decades from persistent poverty related to the decline in the farming, mining, and forestry industries once the economic core of the region. None of those industries is expected to recover. Consequently, while median household income is comparatively high, so is the percentage of households living in poverty.

Sociologically, the community is ethnically diverse. Of particular note is its large and growing Hispanic population. Its psychographic profile has been identified as a mix of "Landed Gentry," elite exurban, small-town executives, and young, middle-class town families, "Affluentials" upwardly mobile, white-collar professional suburban families, and "Heartlanders," farmers, rangers, and tenants. The community is politically liberal with strong support for such issues as immigration rights and the environment. Outdoor activities are popular.

In terms of media, the community has 10 radio stations, all but two owned by national media corporations. The local cable system operator is also the subsidiary of a national cable provider. The system is now fully digital, offers almost 200 channels and broadband services, and sells local advertising. The local daily newspaper is owned by a national newspaper chain and has a household penetration rate above the national average.

Additional Sources

In addition to the data provided, you may wish to do your own research, particularly in order to forecast trends. You may wish to consult the following sources, among others:

> *Statistical Abstracts of the United States* [available in print and online]
> *Veronis & Suhler Communications Industry Forecast*
> *Investing in Television*
> National Association of Broadcasters Web Site
> Current books, trade publications and journal articles on the television industry

Case 8.2 Doing Your Own

Select a newspaper, magazine, radio station, local cable-system operator, television station, or Web company in your community or a nearby community. Conduct your own market analysis of its position in the market. Write your report as if you were writing it for a potential investor.

Make sure that your report includes a detailed analysis of the media company you've selected and its market. Address the issues outlined in the chapter. Make a buy/don't buy recommendation to the investor based upon your market analysis and explain the reasons behind your recommendation.

Case 8.3 An Existing Market

Conduct a market analysis of a selected community and the media already serving it. Try to identify an available media market niche in the community that is not being served. Don't overlook opportunities in the business, trade, travel, or society press. Write your market analysis as a business plan for that media opportunity. Discuss each of the important factors in a market analysis in detail.

Case 8.4 Pitching An Idea

Identify a major project that you would like to pursue: an important long-term investigative news story, a film idea, a television series, etc. Do a detailed market analysis for your project addressing the important factors that need to be considered. Then take one of the two following actions:

1. Use the market analysis process to identify a real media company that might be interested in supporting your project. Describe in detail the factors in the company's market that are relevant to your project idea. Explain why you think your project might be appropriate for that company to support, based upon the analyses you've done for your project idea and for your target investor.
2. Visualize yourself as an employee in a real media company, such as a local newspaper, or television station, that might be interested in your project. Use the market analysis process to identify that company's market. Develop an effective approach that you can use with your supervisor in that company to get his or her support for your idea. Your "pitch" should be based upon the market analysis you have done for your project and for the company, and it should explain to your supervisor how the company's market position will be improved, if you are allowed to pursue your idea.

Additional Sources

Sources you may want to consult as you do your research include,

Bacon's Media Directories
Blair's Television and Cable Factbook
Broadcasting and Cable Yearbook
Editor and Publisher Yearbook
National Association of Broadcasters Television Financial Report
Standard Rate & Data
Statistical Abstracts of the United States [available in print and online]
Veronis & Suhler Communications Industry Forecast
The community's Web site
The local Chamber of Commerce

Current books, trade publications and journal articles
National Association of Broadcasters Web site

There are many other resources, directories, fact books, and sources of information that could provide you with valuable information for a market analysis. Ask your librarian for help in locating them.

Case 8.5 Your Career

Conduct an analysis of the short- and long-term labor market for the career you plan to have. Among the questions you should address in your labor market analysis are the following:

External Conditions

- What are the long-term trends for the job/career that interests you? Is it likely to still exist in 10 years? 15 years? 25 years?
- What are the long-term trends for the industry in which that career would place you? What do those trends mean for your short- and long-term career prospects?
- What technologies are on the horizon that might change the industry in which you would be working, for better or worse?
- What technologies are on the horizon that might change the skill requirements for the job and career you want?
- What are the long-term salary trends in your chosen career?
- What are the costs of getting into your chosen career (examples: moving to a strange place; relocating frequently or traveling a lot on the job; working long hours for low wages and few benefits; working nontraditional hours, so that it's hard to have a social life or family; constant job insecurity, etc.)
- How many jobs of the type you want are available on average each year, and how many different companies offer the type of career track you are seeking (buyer concentration)?
- How much competition is there for the type of job/career you want (seller concentration)?
- What kinds of entry-level jobs will help you move into the career track that interests you?
- What types of education, skills, and experiences do employers expect you to have for those entry-level jobs (consumer demand/uses and gratifications)?
- What types of education, skills, and experiences will you need to get your ultimate dream job 5 or 10 years from now?

- What unique skills, talents, and experiences do you have that your competitors for entry-level jobs might not have (product differentiation)?
- How much competition is there for those entry-level jobs, and what skill sets do your colleagues and classmates have that you don't?

Internal Conditions

- Do you have the skill sets required to get an entry-level job on the career track you are seeking?
- Do you have the personality, abilities, and personal attributes that success in your dream career requires? For example, someone who has trouble handling stress or who doesn't like pushing other people in order to get something they need, will not do well as a journalist. A person who is afraid of public speaking will have trouble as an actor. Physical, learning, or other types of disabilities can also be barriers to success in certain jobs and need to be carefully and realistically assessed for their likely impact on your career.
- Are you willing to pay the costs and make the sacrifices you identified in your external-conditions analysis as being required for success in your chosen career?
- Will your career choice allow you to have other things in life that also are important to you such as a family, involvement in the community, and time for hobbies? If not, is your career important enough to you so that it is worth it to you to give up those other things?

Financial Conditions

- What will your financial obligations be on a monthly and annual basis when you start your career? (Calculate rent, food, utilities, car payments, insurance, gas, clothing, student loans, medical bills and health insurance, emergency costs, and any other expenses you may personally face. These are your fixed costs.)
- What variable costs will you have? (Entertainment; vacation, eating out, buying nonessential items).
- Will an entry-level job in this career track pay enough so that you will be able to cover your fixed costs?
- If not, how will you finance the monthly or annual deficit, and what impact will the finance costs of those subsidies have long term on your personal finances?
- What benefits will your employer cover? Will you also need to pay for your own health insurance or medical bills? Does the employer contribute to retirement, or will you need to save money from each paycheck for that?

- Are there hidden costs to the job that will come out of your salary? Will you be expected to use your own car daily on company business? Will business travel be reimbursed only on a fixed cost and not actual cost basis? Will you be expected to pay for your own cell phone but use it for company business? Will you have to pay for child care in order to take the job? Will you have to pay the cost of a long commute to and from work each day in order to find affordable housing or so that your partner or spouse also can work?
- If eventually getting your dream job will require special advanced education or training, will the job generate enough additional salary over the life of your career to justify the educational expense? For example, if you have to take out $100,000 in student loans to earn the masters degree required to be in a job that will never pay much over minimum wage, the investment isn't worth it.

Additional Sources

The following sources may be helpful for this assignment:

- Annual Surveys of Journalism and Mass Communication Graduates. Provides data about the education, skills, qualifications, job-seeking and employment experiences, starting salaries and benefits for journalism and mass-communication graduates throughout the United States since the mid-1980s. Specific information is available by mass communication major, race and gender. Available on line at http://www.grady.uga.edu/service_&_outreach.php?page=frame|http://www.grady.uga.edu/coxcenter/
- Analyze the help-wanted ads in the trade publications and association Web sites that serve the industry in which you want to make your career. Systematically identify where most of the jobs of interest to you are located geographically; what types of companies are hiring; what education, skills, and experience employers are demanding at different levels along your desired career track; and what salary levels are.
- Use community Web sites, U.S. Census data, and other sources to estimate the cost of living in cities where you are likely to apply for jobs.
- Identify and interview someone who currently holds your dream job.
- Interview a senior executive in the type of company for which you would like to work.

9

MARKETING AND RESEARCH

The market analysis chapter discussed how media managers must understand the interaction of supply and demand in the advertising, information, and intellectual markets. Market analysis is central to managerial decision making because it yields information and analysis to use in decision making. Managers need to understand research to identify whether the information or data obtained from a research study for use in market-analysis or other decision-making tasks is of the proper nature and quality. Managers need to understand the basic steps of the research process and the factors to consider when deciding whether a research study was conducted properly and yields the appropriate data to fit the decision being made.

Managers often hire research firms or expect a research director at their media organization to conduct research to solve problems or help in conducting a market analysis. A manager who does not understand the research process or the important factors to consider in evaluating research is at a disadvantage. If a manager cannot evaluate the quality of information used to make a decision, that manager cannot tell whether the appropriate information is being used to solve a problem or make a decision.

Once a manager decides upon the appropriate content changes for a media organization, potential audiences to consume that content, and potential advertisers who seek to reach those audiences, are identified and targeted. Understanding marketing and advertising enables a manager to promote that content effectively to the right audiences and advertisers. It enables the manager to provide the appropriate information to advertisers, so they will purchase time or space on the media outlet to reach the audience.

The goal of this chapter is to encourage you to develop a broad perspective on marketing and research and to develop the habit of following research trends in the media trade press. Many marketing decisions, research questions, methods, and information gathered are common across media organizations. Therefore, the basic types of research questions and methods used by media organizations are discussed.

With the increasing competitiveness and constantly changing technologies of the media industry, marketing and research activities are central to the job of media management. Marketing activities revolve around decisions about the marketing mix or four Ps—*product, pricing, placement* (distribution), and *promotion*. To make these decisions, managers need answers to questions about their customers. For media managers, the two types of customers are consumers or audiences (readers, viewers, or listeners) and advertisers. One way media managers use research is to develop profiles of their audiences to market their space or time to advertisers.

Marketing and Advertising in Today's Media Environment

Marketing is the "process of planning and executing the conception, pricing, promotion, and distribution of ideas, goods, and services to create exchanges that satisfy individual and organizational objectives" (AMA Board, 1985, p. 1). Marketers consider the correct blend and emphasis of marketing mix elements needed to attract and satisfy their primary customers or target segments. These marketing mix decisions are crucial to determining the message content and media placement of advertising.

Advertising's role in the marketing mix is to communicate the value a brand, product, service, or media outlet has to offer to the desired target segment. An advertising campaign is "a series of coordinated advertisements and other promotional efforts that communicate a reasonably cohesive and integrated theme" (O'Guinn, Allen, & Semenik, 2006, p. 12). However, most advertising campaigns would make little sense without the audience's knowledge about the advertised brand or product from previous campaigns. While an ad campaign has a coordinated theme and message for the short term, advertisers recognize that audiences learn about their products from multiple ad campaigns and other sources over the long term.

Consequently, advertisers use integrated brand promotions (IBP) and/or integrated marketing communications (IMC) for promotional planning. *IBP* is defined as,

> The use of many promotional tools, including advertising, in a coordinated manner to build and then maintain brand awareness, identity, and preference.

When marketers combine contests, a Web site, event sponsorship, and point-of-purchase displays with advertising, this creates an integrated brand promotion (O'Guinn et al., 2006, p. 12)

IMC is "the process of using promotional tools in a unified way so that a synergistic communication effect is created" (O'Guinn et al., 2006, p. 38). The shift from IMC to IBP is based on the current thinking that the emphasis should be on the brand itself rather than the communication. The overall focus is to build brand awareness, identity, and ultimately preference. Therefore, coordinated messages must have communication and brand-building effects.

The need for coordinated brand building grew because mass-media audiences became more fragmented and advertisers began using new methods to reach specific audiences or target markets. For example, some have advertised on viral video Web sites such as YouTube.com offering the audience's home-made video content. MasterCard invited consumers online to write copy for its Priceless campaign contest (Viral Marketing, 2006). Brands are integrated into video games, where the player drives a specific make of vehicle throughout the game because an advertiser paid for that make to be featured (McClellan, 2005).

Viral video and video games reach the elusive young male demographic, which is difficult to reach through TV and other traditional media such as radio, newspapers, and magazines. Research enables advertisers and media outlets to assess audience involvement in viral video and video games. A recent study found 150 million or 63% of the U.S. population play video games. Advertisers also use video-game brand placement because research suggests the audience is engaged or involved with the game (McClellan, 2005). Certain advertising agencies measure engagement by ranking broadcast and cable TV networks based on their levels of ad clutter (or how many minutes of ads air per hour), the length in minutes and seconds of advertising pods or commercial breaks in programs, and the number of different elements within those pods or breaks. Presumably, programs with more commercials, breaks, and elements garner less consumer engagement (McClellan, 2006b).

Engagement is important because audiences often multitask when consuming media. On average, U.S. adults participate in 3 additional activities while they surf the Internet and 2.5 activities while watching TV. Advertisers want to know what primary media audiences consume while multitasking and why. TV is still the dominant medium based on usage; 97% of respondents to a media engagement study reported watching TV. The Internet was the second most widely used medium as 92% reported surfing the Web. However, high usage does not necessarily translate into high engagement (McClellan, 2006a). Media managers use research to determine which advertising venues highly engage various target segments.

Research also suggests consumers increased their total media consumption by embracing newer options and technologies without cutting back on traditional media. The study's respondents reported media consumption takes 9 hours, while sleeping consumes 6.8 hours and working 7.5 hours. Yet, 30% complained about the growing number of ads or unwanted interruptions, and "do not want traditional forms of advertising on their cell phones, PDA, or even on the Internet" (McClellan, 2006a, p. 10). Research may help managers determine ways to reach consumers on cell phones or PDAs that will not annoy them.

The growth of cable, direct satellite channels, video on demand, cell phones, PDAs, and the Internet increasingly fragment mass-media audiences. In 2005, cable had a higher primetime household audience share than broadcast networks. Cable had a 53.1 primetime household share (or the percent of households watching divided by the total number of households using television) while the broadcast TV networks had a 46.6 share. ESPN was the top-ranked cable network with a 2.5 rating or number of households watching divided by all TV households.

This fragmentation is evidenced by the fact that the cable network with the largest audience only reached 2.5% of all U.S. TV households. And the network TV audience decline continued from an audience of 46% in 2002, down from 72% a decade earlier (Green, 2002). IBP and IMC increased in importance because advertisers must define and attract smaller, more precise segments of consumers who share similar characteristics.

Fragmentation results in advertisers considering a wider range of options for advertising placement besides those mentioned already including TV screens in airport waiting areas, posters at public events, grocery store cart or floor advertising, subway posters or car cards on buses, trade shows, convention exhibits, and video on demand online. Traditional mass media may offer larger audiences in popular primetime programming and major sporting events such as the Super Bowl. However, media managers must respond and plan based on the reality that advertisers now consider many communication options when deciding where to place advertisements (Katz, 2007).

Positioning involves designing and representing one's product, service, or brand so it occupies a distinctive and valued place in the target consumer's mind relative to other brands (O'Guinn et al., 2006, p. 214). Positioning develops a perceptual space or perception as to how a brand (or newspaper, station, or Web site) is perceived on a variety of dimensions, such as quality or social display value. For example, *The New York Times* positions itself as a high-quality, in-depth, informative paper for educated, sophisticated, affluent readers. Advertisers communicate the position of the brand or product, media or otherwise, using advertising, IBP, and/or IMC to create the desired image in the minds of consumers it targets.

Media develop content to attract a specific target audience, just as manufacturers create products designed to attract a target segment of consumers. Often media products are designed for audiences that advertisers desire to reach (e.g., the TV program *American Idol* targets young-adult viewers). In this case, the advertiser and media manager target the same audience, and the media manager also targets the advertiser by targeting the advertiser's audience. Alternatively, the media manager may accept the audience attracted by the editorial content of the media vehicle and then find advertisers interested in communicating with that audience.

Since the 1960s, the development of marketing, IBP, IMC, and positioning created the need for a new organizational function—marketing research, which enables media managers to discover their audience's needs and wants and determine how best to meet them. Once a manager decides on a change of content, perhaps as the result of a market analysis, that new content must be marketed to audiences and advertisers. Marketing research is conducted to help managers identify their audiences, identify the content those audience might prefer, or provide other information to help in the advertising and marketing process. This chapter discusses the marketing research process, how to develop and design research, and some of the major media research companies.

The Marketing Research Process

It is important to conduct research systematically and objectively to ensure the quality of the information obtained. No manager wants to spend thousands of dollars gathering information unless it accurately reflects reality. *Systematic research* is well planned and organized. All details are outlined in advance of data collection. *Objective research* is void of bias, which appears in many forms but often results from a researcher's preconceived desires or expectations for the outcome of the research study. The Advertising Research Foundation (2003) developed its Guidelines for Market Research to demonstrate how to conduct systematic, objective, and unbiased studies.

Stages of Marketing Research

The marketing research process resembles the research process in other areas of study. It has eight stages.

Research question.   Also referred to as setting research objectives, this stage may concern a particular problem such as, why do consumers buy one product rather than another? Which newspaper design do readers prefer? Some researchers prefer to set objectives rather than state questions. For example, the second question phrased as an objective is, determine the newspaper design readers prefer.

Secondary research review.   A researcher reviews the available information on a topic of interest before conducting research. Often enough data are available to save the time and money necessary for a new research study. Media managers often use secondary research, a fact discussed later in the chapter.

Primary research design.   The researcher develops a plan or *design* for the study. Will the study be qualitative and use intuitive data collection, or quantitative and use specific measurement techniques like surveys? What type of quantitative or qualitative research would be best? Why? The design for the study is driven by the research questions.

Data-collection procedure.   The researcher identifies the specific data needed to answer the research question and creates a plan to appropriately collect the data.

Sampling design.   Due to financial and time constraints, researchers study a subset of the population of interest. This smaller group, a *sample*, must be representative of the population of concern. A design for obtaining a representative sample must be outlined.

Data collection.   The data are collected. This is often the most time consuming and costly part of a research study.

Data processing and analysis.   Researchers typically edit or verify data before analyzing it. Verification reviews the data for completeness and bias. Then the researcher interprets or analyzes the data and enters them into a computer program.

Report writing. Finally, the researcher writes a report that clearly details the study, the results obtained, and how the results answer the research question(s).

Types of Research and Research Questions

Media managers must understand certain basic research concepts to develop objective and systematic research or assess whether they need a research firm. Media research examines variables or factors, defined as phenomena or events measured or manipulated, such as the characteristics of a newspaper's readers or TV program's viewers. A researcher systematically varies independent variables to see how they affect dependent variables or what the researcher wishes to explain. For example, do full- or half-page ads (independent variable: ad size) attract more readership (dependent variable: number of readers who recall information from each different ad size)? The values of the dependent variable are not manipulated, but rather measured or observed. Reliability or a reliable measure is dependable, stable, and consistently gives the same answer over time. Validity or a valid measure actually measures what it is designed to measure (Wimmer & Dominick, 2006). A manager considers all these factors when evaluating the quality of research.

The type of research problem suggests the method to use. Having knowledge of research methods enables managers to select between competing research proposals submitted by outside suppliers (including evaluating the research design, methods, questionnaires, and sampling techniques used) or to design and implement research in house. Managers also must understand and interpret research findings to use the results effectively.

Consider three issues before designing a research study. (a) How much is already known about the problem at hand? (b) How much information is needed about each audience member? (c) How important is it that the study results generalize or apply to other people and situations? The answers direct the researcher to some types of research and not others. The following is a discussion of the different categories of research available and some considerations for choosing any of them. (For more information on research methods, conducting research and analyzing research see sources such as Babbie, 2004, 2005; Keppel & Wickens, 2004; Livingston & Voakes, 2005; Rubin, Palmgreen, & Sypher, 2004; Williams & Monge, 2001; Wimmer & Dominick, 2006; Zikmund & Babin, 2007).

Primary Versus Secondary Research

The researcher conducts *primary research* for a specific purpose and designs it to answer a specific question. *Secondary research* is conducted for purposes other than the researcher's specific purpose, is often cheaper and easier to collect than primary research, more quickly accessible, and provides sufficient, if not perfect, information. For example, many TV stations and advertisers use Nielsen ratings books to evaluate TV program audiences.

Media managers often use secondary research, especially syndicated research, which is used to answer research questions about the audience (e.g., a publication's readership or the surfers of a Web site), the effectiveness of an advertising message (message or evaluative research), and the placement of advertising by advertisers (advertising activity or media planning research). Syndicated research is conducted on an ongoing basis by a specialized firm to serve a group of companies in the industry rather than contracted to meet the needs of one company. Major providers of syndicated research include Nielsen (www.nielsenmedia.com), Arbitron (www.arbitron.com), Mediamark Research Inc. (www.mediamark.com), and Simmons Market Research Bureau (www.smrb.com).

Exploratory, Descriptive, and Causal Research

Exploratory research is conducted when a researcher approaches a relatively new topic and little information is available. Research questions may not be well defined, and many issues of interest may exist that cannot be narrowed for study. As such, exploratory research identifies key variables, issues, or ideas that help the researcher better understand the general problem and define more specific research questions.

A TV network might want to create a new podcasting hub based on its own programming to attract the young male audience. For example, ESPN (espn.go.com) has its PodCenter with sports-themed podcasts and offers subscriptions to watch Major League Baseball games live online. Researchers might test options by speaking to small numbers of young men in a focus group. This allows for free thinking and reveals important ideas that network executives failed to envision. The exploratory research identifies directions for developing podcasting or other options as well as a more focused set of research questions to study. Exploratory research used to generate advertising messages is called *developmental advertising research* (O'Guinn et al., 2006).

Descriptive research describes a group or a situation in detail across a set of variables defined in the research questions. A local newspaper interested in making its Web site relevant to potential young readers might analyze which online content would attract readers ages 18–34 and which content to safely drop without losing its core readers ages 45–64. The newspaper polls these demographic groups to identify what content they prefer and what content it could eliminate or edit on the Web site. Descriptive research helps identify audience segmenting characteristics and estimate those segments' sizes.

Managers usually ask questions that are inherently causal. When a manager considers strategic options, he or she really asks, Which strategies will create or cause the outcome I want? Only causal research can answer questions that pose a tailored question about a strategy causing an observable effect on an outcome—typically audience behavior. A broadcast programming executive expects the decision of when to air a program to affect the size and characteristics of that program's audience and the programs appearing before and after it. Television channel G4 wants to know why its partnership with YouTube.com to promote Star Trek 2.0 (its program where action figures reenact classic episodes of the 1960s TV series), attracted YouTube user-generated content for G4's podcast, "The Daily Nut" on G4TV.com (Deeken, 2006).

Causal research is difficult and expensive. It requires data accumulated over time, allowing for multiple causes to be examined and for competing theories (as to why behavior occurs) to be controlled. No single research project can establish causality. Because business decisions often do not allow time for causal research, media managers usually accept the ability to reliably predict behavior as a replacement for understanding causal relationships.

Designs for Data Collection

Once the researcher defines the problem, reviews secondary data, and decides that primary data collection is necessary, he or she develops a study design. Exploratory research typically uses *qualitative research designs* not reliant on the measurement of variables, but which use subjective or intuitive data collection or analysis (for more information see Esterberg, K., 2002; Iorio, 2004; Lindlof & Taylor, 2002; Wimmer & Dominick, 2006). Qualitative research provides a relatively quick insight on a problem to plan further action. It often uses small convenience samples, rather than large representative samples, so you should not base risky decisions on its use. Qualitative research techniques include focus-group and depth-interview techniques.

A *focus group* usually consists of 8 to 12 people, who represent the population of concern, and is facilitated by a trained moderator. Focus groups provide an open-ended response situation where synergy among the participants enhances the generation of ideas. Discussions typically last between 1½ and 2 hours. Information collected during a focus group is valuable, but it cannot be generalized to the greater population with confidence, because of the small sample size and the unique nature of interaction.

Depth interviews are often unstructured personal interviews where a trained interviewer probes a subject's behavior and feeling for up to 2 hours. Depth interviews generate a great deal of information, often unexpected, for any one individual. However, their problems include small sample size, limited generalizability, and higher cost than focus groups and other data-collection methods.

Descriptive research is often conducted using *quantitative* methods or a description of a phenomenon involving the specific measurement of variables via such methods as surveys or observational methods (Wimmer & Dominick, 2006). Quantitative methods use larger, randomly collected samples, allowing researchers to generalize the results to other people and situations.

The *survey* or *self-report method* asks people to report their behaviors, attitudes, opinions, and characteristics relevant to the managerial problem. A survey consists of administering a questionnaire specially designed to answer the research questions. The questionnaire is administered face to face through a phone interview or Web site, or it is mailed or e-mailed to subjects. Results are then compiled to describe the research problem and potential outcomes.

Surveys are often cross-sectional or performed at one moment in time. A longitudinal study is used when data need to be collected at more than one point in time to evaluate the research question. For example, the NPD Group (www. npd.com) collects information from its Online Panel of more than 2.5 million members who agreed to participate in NPD surveys. TNS NFO collects information from its online panel named MySurvey.com (www.mysurvey.com; also see www.tns-global.com)

Observation does not rely on self-reports, but observes consumer behavior using obtrusive (known to the observed individual) or unobtrusive (unknown to the observed individual) methods. Some widely used observational data-collection methods include scanner data and tracking of Internet users' surfing behavior. Scanner data are used at point-of-purchase sites such as grocery stores to collect information on purchase behavior.

Many grocery chains provide preferred customer cards that are scanned each time a purchase is made. The customer receives a coupon, discount, or other reward when the card is used. Because the customer provided demographic information to the grocer to receive the card, the list of purchases is associated with that individual's demographic profile. This same approach is used online, having browsers register at a Web site, providing demographic and lifestyle preferences, to receive coupons and free downloads or conduct searches.

Content analysis provides an objective and systematic means to investigate media content. It is used to describe message composition and content. For example, content analysis is often used to examine typography, layout, and makeup in newspapers and magazines. It is used to study how the media portray minority groups, differences in news coverage, and the level of violence in TV programming. (See Krippendorff, 2004; Neuendorf, 2002; and Riffe, Lacy, & Fico, 2005 for more information about conducting a content analysis).

The ability of descriptive research to accurately describe a large population relies on two elements of research. First, the sample studied must be randomly selected from the larger population the sample represents to prevent biases related to income, gender, ethnic background, and so on. Every subject should have an equal chance of being selected so no group or age is overrepresented. Random sampling allows researchers to reduce and estimate the probability that the biases exist. Second, a large sample size is needed because the larger a random sample is, the less likely it is to be biased. Most samples should be larger than 400, and a sample of more than 1,000 works well for representing millions of people.

Causal research is performed using laboratory experiments when control over extraneous conditions is important and feasible. For example, the same newspaper lifestyle section is tested, whereby one group of individuals reads one version and a second group reads a second version in a controlled setting without disruptions. This makes it more likely that different reactions to the two sections are because of the lifestyle content and not some external factor. Yet, exposure to the lifestyle section in a laboratory setting is contrived and may differ from reading it at home, resulting in a different or less-than-natural reaction to the section.

Field experiments are conducted in natural settings to minimize the disadvantages of experiments. For example, two versions of a newspaper lifestyle section are tested by delivering one version to residents in one geographic region of a city and a second version in another region. Readers' reactions are monitored in both regions to discover which section was preferred more by which readers. Real-life conditions are present, yet a field experiment lacks researcher control, allowing many factors to influence the outcome. The researcher may never be sure that the readers' reactions varied only because of differences in the two lifestyle sections.

An experimental design isolates the cause-effect relationship between the managerial factor of concern (the independent variable) and the desired audience behavioral outcome (the dependent variable) to have internal validity. When an experiment has internal validity, the probability is high that only the independent variable caused the dependent variable to change. An experiment has external validity if its results can be generalized to other situations and people. To increase the likelihood of external validity, randomly select the sample used in the experiment from the larger population.

You cannot have perfect internal and external validity in the same experiment. Internal validity requires control over all factors extraneous to the independent and dependent variables of concern. Controlled lab situations enhance internal validity, but decrease external validity by removing outside factors. External validity requires that extraneous variables not be controlled as in field experiments. However, once extraneous variables are allowed to fluctuate, internal validity suffers. There is always a trade-off between internal and external validity, so the research objectives should guide the balance between the two.

Basic Versus Applied Research

Basic research identifies the general principles of practice and answers general questions for media managers. For example, a question such as, "Which type of advertising strategy creates a more positive attitude toward the advertised brand: comparative or single-sided?" is best answered using a basic research approach. This question appears specific, but it is general because the results of a study designed to answer this question could provide information to apply to a variety of brands, product categories, or advertising media. Basic research helps a manager develop principles of practice to use over time.

Applied research is conducted to obtain information for a specific decision in a unique situation. For example, an online newspaper in New York might conduct a study to identify its readers' reactions to either publishing in a commemorative edition archival photos of the

New York Yankees and New York Mets baseball teams or making the photos available online. Applied research takes fewer resources than basic research and answers the specific question at hand, but is of limited use in other situations.

Types of Applied Media Research

Media companies ask similar applied research questions regardless of the nature of the company. The following discusses five basic types of applied media research, including how the information gained is used by advertisers and how it is used to market the media company.

Audience Research: Secondary Data

Audience research examines the characteristics of present and potential target audiences. A company can perform primary audience research or use the many secondary, syndicated sources of audience data. Audience research often identifies the demographic, geographic, and psychographic characteristics of potential audiences. Demographic characteristics include age, education, gender, race, marital status, occupation, and income. Audiences are segmented by geographics including region of the country, state, city, or neighborhood. Geodemographic segmentation uses data from the U.S. Census Bureau and zip codes to identify neighborhoods around the country that share demographic characteristics. For example, the American Dream segment comprises upwardly mobile ethnic minorities found in metropolitan neighborhoods while the Rural Industria segment comprises young families with one or both parents working at low-wage jobs in small towns (O'Guinn et al., pp. 220–221).

Psychographics describe the individual's lifestyle, activities, interests, and opinions to provide insights into consumers' motivations (O'Guinn et al., 2006). The latest VALS (values and lifestyles) typology divides audience members into eight categories based on demographic and psychographic profiles. VALS categorizes consumers by resources (including age, income, education, intellectualism, novelty-seeking, innovativeness, impulsiveness, leadership, vanity, self-confidence, and energy level) and primary motivations (or motivated by ideals or guided by knowledge and principles; achievement or seeking products and services that demonstrate success to their peers; or self-expression or desiring social or physical activity, risk, and variety). The VALS typology and survey are online (www.sric-bi.com/VALS/). The Lifestyle Market Analyst (www.srds.com/frontMatter/ips/lifestyle/) provides demographic and psychographic data for cities and counties nationwide and lifestyle profiles of various consumer interest and demographic groups. (See pp. 378–381.)

Managers of media outlets should learn how advertisers use secondary data to develop effective ways to sell time or space to advertisers. Advertisers and media planners analyze secondary data to decide how to spend an advertising budget, how much their competitors spend in major media, how many in the target audience should see the ad, and where and when to place the ads to effectively reach the targeted audience. The media planner analyzes secondary data to select vehicles in which to place the ads (e.g., *The New York Times* is a vehicle in the newspaper medium). The media buyer purchases time and space in the vehicles that efficiently reach the target audience. Media firms use these same secondary data to identify their audiences and those of competing media outlets.

Using audience research. Simmons Market Research Bureau (SMRB; www.smrb.com) and Mediamark Research Inc. (MRI; www.media-mark.com, www. mriplus.com) report usage rates of national media and brands to identify heavy, medium, and light users of a product. The information allows advertisers and media managers to define a target segment by demographics, geographics, and media-usage habits. A Public Broadcasting System (PBS) station manager could use MRI data to identify and describe the target segment of major contributors (or U.S. Adults Who Contributed to PBS or public TV or radio—see Table 9.1).

The "Total Adults" column and "All" row show 216,971,000 adults in the United States. The next column and "All" row show the projected estimate of 8,723,000 adults who contributed to PBS in the last 12 months. The first "Contributions" column and the "Educ: graduated college plus" row show an estimated 4,098,000 of contributors to PBS earned a college degree. The "% Down" column under "Contributions" shows that 46.97% of contributors have a college degree (or 4,098,000/8,723,000 PBS contributors = 46.97 percent). The "% Across" column shows that 7.50% of all college graduates contribute to PBS (or 4,098,000 contributors with college degrees/54,599,000 total U.S. college graduates = 7.50%). (An asterisk next to a column indicates fewer than 50 subjects responded, so consider these results cautiously.)

The "Index" column shows an index of 187 for PBS contributors who graduated from college. Many secondary research reports use indexes so they are now explained. An index shows a relationship between two percentages, as shown in the following formula for calculating index numbers (Sissors & Baron, 2002, p. 164):

$$\text{Index number} = \frac{\text{Percentage of users in a demographic segment}}{\text{Percentage of population in the same segment}} \times 100$$

Therefore, the 187 index represents the 46.97% of major contributors who have a college degree divided by 25.16% of all U.S. adults who are college graduates (or 54,599,000 total U.S. adults with a college degree divided by the total of 216,971,000 adults in the United States), rounded and multiplied by 100 or,

$$187 = \frac{\text{46.97\% of PBS contributors who earned a college degree or more education}}{\text{25.16\% of U.S. adults who earned a college degree or more education}} \times 100$$

Sissors and Baron (2002) said indexes provide a common method for comparison. An index of 100 is equal to the average, 150 is 50% above average, and 70 is 30% below average. Therefore, the 187 index tells us that college graduates are 87% more likely than the average U.S. adult to be PBS contributors. Index numbers are viewed as central tendencies such as averages or means. An index, like an average, describes the group as a whole rather than one person. "It is also important to note that index numbers between 90 and 110 are generally insignificant" (Sissors & Baron, 2002, p. 167). Therefore, the Mediamark data suggest that adults who are college graduates (with an index of 87) or earned post-graduate degrees (with an index of 256) are more likely to contribute to PBS.

Demographic or other characteristics having indexes over 100 are not necessarily the best to select. Consider segment size, level of use or consumption, and other primary or secondary research when selecting a target segment. Sometimes several categories of the same demographic or characteristic are included in the target segment. For example, the age 65 or older group has the highest index of 181 and comprises 29.25% of PBS contributors. Yet, if the manager only targeted person 65 years and older, most major contributors would be omitted. By adding contributors ages 55 to 64 (23.34% with an index of 174) the total percentage of contributors targeted would be 52.59% (29.25% + 23.34%—only mutually exclusive categories within the same characteristic such as

TABLE 9.1 Mediamark Data on Contributions to Public TV/Radio

Mediamark Research Inc., Spring 2006	Total Adults		Contributions to Public TV/Radio: Contributed to PBS Past 12 Months			
* Based on fewer than 50 respondents	(000)	'(000)	% Down	% Across	Index	
All	216971	8723	100.00	4.02	100	0
Men	104577	3754	43.04	3.59	89	1
Women	112394	4969	56.96	4.42	110	2
Household Heads	134395	5603	64.23	4.17	104	3
Homemakers	134809	5771	66.16	4.28	106	4
Educ: graduated college plus	54599	4098	46.97	7.50	187	5
Educ: attended college	59077	2096	24.03	3.55	88	6
Educ: graduated high school	69062	2041	23.39	2.95	73	7
Educ: did not graduate HS	34233 *	489	5.60	1.43	36	*8
Educ: post graduate	17918	1841	21.11	10.28	256	9
Educ: no college	103295	2530	29.00	2.45	61	10
Age 18–24	28021 *	399	4.58	1.42	35	*11
Age 25–34	39430	665	7.62	1.69	42	12
Age 35–44	43656	1293	14.82	2.96	74	13
Age 45–54	41680	1779	20.39	4.27	106	14
Age 55–64	29077	2036	23.34	7.00	174	15
Age 65+	35108	2551	29.25	7.27	181	16
Adults 18–34	67451	1064	12.20	1.58	39	17
Adults 18–49	133225	3325	38.12	2.50	62	18

Adults 25–54	124765		42.83	2.99	74	19
Men 18–34	33836		6.45	1.66	41	20
Men 18–49	66218		16.50	2.17	54	21
Men 25–54	61584		17.33	2.45	61	22
Women 18–34	33615		5.75	1.49	37	23
Women 18–49	67007		21.62	2.81	70	24
Women 25–54	63181		25.51	3.52	88	25
Employment: working full time	114836		45.11	3.43	85	26
Employment: working part time	24862		10.44	3.66	91	27
Employment: not working	77272		44.45	5.02	125	28
Occupation: professional and related occupations	28822		18.66	5.65	141	29
Occupation: management, business and financial operations	20643		12.96	5.48	136	30
Occupation: sales and office occupations	34842		10.73	2.69	67	31
Occupation: natural resources, construction and maintenance occup.	15072	*	3.75	2.17	54	*32
Occupation: other employed	40320		9.44	2.04	51	33
Wage earner status: sole earner	39966		17.32	3.78	94	34
HHI $150,000+	17148		15.09	7.68	191	35
HHI $75–149,999	53536		34.26	5.58	139	36
HHI $60–74,999	24239		9.86	3.55	88	37
HHI $50–59,999	18892		7.76	3.58	89	38

(continued)

TABLE 9.1 Mediamark Data on Contributions to Public TV/Radio

Mediamark Research Inc., Spring 2006	Total Adults	Contributions to Public TV/Radio: Contributed to PBS Past 12 Months				
HHI $40–49,999	20910	722	8.27	3.45	86	39
HHI $30–39,999	23035	745	8.55	3.24	80	40
HHI $20–29,999	23927	693	7.94	2.90	72	41
HHI <$20,000	35284	722	8.27	2.05	51	42
Census Region: Northeast	41258	1732	19.86	4.20	104	43
Census Region: South	78621	2454	28.13	3.12	78	44
Census Region: North Central	48848	1984	22.74	4.06	101	45
Census Region: West	48244	2554	29.28	5.29	132	46
Mktg Region: New England	10827	656	7.52	6.06	151	47
Mktg Region: Mid Atlantic	34555	1438	16.48	4.16	103	48
Mktg Region: East Central	27791	1013	11.62	3.65	91	49
Mktg Region: West Central	32702	1349	15.46	4.12	103	50
Mktg Region: Southeast	43334	1274	14.61	2.94	73	51
Mktg Region: Southwest	25421	686	7.86	2.70	67	52
Mktg Region: Pacific	42342	2307	26.44	5.45	136	53
County size A	89650	4120	47.23	4.60	114	54
County size B	64984	2723	31.22	4.19	104	55
County size C	31480	1246	14.29	3.96	98	56
County size D	30858	* 634	7.26	2.05	51	57
MSA central city	72989	3141	36.01	4.30	107	58
MSA suburban	102756	4590	52.61	4.47	111	59

Non-MSA	41226		992	11.37	2.41	60	60
Marital status: never married	53847		1285	14.73	2.39	59	61
Marital status: now married	122471		5691	65.24	4.65	116	62
Marital status: legally separated/widowed/divorced	40654		1747	20.03	4.30	107	63
Marital status: engaged	10382	*	208	2.39	2.01	50	*64
Parent	73996		2088	23.94	2.82	70	65
Working Parent	56742		1669	19.13	2.94	73	66
HH size: 1	29992		1522	17.45	5.08	126	67
HH size: 2	71150		3653	41.88	5.13	128	68
HH size: 3–4	82128		2829	32.44	3.45	86	69
HH size: 5+	33702		719	8.24	2.13	53	70
Children: any	89253		2571	29.48	2.88	72	71
Children: 1	35849		1031	11.81	2.87	72	72
Children: 2	32426		1013	11.61	3.12	78	73
Children: 3+	20979		528	6.05	2.52	63	74
Child age: <2 years	17085	*	385	4.41	2.25	56	*75
Child age: 2–5 years	32628		784	8.98	2.40	60	76
Child age: 6–11 years	40728		1190	13.64	2.92	73	77
Child age: 12–17 years	43107		1314	15.06	3.05	76	78
Race: White	168065		7571	86.79	4.50	112	79
Race: Black/African American	24815		755	8.65	3.04	76	80
Race: American Indian or Alaska Native	2603	*	49	0.56	1.88	47	*81

(continued)

TABLE 9.1 Mediamark Data on Contributions to Public TV/Radio

Mediamark Research Inc., Spring 2006	Total Adults		Contributions to Public TV/Radio: Contributed to PBS Past 12 Months				
Race: Asian	6312	*	145	1.67	2.30	57	*82
Race: Other	16965	*	243	2.78	1.43	36	*83
Race: White only	165897		7537	86.40	4.54	113	84
Race: Black/African American only	24278		720	8.25	2.96	74	85
Race: Other race/Multiple classifications	26795		467	5.35	1.74	43	86
Spanish speaking (in an english language capable HH)	29810		709	8.13	2.38	59	87
Home owned	152401		7334	84.08	4.81	120	88
Media Quintile/Tercile Codes: Outdoor I (Heavy)	43400		1558	17.86	3.59	89	89
Media Quintile/Tercile Codes: Outdoor II	43394		1983	22.73	4.57	114	90
Media Quintile/Tercile Codes: Outdoor III	43397		1892	21.69	4.36	108	91
Media Quintile/Tercile Codes: Outdoor IV	43394		1962	22.49	4.52	112	92
Media Quintile/Tercile Codes: Outdoor V (Light)	43386		1328	15.22	3.06	76	93
Media Quintile/Tercile Codes: Magazines I (Heavy)	43355		1956	22.42	4.51	112	94
Media Quintile/Tercile Codes: Magazines II	43396		2141	24.55	4.93	123	95
Media Quintile/Tercile Codes: Magazines III	43409		1904	21.83	4.39	109	96
Media Quintile/Tercile Codes: Magazines IV	43399		1577	18.08	3.63	90	97
Media Quintile/Tercile Codes: Magazines V (Light)	43413		1145	13.12	2.64	66	98

Media Quintile/Tercile Codes: Newspaper I (Heavy)	43392	2852	32.69	6.57	163	99
Media Quintile/Tercile Codes: Newspaper II	43394	2256	25.86	5.20	129	100
Media Quintile/Tercile Codes: Newspaper III	43399	1405	16.10	3.24	81	101
Media Quintile/Tercile Codes: Newspaper IV	43392	1257	14.41	2.90	72	102
Media Quintile/Tercile Codes: Newspaper V (Light)	43394	954	10.93	2.20	55	103
Media Quintile/Tercile Codes: Radio I (Heavy)	43376	1478	16.94	3.41	85	104
Media Quintile/Tercile Codes: Radio II	43407	1810	20.76	4.17	104	105
Media Quintile/Tercile Codes: Radio III	43402	1894	21.71	4.36	109	106
Media Quintile/Tercile Codes: Radio IV	43389	1922	22.03	4.43	110	107
Media Quintile/Tercile Codes: Radio V (Light)	43397	1619	18.55	3.73	93	108
Media Quintile/Tercile Codes: TV (total) I (Heavy)	43364	1434	16.44	3.31	82	109
Media Quintile/Tercile Codes: TV (total) II	43392	1898	21.76	4.37	109	110
Media Quintile/Tercile Codes: TV (total) III	43411	1794	20.57	4.13	103	111
Media Quintile/Tercile Codes: TV (total) IV	43397	1767	20.26	4.07	101	112
Media Quintile/Tercile Codes: TV (total) V (Light)	43407	1829	20.97	4.21	105	113
Media Quintile/Tercile Codes: Internet I (Heavy)	43372	2078	23.82	4.79	119	114
Media Quintile/Tercile Codes: Internet II	43411	2113	24.22	4.87	121	115
Media Quintile/Tercile Codes: Internet III	43407	1778	20.38	4.10	102	116
Media Quintile/Tercile Codes: Internet IV	43394	1573	18.03	3.62	90	117

(continued)

TABLE 9.1 Mediamark Data on Contributions to Public TV/Radio

Mediamark Research Inc., Spring 2006	Total Adults		Contributions to Public TV/Radio: Contributed to PBS Past 12 Months				
Media Quintile/Tercile Codes: Internet V (Light)	43387		1181	13.54	2.72	68	118
Media Quintile/Tercile Codes: Yellow Pages I (Heavy)	31994		1326	15.21	4.15	103	119
Media Quintile/Tercile Codes: Yellow Pages II	31940		1532	17.56	4.80	119	120
Media Quintile/Tercile Codes: Yellow Pages III (Light)	31949		1408	16.14	4.41	110	121
Radio Cume: Wkday 6–10A	111343		4813	55.18	4.32	108	122
Radio Cume: Wkday 10A–3P	81096		3125	35.83	3.85	96	123
Radio Cume: Wkday 3–7P	96647		3951	45.29	4.09	102	124
Radio Cume: Wkday 7P–Midnight	34754		1258	14.43	3.62	90	125
Radio Cume: Wkday Midnight-6A	12381		405	4.64	3.27	81	126
Radio formats: Adult Contemporary	39467		1304	14.95	3.30	82	127
Adult Standards	4088	*	261	2.99	6.38	159	*128
All News	10938		902	10.34	8.24	205	129
All Talk	8310		486	5.57	5.85	145	130
Alternative	16268		543	6.23	3.34	83	131
CHR	36897		802	9.20	2.17	54	132
Classic Hits	8546	*	276	3.16	3.23	80	*133
Classic Rock	21344		675	7.74	3.16	79	134
Classical	7224		1157	13.26	16.01	398	135

Country	49894		1275	14.61	2.55	64	136
Easy Listening	904	*	55	0.63	6.11	152	*137
Ethnic	945	*	47	0.54	5.00	124	*138
Gospel	4841	*	90	1.03	1.85	46	*139
Hispanic	14558	*	369	4.23	2.53	63	*140
Jack	4785	*	206	2.36	4.30	107	*141
Jazz	8561		535	6.13	6.25	155	142
Mexican/Tejano/Ranchera (subset of Hispanic format)	6478	*	186	2.13	2.86	71	*143
News/Talk	24724		1972	22.61	7.98	198	144
Oldies	21183		913	10.47	4.31	107	145
Public	6574		833	9.54	12.66	315	146
Religious	13761		447	5.13	3.25	81	147
Rock	21826		553	6.34	2.53	63	148
Soft Adult Contemporary	13962		538	6.17	3.85	96	149
Spanish AC (subset of Hispanic format)	3709	*	120	1.37	3.23	80	*150
Sports	9703		519	5.95	5.35	133	151
Tropical (subset of Hispanic format)	2054	*	23	0.27	1.13	28	*152
Urban	29501		703	8.06	2.38	59	153
Variety/Other	18737		576	6.60	3.07	76	154
ABC Advantage	13375		445	5.11	3.33	83	155
ABC Daytime Direction	30816		1642	18.83	5.33	133	156
ABC ESPN	5172	*	234	2.68	4.53	113	*157
ABC FM Connection	15608	*	410	4.70	2.62	65	*158
ABC Hot FM	28145		932	10.69	3.31	82	159

(continued)

TABLE 9.1 Mediamark Data on Contributions to Public TV/Radio

Mediamark Research Inc., Spring 2006	Total Adults		Contributions to Public TV/Radio: Contributed to PBS Past 12 Months				
ABC Information Network/ABC Information Weekend Network	9281		674	7.73	7.27	181	160
ABC Morning News	26686		1527	17.50	5.72	142	161
ABC Music	5684	*	175	2.01	3.09	77	*162
ABC News/Talk Production	19041		1234	14.14	6.48	161	163
ABC Prime Access	25600		1392	15.96	5.44	135	164
ABC Prime Reach	26686		1527	17.50	5.72	142	165
ABC Urban Advantage	11141	*	348	3.98	3.12	78	*166
ABC Young Adult	30295		842	9.65	2.78	69	167
AURN (American Urban Radio Network)	20137		533	6.11	2.65	66	168
Bloomberg Network	5120		435	4.99	8.50	211	169
Dial Global Complete FM Network	59602		1885	21.61	3.16	79	170
Dial Global Contemporary Network	42243		1305	14.97	3.09	77	171
Dial Global News & Information Network	32909		1168	13.39	3.55	88	172
Dow Jones Money Report	3040	*	234	2.68	7.69	191	*173
Dow Jones/Wall Street Journal Reports	11622		867	9.93	7.46	185	174
NPR (Nat'l Public Radio)	11753		1695	19.43	14.42	359	175
Premiere Diamond	31797		1023	11.73	3.22	80	176
Premiere Emerald	30097		620	7.11	2.06	51	177
Premiere Female Focus	13750		506	5.80	3.68	92	178
Premiere Fox News	8495		481	5.51	5.66	141	179

Premiere Male Focus		29711	710	8.14	2.39	59	180
Premiere Mediabase Network		51235	1242	14.24	2.42	60	181
Premiere Morning Drive AM		21356	1245	14.27	5.83	145	182
#Premiere Morning Drive FM	*	9813	227	2.60	2.31	58	*183
Premiere Pearl Network		27703	923	10.58	3.33	83	184
Premiere Sapphire		21787	1105	12.66	5.07	126	185
#Premiere Select		17224	640	7.34	3.72	92	186
#Premiere Spectrum		35587	915	10.48	2.57	64	187
Premiere Urban One		16393	380	4.35	2.32	58	188
#Premiere Urban Two	*	9961	236	2.70	2.37	59	*189
Wall Street Journal Report		8828	657	7.53	7.44	185	190
Westwood: CBS FM		24170	1077	12.34	4.45	111	191
Westwood: CBS MarketWatch		12261	752	8.63	6.14	153	192
Westwood: CBS Mix Weekend		58424	2529	28.99	4.33	108	193
Westwood: CBS News Max		26145	1334	15.30	5.10	127	194
Westwood: CBS News Primetime		30006	1490	17.08	4.97	124	195
Westwood: CNN News Reach		29359	1524	17.47	5.19	129	196
Westwood: Digital 24/7 Music	*	7133	269	3.09	3.77	94	*197
Westwood: FM Weekend Source		29459	731	8.37	2.48	62	198
Westwood: Metro Network		106313	4518	51.80	4.25	106	199
Westwood: NBC Lite FM		19895	822	9.42	4.13	103	200
Westwood: NBC Lite FM Max		12709	359	4.12	2.83	70	201
Westwood: NeXt FM		22989	533	6.11	2.32	58	202

(continued)

TABLE 9.1 Mediamark Data on Contributions to Public TV/Radio

Mediamark Research Inc., Spring 2006	Total Adults			Contributions to Public TV/Radio: Contributed to PBS Past 12 Months			
Westwood: Power FM	20972		415	4.75	1.98	49	203
Westwood: Power FM Max	10476	*	285	3.27	2.72	68	*204
Look at or used/past 30 days: America Online (AOL)	36095		1777	20.38	4.92	122	205
Look at or used/past 30 days: AT&T online service	4302	*	226	2.59	5.24	130	*206
Look at or used/past 30 days: Bell South	5331	*	212	2.44	3.98	99	*207
Look at or used/past 30 days: Earthlink	7038		538	6.17	7.64	190	208
Look at or used/past 30 days: MSN (Microsoft Network)	31754		1336	15.32	4.21	105	209
Look at or used/past 30 days: NetZero/Juno	5000	*	302	3.46	6.04	150	*210
Look at or used/past 30 days: SBC Yahoo!	30724		1598	18.32	5.20	129	211
Look at or used/past 30 days: Verizon Online	9997		392	4.49	3.92	97	212
Look at or used/past 30 days: Other Online Service	44547		1821	20.87	4.09	102	213
Web Sites visited in last 30 days: abc.com	7191		373	4.28	5.19	129	214
Web Sites visited in last 30 days: aol.com	27349		1385	15.88	5.06	126	215
Web Sites visited in last 30 days: Ask.com (formerly askjeeves)	8571		395	4.52	4.60	114	216
Web Sites visited in last 30 days: bankrate.com	2131	*	161	1.84	7.55	188	*217
Web Sites visited in last 30 days: cbs.com	5899	*	222	2.54	3.76	93	*218
Web Sites visited in last 30 days: CBS sportsline.com	4402	*	242	2.78	5.50	137	*219
Web Sites visited in last 30 days: CNET.com	3515	*	220	2.52	6.26	156	*220

Web Sites visited in last 30 days: CNN.com	16755		1001	11.47	5.97	149	221
Web Sites visited in last 30 days: disney.com	8566	*	283	3.25	3.31	82	*222
Web Sites visited in last 30 days: ESPN.com	16669	*	744	8.53	4.47	111	223
Web Sites visited in last 30 days: Excite.com	2193	*	112	1.28	5.09	127	*224
Web Sites visited in last 30 days: fox.com	5585	*	257	2.95	4.60	114	*225
Web Sites visited in last 30 days: #foxsports.com	3713	*	168	1.92	4.51	112	*226
Web Sites visited in last 30 days: foxnews.com	10321		462	5.29	4.47	111	227
Web Sites visited in last 30 days: google.com	85946		4421	50.68	5.14	128	228
Web Sites visited in last 30 days: hotmail.com	28894		978	11.21	3.38	84	229
Web Sites visited in last 30 days: iVillage.com	1763	*	65	0.75	3.71	92	*230
Web Sites visited in last 30 days: Lycos.com	2333	*	109	1.26	4.69	117	*231
Web Sites visited in last 30 days: monster.com	11992	*	251	2.87	2.09	52	*232
Web Sites visited in last 30 days: msnbc.com	11851		678	7.78	5.72	142	233
Web Sites visited in last 30 days: msn.com	37243		1571	18.01	4.22	105	234
Web Sites visited in last 30 days: MTV.com	5669	*	193	2.21	3.41	85	*235
Web Sites visited in last 30 days: nbc.com	6456		402	4.61	6.23	155	236
Web Sites visited in last 30 days: Netscape.com	8542		470	5.39	5.50	137	237
Web Sites visited in last 30 days: nytimes.com	5569		646	7.40	11.60	288	238
Web Sites visited in last 30 days: pbs.org	6075		831	9.53	13.68	340	239
Web Sites visited in last 30 days: USA Today.com	4893	*	310	3.56	6.34	158	*240
Web Sites visited in last 30 days: Weather.com	40459		2041	23.40	5.04	125	241

(continued)

TABLE 9.1 Mediamark Data on Contributions to Public TV/Radio

Mediamark Research Inc., Spring 2006	Total Adults		Contributions to Public TV/Radio: Contributed to PBS Past 12 Months				
Web Sites visited in last 30 days: weatherbug.com	7613	*	287	3.29	3.77	94	*242
Web Sites visited in last 30 days: WebMD.com	7689		423	4.85	5.51	137	243
Web Sites visited in last 30 days: wsj.com	1700	*	149	1.71	8.78	218	*244
Web Sites visited in last 30 days: Yahoo.com	85153		3782	43.36	4.44	110	245
Web Sites visited in last 30 days: ZD Net.com	1998	*	201	2.30	10.05	250	*246
TV Avg 1/2 hr aud - Wkday 7–9A	25692		1084	12.42	4.22	105	247
TV Avg 1/2 hr aud - Wkday 9A–Noon	25693		815	9.34	3.17	79	248
TV Avg 1/2 hr aud - Wkday Noon–4P	30499		1020	11.70	3.35	83	249
TV Avg 1/2 hr aud - Wkday 4–6P	43504		1567	17.97	3.60	90	250
TV Avg 1/2 hr aud - Wkday 6–7P	70007		2936	33.66	4.19	104	251
TV Avg 1/2 hr aud - Wkday 7–8P	87890		3589	41.14	4.08	102	252
TV Avg 1/2 hr aud - Wkday 8–11P	101351		4169	47.80	4.11	102	253
TV Avg 1/2 hr aud - Wkday 11–11:30P	59994		2437	27.94	4.06	101	254
TV Avg 1/2 hr aud - Wkday 11:30P–1A	28931		1128	12.93	3.90	97	255
TV Avg 1/2 hr aud - Wkday 1–6A	5407	*	225	2.57	4.15	103	*256
TV: Primetime Cume	181198		7361	84.39	4.06	101	257
Adventure/Westerns/Scifi -Prime	5154	*	222	2.54	4.30	107	*258
Auto Racing-Specials	11898	*	421	4.82	3.54	88	*259
Awards-Specials	10608		611	7.01	5.76	143	260
Baseball Specials	36722		2172	24.90	5.91	147	261

Basketball-Wkend-College	25661		1583	18.14	6.17	153	262
Basketball Specials-College	16200		1023	11.72	6.31	157	263
Basketball Specials-Pro	21213		1159	13.28	5.46	136	264
Comedy/Variety	8450	*	324	3.71	3.83	95	*265
Daytime Dramas	6414	*	229	2.63	3.57	89	*266
Daytime Talk/Variety	4856	*	347	3.98	7.15	178	*267
Documentary/Informational Prime	11153		624	7.15	5.60	139	268
Early Eve Network News - Mon-Fri	15032		870	9.97	5.79	144	269
Early Eve Network News - Wkend	15033		865	9.92	5.75	143	270
Early Morning News	16379		681	7.80	4.15	103	271
Early Morning Talk/Information/News	15904		778	8.92	4.89	122	272
Entertainment Specials	12106		772	8.85	6.38	159	273
Feature Films - Prime	4856	*	183	2.10	3.78	94	*274
Football - College Wkend	30900		1581	18.13	5.12	127	275
Football - Pro Wkend	46675		1958	22.45	4.20	104	276
Football Bowl Games - Specials	21515		1112	12.75	5.17	129	277
Football Specials - Pro	41507		1839	21.08	4.43	110	278
Game Shows - Prime	6963	*	126	1.45	1.81	45	*279
General Drama - Prime	12470		632	7.25	5.07	126	280
Golf	4756		392	4.49	8.24	205	281
Gymnastics	5448		483	5.53	8.86	220	282
Horse Racing	11896		969	11.10	8.14	203	283
Late Night Network News/Info M–F	3889	*	319	3.66	8.21	204	*284
Late Night Talk/Variety	6614		362	4.15	5.48	136	285

(continued)

TABLE 9.1 Mediamark Data on Contributions to Public TV/Radio

Mediamark Research Inc., Spring 2006	Total Adults	Contributions to Public TV/Radio: Contributed to PBS Past 12 Months				
News - Specials	17195	1201	13.77	6.98	174	286
Pageants - Specials	9991	548	6.28	5.48	136	287
Private Detective/Suspense/Mystery/Police-Prime	17089	748	8.58	4.38	109	288
Reality-based	8154 *	262	3.00	3.21	80	*289
Situation Comedies - Prime	8255 *	293	3.36	3.55	88	*290
Skating - Specials	5657	636	7.29	11.24	280	291
Soccer	6962	373	4.27	5.35	133	292
Sports Anthologies - Wkend	9558	492	5.64	5.15	128	293
Sunday News/Interview	7148	521	5.97	7.29	181	294
Syndicated Adult General	6147 *	256	2.93	4.16	103	*295
Tennis	9489	1042	11.94	10.98	273	296
Track & Field	5698	445	5.10	7.81	194	297
Cable available in neighborhood	194066	8125	93.15	4.19	104	298
HH subscribes to cable	128137	5652	64.79	4.41	110	299
HH subscribes to digital cable	55154	2488	28.52	4.51	112	300
HH has satellite dish	52662	1632	18.71	3.10	77	301
DirecTV	26911	794	9.10	2.95	73	302
Dish Network	24566	794	9.10	3.23	80	303
Other satellite dish programming company	809 *	54	0.62	6.67	166	*304
Any premium channel viewing/past 30 days	68693	2522	28.91	3.67	91	305

Watched any pay per-view/past 12 mos	35192		1141	13.08	3.24	81	306
Watched any Video-On-Demand/past 12 mos	18204		759	8.70	4.17	104	307
Any cable viewing/past wk	172055		6912	79.24	4.02	100	308
Heavy cable viewing/15+ hrs past wk	132001		5138	58.90	3.89	97	309
HH has a Digital Video Recorder (DVR)	24308		1083	12.41	4.45	111	310
ABC Family Channel	52715		1876	21.51	3.56	89	311
#Adult Swim	12087	*	297	3.40	2.45	61	*312
A&E	52369		2715	31.12	5.18	129	313
AMC (American Movie Classics)	35783		1801	20.64	5.03	125	314
Animal Planet	55291		2119	24.29	3.83	95	315
BBC America	10149		735	8.42	7.24	180	316
BET (Black Entertainment TV)	22085		577	6.62	2.61	65	317
#Biography Channel	20879		991	11.36	4.75	118	318
Bloomberg Television	3378	*	276	3.17	8.17	203	*319
Bravo	22271		1190	13.64	5.34	133	320
Cartoon Network	26021		712	8.16	2.73	68	321
CMT (Country Music Television)	23937		677	7.76	2.83	70	322
CNBC	35446		1834	21.02	5.17	129	323
CNN	73305		3679	42.18	5.02	125	324
Comedy Central	48028		1765	20.23	3.67	91	325
Court TV	26691		987	11.32	3.70	92	326
#CSTV (College Sports Television)	2258	*	32	0.37	1.43	36	*327
Discovery Channel	74985		3176	36.41	4.24	105	328

(continued)

TABLE 9.1 Mediamark Data on Contributions to Public TV/Radio

Mediamark Research Inc., Spring 2006	Total Adults			Contributions to Public TV/Radio: Contributed to PBS Past 12 Months			
Discovery Health	19391		719	8.25	3.71	92	329
Discovery Home	9341		422	4.83	4.51	112	330
Discovery Times	6869		332	3.80	4.83	120	331
Disney Channel	32864		1120	12.84	3.41	85	332
DIY (Do It Yourself Network)	8982		398	4.56	4.43	110	333
E!	35749		1323	15.17	3.70	92	334
ESPN	60764		2602	29.83	4.28	107	335
ESPN 2	38435		1428	16.37	3.72	92	336
ESPN Classic	15125		423	4.85	2.80	70	337
ESPNews	23243		831	9.53	3.58	89	338
Fine Living	3007	*	139	1.59	4.63	115	*339
FitTV	2582	*	40	0.45	1.54	38	*340
Flix	2700	*	76	0.87	2.82	70	*341
Food Network	43087		2044	23.43	4.74	118	342
Fox News Channel	72370		3015	34.56	4.17	104	343
FSN (Fox Sports Net)	14477		606	6.95	4.19	104	344
Fuse	2698	*	66	0.76	2.44	61	*345
FX	39800		1180	13.53	2.97	74	346
G4	2005	*	41	0.48	2.07	51	*347
GSN (Game Show Network)	7264	*	197	2.26	2.71	67	*348

Golf Channel	8812		481	5.52	5.46	136	349
GAC (Great American Country)	5592	*	94	1.07	1.68	42	*350
Hallmark Channel	27204		1339	15.35	4.92	122	351
Headline CNN News	46707		2253	25.83	4.82	120	352
History Channel	58142		2937	33.66	5.05	126	353
HGTV (Home & Garden Television)	38555		1793	20.56	4.65	116	354
HSN (Home Shopping Network)	6749	*	304	3.48	4.50	112	*355
IFC (Independent Film Channel)	4206	*	126	1.44	2.99	74	*356
I-Life TV	1557	*	52	0.60	3.35	83	*357
INSP (Inspiration Network)	2503	*	74	0.85	2.96	74	*358
Lifetime	47638		1724	19.76	3.62	90	359
Lifetime Movie Network (LMN)	27202		934	10.71	3.44	85	360
Military Channel	8593	*	304	3.48	3.53	88	*361
MSNBC	46675		2292	26.28	4.91	122	362
MTV	35201		867	9.94	2.46	61	363
MTV2	15903	*	403	4.62	2.53	63	*364
Music Choice	7199	*	189	2.17	2.63	65	*365
National Geographic Channel	28573		1251	14.34	4.38	109	366
Nick at Nite	24355		783	8.97	3.21	80	367
Nickelodeon	24253		754	8.64	3.11	77	368
OLN (Outdoor Life Network)	8946	*	330	3.78	3.69	92	369
Outdoor Channel	10082	*	329	3.77	3.26	81	*370
Oxygen	17227		707	8.11	4.11	102	371
QVC	10826		531	6.08	4.90	122	372

(continued)

TABLE 9.1 Mediamark Data on Contributions to Public TV/Radio

Mediamark Research Inc., Spring 2006	Total Adults		Contributions to Public TV/Radio: Contributed to PBS Past 12 Months				
Science Channel	11800		428	4.90	3.62	90	373
Sci-Fi Channel	35006		1130	12.95	3.23	80	374
Shop at Home	4437	*	162	1.86	3.65	91	*375
Soap Net	8551	*	266	3.05	3.11	77	*376
Speed Channel	14651		393	4.51	2.68	67	377
Spike TV	37283		1263	14.48	3.39	84	378
Style	4797	*	220	2.53	4.60	114	*379
Sundance	3934	*	245	2.81	6.23	155	*380
Superstation WGN	20808		760	8.72	3.65	91	381
TBS	54433		1768	20.27	3.25	81	382
TLC (The Learning Channel)	38936		1530	17.54	3.93	98	383
Toon Disney	16427	*	419	4.80	2.55	63	*384
Travel Channel	29799		1514	17.36	5.08	126	385
Trio	682	*	28	0.33	4.16	103	*386
TNT (Turner Network Television)	70751		2650	30.38	3.75	93	387
TCM (Turner Classic Movies)	25388		1361	15.60	5.36	133	388
TV Guide Channel	21074		800	9.17	3.79	94	389
TV Land	25844		881	10.10	3.41	85	390
USA Network	57372		2007	23.01	3.50	87	391
VH-1	29533		813	9.32	2.75	68	392

VH-1 Classic	8698	*	268	3.07	3.08	77	*393
Weather Channel	83501		3695	42.36	4.42	110	394
WE (Women's Entertainment)	14088		606	6.94	4.30	107	395
Pay service: watched Cinemax/past 7 days	17498		570	6.54	3.26	81	396
Pay service: watched Encore/past 7 days	15362		585	6.71	3.81	95	397
Pay service: watched HBO/past 7 days	45271		1597	18.31	3.53	88	398
Pay service: watched The Movie Channel/past 7 days	9978		428	4.90	4.29	107	399
Pay service: watched Showtime/past 7 days	20524		711	8.16	3.47	86	400
Pay service: watched Starz!/past 7 days	18780		668	7.65	3.55	88	401
4 Wheel & Off Road	2889	*	20	0.22	0.68	17	*402
AARP The Magazine	28452		2561	29.36	9.00	224	403
Allure	5393	*	226	2.59	4.19	104	*404
American Baby	6774	*	160	1.84	2.37	59	*405
American Hunter	4002	*	153	1.76	3.83	95	*406
American Legion	3729	*	329	3.77	8.83	220	*407
American Photo	1574	*	115	1.32	7.31	182	*408
American Rifleman	4034	*	148	1.70	3.68	92	*409
American Way	1627	*	116	1.33	7.12	177	*410
American Woodworker	3568	*	169	1.93	4.72	117	*411
Architectural Digest	5070		442	5.06	8.71	217	412
Arthritis Today	4031	*	340	3.89	8.43	210	*413
Arthur Fromm Bud Trv	1973	*	98	1.12	4.94	123	*414
Atlantic Monthly	1261	*	237	2.72	18.81	468	*415
Audubon	1633	*	278	3.19	17.02	423	*416

(continued)

TABLE 9.1 Mediamark Data on Contributions to Public TV/Radio

Mediamark Research Inc, Spring 2006	Total Adults		Contributions to Public TV/Radio: Contributed to PBS Past 12 Months				
Automobile	4127	*	103	1.18	2.50	62	*417
Autoweek	2956	*	45	0.51	1.51	38	*418
Baby Talk	5588	*	122	1.39	2.18	54	*419
Barron's	950	*	68	0.78	7.20	179	*420
Bassmaster	3892	*	82	0.94	2.11	53	*421
Better Homes & Gdns	38388		1810	20.75	4.72	117	422
Bicycling	1825	*	60	0.69	3.31	82	*423
Black Enterprise	3881	*	147	1.69	3.80	94	*424
Blender	1801	*	24	0.28	1.35	34	*425
Boating	2724	*	90	1.03	3.31	82	*426
Bon Appetit	6193		558	6.39	9.01	224	427
Bridal Guide	4334	*	121	1.39	2.79	69	*428
Brides	6408	*	241	2.76	3.75	93	*429
Business Week	4758		312	3.57	6.55	163	430
Car And Driver	10585	*	274	3.14	2.59	64	431
Car Craft	2974	*	87	0.99	2.91	72	*432
Catholic Digest	2518	*	212	2.43	8.41	209	*433
Chicago Tribune Sun.	2377	*	147	1.69	6.20	154	*434
Child	4990	*	121	1.39	2.42	60	*435
Cigar Aficionado	1840	*	87	1.00	4.73	118	*436
Coastal Living	3389	*	201	2.31	5.94	148	*437
Computer Gaming Wrld	1939	*	22	0.25	1.15	29	*438
Computer Shopper	2199	*	80	0.91	3.63	90	*439

Magazine							
Conde Nast Package		88884	5348	61.31	6.02	150	440
Conde Nast Traveler		3330	287	3.28	8.60	214	441
Consumer Reports		18172	1590	18.23	8.75	218	442
Continental	*	1999	89	1.02	4.44	110	*443
Cooking Light		10272	773	8.86	7.52	187	444
Cooking Pleasures	*	5048	220	2.52	4.35	108	*445
CosmoGIRL!	*	4669	123	1.41	2.64	66	*446
CosmoGIRL/Seventeen	*	12870	412	4.72	3.20	80	*447
Cosmopolitan		17362	424	4.86	2.44	61	448
Country Home	*	8288	299	3.43	3.61	90	*449
Country Living		11153	604	6.93	5.42	135	450
Country Sampler	*	2674	87	1.00	3.25	81	*451
Country Weekly	*	3358	129	1.48	3.86	96	*452
Cycle World	*	3047	57	0.65	1.87	46	*453
Delta's SKY Magazine	*	3949	149	1.71	3.77	94	*454
Diabetes Forecast	*	4115	159	1.83	3.88	96	*455
Dirt Rider	*	1837	28	0.32	1.52	38	*456
Discover		5848	306	3.51	5.24	130	457
Ducks Unlimited	*	2944	77	0.88	2.62	65	*458
Easyriders	*	2972	20	0.22	0.66	16	*459
Ebony		10927	489	5.61	4.48	111	460
Economist, The	*	1809	215	2.46	11.88	296	*461
Electronic Game Mnth	*	3428	77	0.89	2.26	56	*462
Elle	*	4793	278	3.18	5.79	144	*463
Elle Decor	*	1765	150	1.72	8.49	211	*464

(continued)

TABLE 9.1 Mediamark Data on Contributions to Public TV/Radio

Mediamark Research Inc., Spring 2006	Total Adults		Contributions to Public TV/Radio: Contributed to PBS Past 12 Months				
Endless Vacation	2741	*	140	1.60	5.10	127	*465
Entertainment Weekly	11407		322	3.69	2.82	70	466
Entrepreneur	2452	*	55	0.62	2.22	55	*467
ESPN The Magazine	12717	*	346	3.96	2.72	68	*468
Esquire	2957	*	106	1.22	3.59	89	*469
Essence	7721	*	329	3.77	4.26	106	*470
Family Circle	20255		1061	12.17	5.24	130	471
Family Handy/Am Wood	7925		402	4.61	5.07	126	472
Family Handyman	4357	*	233	2.67	5.35	133	*473
FamilyFun	4513	*	161	1.85	3.57	89	*474
FHM	5562	*	113	1.29	2.03	50	*475
Field & Stream	9594	*	271	3.10	2.82	70	*476
Field&Stream/Outdoor	15114		531	6.09	3.52	87	477
First For Women	3985	*	95	1.09	2.38	59	*478
Fit Pregnancy	2269	*	25	0.29	1.11	28	*479
Fitness	6808	*	212	2.43	3.12	78	*480
Flying	1330	*	115	1.32	8.63	215	*481
Food & Wine	6639		450	5.16	6.78	169	482
Forbes	4652		354	4.06	7.62	189	483
Fortune	4078	*	243	2.79	5.96	148	*484
Four Wheeler	2927	*	28	0.32	0.97	24	*485
Game & Fish	3316	*	77	0.88	2.32	58	*486

Game Informer	4201	*	48	0.55	1.15	29	*487
GamePro	3026	*	38	0.43	1.25	31	*488
Garden Design	3681	*	166	1.90	4.51	112	*489
Gardening How-To	4784	*	136	1.56	2.85	71	*490
Glamour	12826	*	417	4.78	3.25	81	*491
Globe	1334	*	49	0.56	3.68	92	*492
Golf Digest	6027	*	224	2.57	3.71	92	*493
Golf Magazine	6115		368	4.22	6.02	150	494
Good Housekeeping	24266		1138	13.04	4.69	117	495
Gourmet	5530		629	7.21	11.38	283	496
GQ (Gent's Qtrly)	5871	*	236	2.71	4.03	100	*497
Guideposts	8062		490	5.62	6.08	151	498
Guns & Ammo	5694	*	189	2.16	3.31	82	*499
Hachette Men's Pack	26612		927	10.63	3.48	87	500
Handguns	5206	*	145	1.66	2.79	69	*501
Handy	2713	*	164	1.88	6.06	151	*502
Harper's Bazaar	3070	*	153	1.75	4.98	124	*503
Health	7021	*	263	3.01	3.74	93	*504
Hearst Magazine Grp	126127		5532	63.41	4.39	109	505
Hemispheres (United)	2064	*	201	2.30	9.73	242	*506
Home	3831	*	88	1.01	2.30	57	*507
Hot Rod	6761	*	73	0.83	1.07	27	*508
House & Garden	13934		712	8.16	5.11	127	509
House Beautiful	7242		523	6.00	7.22	180	510
Hunting	2780	*	135	1.54	4.85	121	*511

(continued)

TABLE 9.1 Mediamark Data on Contributions to Public TV/Radio

Mediamark Research Inc., Spring 2006	Total Adults		Contributions to Public TV/Radio: Contributed to PBS Past 12 Months				
In Style Mag	9661		446	5.12	4.62	115	512
In Touch Weekly	4850	*	155	1.78	3.20	80	*513
Inc.	1086	*	70	0.81	6.47	161	*514
Jane	1781	*	98	1.13	5.51	137	*515
Jet	8375		412	4.72	4.92	122	*516
Kiplinger's Pers Fin	2201	*	202	2.32	9.19	229	*517
L. A. Times (Sun)	3210		367	4.21	11.44	285	518
Ladies' Home Journal	13565		737	8.45	5.43	135	519
Life Carrier Nwspapr	26166		1417	16.24	5.42	135	520
Lucky.	2610	*	93	1.06	3.56	88	*521
Macworld	1247	*	122	1.40	9.78	243	*522
Marie Claire	3533	*	82	0.94	2.32	58	*523
Martha Stewart Livng	11802		748	8.58	6.34	158	524
Maxim	13703	*	305	3.50	2.23	55	*525
Men's Fitness	6054	*	146	1.67	2.41	60	*526
Men's Health	10986		339	3.88	3.08	77	527
Men's Journal	3284	*	170	1.95	5.19	129	*528
Meredith Magazine Gr	122496		5333	61.14	4.35	108	529
Metropolitan Home	2516	*	164	1.88	6.51	162	*530
Metro-Puck Carr Nwsp	73089		3945	45.23	5.40	134	531
Midwest Living	3748	*	227	2.61	6.07	151	*532

Modern Bride	5440	*	163	1.87	2.99	74	*533
Money	7707		443	5.08	5.74	143	534
Motor Boating	1332	*	34	0.39	2.55	63	*535
Motor Trend	6519	*	197	2.26	3.03	75	*536
Motorcyclist	2661	*	44	0.50	1.65	41	*537
Muscle & Fitness	6221	*	224	2.57	3.60	90	*538
NA Fishmn/NA Hunter	8515	*	260	2.99	3.06	76	*539
Nat. Geo. Traveler	6718		329	3.77	4.89	122	540
National Enquirer	8895	*	223	2.55	2.51	62	*541
National Geo Adven	1719	*	74	0.85	4.33	108	*542
National Geographic	30704		2199	25.21	7.16	178	543
National Wildlife	4924	*	410	4.71	8.34	207	544
Natural History	1635	*	153	1.76	9.37	233	*545
New York Magazine	1584	*	129	1.47	8.12	202	*546
New Yorker, The	3690		431	4.94	11.67	290	547
Newsweek	18944		1208	13.85	6.38	159	548
Nick Jr. Family Mag	5016	*	217	2.48	4.32	107	*549
North Am. Fisherman	3656	*	98	1.12	2.67	66	*550
Nrth American Hunter	4858	*	163	1.87	3.35	83	*551
NWA WorldTraveler	2116	*	153	1.76	7.24	180	*552
NY Times (Sunday)	4994		602	6.90	12.05	300	553
O, Oprah Magazine	16290		813	9.33	4.99	124	554
Off US Playstation	4931	*	47	0.53	0.94	23	*555
Official Xbox Mag	4164	*	63	0.72	1.50	37	*556
Outdoor Life	5520	*	261	2.99	4.72	117	*557
Outside	2142	*	122	1.40	5.70	142	*558

(continued)

TABLE 9.1 Mediamark Data on Contributions to Public TV/Radio

Mediamark Research Inc., Spring 2006	Total Adults		Contributions to Public TV/Radio: Contributed to PBS Past 12 Months				
Pace Airline Media	7220		456	5.23	6.32	157	559
Parade Carrier Newsp	76825		3926	45.00	5.11	127	560
Parenting	11094	*	229	2.63	2.07	51	*561
Parent's Magazine	15520		447	5.12	2.88	72	562
PC Gamer	2713	*	64	0.74	2.37	59	*563
PC Magazine	4777	*	302	3.46	6.32	157	*564
PC World	4735		297	3.41	6.27	156	565
Penthouse	3147	*	48	0.55	1.52	38	*566
People	40904		1585	18.18	3.88	96	567
People en Espanol	5622	*	108	1.24	1.93	48	*568
PGA Tour Partners	1613	*	83	0.95	5.14	128	*569
Playboy	10119	*	235	2.70	2.32	58	*570
Popular Hot Rodding	3501	*	42	0.48	1.19	30	*571
Popular Mechanics	8588		351	4.02	4.08	102	572
Popular Photo & Imag	1901	*	94	1.08	4.97	124	*573
Popular Science	6595		313	3.59	4.75	118	574
Premiere	1164	*	92	1.05	7.87	196	*575
Prevention	10765		649	7.44	6.03	150	576
PSM:Playstation 2	1727	*	39	0.45	2.28	57	*577
Psychology Today	3561	*	256	2.94	7.20	179	*578
Reader's Digest	38112		2184	25.04	5.73	143	579

Magazine							
Real Simple	5835		424	4.86	7.26	181	580
Redbook	9838		326	3.74	3.32	82	581
Road & Track	5451	*	182	2.08	3.33	83	*582
Rodale Mag. Network	26898		1212	13.89	4.51	112	583
Rolling Stone	10742		408	4.68	3.80	95	584
Runner's World	2125	*	98	1.13	4.63	115	*585
Salt Water Sportman	1353	*	27	0.31	2.02	50	*586
Sat. Evening Post	3190	*	207	2.37	6.49	161	*587
Schol Parent & Child	7549	*	358	4.10	4.74	118	*588
Scientific American	2940		308	3.53	10.46	260	589
Scouting	1699	*	38	0.43	2.23	55	*590
Selecciones	2659	*	49	0.57	1.85	46	*591
Self	5273	*	259	2.97	4.91	122	*592
Seventeen	8200	*	289	3.31	3.52	88	*593
Shape	5933	*	198	2.27	3.34	83	*594
Sierra	1350	*	252	2.88	18.64	464	*595
Ski	1511	*	62	0.71	4.08	102	*596
Skiing	1201	*	73	0.83	6.05	151	*597
Smart Money	3734	*	250	2.87	6.69	167	*598
Smithsonian	6433		850	9.74	13.21	329	599
Soap Opera Digest	5306	*	155	1.77	2.91	72	*600
Soap Opera Weekly	4063	*	149	1.71	3.67	91	*601
Southern Accents	2477	*	154	1.77	6.23	155	*602
Southern Living	15722		757	8.68	4.82	120	603

(continued)

TABLE 9.1 Mediamark Data on Contributions to Public TV/Radio

Mediamark Research Inc., Spring 2006	Total Adults			Contributions to Public TV/Radio: Contributed to PBS Past 12 Months			
Southwest Spirit	3435	*	238	2.73	6.93	172	*604
Spin	2250	*	66	0.75	2.92	73	*605
Sport Truck	2000	*	17	0.20	0.86	21	*606
Sporting News	3998	*	120	1.38	3.01	75	*607
Sports Illustrated	21206		749	8.58	3.53	88	608
Sports Weekly	2857	*	61	0.69	2.12	53	*609
Star	9501	*	273	3.13	2.88	72	*610
Stock Car Racing	2575	*	23	0.26	0.88	22	*611
Street Rodder	2451	*	60	0.69	2.46	61	*612
Stuff	5707	*	118	1.35	2.06	51	*613
Sun Mag/Net Carr Nsp	22159		1717	19.69	7.75	193	614
Sunset	4707		557	6.38	11.83	294	615
Super Chevy	2969	*	66	0.75	2.21	55	*616
Teen People	8430	*	162	1.86	1.92	48	*617
Tennis	1282	*	79	0.90	6.16	153	*618
Texas Monthly	1938	*	112	1.28	5.77	144	*619
This Old House	6062		389	4.46	6.41	159	620
Time	21508		1439	16.50	6.69	166	621
Time4 Media	40321		1865	21.38	4.63	115	622
Town & Country	3903	*	201	2.31	5.16	128	*623
Traditional Home	4161	*	258	2.96	6.20	154	*624

Travel & Leisure	5040		359	4.11	7.12	177	625
Truckin'	3046	*	40	0.45	1.30	32	*626
US News & World Rpt.	10947		668	7.65	6.10	152	627
Us Weekly	10713	*	376	4.31	3.51	87	*628
USA Weekend Carr Nsp	49275		2638	30.25	5.35	133	629
Vanity Fair	6238		470	5.39	7.53	187	630
Veranda	1322	*	148	1.70	11.22	279	*631
VFW Magazine	2921	*	131	1.51	4.50	112	*632
Vibe	7934	*	207	2.37	2.61	65	*633
Vogue	10667		502	5.76	4.71	117	634
W	1650	*	145	1.66	8.78	218	*635
Weight Watchers	8219		470	5.38	5.71	142	636
Wine Spectator	2298	*	243	2.78	10.56	263	*637
Wired	2256	*	87	1.00	3.87	96	*638
Woman's Day	20914		843	9.66	4.03	100	639
Woman's World	8588	*	185	2.12	2.15	53	*640
Workbench	2503	*	150	1.72	5.99	149	*641
Working Mother	2070	*	71	0.81	3.43	85	*642
Yachting	1038	*	68	0.78	6.55	163	*643
Yankee	1776	*	82	0.95	4.64	116	*644

Source: Mediamark Research Inc., Spring 2006

Age in the categories 18–24 through 65 or over when using MRI. The Age categories Adults 18–34 through Adults 25–54, and so forth, comprise separate sets of Age categories; Sissors & Baron, 2002).

Which characteristics best exemplify the national target segment of contributors to PBS? The MRI data in Table 9.1 suggest major contributors are adults ages 55 or older who earned college or post-graduate college degrees and have annual household incomes of $75,000 or more. Contributors appear likely to be employed in professional, management, business, and financial occupations and may be empty-nesters who own their homes and use various online services to connect to the Internet. They tend to read *The New York Times* on Sunday and visit nytimes.com. They listen to all news and public-radio stations. Their TV preferences include golf, gymnastics, horse racing, ice-skating specials, and tennis programming. Their magazine preferences include in-flight airline, gourmet cooking, business, scientific, and travel magazines. Although these are national data, a local public-station manager could conduct research to assess whether these characteristics hold true locally. For example, the station's printed or online contribution forms could include a brief demographic and media usage questionnaire for obtaining local data.

Managers of media outlets should understand the concepts of reach and frequency because advertisers and media planners use them when developing media schedules or plans. *Reach* refers to the percentage of the target segment exposed to a vehicle, ad, or program at least once in a given period. Reach is a measure of dispersion or how widely the message is received. *Frequency* is a measure of repetition and refers to how often the audience segment is reached on average (Katz, 2007). An advertiser may select a particular medium or combination of media based on whether the product is sold to the public at large or a specialized segment (such as major contributors to public TV/radio).

Advertisers and media planners also consider cost per thousand (CPM) when making advertising placement decisions. *CPM* is the cost to deliver 1,000 people or households to an advertiser. It is an estimate of media efficiency for reaching the desired segment. CPMs are used for intermedia (or comparing different media) and intramedia (or comparisons among vehicles in the same class like newspapers or magazines) comparisons. Although intermedia comparisons are made to select among different media classes, remember these media are not directly comparable in terms of how the audience is measured and commercial impact. Intramedia CPMs compare ads of the same sizes and types (e.g., compare full-page, four-color ads among magazines or compare

30-second ads among primetime TV shows). The basic CPM formulas are as follows (Sissors & Baron, 2002, p. 52).

For Newspapers

$$CPM = \frac{\text{Cost of ad}}{\text{Circulation}} \times 1000$$

For Print Vehicles When Audience Data Are Available

$$CPM = \frac{\begin{array}{c}\text{Cost of one page black \& white ad}\\\text{(or appropriate size and color)} \times 1000\end{array}}{\begin{array}{c}\text{Number of prospects}\\\text{(or readers in the target segment) reached}\end{array}}$$

For Broadcast Media (Based on Audience or Households Reached by a Given Program or in a Given Daypart or Standard Broadcast Daytime Period)

$$CPM = \frac{\begin{array}{c}\text{Cost of 1 unit of time}\\\text{(e.g., 30-second spot)} \times 1000\end{array}}{\begin{array}{c}\text{Number of households or persons reached}\\\text{by a given program, daypart or time period}\end{array}}$$

Advertisers and media planners evaluate factors including CPMs, reach, frequency, indices, number and percentage of target readers, and target subsegments to select the most effective mix of vehicles to reach as many different members of the target segment as possible. A media planner considering where to place ads for a firm that wants to inform contributors of its sponsorship of PBS programs could use the MRI data to select particular vehicles. Which combination of publications appears to best reach major contributors to public TV? An estimated 6.39%, or 558,000 PBS contributors (with an index of 224) reported reading *Bon Appetit*, while 7.21%, or 629,000 (with an index of 283) read *Gourmet*. Using one or both these magazines would reach the PBS contributor subsegment with epicurean interests. By adding *Scientific American* (3.53%, 308,000, index of 260) the contributor subsegment with scientific interests is added. By adding *Smithsonian* (9.74%, 850,000, 329) contributors with interests in art, architecture, nature, culture, technology, and travel are added. Finally, by adding *Fortune*

(2.79%, 243,000, 148) and *Forbes* (4.06%, 354,000, 189) contributors in the business subsegment are included in the media plan. Obviously, some major contributors may subscribe to more than one of these vehicles, increasing the frequency of exposure to the ad or campaign.

CPMs help ensure that the media plan or schedule is as cost-efficient as possible in reaching the desired target segment. Assume that the advertiser gave the media planner a limited budget so choices must be made on maximizing reach among various target subsegments. The media planner decides only one business-oriented magazine can be used because many in the target audience work in management and business occupations. *Forbes* with an index of 189 reaches 354,000 or 4.06% of major contributors (see www.forbesmedia.com or www.forbes media.com/forbes and register free for rate information, an editorial calendar, and demographic information). *Forbes* charges $96,150 for one full-page, four-color ad. *Fortune* with an index of 148 reaches 243,000 or 2.79% of major contributors (see rate information, an editorial calendar and reader profile at www.timeinc.net/fortune/mediakit/ or www. fortunemediakit.com). *Fortune* charges $92,500 for one full-page, four-color ad. Yet how do these vehicles stack up in terms of cost efficiency? The intramedia CPMs for a full-page, four-color ad in each business magazine vehicle are the following:

Forbes CPM

$$\text{Full-page, 4-Color Ad CPM} = \frac{\$96{,}150 \times 1000}{354{,}000} = \$271.61$$

Fortune CPM

$$\text{Full-page, 4-Color Ad CPM} = \frac{\$92{,}500 \times 1000}{243{,}000} = \$380.65$$

Typically, differences of $10 or more are meaningful in comparing CPMs. The CPM analysis suggests *Forbes* has a significantly lower cost per thousand among the target market than *Fortune*. In addition, the *Fortune* results are based on fewer than 50 respondents. Therefore, Mediamark is indicating to the media planner that the results regarding *Fortune* are not based on a sufficient sample size. Therefore, a higher index, a higher number of target-market readers, cost efficiency, and questionable data due to a small sample size all point to using *Forbes* in the media plan. In contrast, if the CPMs were similar and all data were reliable and valid, the media planner would evaluate audience and other data to discern if one vehicle is better than the other is for reaching contributors or for garnering reader involvement or engagement. Media planners also consider whether either magazine has a longer issue life or is saved, read again by the subscriber or other people, thus having a larger secondary audience through pass-along readership (Katz, 2007).

Advertisers and media planners analyze the viewing and listening levels of various programs on different stations and channels to decide which broadcast vehicles best reach the target segment. In many markets, the level of program viewing and listening, as well as demographic and other data, are measured by Nielsen (www.nielsenmedia. com) or Arbitron (www.arbitron.com) during the *sweeps* periods. The most important periods for measuring ratings, called *sweeps*, occur in February, May, July, and November.

Arbitron and Nielsen assign stations to only one viewing or listening market area where they receive the largest audience share. Nielsen calls these nonoverlapping, mutually exclusive market areas comprised of counties grouped around cities or towns, *designated market areas (DMAs)*. Each county or parish in the continental United States is assigned to only one DMA. Households using TV (HUT) or persons using TV (PUT) is the total percentage of homes (or persons) in a DMA watching TV during any daypart, such as morning, primetime, and late night or after 11:30 P.M. Eastern time (Sissors & Barron, 2002).

Broadcast managers worry about sweeps results because the price of advertising time is based on ratings and shares. A TV *rating* is the number of households (or persons) that watch a TV show divided by all TVHH or TV households (or persons) in that market area with a TV set. Ratings measure overall reach. A *share* is the estimated percentage of HUTs or PUTs during a specified time watching a program. A *share* is the number of households (or persons) watching a particular program, divided by the total number of households (or persons) with TV sets actually turned on when the program airs. Shares are always larger than ratings because there is never a time when every single household has a TV on. Shares measure comparative performance from program to program, station to station, and network to network. (See Webster, Phalen, & Lichty, 2006, for more information.)

Shares help evaluate how one program fares against its competition and whether it gained or lost audience members over different times of the year. A program's rating depends on its popularity and the daypart when it airs. The rating of a show that airs during the day is normally much smaller than a primetime show airing between 8 P.M. and 11 P.M., Eastern time. Yet, that daytime show may have a higher share of viewers using TV in its time period or daypart. HUTs and PUTs are lower in the summer when fewer people watch TV and higher in the winter when more time is spent indoors watching TV. If you looked only at ratings, you would miss the differences in viewing levels at various times of year (Sissors & Baron, 2002; see also Nielsen's home page at www. nielsenmedia.com and click on the Inside TV Ratings link to learn how ratings data are collected and top-rated programs.)

Media managers must identify the population base on which a rating is based. Cable channels may report ratings as a percentage of their own coverage rather than the total United States to make a stronger sales pitch to advertisers. Assume a cable channel reaches 15 million homes and has a program watched in 1,500,000 homes. The cable channel may report a rating of 10 for the program based on the channel's coverage area (or 1.5 million/15 million) rather than a rating of 1.4 based on all U.S. TV households (or 1.5 million/105.5 million USTVHH). Some Web sites do the same and express audience size as a percentage of Internet users rather than the U.S. population (Sissors & Baron, 2002).

Ratings and shares are used in a local DMA to analyze the performance of local programs. The general manager at the ABC-affiliated station in the Port City DMA is analyzing the performance of her 6 P.M.

TABLE 9.2 Using Ratings and Shares Sweeps Period

	February 2007	May 2007	July 2007	November 2007
ABC Action 2 News				
Rating	15	15	16	20
Share	25	28.8	33.3	35.7
NBC Ch. 7 Hometown News				
Rating	25	23	21	21
Share	41.6	44.2	43.8	37.5
CBS Ch. 12 News You Can Use				
Rating	8	7	7	7
Share	13.3	13.5	14.6	12.5
Port City HUT Levels 6–6:30 P.M.	60	52	48	56

newscast. She may conduct primary research if the analysis suggests her investment in a new anchor and equipment may affect the ratings. From Table 9.2, it appears that her newscast's audience size increased over the past year, especially in July. Had she considered only ratings, she would miss that her audience share increased in May, although the rating did not increase due to a smaller HUT level. (Shares for each sweeps period do not add up to the HUT levels because some local viewers were watching other local stations and cable channels from 6:00–6:30 P.M.)

Advertisers, media planners, and broadcast managers use the cost per point (CPP), which "measures the cost of one household or demographic rating point in a given market" (Sissors & Baron, 2002, p. 54). A CPP is an estimate of the dollars required to deliver one rating point (or one percentage of the audience) of any DMA. The formula is

$$CPP = \frac{\text{Cost of a commercial}}{\text{Rating}}$$

SQAD (www.sqad.com) is a media cost forecasting company that provides CPPs and CPMs for TV and radio market areas nationwide. Therefore, a media planner having a SQAD report and ratings books can estimate the cost of ads and media plans, as well as evaluate the cost efficiency of shows in different markets. Managers use CPMs to compare different vehicles' efficiencies while they calculate a broadcast media plan via CPP (Sissors & Baron, 2002).

Although measurement methods change continually as new technologies develop, broadcast media usage has generally been measured using diaries (surveys) and meters (observation). *Diaries* are booklets in which viewers and listeners write the stations they watch or listen to and when. National TV audiences are measured using people meters that automatically register the channel numbers tuned in, day of week, and time of day. Sample household members push a button to indicate when they view. Set meters logging set-tuning information only and diaries for demographic data measure local TV viewing in large- to mid-size markets. The other local TV and radio markets are measured using diaries. (Sissors & Baron, 2002; Wimmer & Dominick, 2006).

Arbitron implemented its personal people meter (PPM) measurement to measure what radio stations consumers listen to, what they watch on cable, satellite and broadcast TV, what Internet media they stream, and what they hear in retail and entertainment venues. Throughout the day, consumers wear the mobile-phone-sized PPM that detects identification codes embedded in the audio portion of any transmission. (See www.arbitron.com/portable_people_meters/home.htm for more information.) The PPM was designed to measure the wide variety of media to which consumers are exposed in and out of the home on a typical day.

Industry dissatisfaction with the lack of out-of-home ratings and technology are leading to changes in how audiences are measured. Advertisers are demanding accurate measurement of media consumption in the car, at work, while commuting, and on the beach, etc.

Competing companies such as Media Audit/Ipsos claim its "smart cell phone," which runs an operating system similar to a PDA, allows detailed radio and multimedia audience tracking. Cell phones already are Global Positioning System or GPS-enabled, allowing measures of radio listening to be quantified by time, date, and location. In other words, smart cell phones could provide audience data indicating exactly where the individual is traveling to work in the car and which radio station is tuned in at 8:25 A.M. in the morning (Walsh, 2006). The company claims it will provide demographic, psychographic, and retail shopping data using multimedia measurement of radio, broadcast TV, cable, newspaper, outdoor, radio listening, and TV viewing on digital music players, satellite TV and radio, and TV and radio Internet streaming. (See www.themediaaudit.com for more information.)

To compete, Nielsen plans to add Internet measurement to existing People Meter samples to create a TV/Internet measurement panel examining the relationship between TV, Web site and streaming video consumption. The goal is to help advertisers determine how well their online and TV advertising drives traffic to their Web sites. Nielsen also plans to measure out-of-home media consumption and video viewed on portable media devices, digital-video recorder viewing and video on-demand viewing (see www.nielsenmedia.com). Mediamark is introducing MediaDay to measure a consumer's 24-hour media consumption detailed by place, time, other activities while consuming and level of engagement (Mediamark Research, 2006).

Advertisers also want audience and usage data for podcasts. *Podcasts* are downloadable files that can be listened to on MP3 players or computers (Shields, 2005, 2006b). Podtrac (www.podtrac.com) provides measurement and demographic profiles of podcasts and assists advertisers with implementing podcasts, placing ads in podcasts to reach specific audiences and media planning. Podbridge (www.podbridge. com) provides information on demographics and location, reach, and listening time.

Nielsen offers its Product Placement Service using Place*Views software to assess product or brand placement in television programs. Product placement or brand integration is when advertisers pay program producers to include their brand in the content or storyline of TV programs. Brand integration examples include overt placements as when GM's G6 car was given away to all members of Oprah's audience and when Burger King paid for *The Apprentice* TV show contestants to run a BK restaurant in New York while a new sandwich was launched. With placement, the product is less prominent as when an advertiser pays the producer to have a character opens a box of Cheerios rather than a different brand (Katz, 2007). Nielsen data identify uses brand placement, when and where those placements occur, and the types of placements used. The database allows subscribers to search by advertiser, brand, product category, network, program, episode, date, and time of airing. Data also indicate details about the audience size at the time of the product placement and on-screen location (or foreground vs. background; see www.nielsenmedia.com).

The Audit Bureau of Circulation provides information on the number of copies of a newspaper or magazine circulated (see www.access-abc.com). Magazine and newspaper audiences are often measured using three techniques: (a) recent reading and (b) frequency of reading of magazines and (c) yesterday reading for newspapers.

With recent reading, a subject is shown more than 200 cards with the logos of magazines, each card one at a time, and asked whether the magazine was read or looked at in the past month or other publication period. Frequency of reading is measured by showing a list of about 50 magazine logos or cover pictures and asking the number of copies of each magazine that a subject read out of the last four issues. Yesterday reading is measured by asking a selected sample which newspapers they read yesterday.

Syndicated research services provide information on readership of individual magazines such as which days and where it is read, the average number of minutes spent with the vehicle, and what actions were taken after reading it. Newspaper readership data may include demographics, product usage data, and duplication of readership among the various newspapers in a geographic area (Katz, 2007; Sissors & Baron, 2002).

Initially, Internet advertising was sold based on click-throughs or the percentage of users clicking on a Web ad to link to an advertiser's site. Most sites now price their advertising based on CPM or cost per thousand (Katz, 2007). CPM is the cost per thousand for a particular site. A Web site that charges $15,000 per banner and guarantees 600,000 impressions has a CPM of $25 [$15,000 divided by 600 (for 600 thousands)]; (O'Guinn et al., p. 508). Many other audience measures are used. With CPC or cost per click, advertisers pay Internet sites based on the number of clicks a specific banner ad gets, such as $.10 to $.20 cents per click. Hits are defined as the number of elements requested from a particular Web page (O'Guinn et al., 2006).

The Interactive Advertising Bureau (IAB, 2004) issued Internet audience measurement guidelines and defined other terms. IAB defines a visit as,

> one or more text and/or graphics downloads from a site qualifying as at least one page, without 30 consecutive minutes of inactivity, which can be reasonably attributed to a single browser for a single session. A browser must "pull" text or graphics content to be considered a visit. (IAB, 2004, p. 15)
>
> Unique users represent the number of actual individual people, within a designated reporting timeframe, with activity consisting of one or more visits to a site or the delivery of pushed content. A unique user can include both: an actual individual that accessed a site (referred to as a unique visitor), or an actual individual that is pushed content and or ads such as e-mail, newsletters, interstitials and pop-under ads. Each individual is counted only once in the unique user or visitor measures for the reporting period" (IAB, 2004, p. 16).

Developing these standardized measures means advertisers and Web publishers all understand what the research data they analyze means and how it is collected.

Nielsen/Net Ratings (www.nielsennetratings.com) measures visits to Web sites. Nielsen places software on the computers of a nationally representative sample of about 60,000 subjects to record all sites they visit. Data gathered include the number of unique visitors to a site, how deeply they go into the site, how long they stay on each page, and how often they return. ABCi or ABC Interactive (ABCi; www.abcinteractive-audits.com) conducts audits for Web sites, search engines, and Internet broadcasters and posts audit reports online in its report library. ABCi posts guidelines on reading its audit reports (www.abcinteractiveaudits.com/3rdparty/howtoread.htm).

Many other companies provide information about print, broadcast, and out-of-home media audiences and their characteristics. For example, learn more online about the Standard Rate and Data Service (at www.srds.com), Simmons Market Research Bureau (www.smrb.com), TNS Media Intelligence (www.tns-mi.com), and BPA Worldwide (www.bpaww.com). Major international research firms with varied capabilities have been formed through acquisitions. For example, by 2006 GFK had acquired Roper Reports Worldwide, Starch Ad Readership, and Mediamark Research Inc., which had been important research firms when independent. Other major national and international research firms include TNS Global (see www.tns-global.com), Mintel International (www.mintel.com), and IPSOS (ipsos.com).

Various organizations help to set standards and guidelines for media research. Again, the Interactive Advertising Bureau (www.iab.net) evaluates and recommends guidelines, standards, and practices for interactive media. The Traffic Audit Bureau for Media Measurement (www.tabonline.com) audits the circulation of out-of-home media and supports research initiatives. The Media Rating Council (www.mrc.htsp.com) accredits audience measurement firms. The Online Publishers Association offers a Primer on Online Video Viewing (www.online-publishers.org/pdf/opa_online_video_study_mar06.pdf) and guidelines on Measuring Local Audiences Online (www.online-publishers.org/pdf/OPALocalWhitePaper.pdf). It publicizes other guidelines including the Streaming Video Advertising Guide (www.pointroll.com/docs/Accu StreamStreamingVideoGuide2006.pdf).

Audience Research: Primary Data Collection

A media manager may conduct primary audience research to answer questions unanswered by syndicated data. For example, more specific information on the audience's demographic or lifestyle characteristics may be needed. Or a newspaper or Web-site manager may need to discover which sections are preferred, and why, by important audience segments such as young professionals ages 18–34 with household incomes of $75,000 or more. The major types of research used by newspaper managers include circulation, readership, and advertising studies.

Circulation studies. Geography is important to local newspaper managers because it defines the area where readers are attracted. Circulation studies reveal the newspaper's market share, market share of competing media, existing circulation patterns, and areas of potential circulation growth. A newspaper manager then conducts a situation or market analysis to determine which areas to target for increasing circulation.

Readership studies. Readership studies describe the people living in the target areas. They often include questions about demographics, psychographics, and media usage to discover who reads the newspaper, why, the sections they prefer, and the benefits they obtain from reading it. A large metropolitan newspaper might develop a lifestyle section appealing to upper-income city residents moving to a particular zip code. A small town newspaper might increase soccer coverage in the sports section when research shows many local children and parents participate in soccer.

Studies incorporating demographics, psychographics, and media usage are used to measure the audience characteristics of competing media. Information about who exclusively reads each local daily, weekly, and shopper; who reads a combination of these publications and why; and how these and other publications are used may reveal untapped readership segments.

Advertising studies. The media manager or media representative sells media time or space to media buyers using a media kit. A media kit positions the media product as an ideal vehicle for the advertiser. Media outlets may conduct research to accurately describe the demographic and psychographic composition of their audiences. Industry groups provide advertising advice and data for media kits. The Chamber of Commerce, other local economic development offices, or state agencies concerned with economic development provide market information. State or regional press associations may compile primary and secondary market information. Include CPM data in media kits or make them available to advertisers.

Many vehicles with online sites include a media kit, rate card, and information on their audiences. MRI (www.mriplus.com) consolidates searchable databases used to evaluate magazines that include information used in media kits when one registers with the free service. Many media outlets list media kits on their Web sites, including *Forbes* and *Fortune,* noted previously.

Various media and marketing trade organizations provide information as well. These include the Television Bureau of Advertising (www.tvb.org), Cabletelevision Advertising Bureau (www.onetvworld. org), Radio Advertising Bureau (www.rab.com), Magazine Publishers of America (www.magazine.org), Newspaper Association of America (www.naa.org), Interactive Advertising Bureau (www.iab.net), Electronic Retailing Association (www.retailing.org), Outdoor Advertising, Association of America (www.oaaa.org), Direct Marketing Association (www.the-dma.org), POPAI Marketing at-Retail (or at point of purchase—www.popai.com), Promotional Products Association International (www.ppa.org), Promotion Marketing Association (www. pmalink.org), Entertainment Resources & Marketing Association (www.

erma.org), and Online Publisher's Association (www.online-publishing.org).

Advertisers purchase data on their own and competitors' past and present media activity from TNS Media Intelligence (www.tns-mi.com). TNS-MI provides current and trend data on TV, radio, cable, syndication, magazines, newspapers, Internet, outdoor, and various ethnic media for millions of brands searchable by product category, parent company, brands, ad size or spot length, medium or vehicle, national or local media and market. Nielsen Monitor-Plus (www.nielsenmedia .com/monitor-plus) also provides advertising activity information. Media managers use these data to identify an advertiser's buying patterns and gain insights into media buys.

Positioning research includes studies of audience perceptions to discover a brand or product's unique attribute (or combination of attributes) to better meet consumers' needs. Positioning research diagnoses why audiences are not attracted to a product and includes other factors such as how a product compares to competitors. It often uses exploratory and descriptive methods such as focus groups or surveys. Identifying consumer habits, lifestyles, behaviors, and desires through primary target-segment research provides the information basis for product positioning.

For media organizations, positioning concerns the audience's image of the media outlet or company, or the *product* in this case. A new Web site's name is critical to its successful positioning because it may be the only information the audience hears about it. At the media content level, studies of audience reactions to and preferences for broadcast and cable programming, news and magazine articles and format, and the structure and content of Web sites are critical to maintaining audience commitment. A manager conducts a mail or telephone survey, focus group, or personal interviews to determine whether the local community favors the news talent and newscast. Results may be used to determine local news anchor changes.

Media Content: Evaluative, Formative, and Summative Research

Evaluative research determines how well the media content conveys what it is intended to convey. Causal research methods such as experiments are often used to conduct this research. Advertisers and their advertising agencies use evaluative research to test messages before (pretesting) and after (posttesting) ads are conveyed to the general public.

Test marketing evaluates audience tastes for broadcast and cable programming, print editorial content, Web site structure and content, and advertising. An ad might be aired in one market before it airs nationally to project what its effect on consumer behavior might be. Ads might be shown in two different markets or on a two-way cable system in one city, with subscribers in one part of the city seeing one version of a program or commercial and those living in another area seeing another version. Results of a random telephone survey reveal which program version earned higher ratings or which commercial spurred more sales.

With formative research, production companies and TV networks pretest programming and advertisers pretest ads before committing full resources to them. Concept testing assesses a program's potential popularity or the potential effectiveness of an ad's key selling concept before exposure to the general public. A concept is tested by having subjects read a one-page program summary or showing them a mock-up of a commercial. Subjects may be invited to a theater to view a pilot program. After viewing, they report their feelings about the program to help network executives determine how popular various characters and endings might be (Wimmer & Dominick, 2006).

Summative research examines whether the appropriate message is conveyed to the target market. This allows the media or advertising manager to evaluate whether the media or advertising content objectives were actually accomplished. Summative research can be performed in the field during a campaign or purchased as secondary data. For example, Starch Ad Readership Studies (www.gfkamerica.com/products/StarchAdReadershipStudies.htm) evaluate advertising success by comparing ads to competitors and readership norms. Its measures include reader interest and reactions to magazine editorial content and advertising

Summary

All media managers must understand research from a broad perspective to use it effectively. It is important to understand research methods and concepts like variables, reliability, and validity to conduct or effectively assess research.

Before designing a research study, a manager considers three issues: (a) How much is already known about the problem at hand? (b) How much information is needed about each audience member? (c) How important is it that the study results generalize to other people and situations? The answers direct the researcher to some types of research and not to others.

Advertising, print, broadcast, cable, and online managers use similar kinds of data, research sources, and research techniques in different ways. Media outlet managers must comprehend how advertisers use audience data and media-planning concepts such as indexes, reach, frequency, CPMs, and CPPs to select media vehicles for advertising buys. Understanding how advertisers and agencies use these concepts helps a manager sell advertising time or space effectively.

Some of the research categories that are important to effective media management are primary, secondary, syndicated, exploratory, descriptive, and causal research. Applied research methods include audience, positioning, formative, and summative research. Data-collection designs available to the researcher include focus groups, in-depth interviews, surveys, and experiments. By collecting information about the consumer, the media manager makes more informed strategic decisions and thus markets the media vehicle more effectively to advertisers.

Case 9.1 The Case of the Ratings Increase

Sue Al-Matrouk, general manager of WPRT-TV 2 in Port City, was delighted to receive the latest sweeps report showing the ratings and shares for Action News at 6 P.M. appeared to increase over the past four sweeps periods (see Table 9.2). She wondered whether the increase was because of her investment in a new anchor and set, additions to the Web site, or new equipment like the Doppler radar, news helicopter, and remote truck. It was expensive to retain the news helicopter, so she would cut that expense if it was not a factor in the ratings increase. Yet, News Director John Small said he had received a great deal of positive feedback about it. Perhaps she could share the cost of the helicopter with another media outlet. She also wondered whether the new promotional campaign by Promotions Director Janice Biaggi had had an effect.

Sue noted the ratings and shares of the long-standing newscast leader in the market, NBC's "Hometown News," appeared to be declining since May. She wanted to know why. The CBS "News You Can Use" newscast remained solidly in third position and could be losing viewers. She wondered whether these changes were because of improvements in her newscast, factors related to the competing newscasts, other factors in the market, or a combination of all these factors. She planned to call Robert Howard, her station's group owner, to inform him of the ratings increase and ask him to support a research project to discover what contributed to the newscast's success.

Avery Atkin, sales manager at WPRT, came into her office with a big smile on his face. "In all my years in this market I've never seen a book like this. I've never seen us so close to Hometown News. We may have the best sales quarter ever after my team and I go out and sell advertising based on this book."

"I'm excited too," Sue replied. "I'm really proud of our team because all the hard work paid off. And I know you and the sales staff will do a great job selling us based on this book. But I want to be sure we stay on this upward track. We may be able to overtake and pass Hometown News and I don't want to squander this opportunity."

"Yeah," Avery agreed. "This is great, but we really do need to understand why this is happening so we can keep it up."

Just then, John and Janice came in looking quite happy.

"Good news sure travels fast," Sue said. "Great job, gang! I know how hard you've worked and I'm so proud of what we've accomplished."

"Thanks! Yeah, this is great. I just want to keep this train on the track, so to speak," Janice said.

"Thanks and me, too," said John. "I've been in the news business too long to sit on my laurels."

Sue thought for a moment and said, "Let's plan to have a meeting tomorrow. I want each of you to tell me why you think this is happening and what we need to do to maintain this success. I also want each of you to propose ideas and objectives for a research study. We need some good research to plan and maintain this success in the future. I think Robert will support a study and might even give us some extra money if we give him a good research proposal."

Assignment

1. Evaluate the ratings, shares, and HUTS in Table 9.2 carefully. Write a paragraph or two explaining what these ratings and shares appear to suggest about each station's performance and why. Explain whether it appears viewership for each station is increasing, declining, or staying the same, and why.
2. How much confidence do you have in your answers to Question 1? What do the ratings and share data really reveal? Do the data in Table

9.2 tell us why the ratings and shares of the station have changed? Why or why not?

3. Write a few detailed paragraphs that answer the following questions: (a) How can Sue determine whether the ratings and shares for her 6 P.M. newscast are improving due to the investments she's made in talent, her online edition, and equipment? (b) Can she answer this question? (c) Why or why not? (d) What can Sue realistically do to get ideas about why viewership of her newscast may be increasing?

4. What type of research study should each of the following managers propose to Sue? What type of research study is needed to determine external factors that may be having an effect? Name and describe the research objectives, type of study or research, methods, and data analysis techniques to use, and so on, to answer Questions 4a through 4d.

   a. What type of research study should the news director propose? Why?

   b. What type of research study should the sales manager propose? Why?

   c. What type of research study should the promotions manager propose? Why?

   d. What type of research study should be developed to discover what other factors (e.g., changes in the other stations' newscasts, etc.) may have an influence?

5. Using your answers to Question 4, design a research plan for Sue to present to the station's owner. For what type of research study or studies should Sue contract? What type of study or studies could Sue contract for to serve the needs and meet the research objectives of news, promotions, and sales and examine external factors? Should she contract for more than one study? If yes, which ones should she contract for and in what order?

Case 9.2 Evaluating Contributors to Public TV/Radio

Assume you are the general manager of the public TV or radio station in your city or the nearest major city. You just completed your latest fundraising campaign and are dissatisfied with the results. You want to discover why your fundraising campaign was not as successful as you had anticipated.

Review the Mediamark data for Contributors to Public TV/Radio (see Table 9.1). Evaluate Simmons or more recent Mediamark data if available. If the SRDS Lifestyle Market Analyst (LMA) is available in your library, review data on the relevant demographic segment and lifestyle profiles. Evaluate any other available data about the target segment of contributors to PBS or public TV.

Check Mediaweek to see if an analysis of your city has been published recently (for example see Hudson, 2005a, 2005b). Review the census data for demographic and economic information about your city or the nearest major city. Try to find out who major individual and business contributors might be. If the LMA is available in your library, review data for your city or the nearest major city in the Market Profiles section. (See the examples on pp. 378–381).

See if the Demographics USA—County Edition (2005) is available in your library and obtain the basic demographics, occupation employment data, 5-year projections, effective buying income, population by age and sex, household data and other relevant information contained there.

Look for other sources of secondary or syndicated media research that provide information about your city or market. Ask your reference librarian for other sources of information. In other words, conduct a thorough secondary research review on contributors to public TV/radio and your market or city. (Note: Published sources of secondary or syndicated research tend to have instructions on how to use and interpret their data at the beginning or end of the report or in a separate pamphlet or publication that may accompany the report. Some include instructions, advice, or answers to frequently asked questions [FAQs] on their Web sites.)

Assignment

Write a report detailing the primary target segment of contributors to public TV/radio nationwide, including demographics, geographics, psychographics, and any other information you find. Identify and describe the major potential corporate contributors or supporters in your city (including the major companies and industries located there). Then write a proposal for a research project to assess why your most recent fundraising campaign was unsuccessful and whether local contributors have similar characteristics to contributors nationally. Include each of the following sections in your final report and research proposal.

1. Provide a description and analysis of the target segment of contributors to public TV/radio. Include all major characteristics including demographics, geographics, and psychographics. If possible, identify how many persons or households appear to be in the major public TV/radio contributors target segment (e.g., the number of house-

holds in your city headed by college graduates and adults with post-graduate degrees, persons 55 or older, and/or households having incomes of $75,000 or more, etc., from the LMA). Write a detailed and concise report on the target segment of national public TV/radio contributors.

2. Provide a detailed-yet-concise description of your market area or major city. Provide information about the city's major economic conditions, industries, characteristics, and so on. The goal is to describe your city accurately, describe local economic conditions, and identify major local industries, companies, and so on (and identify and describe potential corporate contributors in the next question).

3. Provide a detailed-yet-concise description of potential corporate contributors. Identify the major companies and industries in your city, and describe how and why each might be persuaded to contribute to or support your local public TV/radio station.

4. Write a research proposal to discover why your most recent fundraising campaign was not as successful as hoped and the characteristics of present and potential local individual contributors (or whether they are similar to the national target segment of individuals who contribute to public TV/radio). Develop a part of your research proposal to discover the major local companies and industries who have/have not contributed to the local public TV/radio station and why.

Your research proposal should discuss the major aspects of the marketing research process, including research questions, a secondary research review, primary research design, data-collection procedures, sampling design, data collection, data processing and analysis, report writing, and potential research firms to contact about conducting the study. Identify local or national research firms you might hire to conduct the research you propose. Explain why the research company or companies are qualified and appropriate choices for the type of study you propose to conduct. Identify which research company is the best to hire to conduct your research and why. Provide an appendix in your report that includes examples of the types of questions to ask individual and corporate contributors in your study.

Case 9.3 Developing A New Magazine

Assume you work at a major national magazine publishing firm. Your task is to develop a proposal for a new magazine. Your magazine may have a national audience or be targeted to a certain region (e.g., *Southern Living*), state (e.g., *Texas Monthly*), or city. You may propose a general-interest magazine or one tailored to a certain interest segment (e.g., *Forbes, Gourmet*, etc.). Your primary criteria are that a significant and viable audience segment and group of major advertisers exist to support the magazine. You must provide supportive data that are realistic and suggest the magazine you propose could survive and prosper.

You might begin by evaluating data such as recent magazine launches and industry trends at the Magazine Publishers of America (MPA) home page (www.magazine.org) or Magazine Handbook (www.magazine.org/content/Files/MPAHandbook06.pdf) or Advertising and PIB (www.magazine.org/advertising_and_pib). If your library has the appropriate Standard Rate and Data Service publication (e.g., SRDS Consumer Magazine Advertising Source or Business Publication Advertising Source), review it to see which magazines already exist in the categories you are considering, what their editorial descriptions are, their regular features and sections, who they target, how much they charge for advertising, and so on. Advertising industry publications such as *Advertising Age* or *Adweek* or *Mediaweek* often publish articles or data about magazines. Conduct a search on ABI Inform/ProQuest, Lexis-Nexis Academic Universe, or Ebsco for other articles and data on magazine launches and the magazine industry.

Once you have narrowed your ideas to a few categories, evaluate the relevant data in Mediamark, Simmons, and the SRDS Lifestyle Market Analyst (LMA) if available. For example, if you are considering a magazine targeted to dog owners, check dog food product sales data in Mediamark and/or Simmons. Then review the demographics, geographics, and media usage data for people who buy dog food.

These reports contain the brand names of major companies in the category (e.g., major dog food companies like Purina its brands). Write down those company and brand names and look in the Ad $ Summary if it is available in your campus library (it lists brands and parent companies plus the amount they spent in major media during the past year alphabetically in the brand index; also check for spending data for the category in the volume). Check to see which major advertisers advertised in magazines and copy the names and amounts of those that did. Conduct a search of those major advertisers using online databases to find out how much they spent and in which magazines they advertised.

Then review the LMA lifestyle segment Own A Dog (or the appropriate segment for the type of magazine you propose) for demographic data on dog owners (or your lifestyle segment) nationwide and information about the other lifestyle activities they enjoy. This helps you identify potential features or sections and other potential advertisers for your proposed magazine. Review the instructions at the front of the LMA volume to see whether there is other information of interest. If you are thinking about proposing a city magazine, check out the LMA demographic and psychographic data from the Market Profiles section for ideas and data to help justify your choices of sections and features to offer. (See pp. 378–381.)

Then visit a local library, bookstore, or newsstand to review copies of existing magazines in your proposed category. Check their Web sites. Review their sections, advertisers, rate information, and so on. Also search the Advertising Media Internet Center (www.amic.com) and MRI online database (www.mriplus. com) if desired (you will need to register to use these sites). Also review the ARF's Magazine Prototyping Guidelines (www.arfsite.org/downloads/MagPrototypingGuidelines.pdf) to get a sense of the types of information advertisers want a magazine to provide.

In other words, find and evaluate as much information, research, and data as possible to develop a thorough magazine proposal and a comprehensive understanding of the category in which you wish to launch your magazine. Ask your professor and reference librarian for suggestions of available information sources or databases to use. Use your imagination to develop original and useful information to include in your proposal.

Assignment

After conducting a thorough and detailed information search, write a proposal to start a new magazine. You must support your proposed magazine and recommendations with information and data. Your proposal must include each of the following sections.

1. A title and overall description of the proposed magazine, including its editorial mission and descriptions, features and sections, types of articles to include, and so on. Explain why you propose the title you selected. Provide as much detail as you can about the proposed magazine and its content. Provide data and information to support why you selected the magazine, magazine type, and magazine category you selected for your proposal. Explain how and why it is different from other existing magazines in the category. Identify the unfilled niche or position it fills. Make a strong case based on actual recent data and information.

2. Identify and describe your target segment of readers in as much detail as possible. Provide an estimate of the number of potential readers or subscribers nationwide (e.g., the number of persons or households owning a dog from the LMA) or in your region, state, or city of interest. Provide as much detail as possible about the major characteristics of your target segment of potential subscribers or readers, including demographics, geographics, psychographics, and so on. Explain how and why your proposed magazine will be of interest to your target segment. Explain how and why it matches them and their interests. Provide information and data to support your recommendations.

3. Identify and describe a minimum of five potential advertising categories and examples of advertisers in each (e.g., dog food advertisers such as Purina for a dog magazine, etc.). Provide data on how much is spent in magazine advertising in the category. If possible, provide data for how advertising spending in the category increased over the past 5 years or decade (this information may be available in the Ad $ Summary). Provide information about how much each company/ brand that advertises in magazines spent (or spent on advertising in general if specific magazine data are unavailable). If possible, identify the magazines in which these advertisers have placed ads. Explain why your proposed magazine will be an attractive advertising vehicle for these advertisers, providing as much detail, data, and support as you can.

Case 9.4 Developing or Updating an Online Media Kit

Assume you work for a major daily, weekly, ethnic, or community newspaper in your town or the nearest city. Your job is to develop data to include in an online media kit for that paper's Web site. Begin by reviewing the Web page and newspaper media kits for major newspapers like *The New York Times* (http://www.nytmarketing.com/media-kit2), *USA Today* (go to www.usatoday.com and click on the Media Kit link at the bottom of the page), *Los Angeles Times* (www.latimes.com/ extras/mediakits/latdotcom), and the *Chicago Tribune* (www.tribune interactive.com/chicago/mediakit/).

Then review pertinent information about interactive marketing and advertising at the Interactive Advertising Bureau's (www.iab.net) Web site. Visit the Online Publishers Association site (www.online-publishers.org) for reports and data. Also, review the Electronic Publishing link at the Newspaper Association of America's home page (www.naa. org). Next, review the Web sites of the existing major media outlets in your city or market (e.g., those for TV stations, radio stations, cable outlets, magazines, other newspaper sites, online sites, etc.). Review the types of information and data they include as well as how they describe the benefits of advertising in each medium or vehicle. Develop your own list of pros and cons from surfing these Web sites. Obtain ideas for what to include, what not to include, what to do, and what not to do in the Web site you are developing or updating for the paper. Also, consider the pros and cons of the vehicle's existing media kit and Web page. Also, review the trade publication Web sites noted earlier in the chapter to see the kinds of information available for media kits in other media.

Assignment

Develop a media kit or provide recommendations for updating and for improving your paper's online site that includes the following sections. Provide details, data, and specific information where possible. At the end of each question, provide a section on how the paper's media kit or Web site should be improved or changed. (See the comments in parentheses after Questions 1 and 2 for examples.)

1. About the online paper: Provide background information about the paper, its mission, and descriptions of major pages or features on the site. (Then discuss what should be added, changed, dropped, etc.)
2. Online editorial sections and descriptions: Provide a brief overview of each section of the paper and the kinds of articles often found in each section. Identify whether each section targets any specific or special reader segments. (Then discuss which sections should be added or dropped, any new reader segments that should be targeted, etc.)
3. Online editorial calendar: Provide an editorial calendar showing when special issues will be published during the year (if available or applicable).
4. Online audience data: Provide an audience profile of readers including demographics, psychographics, and all other information available. Provide any information you have on reader loyalty, how long readers visit the site, and so on. Compare and contrast the online and regular newspaper readers.
5. Comparative data on other local media Web pages: provide any information that identifies the advantages of advertising on the paper's

Web site versus the Web sites of other media outlets. Explain why advertisers should advertise on your paper's site rather than or in addition to other local Web sites.

6. Online rate information: Provide information about Web rates, advertising acceptability standards (or what ads the paper will/will not accept for publication), and other information for selling the site not included in Number 7.

7. Online advertising units: Recommend the types of online ads to offer for sale to advertisers. Justify and support your choices.

8. Obtaining reader information: Provide ideas and suggestions for obtaining demographic, psychographic, or other information from readers. For example, should you require readers to register when first visiting your site and obtain demographic and other information then? What other ways could you collect information for your media kit online that respect the privacy of your readers? What information should you try to collect (e.g., age, income, zip code, education, etc.) and why (especially information that is not already being collected by the newspaper)?

9. Discuss any other improvements or changes that are needed. Provide any other advice or guidance for developing or updating the online media kit for the paper. Provide any other data, design advice, methods, resources, and so on that might be helpful in developing or improving the site so it is useful to advertisers.

Case 9.5 Dealing With Cable Customer Dissatisfaction

You are the manager of the cable system in your city (or the nearest city). You are concerned about constant complaints from customers regarding service. You received 20 letters this week alone; you shudder to think how many complaints the receptionist received by phone. You are also concerned because the local city government is beginning to make noise about the poor level of service the cable company provides.

You decide to conduct a survey of subscribers to identify the major service problems and determine how they might be solved. You have never conducted a survey and cannot afford to hire a research firm. You must design a study that can be conducted by you and your employees.

Assignment

Prepare a report describing how you could design and conduct such a survey from scratch using only company employees and resources. Include the following in your report:

1. Identify and describe the appropriate method to use to conduct the survey and how it can be handled in house. In other words, what kind of survey can be handled by local cable employees and why?
2. Discuss the sources of free or low-cost information to consult for developing your consumer survey. Explain how these sources can be used and why they are appropriate for this situation.
3. Explain how questions for the questionnaire will be developed. In other words, how can you find out what the major problems are before you conduct the survey? How can you decide which questions to include in the survey and why? How can you allow for employee input on which questions to include? How can you allow for community input on which questions to include?
4. Provide examples of the types of questions that accurately measure what your major service problems are.
5. Suggest other questions to include, if any, besides questions regarding the problems and their solutions. Describe the other types of questions to include and explain why they are needed.
6. Make a decision regarding the kind of survey to conduct. Explain and support your decision.

Case 9.6 Analyzing Research Methods for Measuring Online Audiences

Visit the Online Publisher's Association (OPA) and download the White Paper entitled Measuring Local Audiences Online (www.online-publishers.org/pdf/OPALocalWhitePaper.pdf). Read the report (or a newer version, if available). Check if OPA has posted other more recent reports on the topic.

Then visit the Web sites of the research companies analyzed in the report and read about these services [including comScore Media Metrix (www.comscore.com/metrix), Nielsen//NetRatings (www.nielsen-netratings.com), Scarborough Research (www.scarborough.com), and The Media Audit (www.themediaaudit.com) in the October 2005 white paper].

Conduct an online database search for articles or additional information about how local online audiences are measured. Find and read about any other relevant research companies that offer online measurement services.

Assignment

Select a market and Web site (that is not used in the white paper) or use those assigned by your professor. Review the site itself and consider which aspects of the site should be measured. Review the site's media kit to discover the type of information currently provided to advertisers online. Think about any other information that should be measured or provided to advertisers.

Then write a paper assessing the report(s) and research company Web sites you've analyzed. Recommend which research service(s) the Web site in your market or city should use and why. Recommend any new information or data that should be measured and explain why. At minimum, answer the following questions in your report.

1. Which measurement service is the best to use for your market and Web site? Why? Explain your choice in detail and explain why its methods and measures were the best for your site.
2. What are the major advantages of the online measurement service you selected?
3. What are the major disadvantages of the online measurement service you selected?
4. Would it be helpful to hire more than one online measurement service if you could? Why or why not? What additional information could the other online measurement services provide?
5. What information do you need to make it easier to make this decision about which measurement service to hire?
6. What other ideas or recommendations do you have?

10

MAKING SENSE OF IT ALL: MANAGING KNOWLEDGE

You're an online content provider on the five-person newspaper Website staff and your job is to put local and wire stories up on the site as they come in. You need to keep the site fresh with stories and art.

After working there several weeks you realize that you don't really know what the audience wanted as far as news stories. You are basically using your own news judgment when it comes to choosing wire stories to put on the site. When you think a story merits bigger play, meaning up high on the site, you ask someone on the online desk, usually the supervisor, if it merits such play, just to get a second opinion. However, usually the staff stories play up high.

You ask the online editor if you can do a survey, one that you could post online and have users complete to find out what stories they like to read online. You would like to know how they like the design/navigation of the Web sites, and how do they read the site (top down, straight to local news, etc.)? You feel confident in your survey-writing ability, since you are taking a survey-research course and this would fulfill a course requirement.

Your boss likes the idea. (He oversees all six people on the staff.) During down time at work, you write the questions as you think of them. When you finish, you give him a copy. Later, four of you (including your immediate supervisor) go outside for a couple hours, look over the survey, fine tune it, add questions (such as what type of content would the online readers be willing to pay for). You then make all of the group's corrections and the survey is finished. All you have left to do is to sell it to "the big boss," the general manager (GM), who oversees all of the online sites that the newspaper runs (the entertainment site, classifieds, etc.). You set up a meeting and your supervisor accompanies you. The GM receives a copy of the survey a week prior to the meeting, so that he could look over it.

At the meeting, the group sits down and you start your sell. The GM tells you the survey is a good idea, but says, "We already survey our readers." Your initial, internal reaction is, "We do?" but you don't say it, of course.

He continues, "When users log in to the site for the first time we ask them all of these same questions—what types of content they like." He uses the example of how a lot of users like to read about travel. You know that travel is the least-hit topic on the site.

"This isn't a marketing survey," you say. "It's a reader survey, strictly to learn what readers want news-wise."

This doesn't seem to make sense to the GM. You try to be as professional as you can and your supervisor tries to reinforce your point but is just as dumbfounded as you are. The survey is essentially a no-go. Your supervisor apologizes to you on the walk back to your desks. There was nothing he could really do, he says. He later writes an e-mail to your professor (the evaluation e-mail at the end of your class) apologizing that your survey won't be used.

Here you are, willing to do something to improve the news site. Basically, free labor. And you were shot down, even though you have the backing of the entire online desk and your supervisor. You feel the GM was a little out of touch with the whole news process and what readers really wanted, but who are *you* to say this?

Welcome to the real world! Just as the content provider discovered that "things happen," so too, do media managers as they try to use several types of information to make decisions. For example, a sports reporter discovered his newspaper's star sports editor/columnist (and his immediate boss) plagiarized quotes from a news service. The reporter told the paper's editor, who then *fired the reporter*. The paper's editor, who realized proper channels had not been followed (the sports reporter also had told several other reporters and staffers), considered the reporter's behavior a bigger threat to internal morale and organizational authority than that of the columnist. The sports editor subsequently was disciplined and eventually demoted (but his career was saved) while the rest of the staff was outraged!

This chapter discusses how media managers use (or don't use) information for planning and controlling organizational behavior. More importantly, it suggests that information can come in any form, at any time, and that a good media manager transforms that information into knowledge—a proactive management tool that sorts, classifies, evaluates, and socially tests situations and people, thereby allowing a manager to make a more sound decision (see a full definition later in this chapter).

This chapter offers reasons knowledge for and procedural contexts in which media managers can comfortably use knowledge. As a reward for reading this text's first nine chapters, you deserve to know—assuming you haven't already come to the conclusion—that not everything we say or suggests works all the time. Decisions (chapter 1) go wrong; leadership (chapter 2) can be flawed; motivation (chapter 3) can be elusive and misfire; global markets (chapter 4) are complex and unpredictable; technology (chapter 5), market analysis (chapters 8 & 9) are just two tools; laws can be restrictive and ethics can be violated (chapter 6); and, finally, planning (chapter 7)—while another tool—cannot anticipate every reality.

The *harsh* reality, then, is that managers and their subordinates often behave in ways that seem unexplainable—much of it based on the types of information they have received and how they perceive it. As you'll discover in the Extended Cases chapter following this chapter, not every situation arrives with a full set of data and information; often you'll have to find more information online or in a library or a pamphlet or via talking to someone more experienced. As this chapter illustrates (and as the extended cases will test), media managers must learn to improvise and manage on the fly.

Certainly, managers can select from a wide range of information, depending on several factors, including the manager's level in the organization, the long- or short-term nature of the decision, the organization's size and complexity, and the nature of the firm. However, regardless of the information's quality or source, some things just don't seem to make sense. The next section discusses the thinking processes that often result in seemingly nonsensical managerial moments.

Facing "Unreality"

People are never dull and are full of surprises. However, fortunately, nothing is new under the behavioral sun. The following describes the cognitive theories or approaches that a media manager should include in his or her tool kit (or at least have in a filing cabinet under "huh?").

Cognitive dissonance. Psychologists describe thoughts, or "cognitions" that contradict each other as "dissonant," while cognitions that agree are "consonant." Cognitions that neither agree nor disagree with each other are said to be "irrelevant." Having a new cognition in opposition to a current cognition creates a state of "dissonance," that IS great or small depending on the cognitions involved. You can reduce dissonance either by abolishing the dissonant cognitions, or by adding new consonant cognitions. When the dissonance level exceeds the resistance of one of the cognitions involved, you will change or abolish that cognition and, thus, reduce dissonance. Therefore, subordinates (or superiors) experiencing dissonance may look for information that will reduce dissonance. They will seek dissonance-reducing information and avoid dissonance-enhancing information. Some involuntarily exposed to dissonance may very well write off that information by overlooking, misjudging, or refuting it (Festinger, 1957).

This may sound similar to equity theory (Adams, 1963), which says inequity is a motivator. For example, employees who feel unfairly treated will attempt to achieve a sense of equity. A reporter could "satisfice" a story if he knows comparable reporters in the newsroom earn more money; changing how much he works, increasing his pay, changing how he compares himself, among other methods, may decrease the dissonance. However, this theory also has been seen (Aronson, 1969) as a connection to how people view themselves; e.g., cognitive dissonance arises not when people have conflicting thoughts, but instead, when they see their behavior as conflicting with their self-concept. Therefore, in this view, dissonance between "I'm a good reporter," and "I plagiarized a story," would not occur if the person viewed him- or herself as a liar.

To follow that thought, an editor may have various doubts about a story's truthfulness, but she has to either publish or kill the story. But to work over time believing the story's author always plagiarizes would be intolerable. Therefore, working conditions themselves prompt many managers to see what they want to see, or, technically speaking, to reduce dissonance. That's not to excuse misbehavior, however; Macarena Hernandez could have used the same thought process when she noticed *The New York Times* 2003 story about a Texas woman whose soldier son was missing in Iraq. Instead, she notified her *San Antonio Express-News* editors that the story had elements "word for word" from her own story about the woman; this marked the beginning of the fall of renowned plagiarist Jayson Blair. The Blair scandal showed how well-intentioned editors can improperly use information. However, such celebrated cases—and plagiarism incidents—aren't the norm when it comes to dissonance. Media managers create quite a bit of dissonance, for example, each time they critique someone's work (What writer hasn't thought their writing was perfect?) or decide *not* to choose someone for a promotion. Dissonance, in a sense, comes with the territory.

That's especially true in this age of change and convergence. For example, it's not uncommon to think negatively about employees in departments other than your own. Many advertising sales people, for example, believe journalists are spoiled, "prima donnas," or elitist toward others in the organization. Journalists, for their part, may view non-newsroom personnel as being less educated, lower class, or less trustworthy. Imagine the dissonance—positive and negative—when such employees are thrown together on a task force or team venture. That's what happened when a group of Swedish journalists merged with some of their newspaper's advertising sales staff to create the paper's Web site. The groups came to respect each other; close working conditions meant old-group identities were renegotiated and reformed, but not before difficulty arose between members of the merged departments (Fagerling & Norbäck, 2005). Employees naturally seek a stable state where minimal dissonance exists, and change may threaten that state. In organizations with a culture of trust, where change is frequent, and employees expect positive outcomes, employees tend to already be receptive to change (Burnes & James, 1995). Any kind of management-imposed compliance with new rules or ideals, then, can expect to generate dissonance.

If you're a student, you no doubt recall a time when you believed your performance in a class or on a test was top notch. If you're like most people, that performance may actually have been less sterling than you imagined or expected, at least in the eyes of your instructor. Such personal or near-personal interactions frequently make solid opportunities to sow the seeds of emotional dissonance and stress, particularly when it involves role evaluations (self-evaluations and those of supervisors and/or subordinates) and self-esteem (Abraham, 1999). However, many editors avoid these opportunities because of feelings similar to those vented below by a former *Washington Post* reporter (Downie, Bennett, & Coleman, 2006, p. 20):

> "I found the experience frustrating and humiliating," said a former education reporter, who left in 2004. "My assignment editor asked me for feedback after she gave me my evaluation and then cut me off and argued with what I was saying. I never finished. She then told me to sign the evaluation that day because she was in a hurry. I got the impression that my input was unnecessary and my involvement a formality."

And if you're soon graduating, you most likely know about the notoriously low beginning pay scales of many journalistic positions. We know that job satisfaction has a big impact on dissonance; we also know that older journalists are more satisfied than younger journalists (Weaver & Wilhoit, 1996), with higher pay a probable influence. So it's not unusual to—in your first two years as a professional—discover considerable dissonance when you ponder your situation: a low-paying job, probably in a smaller locale with limited nightlife, away from your primary family, possessing a burning desire to move up the professional ladder in pay and status. Now, consider your supervisor's dilemma in that situation: train you so you're ready when it's time to move up but understand your behavior and try to keep you motivated until then. That may explain why they're sending you to cover that energy conference that you didn't ask to attend but for which you're grateful to get away from the office!

As the manager in that scenario, you may find yourself scratching your head, flipping a coin, and hoping for the best. At least employee evaluations usually come only once a year. Seriously, such situations—in addition to testing your patience—will test your knowledge of motivational theory and your ability to clearly communicate with the involved employees. You should be prepared for both and manage such information accordingly.

Prospecting.   Matt prided himself on his recruiting ability. As the managing editor of one of the top 10 newspapers in the country, he was intent on diversifying the newsroom—starting with the kid in front of him. Deep South native Earl was 4 years into his career at a little southern afternoon daily, having worked his way up the ladder to an assistant city editor position there but feeling overwhelmed and looking for a change. Matt's big-city daily beckoned—a general assignment reporting job, nice, union-based pay, and a chance to see the rest of the country. But the visit had left him cold: The paper's newsroom looked like any other, the city's downtown was cold and dirty (it was late February), minorities were hard to find, and reporting meant starting over again, with editors in control of your fate. Still, this was a chance at the big time.

Before you try to determine whether Earl will take the job, you need to understand prospect theory (Kahneman & Tversky, 1979), which concerns the behavior of individuals faced with two alternatives. Often, people make irrational choices—some might say "gambles"—in such situations. Prospect theory predicts that preferences will depend on how a choice is framed or presented. If the reference point—the issue as it's framed (usually seen as the *status quo*)—is viewed as positive, then the opposing choice will be seen as a risk to avoid. If the issue's framed negatively, then the opposing choice will be seen as a risk to be sought and taken. In some respects, this resembles a costs-benefits analysis with an added, emotional factor.

You can probably foresee that prospect theory potentially has much larger implications in managing. It points to the power managers may have in framing events or issues and the degree to which the frame gets accepted (e.g., see George, Chattopadhyay, Sitkin, & Barden, 2006). In media managing, prospect-theory applications may arise in many settings: strategizing and planning, motivating, organizing—in short, any time risk is perceived, which usually is every day. Editors always take risks in deciding what's news, for example, with the fear of being scooped, embarrassed or seen as the top risk. Of greater concern, as seen in Matt and Earl's dilemma, are those key or pivotal instances when perceptions of risk vary and may provide a difference of opinion or differing behaviors.

Of greater concern, as seen in Matt and Earl's dilemma, are instances when perceptions of risk vary and may provide a difference of opinion or differing behaviors that puzzle or confuse managers. For example, why do some reporters fabricate and plagiarize and most don't? Why do some people see teams (or any other kind of change) as a threat? Why do some people conform to group pressures while others chafe? Why do some people quit while others persist? Many such questions will never have a satisfactory, clear-cut answer. However, the media manager must continue to ask these questions in order to effectively manage. For instance, some reporters know more (or at least their news copy seems to indicate as much) about the legal restrictions on journalism than others. But a manager can only provide so much education, which by itself can prevent only so much behavior. Apparently frequent and informal discussions of legal problems raise awareness of the law—even the law's more formal aspects (Voakes, 1995). Therefore, an editor or news director should seek to foster discussion and work to incorporate positive, enabling framing at every opportunity.

Overcoming assumptions plays an important role in this approach. For example, simply because a person has a college journalism degree does not mean that person's supervisor should presume that the person is fully ready to do the job when hired. Yet, a national survey of TV news directors asking about their employees' abilities in story development, available training programs, and training areas in which news directors have interest indicated that TV stations have relied too heavily on higher education to provide all the knowledge and skills TV journalists need to function in the profession (Ellis & Jabro, 1997). Too often, managers assume that they and their subordinates carry the same attitudes and values, when research has shown that even managers have different values (Sylvie & Huang, 2006).

Assumptions also stem from selective perception, or how individuals perceive things differently according to their expectations. An assignment editor who's been to dozens of school-board meetings believes that a reporter should never leave a meeting early because important issues sometimes get decided late in the meeting. A brand new reporter who's never covered a school-board meeting doesn't necessarily know that and assumes all the important issues have been covered, especially when there's nothing controversial left on the agenda. Therefore, it may seem to the assignment editor that the reporter should have stayed at the meeting until the bitter end (when the school board decided, after an executive session, to file for bankruptcy), but the reporter may believe the meeting was "essentially" over, the bankruptcy news was "just one of those things" and that nothing was wrong. Selective perception is just one bias among many, as Fig. 10.1 illustrates.

Therefore, although media managers can never completely eliminate surprise judgments, evaluations or decisions by subordinates, they can at least understand what elements influence such results. That's why Matt was not surprised when Earl rejected the job offer, which he saw as a step down from the mental challenges of editing. Matt suspected as much by listening to Earl discuss his hopes for the future and by understanding that not everyone is the same. Earl wound up going to graduate school, while Matt became editor of the paper.

Myth-making. The headline said it all: "Board probes special ed director's use of funds." It was the talk of talk radio, the lead story on the six o'clock news, and a juicy *whodunit* with all the makings of a soap opera. Did she or didn't she? Was she really cashing in on less-privileged kids? Jorge should have been happy that such a hot item was *the story* everyone on his beat wanted to discuss. There was only one thing wrong: Jorge didn't write the story; his own city editor scooped him.

BillyBob Turner was no ordinary city editor; a Pulitzer-finalist as a city hall reporter and a legendary investigative writer, he was known for his exposés on everything from vote buying in rural counties to gambling in the police department. No local politician wanted to get a call from him because it could only mean bad news. However, BillyBob was pursued by a competing organizaton for its city editor position, and he took it because it doubled his salary and he was challenged with making the paper a hard-hitting local-news leader. He still enjoyed

Bandwagon effect – doing or believing things because others do/believe the same
Bias blind spot – not compensating for your own cognitive biases
Choice-supportive bias – remembering your choices as better than they actually were
Confirmation bias – searching for or interpreting information that confirms your preconceptions
Congruence bias – the tendancy to test hypotheses exclusively through direct testing
Disconfirmation bias – uncritically believing information congruent to your prior beliefs while being critical of
Focusing effect – placing too much importance on one aspect of an event, thereby causing error in predicting the
Hyperbolic discounting – occurs when people discount the future consequences in preference for more immediate
Illusion of control – thinking you can control or influence outcomes you clearly cannot
Impact bias – the tendency to overestimate the intensity of your emotional responses to circumstances
Information bias – the tendency to seek information even when it cannot affect action
Loss aversion – the tendency to strongly prefer avoiding losses over acquiring gains
Neglect of probability – the tendency to disregard probability when deciding under uncertainty.
Mere exposure effect – the more we are exposed to something, the more we like it
Omission bias – judging harmful actions as worse, or less moral than equally harmful omissions (inactions.)
Outcome bias – judging outcomes in a way irrelevant to a decision's quality; judging a decision by its eventual
Pseudocertainty effect – selecting a less effective option because of the illusion of risk in another option
Rosy retrospection – rating the past more positively than you rated it when it occurred
Selective perception – the tendency for expectations to affect perception
Status quo bias – the tendency for people to like things to stay relatively the same
Von Restorff effect – remembering something moreso because it stands out more than other memories
Zero-risk bias – preferring to eliminate a small risk than more greatly reducing a larger risk

FIGURE 10.1. Decision-making and behavioral biases.

reporting, however, and he had pursued the special ed story for a year, finally breaking it in yesterday's paper. Unfortunately for Jorge, Billy-Bob never told him about it. In fact, the day the story broke, he gave Jorge a paternal pat on the back and said, "Yep, Jorge, that was a good story; let me tell you how I did it."

Media managers like to believe they know what they are doing—they have their work situations fairly under control, their subordinates usually do their jobs and as they're told, they (the managers), for the most part, get along with others in an atmosphere constructive for working, and, they represent models of reasonable management; e.g., they make sound, rational, and logical decisions. They strongly hold this belief and behave accordingly. However, some of the same managers will sell their souls for a promotion or pay raise, or arbitrarily and capriciously decide to fire or transfer a subordinate, or tear apart your social plans on a moment's whim of "planning" or routinely make decisions without input from others. Those lofty self-beliefs? Myths, theories, and things we all espouse to be. The "real" manager is the one who just refused to listen to your appeal of her decision to send you to the electric-company office with a drug-store thermometer to see "if those folks practice what they preach on energy saving"? That, unfortunately, was real—a "theory in use" (Argyris, 2000).

In short, we often *say* one thing and *do* another. Such "Model I" behavior springs from our desire to be in unilateral control, to win, to suppress negative feelings, and to act as rationally as possible, which leads us to (Argyris, 2000, p. 5):

> . . . advocate our position, make evaluations of performance, and offer attributions about others' intentions in such a way that we remain in control, maximize our chances to win, and suppress negative feelings. In practice, this means that we act in ways that encourage neither inquiry into our views nor the robust testing of the claims that we make. Indeed, the only test possible under these conditions is one that uses self-referential logic: "Trust me; I know what I am doing."

Model I practitioners defensively project blame for errors on others and on the system, which results in defensive dialogue and—astoundingly—an unawareness that they behave as such. They tend to advocate general, vague benchmarks, or goals while simultaneously avoiding any challenge or attempt to accurately measure progress via the use of more projection or, worse, repressing any negative responses or assessment. Let's use a perennially underachieved goal—diversification of content and of the newsroom—to show how this works.

All Model I behavior springs from a set of general, underlying governing conditions (the lack of diversity, political, and economic pressure from interested parties [e.g., advertisers and readers], and the lack of effective retention tools). These variables prompt action strategies that media managers and their subordinates use in reaction. A typical management reaction might include "The newsroom's not minority friendly. We're not nurturing minority journalists' creativity." Supervisors should more actively and regularly address career-development and advancement issues for journalists of color; and since minority journalists themselves are diverse, the company must tailor recruitment and retention efforts more to the individual (based on McGill, 2000).

Subordinates, on the other hand, might say, "The pay is too low, and the hours are too long." Minorities feel as if they have to work harder than nonminorities to get ahead; minorities leave because they feel more pressure than nonminorities to cover racial/ethnic stories, the company "has bent over backward" to hire Blacks and women for high-profile jobs at the expense of equally or more qualified White males. They also might say, "There's not enough time to properly recruit. This is just a political thing, for appearances' sake (e.g., diversity doesn't really matter). We have to lower our standards to find minorities, and the bigger media companies get the lion's share of minorities while smaller outfits have to fight over the crumbs." Note that both management's and subordinates' responses are somewhat vague and, to a large degree, untestable.

There's nothing out of the ordinary or nonsensical about these responses. However, the problem is that they can be self-fulfilling; they're defensive because no one wants to look as if it's their fault (they all want to "win"). For example, mid-level editors see their supervisors as unrealistic and not mindful of the degree of work involved in retaining minorities, and as sending mixed messages ('We want you to hire more minorities but we're not going to give you any additional resources to do it."). Top-level editors see mid-level editors as lazy, satisficing, always wanting money thrown at problems, and also sending mixed messages ("We want to hire more minorities, but we're unwilling to take the time to do it."). Such feelings create cynicism and further mistrust while, more importantly, discourage constructive action by making employees believe they'll get "burned" for doing so ("Even if I hire more minorities, the nonminorities will get angry, and my bosses will be on my back for not promoting the minorities fast enough or not being able to make everybody happy. To hell with that!"). This essentially creates silence or an absence of action that can be misinterpreted as a lack of caring or a lack of ability, which then continues to feed the negative cycle. Eventually, no change or learning occurs because no one wants to talk about it for fear of "losing control" or being on the losing side.

To avoid such an end, managers need to engage in Model II behavior (Argyris, 2000). This involves a conscious testing of the vaguely worded, untestable assumptions or rationales people offer when faced with an issue or problem. For example, "How do we know money is a problem in retaining minorities? Have we asked? Have we studied the issue by comparing salaries of minorities and nonminorities?" If the answers indicate these are valid points, the manager acts accordingly and works to correct the problem.

Too often, however, the answers also are vague, untestable, defensive statements (e.g., "What else could it be?" or "I just know! Trust me."). In that case, the manager advocates (and validates) his or her own views while insisting on valid measures or reasons, taking care not to put others on the defensive. Using this approach means you are willing to share power with "anyone who has competence and is relevant to deciding" the issue or problem (p. 76). This approach not only encourages honest dialogue, but also requires participants to engage in authentic dialogue and leave their Model I "comfort zone." Only then can a media manager hope her employees will incorporate *her* goals in *their own* personal set of motivational drives and that productive behavior will follow.

Model II behavior is an example or end-product of hard work and willingness to share. If BillyBob had shared with Jorge, perhaps Jorge would not have withheld all the information *he* knew about the special ed director's romantic involvement with the superintendent. And perhaps BillyBob wouldn't have believed that Jorge was "just a blind, naïve rookie." Either way, reality would seem less harsh and easier to swallow and BillyBob's managerial techniques would approximate those advocated in the following section.

Harsh Realities

As the prior discussion illustrated, reality is more complex than it initially appears. In the highly competitive media industry where technology and markets constantly change to adapt to ever-increasing competition, media managers must be adept at handling change and prepare their subordinates (and superiors) to handle that change. To do so requires solid decision making based on reliable, manageable, useable, and resourceful information. In other words, media managers need to supervise knowledge as well.

Knowledge is a specific kind of information suited to solving a problem or enabling decision making that is developed through experience and conducting research. Hislop (2005) distinguished between information and knowledge by saying knowledge is something we possess and can make explicit and is derived from information or its use. Knowledge is not only an idea but, rather, embedded in practice (pp. 27–40), much like a newsroom represents a level of knowledge about a local community. Knowledge obviously is embodied in people, but it's also socially constructed because the routines, behavior, and interactions between people create knowledge. To continue the newsroom analogy, think of reporting "beats" as socially constructed knowledge or as group subcultures having culturally embedded knowledge. The information these group members share is developed via the everyday group routines.

People can choose to share, or choose not to share, knowledge or contest the information contained in knowledge. Not sharing makes knowledge something personal, subjective, and—as in the case of Billy Bob and Jorge—something that creates tension or conflict between manager and subordinate. Finally, knowledge is multidimensional due to all the biases and possible categories of knowledge. For example, in addition to individual and group knowledge, knowledge can be situational, abstract, implicit, explicit, verbal, and nonverbal, among other categories.

Therefore, knowledge has its fundamental roots in human, social, and cultural elements. It should come as no surprise that managing and sharing knowledge carries with it social and cultural issues (Hislop 2005, pp. 41–55) a media manager should grasp and use wisely.

Motivation to share.   This text has dealt at length with motivation (see chapter 3), so you're familiar with the many rationales that employees can use for hoarding or not sharing information. They can range from the selfish to the defensive to fear, to issues of trust and commitment—no surprises there. However, in a media setting, particular, "media-centric" elements arise, such as autonomy.

Obviously, so much of what the media produce comes from the hand of one or two individuals or—in the case of a mass effort—the interdependence of tasks conducted by one person or by a small group of persons who basically do so with little or no supervision. That degree of autonomy may be specific to only one or a set of tasks, but the sense of autonomy that it bestows may "leak"—intentionally or not—to other tasks. Attempts to change or modify that autonomy can create a high level of anxiety or resentment, thus affecting the employee's motivation to share knowledge and possibly generating concerns about expertise, status, or power. As we've seen in the previous section, this may generate cynicism, lack of trust, miscommunication and other, unproductive, Model I behaviors.

Media managers, especially in the era of increasing convergence, changing markets, and ever-evolving technology, work to persuade their subordinates in all departments that multimedia platforms and formats, new forms of storytelling, citizen journalism, and changing tastes can be used in their best interests and with no substantial changes in autonomy. As we saw in chapters 3 and 5, without clear feedback from employees—who believe the change you're trying to implement is vital to how well they can do their jobs—media managers are unable to successfully facilitate or take advantage of innovation.

Communities of practice.   Informal groups that have some common activities typically will develop a common body of knowledge as well. This not only includes cliques of certain types of workers, but perhaps also a group of managers. They support each other and the knowledge they generate but also develop ways of sharing information among the group. For example, a group of reporters may take a new reporter to a local after-hours bar for "indoctrination," while some managers may invite the newest of their group to play golf on Saturday morning. Either venue helps the group develop a sense of identity and strengthen personal relationships and mutual trust.

Chapter 3 mentions these communities indirectly when discussing culture (as does chapter 5), but the media manager also should recognize such groups as crucial tools in the constructive management of knowledge. For example, the introduction of a new technology may want to feature training sessions tailored specifically for certain practice communities. For instance, copy editors learning a new editing system may want to learn as a group in order to assure no questions specific to the group's tasks go unanswered. Such sessions not only would generate priceless peer support for learning the technology, but also would illustrate management's understanding of the group's needs as well as reinforce the group's sense of autonomy and interactive mechanisms.

Power and conflict.   Similar to previous discussions on Model I behavior, it's wise to admit that conflict exists in all organizations, most notably in media companies: journalists vs. management, advertising staff vs. journalistic staff, online vs. print/broadcast, upper management vs. middle management, and so on. Different people will always have divergent interests; managers have to account for power and conflict when managing knowledge processes (Hislop, pp. 88–89):

> . . . The requirement of organizations to appropriate economic value from their workers' knowledge may conflict with their workers' individual objectives in this respect. For example, while there are economic benefits to organizations from having their workers share or codify their knowledge, workers may be unwilling to do so if they feel such a process may dilute and diminish their expertise.

This would be obvious to see, for example, that in instances of convergence or convergence initiatives, one group not only learns a new skill, but also has to share its expertise with other groups. Not only does that group's specific knowledge implant the group with power, so does the relative lack of the group's knowledge in other areas of the organization. Therefore, power influences *and is influenced by* knowledge and how it's managed. Some (e.g., Foucault, 1980) would go so far as to say knowledge *is* power; e.g., the mere fact that a subordinate is "the subordinate" means he can never be sure when he is being evaluated when in the presence of "a superior" and, thus, he can never totally let his guard down.

In effect, then, a media manager must always be cognizant—when trying to manipulate or overcome these "harsh realities" of organizational life—that she's also playing somewhat of a "power game" with subordinates. Managing knowledge, in a sense then, means using power to produce, select, or harness knowledge, which produces more power for someone. Recall that the GM in our online newspaper scenario in this chapter's introduction had power to accept or reject the readership survey. By arbitrarily refusing to recognize the proposal as new knowledge, he not only exercised his power, he figuratively whipped his subordinates with it, generating the knowledge that he was in charge and that knowledge had no place in his organization.

While understanding the roles that employee motivation, communities of practice, and power have in your attempt to navigate the turbulent seas of organizational knowledge, "lifesavers" exist. The next section will attempt to illustrate that the course you chart still is very much in your own hands.

"Preventive Remedies" for Knowledge Management

When last we saw you, you had just been devastated by your online site GM's veto of your readership study proposal. "Things happen," you said to comfort yourself. Unfortunately, there's nothing to immediately change matters in such a situation. However, that does not preclude using this instance as a stepping stone to more successful and proactive knowledge management for the future. Others will excuse your seemingly undeserved rosy outlook because a media manager's ultimate intent concerns productivity—solving problems and learning from mistakes. Of course, one way of doing so involves making good decisions; but that didn't happen, if the GM's decision is any indicator. Therefore, let's lay the groundwork for the next decision, taking advantage of two remaining tools.

Creating knowledge. As the content provider and probable manager in training at the online site, your power's limited to getting the ear of your editor, who seems willing enough. Your aim—to help the GM "unlearn" his current thinking toward your idea—obviously carries merit. However, to create knowledge—essentially earn a change of mind—you first have to understand what lies ahead.

Recall that we previously mentioned that knowledge comes in different types or forms. An organization's knowledge can be classified as tacit, explicit, and cultural (Boisot, 1998). Employees use *tacit knowledge*—usually inexpressible except via action or skills—to do their jobs; e.g., it's personal, perhaps intuitive, difficult to express, but the employees possess it. By comparison, employees can share, verbalize, or objectively illustrate *explicit knowledge*. It takes various, impersonal, organizational forms, such as reports, budgets, page formats, technical standards, official memos, policies, recordings, publications, and so on. Less frequently, you'll encounter *cultural knowledge* when you discuss the organization's identity, business, customers, values, and goals. In short, employees find cultural knowledge in the beliefs, ideals, and rules they share and understand as their company's purpose, concerns, and circumstances.

To help this knowledge evolve, grow, or change for the better, a media manager most often will have to convert tacit knowledge to explicit knowledge—obviously, because the latter can be shared and, when knowledge is shared, it's more likely to become examined, argued, accepted, rejected, or modified. Therefore, when an editor begins to verbalize his ideas of what makes a good story, his reporting staffers can consider, use, modify, or reject those ideas when they conduct interviews and research. Our content provider knew, for example, that the travel section was one of the site's least-viewed areas, directly contradicting what the GM believed he "knew." The content provider also knew the difference between a marketing survey and a readership survey, but was hesitant (or, at least, made an unsuccessful attempt) to do so. Both instances kept tacit knowledge tacit. So creating knowledge doesn't happen overnight.

An easier avenue entails taking advantage of an organization's *core capabilities,* uniquely held knowledge that makes it superior to other organizations (Leonard, 1995). These capabilities include employees' skills, knowledge entrenched in physical systems, managerial structures that support and reinforce knowledge growth, and values that support or oppose the accrual of knowledge. Therefore, the content provider in our scenario must learn (or ask the online editor to help) to "create knowledge" or find a way within the company's framework to open the GM's eyes.

One method might involve regrouping or asking the online editor to call a meeting to discuss the GM's decision and examine the alternatives. Such *shared problem solving* involves obtaining different viewpoints and skills to develop another, perhaps more innovative, approach. Of course, the problem requires a creative approach because the group has a large hurdle to leap.

Let's say you decide to take the initiative and indirectly force the issue. You know that every day the computer servers record what readers do when they're online. These logs, or raw data, can be mined to determine readership patterns by type of content, span of attention per page, popularity of embedded links, viewing paths (e.g., what a reader reads before and after viewing a site), etc. All the data are there and waiting for someone with the time and patience to compile and analyze these factors. By *implementing and integrating new processes and tools* such as these and presenting the findings in an unsolicited report, you show your initiative and provide valuable analytical measures for the site. The earlier survey proposal may be forgotten if you present this analysis in a different light.

You'd like to analyze the data, but time is money and you're underpaid and overworked enough without taking on a new chore. And let's say no one knows how to mine the data or the capability doesn't exist. In that case, you and your boss have two choices: first, attempt to generate the data by having the technical staff explore how to create the capability or write the software to deliver the capability. Such *experimentation* and *prototyping,* while innovative, could fail. If the technical staff proves incapable, perhaps next year when its budget increases it can *import the knowledge* via new a new software analyst or a new computer server.

Making sense of the environment.   Remember that helpless feeling after the GM's veto? "Ambiguity" probably best describes it. What's next? Where do I go from here? What does this mean besides "no"? We've all been there before, where things are metaphorically spinning. However, ambiguity doesn't necessarily imply "confusion." Businesses constantly try to examine their environment, whether it be the market, the regulatory atmosphere, the economy and interest rates, etc.; newsrooms are masters at this, taking chaos and information and converting them into "stories" and "news."

Of course, sense making has its traits (Weick, 1995): it's subject to interpretation, thus it's more in the realm of plausibility than reality; hence, the ambiguity. It's ongoing, so there's no avoiding it. Because you produce part of the environment, sense making is partly borne of your experience and therefore grounded in your identity. It's often a group activity and it's almost always done in hindsight, after the fact—a view on the past. For a manager, sense making basically means assessing and understanding the challenges ahead. It should be an almost-subconscious activity, meaning it is second nature.

For our content provider in the online newsroom, sense making means getting over the initial shock of the GM's rejection and objectively trying to place the incident within the frame of the tasks ahead. Translation: If the task was easy or obvious, it would have been done before. Get over it, and use it to your advantage. Then sense making becomes an opportunity—a chance to learn from the failure and successfully adjust.

However, to make sense requires placing the GM's decision in the equivalent of a conceptual 360-degree mirror. Get as many perspectives as possible. Ask for advice. Read. Search for ideas and knowledge on the Internet. Read some more. Place personal biases aside, question the previous approach. Ask for or conduct research to find more advice, etc. Such critical thinking and research lead to the development of some meaning or analysis that "makes sense." This approach leads to more productive behavior—in this case, a way to improve the selection of news to place on the Web site.

In essence, then, sense making is selecting a frame of reference with which to view the environment. In practical terms, a good manager needs a reliable and objective viewpoint from which to productively operate. To be productive, that viewpoint must be successfully tested against the experience of others, firm enough to work in most situations, yet flexible enough to be adjusted when necessary. In short, this is *a learning attitude*—again, "Model II" thinking (Argyris, 2000)—that allows you to perform your job *and* learn and adjust to changes in the environment.

Therefore, our content provider, or any media employee who feels "thrown for a loop" by the behavior and decisions of others, needs to learn how to regroup and reevaluate their position. Chances are the situation isn't as dire as first impressions make it seem.

Summary

This chapter discussed how media managers should use or manage information and knowledge. In the sometimes-harsh glare of everyday management, when things often seem to go wrong, textbook advice may not be the appropriate tool to use. However, apparently irrational behavior can be explained and used to the manager's advantage.

Cognitive dissonance, prospecting, and myth-making theories illustrate the complexity of the human mind as it defies simple analysis. Cognitive dissonance sheds light on how people seek to lessen conflicting concepts while prospecting shows how choices, and how we frame them, can test the bounds of logic. Myth-making—with its distinction of what people say vs. what they do—not only allows the manager to understand frustrating consequences but also provides a window on the rationales and self-fulfilling arguments that perpetuate such frustration.

Still, in dealing with these annoying moments, media managers have to understand that employees' motivations in sharing, their communities of practice, and the inherent conflict present in power-tainted situations can either be obstacles or tools. Comprehending the influence of these elements allows the media manager to elicit sincere employee input while being viewed as a supporter of informal groups and a consensus builder.

Finally, the media manager can take proactive steps in managing organizational knowledge via his or her ability to create knowledge and make appropriate sense of the environment. More than just mere buzzwords, these tools allow the manager to convert tacit knowledge to explicit, shared knowledge as well as to put events, decisions, markets, behaviors, and practically everything else in proper perspective—all of which facilitates good decision making, the heart of media management.

Case 10.1 Left-Column/Right-Column

The following assignment (modeled after Argyris, 2001), should help you reflect upon your own defensive reasoning, skilled unawareness, and counterproductive results in specific situations.

Assignment

1. Think a few minutes about dysfunctional higher-education class-room settings. Then complete your own management case using the following steps:
   - Take out a sheet of paper and write one paragraph describing a key, frustrating, structural, procedural, or organizational prob-lem as you see it in most classroom settings.
   - Now, in a paragraph or two, describe the strategy you would use in a meeting between you and whoever you would ideally speak to in order to solve the problem.
   - Draw a line down the center of your sheet. On the right side, describe how you would start the meeting—your actual words and actions. Next, on the same side, put in plain words what you would imagine the other person(s) would logically say or do. Next, describe exactly what you would say in response to the other person. Keep doing this for at least two more typed, double-spaced pages.
   - On the left side, describe how you would feel, what you would think, or why you would not relate to that person. Place each feel-ing or thought in its corresponding place alongside the comment on the right side that would evoke it. Hand in your sheets to your instructor, who, *in exchange*, will give you some handouts. Keep a copy of what you submitted for use in the next step as well.
   - The handouts describe Model II behaviors to be used in the next step 2 below.
2. Using the handouts your teacher distributed and, *for the next class meeting*, change your actions that you listed on the sheets in No. 1 above to illustrations of Model II behaviors. *Do not read the next step until the next class meeting!*
3. Compare what you've done to your instructor's diagnosis and other written comments and answer the following questions (you don't have to share the answers with anyone but the instructor if you don't want) pertaining to your initial case:
   - Are there any attempts to take unilateral control? If so, by whom?
   - Are there any attempts to cover up information or to cover up information that there's a cover up?

- Does anyone evaluate another's actions as wrong?
- Does anyone test (or make an attempt to test) the validity of another's evaluations?
- Is anyone being manipulative?
- Does any suggested strategy require secrecy of any kind?
- How do you explain any of the above?

Case 10.2 He Shoots! He...Airball!

It's NCAA basketball tournament time and you've been assigned the story about former local college hoops great Joe Redd. Redd made himself famous in the championship game by calling a time out with his team ahead by a point but out of time outs. This resulted in turning the ball over to the other team, Duke, which called an in-bounds play with 1.3 seconds left, enough time to sink the winning shot.

You were feeling just as lucky as Duke, and your story lead was out of Hemingway, or, maybe it was Dickens? "Joe Redd is enjoying the best of times," started the story of how Redd used his pain and embarrassment to boost him into an iconic career as a college hoops broadcaster.

A copy editor calls you at home as you're settling in to watch the tournament.

"Are you ill?" he asks, sarcastically repeating your lead: "Joe Redd is enjoying the best of times"?

"Whadduya mean am I ill?" you ask.

"This lead makes me want to blows chunks the size of my Aunt Martha."

You feel whipped. You and he revise it to make it a little more acceptable, e.g., much like those trite things you hate reading from the rest of the staff. He liked it, and said you also should like it. When the story is published, you don't even look at it. You just remember there might have been blood on the carpet that night when you hung up the phone.

Assignment

1. What kind of harsh reality does the above present to the reporter?
2. What could you, the reporter, have said during the phone call that would have resulted in a more pleasant reality for you?
3. What is the editor doing that he might later regret. For example, what future, harsh reality is he inviting?

4. Is the editor's call more likely to force a prospect theory situation, myth making, or cognitive dissonance? Why one more than the other?
5. Is it ever possible to conduct appropriate "sense making" on the spot like this? Why or why not?

Case 10.3 A Little Roll-Play

As assignment editor of the newsroom, you're minding the store as your boss attends a regional meeting for news directors. You're a bit worried, because your daughter battles bipolar disorder—and her treatment plan requires her to take her medicine, which means a parent has to be with the teen. Your work schedule is flexible, which is fortunate because your spouse travels a lot. You're on edge because it's almost your daughter's lunchtime.

But you're not a fan of the current generation of journalists in the newsroom. They're different, and they don't think like you. You get frustrated when they do things you wouldn't, when they need extra instruction, when they do a half-baked job, and when they wonder why they haven't won any awards. They think the newsroom should be a democracy. You remember when dictators were the norm.

You see Mary; she's been here in small-town Texas for 3 months. On her first day, you gave her a brief tour and took her into the lounge for some coffee and a pastry. You used your special knowledge of the vending machine and were able to get a free doughnut dispensed for her. Now you see her getting a cinnamon roll by using your "technique."

"Just a damn minute," you yell. "Who told you that you could do that? Put your quarters in the slot or go buy your own vending machine!"

She explains to you that she likes cinnamon rolls and it was the last one and she didn't have any change.

"What makes you so special?" you ask. "Why can't you just go without, like everyone else would in that case?

"Because I really want this roll," Mary says.

"What are you?" you respond, the disgust dripping with every word.

"I'm a roll person," she says, not getting the hint. "My parents are roll people, my siblings are roll people, my husband's a roll person, so I guess that makes me a roll person."

You're really ticked now; you can feel your blood pressure rising and you're going to miss your daughter's lunch. "That's no reason!" you scream. "What if all those people were thieves? Would that make *you* one? What would you be then?"

Mary thinks a minute, then beams, "I guess I wouldn't be hungry!"

Assignment

1. What kind of harsh reality does the above present to Mary?
2. What could you, the assignment editor, have said during the "discussion" that would have resulted in a more pleasant reality for you?
3. What is the assignment editor doing that might be regretted later? For example, what future, harsh reality is being invited?
4. Does the assignment editor's behavior more likely force a prospect theory situation, myth making, or cognitive dissonance? Why one more than the other?
5. Will it ever be possible for the assignment editor to conduct appropriate "sense making" on the spot like this? Why or why not?
6. What about the assignment editor's daughter? What role does the daughter play in the assignment editor's behavior? What behavioral bias, if any, does the assignment editor display?

Case 10.4 A Baker's Dozen

You're Tom Baker, the editor of a major metropolitan daily newspaper. Most days, things go well: people do their jobs, the paper is full of interesting stories, the publisher's happy, there's good debate at the budget meeting, and you have a little time to work out at the gym. Today is not one of those days.

In the span of one, rainy morning, you had to deal with several disconcerting issues. If you hadn't listed them in the following assignment section, no one would believe these things could happen.

Now, as you're sitting at home, rehashing your day, you're going through them and wondering, one by one, "What was I supposed to do?"

Assignment

After each of the following, determine whether you, Tom, should have created new knowledge (and, if so, what and how?) or whether you should have just soaked it all in and tried to make sense of it all (and, if so, why):

1. Lucy, the city hall reporter turned up in Wichita Falls, Texas, to interview Stu Hanna, your mayor's choice for his new chief executive officer. The trouble is that Hanna lives in Wichita, Kansas.
2. Saul, your entertainment editor, told you first thing this morning that he was diagnosed yesterday with HIV.

3. You couldn't find Sam, your managing editor, and Mariah, your librarian between editions. It turns out they were across the street— in a room, together. Sam's the married father of two while Mariah is a recent divorcee' to whom the staff looks to for personal advice.

4. Joanne, your features section editor, just "out of the blue" walked by ace news reporter Bill's desk and "slapped the fire" out of him. Bill stared at her as she continued walking and then shot a glance at Kathy, who was staring back at him with a smile on her face.

5. Earl, your mild-mannered education reporter, tells you he's weighing an offer from *The New York Times*.

6. Heathcliff, the editorial page editor, wants "a sit down" with you to discuss the singing that he can't help but hear from the sports department.

7. Circulation numbers were down by 1.4% this quarter; the publisher sends you a memo asking for an explanation.

8. We missed deadline again today, the third day in a row. The press-room isn't happy.

9. Another publisher's memo suggested you "get ready to converge" the newsroom.

10. Your administrative assistant forgot to get the slides together for your noon talk to the Optimists Club.

11. Your mid-morning blood sugar count was 195.

12. An old, reliable source called to inform you that General Motors was sealing a deal today to build a plant in your town.

13. Nearly every story in today's first edition was on the 10 o'clock news on one or all of the local stations last night.

EXTENDED CASE STUDIES

Introduction and Preparation

Hoag, Brickley and Cawley (2001, p. 52) argued that the case method of experiential learning "stimulates the same skills managers use: analysis with intuition, integration, decision-making, self-initiative and persuasive communication." A case study tells the story of a problem or problems to be solved based on actual events or decisions concerning firms and managers or a composite of various events or problems in an industry.

In case analysis, students assume the role of the manager featured in the case to learn about situations they are likely to face on the job. It is especially suited to disciplines where theory, research, and principles are applied in the real world. The case method allows students to (a) gain experience in making decisions and solving problems; (b) learn to identify, analyze, and research complex problems, and (c) and integrate theory and prior knowledge to lifelike situations (Chandy, 2004). "The history, discourse, and empirical research on the method suggests (sic) it is an effective form of active, experiential learning and has been successfully adopted across a broad spectrum of disciplines" (Hoag et al., 2001, p. 58).

Students accustomed to lecture classes must learn that the case method requires extensive reading, preparation, and discussion. As Foran (2002, p. 1) argued, unlike lectures, "case discussion demands your ideas and participation." Learned (1980, in Christensen, 1987, p. 13) suggested students could prepare to discuss or write about a case by answering the following questions about it:

1. "What, in your opinion, is the most fundamental, crucial, or urgent issues or problems—or issues and problems—before the company? Why do you think so?
2. "What, accordingly, if anything, should anyone do? Who? When? How? Why do you think so?
3. "How will you communicate your ideas to the top management of the company? Why?" (Learned, 1980, in Christensen, 1987, p. 13)

Often professors want more extensive preparation from students. The following suggestions from Foran (2002), Wertheim (2006), and Preparing (1998) are integrated to provide specific suggestions as to how professors may want students to read a case and prepare for class:

1. Read the case once to get a quick sense of the whole case. Then read it again and consider steps 2 through 7.

2. Identify the who, what, where, when, and how of the case. Who is/are the important decision maker(s)? What is the major problem and/or decision to be made? Who are the important persons in the case? Why? What is the background and important information about the firm? What are the key issues in the case? What important information is lacking? If you could ask the case's main characters questions, what would you ask?

3. Define the problem(s). Where is the problem and why is it a problem? What type of problem is it (e.g., group, leadership, motivation, etc.)? Which chapters in this book address the type of problem? How urgent is the problem? What are the consequences if the problem isn't solved? What information is lacking that is needed to help solve the problem? Find and list all indicators in the case that something is wrong or not as desired or expected. Distinguish between symptoms and the problem. *Symptoms* are indicators of problems that reveal something is not as it should be and help you to identify the problem. *Problems* are the situations or conditions that require a solution before performance can improve. Therefore, your focus should be on figuring out the problem's actual causes.

4. Identify the goals. What is the organization's mission statement? What do the overall goals of the manager(s) involved seem to be? What important statements are made by the managers or others in the case that reveal what is important or motivating factors? Are the goals of firm(s) and individual(s) similar or not? Why or why not?

5. Conduct the analysis. Reread the relevant chapter(s) you identified in section 3 above. Identify the theories, models, ideas, or research that are helpful. Apply these to the situation. As you learn more through research and discussion, review the relevant chapters and concepts again.

6. Diagnose the problem. Identify the primary goals of the organization and individuals. Think about how they relate to the problem. Unless your professor tells you otherwise, select the most important goal and consider alternative solutions to enable managers and employees to achieve that goal. Think about short, intermediate, and long-term actions or steps to be taken to solve the problem. What are the possible alternative solutions? What are the resources needed for each alternative? What constraints or problems are associated with each alternative? What are the likely short- and long-term consequences

of these alternatives? Identify the criteria that are crucial to identify and solve the problem (unless your professor assigned such criteria).

7. Develop an action plan and defend your decision. Identify the criteria used to select an alternative and develop an action plan. Decide upon the best alternative or course of action to solve the problem. Explain why is it the best alternative, identify what resources are needed, identify what the primary manager or important characters in the case must do and how they should change, and identify how or why the firm should change. Be sure to develop a contingency plan. In other words, "select an alternative that leaves other plausible alternatives available if the one selected fails" (Preparing an Effective Case Analysis, 1998, p. 5). Identify what the best plausible alternatives are and explain why they should be implemented if the original plan fails.

Not all cases or assignments require each step. Your professor may ask you to use a completely different approach for class discussions or when writing your assignment. However, these steps provide a good approach for reading cases and preparing for class discussion. Like life, you will never have enough information, cannot always be certain you have identified the real problem, will face ambiguity, will realize there is rarely one right answer, and likely will not have a perfect solution (Foran, 2002; Preparing an Effective Case Analysis, 1998; Wertheim, 2006). Unlike a lecture, conducting a case analysis allows you to feel the frustration and face the difficulty of making hard decisions with imperfect information in difficult and complex situations where the wrong decision could ultimately cost you your job and put your employees out of work.

You may experience these realities because cases often present ambiguous and complex problems and provide misleading and incomplete information. Students often feel overwhelmed when working on a case for the first time. Managers have these same intellectual and emotional experiences, so you can apply what you learn to business situations after graduation. More suggestions for students are available from sources such as Student Tips for Solving Case Problems (2006), Christensen (1987), Foran (2002), Preparing an Effective Case Analysis (1998), and Wertheim (2006).

To the Instructor: About the Cases

Extended Case Studies 1 and 2 feature fictitious characters at fictitious media organizations facing fictitious situations. While each case is based on real-life events representing the types of problems and issues media managers face on the job, neither case represents any real-life person or organization. These cases also provide practice in using concepts covered in all chapters of the book. For more information on teaching using the case method see Using Cases in Teaching (2006), Boehrer and Linsky (1990), Christensen (1987), and Weber and Kirk (2000).

Both cases can be used as major end-of-the-semester assignments, assignments to cover certain course segments, several chapters, or one chapter. Consider the questions from Extended Case 1 for these following examples. Assign Question 1 and/or 4 after covering chapters 1 through 4. Assign question 3 and/or 8 after covering chapters 1 through 6. When covering single chapters at a time, assign question 5 after covering chapter 4, assign question 11 after covering chapter 6, assign question 15 after covering chapter 10, or assign question 17 after covering chapter 9.

One or more questions could be assigned from each extended case only once during the semester. You can use either or both extended cases in a holistic and comprehensive approach to dealing with organizational problems. Assign different questions from one or both cases at several points during the semester. Using the holistic approach allows students to see how changes in one area of the firm affect other departments or decisions in that same organization.

You can also use Extended Cases 1 and 2 for individual and/or group assignments, so students learn and apply the individual and group decision-making aspects covered in the book. For example, have students work individually on one question in a case. Then have them work in teams on other questions in a case at midterm. Have teams work on all or many of the case's questions as a final course project. The goal is to provide the most flexibility to professors and students in using the cases to allow for different teaching and learning styles.

Many sources are included in the next section to teach students to locate, assess, and analyze a variety of data. That is why Extended Case 1 allows you to select a major city close to you if you prefer not to use the market featured in the case. Professors often already have data about nearby cities or media markets to be used for cases. This allows them to tailor the case to meet their own learning goals and use material they already have.

Professors are also urged to examine the sources included in the next section and select those most appropriate to their goals and teaching styles. After publication, some of the Internet addresses in the case will change or disappear. Students will find the number and types of sources in the case overwhelming if they receive little or no guidance in using them.

Extended Case 1 provides information and practice in dealing with managing change in a variety of ways in an organization with several media outlets. Extended Case 2 provides information and practice in online management and dealing with the types of social issues or controversies media managers deal with throughout their careers. Both cases allow students to deal with specific problems in the overall context of the organization and situation. Both involve vexing management situations with no easy or clear answer. Students must consider the managerial, organizational, structural, legal, ethical, and human consequences of the decisions they make.

In summary, the first goal in both extended cases is to give students a chance to consider major problems they are likely to face at various points in their careers. The second goal is to instruct students on how to quickly find good, relevant information to aid in solving problems and making decisions. A third goal is to provide a variety of real-life situations to apply theory, research, and data analysis. A fourth goal is to give students a better perspective on how smaller problems seemingly unique to one department or situation are interrelated with, and not necessarily independent of, larger more complex organizational problems. Next, background information is provided to help you in completing these extended cases.

Backgrounder 1: New Media Trends and Technologies

Media managers are concerned with developing new offerings based on constantly changing new technologies to generate revenue and attract new, and often younger, audience segments. Many media companies or groups also seek managers to lead organizations based on new media offerings or technologies. Anyone considering a future in media management must keep abreast of the new technologies and the offerings they enable media organizations to offer. This section provides information and ideas on such offerings and technologies. However, technologies develop so quickly that this information will soon be dated. Keeping up requires a conscious, continual effort to follow trends in industry and academic research.

Audiences continually incorporate new technologies into their media consumption. For example, McClellan (2006) reported that the 2,500 consumers interviewed increased their media consumption, embracing newer options like the Internet, without cutting back on traditional media consumption. People spend about 9 hours daily consuming all media, more time than they sleep (6.8 hours) or work (7.5 hours). A major concern for media managers is how to market to audiences without angering them for interrupting their private time. McClellan (2006) also reported the second most frequent complaint (or 30%) was the growing number of unwanted interruptions while consuming media.

McClellan (2006) reported multitasking as being more prevalent than previously believed. Respondents said they engage in an average of 3 additional activities while they surf the Internet and 2.5 additional activities while watching television. Television is still the most dominant medium in terms of usage, with 97% of respondents reporting usage. The Internet has become the second most widely used medium, with 92% reporting they recently surfed the Web. Yet, only 15% or fewer report recently watching high-definition TV, watching TV on their computer or handheld device, or using a DVR. Most consumers have been slow to adopt MP3 players, personal organizers, and other handheld units. Only 6% said they download videos to cell phones, video iPods, and other handheld units (McClellan, 2006).

The Mobile Marketing Association or MMA (Mobile Marketing Association, & The NPD Group, 2006) noted that watching video on a mobile phone is in the very early stages of the product life cycle. While 28% of mobile phones offered this capability in 2006, only 1% of consumers watched video on a mobile phone. Of that 1% who did watch, over half watch video on their mobile phones at least once weekly. The MMA also reports that 17% of mobile phones sold in the first quarter of 2006 were Bluetooth-capable (The NPD Group, 2006). Bluetooth allows consumers to pass content directly to each other using their mobile phones. Marketers might use this capability to dispense movie information and tickets or inform consumers or retail sales and transmit coupons on mobile phones.

A research study from the MMA and NPD Group (Mobile Marketing Association, 2006b) reveals consumers use their mobile phones with digital cameras to snap photos of family members (84%), spontaneous moments (72%), friends (69%), outdoor scenery (34%), vacation moments (25%), parties (23%) and birthdays (22%). Most camera-phone users took a few photos each month (32%) and 20% took photos a few times each week. The MMA reported the use of wireless features (Use of Wireless, 2006) included text messaging (38.5%), playing mobile games (38.2%), downloading audio (23.8%), downloading screensavers, or other graphics (15.6%), mobile e-mail (13.2%), Internet access from the handset (12.29%), picture messaging (11.8%), digital-music playing (4.2%), video messaging (4.2%), and watching TV (2.9%).

Media outlets and advertisers have experimented with ways to use these and other capabilities. For example, *Maxim* magazine encouraged its readers to send in text messages and phone camera pictures, essentially asking readers to serve as reporters or share funny and crazy items. Various editorial "bugs" were placed to invite users to respond to poll questions or send in contributions using mobile phones. *Seventeen* and *CosmoGirl* also sold ringtones and wallpapers, for example (Mobilizing the Magazines, 2006). Some newspapers continually update local restaurant inspection results online to encourage site visits (Okada, 2006).

ABC and NBC sold downloads or streamed popular programs on their Web sites. CBS's video streaming of NCAA college basketball tournament games had 5 million visitors. The networks offered outtakes, online chats, and cast interviews to attract viewers and build program loyalty. Making full TV episodes available on the Apple iTunes Music Store boosted downloads. The iTunes list includes shows from NBC, Fox, MTV, ESPN, Comedy Central, Nickelodeon, Showtime, the Disney Channel, and the Sci-Fi Channel, for example. Users can also purchase season passes for popular shows. And, for people who only watch a few shows regularly, iTunes downloads are convenient. In addition, the downloads can be watched anytime or transported to a big-screen TV. Thus, purchasers can obtain some cable shows without a cable subscription (Holloway, 2006).

Other companies seek partnerships or ways to cash in on technology. For example, Dallas-based Texas Instruments (TI), whose chips were in about half of all mobile handsets in 2006, wanted to find new business for its semiconductors, likely in video. Companies are offering products to allow users to watch regular TV on any device connected to the Internet such as laptops, PDAs, and mobile phones. TI was developing a processor to allow users to download high-quality video to their phone, which can later be replayed on a TV screen (Koenig, 2006b).

Yet, media companies must consider the legal ramifications of these new services and technologies. A 14-year-old girl who claimed to be assaulted by another user sued MySpace.com for $30 million (Associated Press, 2006b). Because court orders or governments sometimes request such information, AT&T required its Internet and video customers to agree that it owns their account information and can share it with government officials. AT&T will collect customer names, pass-words, charges, payments, and online purchases as well as their clicks on sites operated in partnership with Yahoo. AT&T said its policy is similar to that of other Internet providers, and the company wants to be sure customers know it may release information, possibly without their knowledge, to comply with court orders, subpoenas, or to assist collection agencies (Koenig, 2006a).

These and other privacy or legal issues arise as new technologies or offerings are created. Media managers must consider the legal and ethi-cal issues that may arise when developing ways to use these and other technologies and capabilities. Otherwise, legal liabilities and consumer anger will outweigh any gains from adopting new offerings.

Backgrounder 2: Seeking Information to Solve Problems and Make Decisions

Chapter 9, "Marketing and Research," discussed how managers can-not always conduct primary research to obtain the ideal information to use in problem solving or decision making. Hoag, Brickley, and Caw-ley (2001) pointed out that as convergence increases, managers must skillfully manage rapid change. Knowing how and where to find infor-mation quickly and inexpensively is an invaluable skill for present and future media managers. This, too, can be a difficult and overwhelming process and skill to learn.

Extended Case 1 deals with group owned media outlets in a major city or market, in this case Dallas-Forth Worth, Texas. Here are ideas for finding information about a market quickly: industry publications often publish analyses or profiles of media markets. Start by trying to locate such an article [e.g., see Hudson (2005a) for a profile of the Dallas-Forth Worth market. *Mediaweek* updates these profiles regularly so check to see if a more recent profile has been published for your market or city].

Professors: if you teach your media management course in a computer lab (or could for a short period of time), the class as a whole could take a class day or week to conduct an Internet, database and library search to locate information to share. The professor could organize an efficient search by assigning different search objectives to different students or teams.

For example, have a class discussion to generate an exhaustive list of search objectives and key words or terms to use for searching. Then assign one team to conduct a thorough search in Lexis-Nexis Academic Universe, another team in ABI/Inform ProQuest Direct, and a third team to search EBSCO. Assign a fourth team to conduct a thorough Internet search using Google or similar search engines. Assign a fifth team to go to the library to obtain Mediamark, Lifestyle Market Analyst, data from the Statistical Abstracts of the United States and other relevant published information. Assign a sixth team to make an appointment with a Reference Librarian to locate any other available or newer information or publications. Assignments are made until all major information sources available are covered.

Instruct all students to e-mail any useful articles or citations they find to the professor. Most online databases have an e-mail function for this purpose. If useful Internet sites are found, those Web addresses could be pasted into an e-mail message and sent to the professor. After the research is conducted, the professor can then e-mail the relevant articles and cites to the entire class or provide hard copies of selected materials. By dividing the major search goals and sharing what is found, much information to use in working on the case can be obtained quickly. Then the class is assigned to read all sources or assigned materials to discuss in the next class.

Your professor may divide the following online sources among individuals or teams in the class. These are examples of the types of sources that may be useful to you on the job. While these are for the Dallas-Fort Worth, Texas, market (as you'll use them in Extended Cases 1 to follow), these same types of sources are available for cities and towns nationwide.

Online resources that may be useful for analyzing the Dallas-Forth Worth, Texas, market are listed next. These sources are listed to provide ideas for the types of sources available for other markets or cities. Remember these addresses may change after publication so titles are provided to assist in locating them.

About TexasTexas State Library and Archives Commission.
www.tsl.state.tx.us/ref/abouttx/index.html
Be sure to visit and carefully search this site.

American Indian Chamber of Commerce of Texas
www.aicct.com
Use sites like these to find member lists of ethnic businesses in Dallas/
    Fort Worth.

Arlington City Web Site
www.ci.arlington.tx.us

Arlington Independent School District (2006)
www.arlington.k12.tx.us

Business and Industry Data Center (2006)
State of Texas. http://www.bidc.state.tx.us/
Be sure to visit the BIDC Maproom that provides demographic, employ-
    ment, income, and other information

CEO Express—Connecting busy executives to information that matters
www.ceoexpress.com

City of Dallas Office of Cultural Affairs
www.dallasculture.org

ClickZ Network—Solutions for Marketers
www.clickz.com

Dallas Black Chamber of Commerce
www.dbcc.org

Dallas City Web Portal
www.dallascityhall.com

Dallas/Fort Worth Search Engine Marketing Association
www.dfwsem.org

Dallas Independent School District
www.dallasisd.org

Dallas Morning News
www.dallasnews.com

Dallas Observer
www.dallasobserver.com
See their blogs page at www.dallasobserver.com/blogs/

Dallas Office of Economic Development
www.dallas-edd.org

Dallas Police Department
www.dallaspolice.net

Digest of Education Statistics—NCES/National Center for Education
    Statistics
http://nces.ed.gov/programs/digest/

Federal Bureau of Investigation—Dallas Field Office
http://dallas.fbi.gov/dallas.htm

FBI Uniform Crime Reports
www.fbi.gov/ucr/ucr.htm

Federal Reserve Bank of Dallas
http://dallasfed.org

Federal Reserve Bank of St. Louis
http://stlouisfed.org
There may be a Federal Reserve Bank closer to your city.

Fort Worth City Web Site
www.fortworthgov.org

Fort Worth Chamber of Commerce
www.fortworthcoc.org or www.fortworthchamber.com

Fort Worth Independent School District
www.fortworthisd.org/

Fort Worth Introduction (2006). A statistical profile of Fort Worth
and the Fort Worth-Arlington Metropolitan Division.
www.fortworthcoc.org/eco/docs/Intro2006.pdf

Fort Worth Star-Telegram
www.dfw.com

GDAAC: Greater Dallas Asian American Chamber of Commerce.
www.gdaacc.com/

Greater Dallas Chamber of Commerce
www.gdc.org/
www.dallaschamber.org
Carefully review sites like this for the wealth of online data they typically offer. They may be listed under several addresses.

Greater Dallas Hispanic Chamber of Commerce
www.gdhcc.com/index.html

KTVT CBS 11
http://cbs11tv.com

KDFW FOX TV 4
www.myfoxdfw.com

WFAA ABC TV 8
www.wfaa.com

KXAS NBC 5
www.nbc5i.com

Mobile Marketing Association
www.mmaglobal.com
Data and case studies are available here to give you ideas on mobile or
   digital services and campaigns.

NADbase Newspaper Audience Database Spring 2006—Newspaper Association of America www.naa.org/nadbase/2006_NADbase_Report.pdf

NCTCOG: North Central Texas Council of Governments.
www.nctcog.org
Also click on the Population Estimates link for data.

Real Estate Market Overview 2006. Dallas-Forth Worth-Arlington.
   College Station: Texas A & M University Real Estate Center.
http://recenter.tamu.edu/mreports/DallasFWArl.pdf

Texas Instruments
www.ti.com

Texas K–12 Schools on the Web
www.tenet.edu/schools/texas.html#regxi

Texas Online—Texas at Your Fingertips
www.texas.gov

Top 100 Newspaper Web Sites—Newspaper Association of America
www.naa.org/nadbase/Top_100_Newspaper_Web_Sites.pdf

Total Newspaper Web Site Audience—Newspaper Association of
   America
www.naa.org/nadbase/Nielsen_TotalWebAudience_06.pdf

U.S. Census Bureau
www.census.gov
Check out the Population Finder, Area Profile, and Economic Indicators.

U.S. Census Bureau American Community Survey
www.census.gov/acs/www

U.S. Census Bureau Fact Finder
http://factfinder.census.gov

U.S. Census Bureau—Computer Use and Ownership
www.census.gov/population/www/socdemo/computer.html

U.S. Census Bureau—The 2006 Statistical Abstract
www.census.gov/compendia/statab

U.S. Census Bureau—Computer and Internet Use in the United States:
   2003
www.census.gov/prod/2005pubs/p23-208.pdf
These are updated periodically so check to see if a newer version is available.

Other published or online sources that may be available in your library include:

ACCRA Cost of Living Index
American Chamber of Commerce Researchers Association
Louisville, KY: ACCRA.

Dun & Bradstreet/*D & B Regional Business Directory*
Your library should have the one for your state, group of states, or region.

FBI/Federal Bureau of Investigation, U.S. Department of Justice
Crime in the United States

Often reference librarians prepare checklists of resources for a particular subject area (Daniels, 2005, from which some of these sources are obtained). For example, some useful Journalism and Mass Communication sources include,

Communication Abstracts—indexes and abstracts research in the communications field including journalism and news media, mass media, popular culture and the media and public relations.

Encyclopedias, Dictionaries, Atlases and Almanacs
   Encyclopedia of Associations, Facts on File, Famous First Facts, Rand McNally Commercial Atlas and Marketing Guide, World Almanac, and Book of Facts

Politics and Government—State
   Book of States
   Web site of your state

Politics and Government—Federal
  Almanac of American Politics
  Congressional Dictionary
  Federal Staff Directory
  GPO Access—Government Printing Office online at www.
    gpoaccess.gov
  U.S. Government Manual
  Who's Who in American Politics

International
  CIA Central Intelligence Agency—The World Factbook online at
    www.odci.gov/cia/publications/factbook/index.html
  Europa World Yearbook with current in depth social, political,
    and economic information on all countries
  Market Research Monitor (Electronic Resource)—International
    and European country market and media guides.

Statistics (besides the Census sites noted earlier)
  Education Statistics of the United States
  LexisNexis Statistical (Electronic Resource)
  STAT USA (Electronic Resource) includes the State of the Nation
    section on the economy and various industries and the Glo-
    bus section covering the international economy.
  Statistical Abstract of the United States

Selected Journalist Resources
  CyberJournalist.net (at www.cyberjournalist.net)
  Finding Information on the Internet: A Journalist's Guide at
    www.nilesonline.com/data
  J-Lab: The Institute for Interactive Journalism
    (at www.j-lab.org)
  Journalist Express at www.journalistexpress.com
  The Media Center at American Press Institute (at www.media-
    center.org)
  University of Iowa Journalism Resources at http://bailiwick.
    lib.uiowa.edu/journalism/ Compiled and edited by Karla
    Tonella, University of Iowa
  NAA: Digital Age (at www.digitaledge.org)
  NAA: Electronic Publishing (www.naa.org/Electronic-Publish-
    ing.aspx)
  Pew/Internet: Pew Internet & American Life Project (at www.
    pewinternet.org)
  Poynter Onine (www.poynter.org)

Selected Broadcast Journalism Publications
>   *Broadcasting & Cable Yearbook*
>   *Encyclopedia of Television News*
>   *Gale Directory of Publication and Broadcast Media*
>   *Television & Cable Factbook*
>   *International Television and Video Almanac*

Selected Journalism Industry Publications
>   *American Journalism Review* (also onine at www.ajr.org)
>   *Columbia Journalism Review* (also online at www.cjr.org)
>   *Editor & Publisher*
>   *Editor & Publisher International Yearbook*
>   *Editor & Publisher Market Guide*
>   *Folio*
>   *SRDS Circulation 2006 (or latest edition)*
>   *SRDS Newspaper Advertising Source*
>   *SRDS Consumer Magazine Advertising Source*
>   *SRDS Business Publication Advertising Source*
>   *SRDS Interactive Advertising Source*
>   *SRDS Out-of-Home Advertising Source*
>   *SRDS Print Media Production Source*
>   *SRDS Radio Advertising Source*
>   *SRDS TV & Cable Source*
>   *SRDS International Media Guides*
>   *SRDS Hispanic Media & Market Source*
>   *SRDS Technology Media Source*
>   *SRDS The Lifestyle Market Analyst*
>   *The Quill*

Selected Advertising Industry Publications and Sources
>   *Advertising Age*
>   *Adweek, Mediaweek*
>   *Communication Arts*
>   *Standard Directory of Advertisers*
>   *Standard Directory of Advertising Agencies*
>   *Advertising World* (online at http://advertising.utexas.edu/world)

Selected News Magazines and Newspapers
>   *Christian Science Monitor*
>   *Economist*
>   *Futurist*
>   *Harper's*
>   *MacLeans*
>   *Nation*

New Republic
New York Times
New Yorker
Newsweek
Time
U.S. News & World Report
Wall Street Journal
Washington Post
World Press Review

Selected Journalism & Mass Communication Scholarly Journals
Journalism & Mass Communication Quarterly
Journal of Broadcasting & Electronic Media
Newspaper Research Journal
Journal of Media Management & Economics
Journal of Advertising
Journal of Advertising Research
Public Relations Quarterly

Childhood obesity is another important topic covered in Extended Case 2. It is one example of many social issues or problems for which some blame the media or advertising. Managers often have to make difficult decisions regarding whether to accept advertising for problematic products or services. Media outlets sometimes lose lucrative advertising contracts due to their news coverage of important social issues or consumer interest stories. Thus, you must know how to find information quickly on social issues and problems concerning your market, state, industry, or country.

The following sources are listed to give you ideas on the types of information you may find. The list provides examples of sources only and again is not all-inclusive. The goal is to help you get started and give you ideas on the types of sites you might find for child obesity or other social concerns.

Selected sources of online information on child obesity include,

American Academy of Pediatrics at www.aap.org or its Overweight and Obesity site accessible at www.aap.org/healthtopics/overweight.cfm

American Medical Association at www.ama.assn.org

American Obesity Association at www.obesity.org and its Childhood Obesity page at www.obesity.org/subs/childhood/healthrisks.shtml

American Physiological Society—Obesity at www.the-aps.org/press/disease/womb.htm

California Center for Public Health Advocacy at www.publichealthadvocacy.org

California Department of Education—Childhood Obesity & Diabetes Task Force at www.cde.ca.gov/ls/he/cd

California Department of Health Services at www.dhs.ca.gov

California Endowment at www.calendow.org

California Food Policy Advocates at www.cfpa.net

California Governor's Council on Physical Fitness and Sports at www.activeca.org

California Health Interview Survey at www.chis.ucla.edu

Center for Health and Health Care in Schools at www.healthinschools.org and its Overweight page with other online resources at www.healthinschools.org/sh/obesity.asp and Fact Sheet at www.healthinschools.org/sh/obesityfs.asp

Centers for Disease Control and Prevention at www.cdc.gov and its Overweight and Obesity: Home at http://www.cdc.gov/nccdphp/dnpa/obesity including its Overweight and Obesity: Obesity Trends: U.S. Obesity Trends 1985–2004 at http://www.cdc.gov/nccdphp/dnpa/obesity/trend/maps (or see if a more recent version is available) and the Overweight and Obesity: State-Based Programs: Texas at http://www.cdc.gov/nccdphp/dnpa/obesity/state_programs/texas.htm Children Now at www.childrennow.org including its Childhood Obesity page at http://www.childrennow.org/issues/health/childhood_obesity.html and page on Media and Obesity at http://www.childrennow.org/issues/media/media_obesity.html

City of Los Angeles Commission for Children, Youth, and Their Families at www.ccyf.org

Commercial Alert http://commercialalert.org and its Childhood Obesity page at www.commercialalert.org/issues/health/childhood-obesity

Common Sense Media—Obesity at www.commonsensemedia.org/resources/childhood_obesity.php

County of Los Angeles Department of Health Services at www.ladhs.org

County of Los Angeles Department of Public Health at www.lapublic health.org

Family Doctor—Health information for the whole family from the American Academy of Family Physicians (www.aafp.org) at http://familydoctor.org

FirstGov for Kids Health page at www.kids/gov/k_health.htm

Food and Nutrition Information Center at www.nal.usda.gov/fnic/reports/obesity.html

Future of Children at Princeton University-Brookings Institution at www.futureofchildren.org

Harvard School of Public Health (www.hsph.harvard.edu) offers its Healthy Weight site at www.hsph.harvard.edu/nutritionsource/healthy_weight.html

Helping Your Overweight Child—National Institute of Diabetes and Digestive and Kidney Diseases at http://win.niddk.nih.gov/publications/over_child.htm

Institute of Medicine at www.iom.edu including its Focus on Childhood Obesity at www.iom.edu/CMS/22593.aspx offering numerous fact sheets.

Johns Hopkins Bloomberg School of Public Health at www.jhsph.edu

Kaiser Family Foundation at www.kff.org and its Role of Media in Childhood Obesity site at http://www.kff.org/entmedia/entmedia 022404pkg.cfm and the report at http://www.kff.org/entmedia/upload/The-Role-Of-Media-in-Childhood-Obesity.pdf

Kraft Responsibility at www.kraft.com/responsibility/home.aspx

Los Angeles California City Web Site at www.lacity.org

Mayo Clinic at www.mayoclinic.com and its Child Obesity Overview at www.mayoclinic.com/health/childhood-obesity/DS00698

National Center for Health Statistics—State Data are available at www
.cdc.gov/nchs/fastats/map_page.htm

National Center for Health Statistics at www.cdc.gov/growthcharts.
BMI—Body Mass Index: About BMI for Children and Teens at www
.cdc.gov/nccdphp/dnpa/bmi/childrens_BMI/about_childrens_BMI
.htm. Overweight and Obesity: Home page at www.cdc.gov/nccdphp/
dnpa/obesity.

Overweight Children in California Counties & Communities 2004—Los
Angeles County. www.publichealthadvocacy.org/county/Los_Ange-
les_Fact_Sheet.pdf

California Center for Public Health Advocacy at www.publichealth
advocacy.org/center.html

National Institutes of Health at www.nih.gov and

National Institute of Environmental Health Sciences www.niehs.nih
.gov/kids/weight.htm Obesity and Your Environment Kids Page at
www.niehs.nih.gov/kids/weight.htm

PTA or Parent Teacher Association at www.pta.org including its Parent Resources Health and Wellness page with several obesity-related
links.

PBS Teacher Source—Media Literacy www.pbs.org/teachersource/
media_lit/related_study.shtm

Robert Wood Johnson Foundation—Healthy Eating Research: Building Evidence to Prevent Childhood Obesity at www.healthy
eatingresearch.org. Active Living Research—Designing to Reduce
Childhood Obesity at www.activelivingresearch.org/downloads/
childhoodobesity021105.pdf

School Nutrition Association at www.schoolnutrition.org

U.S. Department of Agriculture—National Agricultural Library—
Weight and Obesity at http://riley.nal.usda.gov/nal_display/index.
php?info_center=4&tax_level=1&tax_subject=271 which has a link
to Adolescent and Childhood Obesity (http://riley.nal.usda.gov/nal_
display/index.php?info_center=4&tax_level=2&tax_subject=271
&topic_id=1308

U.S. Department of Health and Human Services at www.hhs.gov

U.S. Government Accountability Office Childhood Obesity at www.gao.
    gov/new.items/d06127r.pdf

University of California—Los Angeles School of Public Health at www
    .ph.ucla.edu

University of California—Los Angeles School of Public Health
    California Health Interview Survey at www.chis.ucla.edu

University of Michigan Health System Obesity and Overweight at
    http://www.med.umich.edu/1libr/yourchild/obesity.htm

University of Southern California Keck School of Medicine at www.usc
    .edu/schools/medicine/ksom.html

Why Have Americans Become More Obese? Harvard Institute of Eco-
    nomic Research Discussion Paper Number 1994 by David M. Cutler,
    Edward L. Glaeser, and Jesse M. Shapiro (January 2003). http://post.
    economics.harvard.edu/hier/2003papers/HIER1994.pdf

This list may seem formidable, but as you use these sources over time, you begin to recognize which ones to use for certain information needs. Developing your research skills will not be easy and will not happen overnight. However, knowing how to find quality, credible information quickly will be helpful for many professional and personal life issues for years to come.

Backgrounder 3: Childhood Obesity, Media, and Marketing

In 2006, it was reported the highest number of U.S. youth ever recorded were overweight or on the brink of becoming so, representing about a third or 25 million U.S. children and teens. Type 2 diabetes, formerly called adult-onset because of its frequency among overweight adults, also is at an all-time high among children (Third of kids, 2006, 1A), more than doubling in the past decade (McGinnis, Appleton Gootman, & Kraak, 2006). Ominously, children with Type 2 diabetes likely will not achieve their parents' life expectancy (Paskowski, 2006).

Parents must recognize a child has a weight problem to intervene. Yet, they often do not recognize their children are overweight. In a 2006 study, 39% of children were overweight or at risk for being so, yet only 26% of their parents reported being concerned over their child's weight. While 70% picked a picture that accurately reflected their child's weight, only 36% described their child as overweight. The study's authors noted that parents in general must be educated about recognizing when a child is overweight. Unless parents recognize their child's weight problem, they cannot understand the accompanying health risks nor be expected to intervene (How parents, 2006). The American Academy of Pediatrics advised all children ages 2 or older have their body mass index or BMI measured at least once a year after a study reported 49% of responding parents thought their overweight kids were normal (Barnett, 2006).

However, care should be taken in educating parents and children on maintaining healthy weight. A 2006 study at the University of Minnesota found that dieting was associated with increased "extreme weight control behaviors," body dissatisfaction and depression. Girls who said they dieted, whether overweight or not, were more likely to smoke as well as use marijuana and alcohol (University of Minnesota, 2006, p. 189).

A 2006 University of Michigan study reported that three-year-old children exposed to two or more hours of television per day were about three times more likely to be overweight than kids who watched or were in the same room with a TV on for fewer than two hours per day. Children with excessive TV exposure were about three times more likely to be overweight than kids will less TV exposure by age 4½ (Pediatric Obesity, 2006, p. 338).

The Michigan study reported 1 in 4 kids were exposed to 5 or more hours daily of television, exceeding the American Academy of Pediatric recommendation that media exposure for kids 2 and under should be less than 2 hours per day. The TV was on for more than 7 hours daily in the typical U.S. home and kids spend more time watching TV than in school. Kids who watched 2 or more hours of TV daily had more behavior problems, were more likely to have a less-stimulating home environment, and mothers with more depressive symptoms. It was argued that exposure to television should be for preschool children an independent risk factor for obesity (Pediatric Obesity, 2006, pp. 338).

Exposure to television advertising apparently has an effect on youth. Among children ages 2–11, television advertising influences their food and beverage requests, purchase requests and short-term consumption. Among children ages 2–11 and teens 12–18 years old, television exposure is associated with adiposity or body fatness (McGinnis et al., 2006, p. 8–9).

Christakis (2006) found each additional hour of television viewing was associated with increased youth calorie intake and the consumption of foods advertised often on TV. Piaget (1970, 1977) noted cognitive development begins as children acquire sensory-motor skills and direct experience. Through a trial-and-error process, children adapt to failures by reorganizing knowledge of their world. This adaptation spurs their learning to think logically about things that are beyond their direct experience, thus achieving abstract thought.

However, a child's learning process takes time. Van Evra (2004) reported until about age 8 children have difficulty identifying a message as commercial, especially those conveyed verbally. As more attention-gaining effects are used in commercials and programs, it becomes more difficult for children to distinguish between programming and commercials. Although kids may develop the ability to discriminate commercial from programs, or recognize the persuasive intent of advertising, at about 8 years, children as old as 11 years may not activate their defenses unless explicitly cued to do so (McGinnis et al., 2006). Moses and Baldwin (2005) argued although by age 7 or 8 children have well-formed conceptions of advertising's underlying intentions, they cannot apply these concepts effectively until much later in development.

Arnas (2006) reported that 344 of the 775 television advertisements studied were food ads, with most about candy/chocolate, chips, milk, and milk products and breakfast cereals. More than half of the advertised foods had much fat and sugar. Almost 90% of the children typically ate or drank fruits, soft drinks, popcorn, nuts, cake, chips, and chocolate or candy while watching TV. The results also revealed 40.3% asked their parents to buy what they saw on TV ads and 8.9% cried or argued to coerce their parent to buy a desired product. Children in the study tended to ask for sweetened items such as soft drinks, cake, candy, or ice cream. Harrison and Marske (2005) concluded that snack foods, convenience foods, fast foods, and sweets that lack adequate fiber and nutrients and exceed daily recommendations for fat, saturated fat, and sodium continue to dominate the food ads children view.

The Academy of Sciences Institute of Medicine (McGinnis et al., 2006) reported that advertising and marketing of food and beverages influences the diets of youth. Most food and beverage products targeting children are low in nutrients and high in calories, salt, sugar, and fat. Youth are an important target because they spend over $200 billion annually and influence other family food and beverage purchases (McGinnis et al., 2006). It was estimated $10 billion is spent annually on food and beverage marketing to reach children. Advertising and marketing are pervasive in children's lives, reaching them at home, in school or child-care, at the grocery store or shopping mall, in theaters, at sporting events, at airports, and numerous other locations. Children are reached using broadcast and cable television, radio, magazines, computers and the Internet, music, cell phones, and numerous other vehicles. Television advertising is an important promotional vehicle but budgets are shifting to sales promotion, product placement, character licensing, in-school activities, and advergames. In 2004, only 20% of food and beverage marketing was in broadcast, print, outdoor, and Internet advertising (McGinnis et al., 2006, p. 4).

Governments have taken action to deal with the problem. California passed legislation prohibiting full-calorie sodas in middle schools during school hours, and beginning in 2007 grade schools can sell only water and juice. The law also limits the sugar and fat content of items sold through vending machines or school stores. New York and Los Angeles also enacted similar programs in their public schools (Child Obesity, 2005, p. 22).

Marketers are responding because childhood obesity continues to be a top marketing issue of 2005 (Child Obesity, 2005; Lafayette, 2006). Marketers adopted programs and tactics to help solve the child obesity problem and stave off critics. Kraft stopped advertising certain products to children under age 12 but still markets products it says are healthier to children ages 6 to 12 years old. Any product advertised on a TV program where over half of the audience is under 12 must meet the company's nutritional standards. Yet, Kraft continues to advertise on shows young children may watch as long as more than half of the audience is older than 12 years, as well as in certain magazines and on Web sites consumed by kids (Ellison, 2005).

Interestingly, Hein (2005) reported as many as 25% of the viewers of the top five shows for soft drink and fast food product placement were ages 2 to 16 years old. For example, children were 16.9% of *American Idol's* and 11.1% of *The Contender's* viewers, which had 3.461 occurrences of soft drink placements during 5 hours of product exposure. Children were 20% or more of the audience for *The Simple Life: Interns, What I Like About You,* and *Eve.* They saw 140 fast food placements, 2,859 Coke placements, 794 Sierra Mist placements, and 132 Pepsi placements.

PepsiCo planned to spend about half of its advertising budget on its Smart Spot products such as Quaker Chewy Bars, Baked Cheetos, and Aquarine. Products with the Smart Spot logo meet Food and Drug Administration and National Academy of Sciences standards. PepsiCo recommends only its Smart Spot products to elementary schools (Child Obesity, 2005; Reyes, 2005).

Coca-Cola has a fitness program featuring seven-time Tour de France winner Lance Armstrong and other noted athletes that promotes an active lifestyle and healthy food choices. Coca-Cola agreed to limit full-calorie sodas to 50% in high-school vending machines. No Coke products or logos appear in the posters and materials (McGinnis et al., 2005). McDonald's said its Passport to Play fitness program teaching kids about games from around the world reached about 7 million children in 31,000 schools (Child Obesity, 2005, p. 22). The chain introduced healthy food options including its successful Fruit & Walnut Salad. Yet, Wendy's discontinued its fruit cups and bowls due to poor sales (Reyes, 2005).

In 2006, Nickelodeon spent $30 million in 2006 on its Let's Just Play Go Healthy Challenge featured on the nework, a Web site, and community action program. Nick aired the first 30-minute commercial-free episode of this 5-month miniseries documenting the struggles of four actual kids trying to get healthy. The kids' progress was tracked in 12-minute segments airing once a month with the final episode advising kids to turn off the TV and go outside to play. Nick also said it donated $1.2 million to local community groups and schools for exercise equipment (Paskowski, 2006, 10).

Nickelodeon earns about $200 million by licensing its cartoon characters to sell foods and beverages, many of which are unhealthy. Nick licensed SpongeBob SquarePants to promote a Keebler cookie (Paskowski, 2006). Yet, Boskovich Farms (spinach), Grimmway Farms (carrots), and LGS Specialty Sales (citrus fruit) licensed Sponge Bob and other characters, offering temporary tattoos packs of the characters in the packaging (McGinnis et al., 2005). The Institute of Medicine recommends that the food industry designate industry-wide healthy product icons and stop using licensed characters to sell "low-nutrient and high-calorie" products, using them "only for the promotion of foods and beverages that support healthful diets for children and youth" (Ellison & Adamy, 2005, p. B1).

The advertising and marketing industry notes that blaming advertising for child obesity is easy. The obesity problem is complex, and more parental involvement, physical and nutritional education in schools, more time playing, fitness facilities at work, healthier food choices, less TV viewing, and other public and private initiatives should be part of the comprehensive approach to solve the problem (MacLeod, 2006). Yet, critics claim, "Food giants wouldn't spend $11 billion a year on ads if they didn't get a payback. People see the commercials, and don't need a guy in a lab coat to tell them what piles of fatburgers and megagulps do to young bodies" (Ruskin, 2006, p. 18).

Backgrounder 4: Content Analysis of Food and Beverage Television Advertising

The data in this section come from a content analysis of food and beverage television advertising on U.S. networks and cable channels. Warren, Wicks, Chung, Wicks, and Fosu (2006) analyzed a sample of 4,324 advertisements that aired from 2 P.M. to 10 P.M central time in a total of 672 hours of a composite week of programming from January to May 2006 from six U.S. broadcast television networks and five cable networks having the highest numbers of subscribing homes with children and offering child/family friendly programming.

They found pizza/fast food restaurants (23.9%), sweets (16.4%), breakfast foods (13.0%), family restaurants (11.7%), and convenience entrees/meals (9.2%) constituted 74.2% of the sampled ads. No other category was more than 5% of the sampled commercials. This means that 44.8% of the advertisements were for restaurants or convenience meals. Food and beverage products advertised least frequently were fruits/vegetables (0.4%), meat (1.4%), and juices (3.0%).

The researchers reported that when certain products were advertised, they were more often targeted to children than to general audiences. Those product types included dairy products, pasta/bread, breakfast foods, convenience entrees/meals, and juice. There were significant differences in the appeals used in child-targeted versus general-audience targeted advertising. Appeals appearing more often in child-targeted ads included premium offers, mood alteration, speed/strength, action/adventure, magic/fantasy, and peer acceptance. The appeals appearing more often in general audience ads included health/well-being, achievement/enablement, and appearance.

Warren et al. (2006) reported almost three-quarters of food and beverage ads in the sample, which were likely to be viewed by children, were among the five most unhealthy food categories (e.g., pizza restaurants, sweets, breakfast foods, family restaurants, and convenience meals). The results were consistent with previous studies of advertising content (e.g., Harrison & Marske, 2005).

The researchers argued one important study implication was factors governing young children's processing of televised messages may combine to intensify the persuasive effect of advertising. Perceptually based processing is critical to children's interpretive strategies until about age 7. Therefore, animation, lively music and auditory change

TABLE 1 Types of Advertised Products Targeted to Children vs. General Audiences (in percents)[1]

Product Category	Target Audience		
	Children	General	Totals (N)
Dairy	66.7	33.3	147
Meat	39.3	60.7	56
Pasta/bread	79.0	21.0	143
Breakfast foods	65.8	34.2	530
Fruits/vegetables	53.3	46.7	15
Snacks	39.8	60.2	206
Sweets	50.5	49.5	671
Pizza/fast food	47.8	52.2	977
Convenience entrees/meals	68.0	32.0	375
Carbonated/artificially flavored drinks	17.3	82.7	179
Juice	62.9	37.1	124
Fats & condiments	51.7	48.3	178
Family restaurants	30.9	69.1	479

[1] $\chi^2 (12, N = 4080) = 332.79, p < .001$

are likely to influence attention that young children allocate. Seventy-one percent of child-directed ads in their study had animation while only 29% of general audience ads did. Sixty percent of child-directed ads had sound effects and 59% had musical jingles while general audience ads had 40% and 41% respectively. Such attention-getting techniques may divert attention from important product information such as nutritional content. The authors concluded that there is a significant risk that much advertising viewed by children misleads them about the nutritional benefits of the advertised products.

Descriptions of Types of Persuasive Appeals in Food/Beverage Advertisements
(Warren, R. Wicks, Chung, J. Wicks and Fosu, 2006)

   A. Product appeals
     1. Competitive/unique: Presented as better or different than other brands.
     2. Premium offers: Product has associated free gifts or material benefits.
     3. New (introduction of new product or flavor).
     4. Quantity/size/amount: claims about the size or amount of the product (e.g., comes in the gallon-size container; 20% bigger, etc.).

TABLE 2 Types of Persuasive Appeals Targeted to Child vs. General Audiences (in %s)[1]

Primary Appeal	Target Audience		
	Children	General	N
Competitive/Unique	45.5	54.6	143
Premium Offer	68.2	31.8	277
New	40.9	59.1	553
Quantity, size, amount	48.7	51.4	37
Taste, flavor, smell	44.3	55.8	2418
Nutritional content	46.6	53.4	661
Convenience	54.0	46.0	324
Value for money	48.0	52.1	440
Mood alteration	60.6	39.4	966
Health, well being	31.0	69.0	332
Speed/strength	65.5	34.5	139
Achievement/enablement	37.6	62.4	133
Action/adventure	89.4	10.6	198
Magic/fantasy	88.4	11.6	69
Peer acceptance	69.5	30.5	59
Adult approval/disapproval	100.0	0.0	36
Appearance	17.2	82.8	58
Trickery/deceit	97.6	2.4	83
Other	45.8	54.2	24

[1] χ^2 (18, $N = 6950$) $= 514.98$, $p < .001$

5. Taste/flavor/smell/texture (description of product's sensory characteristics).
6. Nutritional content: specific claims about fiber, fat, calories, sugar, protein, and carbohydrates; includes claims about product purity (e.g., 100% juice) or lack of additives (does not include general claims such as "eat right" or "be healthy").
7. Convenience: product is easy to prepare and/or consume (e.g., ready-to-eat or heat & eat).
8. Value for money: Claims of better product value for the money spent (e.g., buy one get one free, free 30% more). Mere mentions of price do not apply here.

B. Emotional appeals
9. Mood alterations: Suggests that product will either create/enhance positive feelings (e.g., happiness, relief) or remove negative feelings (e.g., anxiety, anger over not having product). This does not refer to the viewer's general enjoyment of the ad.

TABLE 3 Production Techniques Used in Combination with Appeal Types, Child-Targeted Advertisements (in %s)

Appeal	Animation[1]		Visual FX[2]		Sound FX[3]		Jingles[4]	
	No	Yes	No	Yes	No	Yes	No	Yes
Competitive/unique	93.8	6.2	35.9	64.1	54.8	45.2	62.3	37.7
Premium offer	64.0	36.0	44.3	55.7	47.6	52.4	47.0	53.0
New	72.1	27.9	43.5	56.5	42.3	57.7	52.1	47.9
Quantity	100.0	0.0	37.5	62.5	16.7	83.3	55.6	44.4
Taste, flavor, smell	74.7	25.3	35.0	75.0	50.0	50.0	55.8	44.2
Nutritional content	88.6	11.4	41.3	58.7	44.1	55.9	52.9	47.1
Convenience	83.4	16.6	37.9	62.1	59.4	40.6	55.0	45.0
Value for money	92.9	7.1	43.9	56.1	62.9	37.1	64.6	35.4
Mood alteration	68.0	32.0	33.2	66.8	47.1	52.9	53.2	46.8
Health, well being	95.1	4.9	45.5	54.5	48.3	51.7	48.3	51.7
Speed/strength	54.9	45.1	35.5	64.5	49.2	50.8	42.0	58.0
Achievement	50.0	50.0	37.3	62.7	47.1	52.9	33.3	66.7
Action/adventure	58.0	42.0	31.0	69.0	34.4	65.6	60.1	39.9
Magic/fantasy	36.1	63.9	43.9	56.1	35.6	64.4	44.4	55.6
Peer acceptance	43.9	56.1	44.4	55.6	42.9	57.1	39.1	60.9
Adult approval	61.1	38.9	39.1	60.9	58.5	41.5	67.5	32.5
Appearance	100.0	0.0	47.1	52.9	10.0	90.0	38.5	61.5
Trickery/deceit	46.9	53.1	48.4	51.6	48.9	51.1	62.2	37.8
Other	100.0	0.0	63.6	36.4	72.7	27.3	75.0	25.0

[1] $\chi^2(18, N = 2146) = 107.69, p < .001$ [2] $\chi^2(18, N = 2146) = 30.40, p < .001$
[3] $\chi^2(18, N = 2146) = 41.73, p < .001$ [4] $\chi^2(18, N = 2146) = 19.51, p < .001$

10. Health/well-being: Product consumption is associated with a general improvement in overall health or well-being as well as claims around weight management or dieting.

11. Speed/strength: Product consumption will enhance physical performance or energy (e.g., sports performance, stamina).

12. Achievement/enablement: Product consumption is linked with being able to obtain a desired goal or achieving control over undesirable aspects of self or the environment.

13. Action/adventure: Product is associated with engaging in daring thrill-seeking activities.

14. Magic/fantasy: Product is associated with producing effects by charms, spells, rituals, slight of hand, or concealed apparatus.

15. Peer acceptance/superiority: Product consumption is associated with peer acceptance or being better than one's peers.

16. Adult approval or disapproval: product consumption is linked to either adult's (or other authority figure's) approval of child, or getting away with something despite disapproval.

17. Appearance: improved appearance as the main reason for having the product.

18. Trickery/deceit: denying, tricking, or deceiving others out of the product.

To professors: In summary, the first goal in both extended cases is to give students a chance to consider major problems that they are likely to face at various points in their careers. The second goal is to instruct students on how to quickly find good, relevant information to aid in problem solving, and decision making. A third goal is to provide a variety of real-life situations to apply theory, research, and data analysis. A fourth goal is to give students a better perspective on how smaller problems seemingly unique to one department or situation are interrelated with, and not necessarily independent of, larger more complex organizational problems. Remember: an organization may not have the resources to conduct a research project to learn about a problem or social issue. Learning how to find relevant information is a valuable skill to aid you in solving smaller as well as larger, more complex, organizational problems.

Extended Case 1: Turmoil at the Granger Group

Amber Jackson, the managing editor of Web, multimedia, digital, and interactive sites and services for the *Dallas-Fort Worth Gazette* and associate managing editor for the print edition, sat in her closed office and thought, "You know, if someone had told me this sequence of events would have happened, I would have pronounced it fiction." Amber pondered how to deal with the events and decisions she faced.

Amber had just returned from the office of the *Gazette*'s group owner and CEO, Arthur Granger, after a meeting with him and *Gazette* publisher William Stahl, and Jose Mendoza, editor and publisher of *DFW Noticias*, the *Gazette*'s Spanish-language edition. The primary group owner and CEO of the Granger Group, Arthur Granger, had asked to meet him in his office downtown. "I'm not satisfied with Granger's profits or its editorial coverage. I take primary responsibility and am committed to changing the culture at the *Gazette* and my other properties. That means some major changes are going to happen at the *Gazette*," Granger said.

Granger continued, "I know employees say that I don't take bad news well. I'm rumored to be unapproachable and to hide in my office. I've been told that our circulation problems developed because we have a culture that discourages candor. Employees say they have a hard time telling the truth to management, including me, you, and others down the line. We all know this has been published by competing and industry publications, who've said our circulation fraud scandal resulted from my setting revenue goals that are too high. I've also been told that the scandal really blew up because our newspaper and reporters didn't cover the story honestly and thoroughly enough.

"We haven't yet cut our investigative reporting unit and I won't. I've been holding Mother off on that for years. I think we need to improve our editorial even more but I don't think our reporting is near as bad as our competitors and critics make it out to be" Granger added. "We haven't been taking on the powerful and comfortable Dallas elites in business, society, and government. We have excellent political coverage and took the Catholic establishment head on after the corruption and priest sexual abuse scandal. My family is Catholic and my mother was very displeased with our coverage. But I convinced her that we must be honest and fair, especially when it's our own church family. She finally turned over control of the group to me last month. Therefore, I want to begin my term as CEO and family owner as I see fit. But I want to do so in a way that is not disrespectful to my mother, the group, and our managers, and employees. I don't want to make it look like a rejection of our past. I see it as building on our successes and failures and going forward into the future.

"As part of building our future, I want to develop additional digital and new media offerings. These can be associated with the *Gazette*, *Noticias,* or our TV and four radio stations, or an entirely new outlet or service that the Granger Group will own and operate. We must grow and try new things. Obviously, given our losses after the circulation fraud scandal, we must rebuild the journalistic reputation and generate significant new revenue. I don't want to repeat the mistakes that employees think they have to do anything to raise revenue, however. I'm thinking we'll need to reorganize the firm's structure to make it more open and responsive to new media ideas and change the culture. I'll want your recommendations on structural changes in your reports. We also need to see whether our personnel and legal documents need to be changed as well," Granger said.

"I'll also be meeting with management at our sister television station as well as our four radio stations in DFW. We're going to improve things there too, building on our DuPont-Columbia, Peabody, and other awards for TV news and documentaries. We've gotten a reputation for not retaining our top news employees. Well that's going to change starting immediately. We're going to retain our older, core audience while finding new ways to attract a younger audience with new-media ventures," Granger looked quite serious when he said this.

Granger paused and then took an even more serious tone. "Obviously this necessitates decisions that are personally and professionally challenging. I've already talked to William and he is stepping down as publisher of the *Gazette*. He's agreed to retire and have his contract bought out. I've already spoken to Jose who has agreed to take over as the *Gazette*'s publisher. I've personally spoken to Bobby Joe Bryant and offered him a buyout. Amber, as you know, both Jose and William have recommended you to be the new managing editor of the *Gazette*, should Bobby Joe accept the buyout. I spoke to him this morning and he refused to give me an answer or stay for this meeting. I've given him a week from today as his deadline for giving me an answer."

Granger noted, "I brought you all here today to charge you to identify and report on the cultural, organizational, and revenue problems we need to solve. I'd like you all to provide a report in a week outlining what you see as the major problems we need to solve and how to do so. William has kindly agreed to provide a report even though he will not participate in the actual implementation due to his retirement. Bobby Joe also has agreed to provide a report but says he doesn't want to be a part of the process."

Granger added, "Another major concern is how to handle the buy-outs and possible layoffs. Please make recommendations to me as to which employees are to be offered buyouts, why, how those buyouts should be handled to avoid negative publicity or further harm to the *Gazette*'s reputation, and what to do if these employees refuse to be bought out. When I receive financial updates, I'll be able to give you a clearer picture of whether and how many employees may have to be laid off. So you should be making contingency plans now to respond if I need recommendations from you soon. William, if you don't mind, I'd like to talk to Amber and Jose alone now."

William left the room and closed the door again. Granger sighed and then concluded. "Obviously, Bobby Joe Bryant is one of our buyout can-didates. I asked William to leave because it appears to me he's been pro-tecting Bobby Joe and providing him inside information. As you know, they're Mother's favorites and I've been trying to explain to her why a change of leadership is needed for years. I can't be sure if Bobby Joe or William has been the source for negative information to the media. Given the amount and type of information leaked, it could be several people in management and nonmanagement positions."

Granger continued, "Bobby Joe's case is not an easy one. He's cer-tainly been an institution in the Dallas-Fort Worth journalistic com-munity, having won numerous awards earlier in his career. My mother loves him. But we all know his reputation has declined and he's been a lightning rod for personnel problems and controversy. Others have accused him and William of leaking information about our predica-ments to competitors. One theory as to why it is them is because noth-ing negative about mother has ever been published, nor has she even been mentioned in the criticism. It's assumed that they wouldn't say anything negative about Mother because they want to protect their power stemming from her favor of them. William has never been able to clearly explain to me why he protects Bobby Joe the way he does. So we all need to carefully think about how to handle his situation, whether or not he accepts a buyout. We have to assume he and William may leak anything we present or say to him. We also have to assume he and William may try to call Mother to rescind their buyouts. Mother will refuse so we must expect that there may now be negative coverage about her. Whatever happens, I want to be sure we treat William and Bobby Joe honorably and fairly."

Granger concluded by saying, "Obviously, I've shared personal informa-tion with you about my family in this meeting that I've never discussed with you before. As my leadership team, I want us to be completely comfortable in discussing anything with each other in a professional way. I expect that you will always keep these discussions of personal family issues that affect the company private and will not leak them to the media. I mean no offense, but because we are a family corporation I have to say that. I want to be sure I've clearly stated that to you so my expectations are clear. I also want to be sure we all have a working relationship where we can trust each other completely and discuss whatever we have to."

Jose replied, "I've worked for large, small, public, and private media group owners. I fully understand why you are saying this and will keep your trust. If I ever felt I had to provide information that you felt I shouldn't, I would talk to you first. Then I would accept the consequences of my decision. I fully understand, respect, and agree with what you're saying. But I'm also telling you, Arthur, that if I ever felt my journalistic integrity was compromised, you'll hear about it."

Amber concurred, adding, "Arthur, you know I feel exactly as Jose does. I am loyal to you and the Granger Group, but I cannot compromise my journalistic integrity. There is concern about the direction the *Gazette* had been taking. I think it would improve morale and help us to retain our best employees if we could share what you're telling us with our employees. Certainly, I understand there will be an appropriate time, way, and place for doing so. But I think if we really want to change the culture and improve morale at the paper we need to improve communication between you and our employees. We need to deal with issues like the circulation scandal in the same way we'd investigate any other paper or organizations. I think outlining how to deal with things like the circulation scandal in the employee manual, as well as improving communication, would go a long way toward reducing or eliminating leaks as well."

Arthur said, "That's why you're my new publisher and will be my managing editor, sooner, or later. Even if Bobby Joe remains in his position for the time being, Amber, you'll be included in upper-management decisions. I have no doubt you both have the kind of journalistic integrity and personal candor I admire and seek in my top managers. I respect and trust you both and want you to stay with us over the long term. I hope you will always give me the chance to retain you."

After the meeting, Amber and Jose met in Jose's office with the door closed to discuss things further. Amber asked Jose, "Why was I called into this meeting even though Bobby Joe has not yet accepted his buyout? That's a bit uncomfortable for me and him. And it seems likely to anger him, knowing his past behavior."

Jose replied, "Well you're the associate managing editor and Granger, William, and I wanted to include the entire top management team in these discussions. Everyone, including Bobby Joe, knows you're being groomed for his job after he retires. But, between you and me, I think Granger is trying to find out who has been the source of the leaks. And we all know William and Bobby Joe are among those who are suspected of leaking negative information. I think he wants to find out quickly whether his mother has truly given up control. And I think he was very upset about the way coverage of our scandals was covered in the *Gazette*."

Jose continued, "Obviously, our jobs are unusual in that, for better or worse, in this company top managers have to consider the family politics of the principal group owners. You and I wouldn't be in these positions if we hadn't walked the fine line well between maintaining our journalistic integrity and understanding how to keep clear of family politics. I don't think William and Bobby Joe ever truly understood how being Mrs. Granger's favorites and playing that angle is a double-edged sword."

Jose concluded, "Now, there's another important factor we need to consider. How we handle what's coming is going to define our reputations. I am committed to rebuilding the paper to its previous role as the journalistic leader in Texas and the region. I was crystal-clear about that to Granger when he offered me the publisher's job. I also told him I would be forthright and honest with him and would not hesitate to go to him with things he may not want to hear. Obviously, I'll be diplomatic, but I won't hesitate to approach him. You heard what he said, so I'll take him at his word."

"That's what I told him too," Amber said, adding, "Between you and me, do you really think his mother will take a background role? She's a smart, strong woman and has deep ties with most community leaders."

Jose replied, "I know Granger has been working toward taking over from his mother for several years. He's been courting the community leaders. And the coverage of the Catholic Church scandal made it pretty clear he'd take on the community establishment. I think most felt the coverage was fair and appropriate. Yes, I do believe he has finally taken over. Mrs. Granger is a pistol, but she's 84 years old. Even though she and Arthur have different philosophies and approaches, I know she's always respected him for taking stands even when he knew she wouldn't approve. I think Arthur's taking the right steps, and he'll find out pretty quickly whether his mother is truly ceding control. While I do believe it's final, we'll all have to keep our eyes open and be prepared to deal with any eventuality. And you and I must remember not to discuss private Granger family matters with anyone else. Nor do I want either of us to try to court favors like William and Bobby Joe have.

"I think you and I need to reconsider our style of working together. I know in the past we've each written separate drafts, and then gotten together, combined our reports, and worked out a final draft together. But if you become the managing editor, there will be times you'll need to take stands. I know you'll be an independent and strong managing editor. I think some employees buy into the female stereotype that you follow my lead. I suspect many employees don't know we disagree but work out our differences and compromise. I'm not sure of the best approach, but we need to consider this carefully and establish our own independent styles and authority at the outset, while maintaining our strong professional partnership."

Amber was a bit taken aback. She'd never heard that rumor. She thought a moment, and then replied, "I appreciate your thoughtfulness on my behalf. I'm not sure if many employees buy into that stereotype. And I think most employees understand our professional working relationship and recognize we are each independent and quite willing to stand up to each other. I also want to keep our partnership strong, agree that we need to consider this carefully, and establish our own independent styles and authority at the outset. I'll think carefully about this and get back to you informally with suggestions. And I assume that you and I, like Arthur, want to be completely candid and be able to trust each other."

"Of course, that goes without saying," replied Jose.

Amber knew she and Jose thought removing William and Bobby Joe was a big step toward solving problems and improving the paper. On numerous occasions, they had tried to talk to Bobby Joe about offering new digital, video, or mobile services or outlets for the paper. And Bobby Joe always refused to consider their ideas. Amber and Jose often had to weigh the pros and cons of going over Bobby Joe's head and meeting with William about their ideas and Bobby Joe's lack of cooperation. Yet both dreaded this option as Bobby Joe was known to retaliate or simply stop speaking when he was unhappy with someone.

Even Jack Hancock, the sports reporter who was universally liked and admired for his award-winning reporting, had had run-ins with Bobby Joe. Bobby Joe held Jack's story on a doping scandal involving a prominent Texas Rangers baseball player because he wasn't satisfied with the supporting sources. A competing paper ran the story first, depriving Jack, the *Gazette,* and *Noticias* of the scoop. While both continued to work together well, it was common knowledge among the staff that it was only because Jack knew Bobby Joe's stubborn nature and decided not to press the issue to the publisher. Both Amber and Jose had smoothed things over, ensuring Jack got a well-deserved raise after his next performance evaluation. Newsroom employees felt the sources were solid and the story held simply due to Bobby Joe's excessive caution. Other staffers wondered who and what Bobby Joe might be trying to protect or if someone behind the scenes was intervening. Most of the staff tried to avoid conflicts with Bobby Joe because they felt he was a friend of the publisher and the elderly Mrs. Granger.

The *Gazette*'s and *Noticias'* management and staff were also on edge because of newsroom buyout rumors. Bobby Joe told staffers he'd heard "from a reliable source" that about 50 positions would have to be cut from the print, online, and digital/new media newsrooms. Word quickly spread among the employees. However, given the papers' new goals for emphasizing multimedia and Internet strategies in the future to generate new revenue streams, the print edition news staff was especially concerned. Only a year and a half earlier about 60 newsroom and circulation department employees had been laid off after the circulation fraud scandal, leaving the company with about 3,000 employees.

William had outlined his goals in a paper-wide assembly and letter to employees several months earlier. William and his senior management had finalized the goals after department and edition managers held focus groups and meetings with employees to develop goals. Amber agreed with William's insistence in including all employees in the goal-setting process and genuinely considering their input. This same process was used for goal-setting at the other outlets as well. William said he wanted to emphasize breaking news and information on the *Gazette* and *Noticias* print and Web editions, add more streaming video feeds and podcasts, and launch demographic or psychographic segment-tailored community, digital or mobile services or sites. Yet, after the goals were formally adopted, every time Amber or Jose tried to talk to Bobby Joe about ideas to meet these goals, he blew them off.

The print and online newsrooms had come close to exploding over Bobby Joe's antics several times. Only loyalty to Amber and Jose, as well as fear over losing their jobs due to layoffs or buyouts, had kept the staff from taking more drastic action. But Amber knew it was only a matter of time. Either someone would file a complaint against Bobby Joe or they'd lose a valued employee who could find a better job. She hoped Bobby Joe would accept a buyout.

Amber knew Bobby Joe would be 65 soon although he'd often said he wanted to work as long as he could, at least until he was 70. He'd won numerous local and state awards earlier in his career as a reporter. He'd been promoted several times and had worked at the paper for more than 35 years. As an entrenched member of the local news media, his buyout would have to be handled carefully. But Amber, Jose and many other news staff felt Bobby Joe was a good ol' boy who didn't change with the times. Many editorial management and staff also felt that Bobby Joe, and to a lesser extent William, tended to protect the community's "sacred cows," such as major corporations and prominent citizens. The *Gazette* had lost several respected reporters over the years and many employees blamed Bobby Joe.

For example, a number of years earlier when Amber and Jose recommended developing blogs for the online edition, they finally had to write a memo to William outlining their ideas that also included Bobby Joe's objections and that the ideas were being submitted despite his failure to recommend them. The blogs they recommended were likely to be successful such as sports-interest blogs for Ranger, Mavericks, and Cowboys fans. The DFW area breaking news, weather and sports opt-in e-mail alerts also were a success. Yet every time they had a new media recommendation, they had to write a memo presenting their ideas and outlining Bobby Joe's objections. Amber and Jose were sick of having to do things this way. It seemed counterproductive and made it harder to maintain good working relationships. All were constantly reminded of their philosophical and editorial differences.

To make matters worse, the best employee in Amber's division, Senior Editor Umberto Martinez who excelled in his strategic development role, had just come to her with a job offer from the *Austin American-Statesman*. Umberto was essentially offered Amber's job at the Austin paper. And the paper offered an investigative reporting position for Umberto's wife, Sheila Kelley.

Umberto told her, "I'd love to stay, but I'm sick of dealing with Bobby Joe. My wife and I would prefer not to work at the same paper, but I want to be in a position where I don't have to argue with Bobby Joe over every idea. And we all know that I've been blamed for leaking to Sheila, but honestly, I'm not the source of the leaks."

Sheila was the investigative reporter on a local alternative newspaper. There she had the luxury of writing long, detailed investigative reports. She was one of the reporters who broke the story on the district attorney's investigation of the *Gazette*'s circulation scandal. The district attorney investigated Granger and the other owners of the *Gazette* for claiming to distribute more newspapers than are actually distributed and charging advertisers a higher rate based on the inflated circulation figures. The case had gone to a grand jury but no indictments resulted.

Rumor had it Bobby Joe had quashed the *Gazette*'s top reporter's story about the district attorney's investigation, allowing Sheila and reporters at other local and regional papers the scoop and embarrassing the *Gazette*'s publisher. That top reporter, Amanda Marshall, left to take a reporting position at *The New York Times* about 2 months after the incident. The group owner had included the investigation in its online quarterly report on the Web and a story appeared on the *Gazette*'s front page the day after Kelley's scoop.

Ultimately, the district attorney did not file charges. But the way the investigation story was handled when it broke embarrassed and humiliated many *Gazette* newsroom employees. Whether it was true, it made it appear the *Gazette* did not adhere to journalistic standards of integrity. It also affected the perceived integrity of the paper's sister television and radio stations in town. Critics claimed it was because the Granger Group did not have a commitment to presenting quality, forthright news, especially when it involved the family company.

Ironically, a few months earlier, the *Gazette* ran a front-page story reporting that Sunday circulation was inflated by about 10% and daily about 5%. A whistle blower had privately informed Arthur Granger of the scandal. Granger kept the whistle-blower's identity a secret. He immediately called a meeting with his mother, the other owners, and the *Gazette*'s top managers, who were all appalled by the scandal.

Arthur got the owners and managers to agree to hire a prominent and respected law firm to conduct an internal investigation. It was rumored that the law firm had documentation that certain employees were responsible. Yet, many in the circulation department were fired and the vice president of circulation resigned. The group charged about $20 million against earnings to compensate advertisers and other related expenses. Arthur Granger sent a letter to all employees explaining the results of the law firm's investigation and the subsequent actions. Granger had been deeply offended and angered that the *Gazette* had not reported about the district attorney's investigation first.

Apparently, the circulation fraud was the result of an incentive program that awarded trips and cash to employees who met goals to increase circulation. Unfortunately, the circulation employees who appeared to be involved in the fraud had been fired about 2 months before other employees were laid off who had no part in the scandal. This unfairly placed under a cloud of suspicion many innocent, good employees who had simply lost their jobs because revenues declined after the scandal.

This was another reason employees were so concerned about the buyouts and possible layoffs. What would happen now? They did not know that Bobby Joe had been offered a buyout. They didn't know about Granger's dealings with his mother behind the scenes. Amber and Jose knew they'd wonder whether employees like Bobby Joe would be retained based on seniority while excellent employees with shorter tenures be let go.

Amber knew she had a lot on her plate. She sat down at her desk and began formulating her thoughts. She knew major changes were coming, and there would be events she could not anticipate, but others she could. She wanted to develop an excellent report and prepare herself as best she could for all that was to come.

She thought, *My organization's, employees', owner's, and personal and professional reputation are at stake.* She knew Arthur and Jose felt the same way.

Assignment

Select a major daily newspaper in the city where your university is located or in a nearby major metropolitan area. Pretend it is the *Dallas-Fort Worth Gazette*. Conduct a market analysis and consider what new media offerings are needed, whether and how to change the organization's structure, culture, communication as well as its legal and personnel documents.

Such major changes require extensive research and planning as well as cultural changes to implement. By carefully planning and considering many factors before these changes are implemented, the ultimate changes should be easier to manage when the process starts. Remember your plans must achieve the Granger Group's goals to (a) be the undisputed multimedia news leader in the state and region; (b) to develop and use new technologies to foster excellence in news and cross promotion among the paper and group owned television station in the market; (c) to achieve this editorial excellence in the Hispanic media outlets owned by the group in the area and region; (d) to achieve this editorial excellence among other major demographic and ethnic segments in the local market; (e) to ensure the organizational culture and policies promote journalistic initiative and integrity to support the goal of being the state and region's news leader; and (f) to use new approaches and technologies to create operational efficiencies and increase revenue.

Before you formulate plans, begin by conducting a market analysis for the *Gazette* (and pretend it is the major paper you have selected in a nearby city). Start by reading the most recent profile of the Dallas-Fort Worth market (or your assigned market, if available) in *Mediaweek* (see Hudson, 2005b). Use the sources and suggestions provided in the section entitled Information Searching for Problem Solving and Decision Making to conduct your analysis and research of the market.

Also, obtain as much information as you can about the demographics, psychographics, and other characteristics of the city's residents. If available in your library, obtain the SRDS Lifestyle Market Analyst and copy the demographic and lifestyle pages for your city. Analyze the major demographic and lifestyle characteristics of residents. If Mediamark or Simmons are available in your library, check to see whether a report on your city is included.

Use the information and data obtained from all sources and the text to answer the following questions:

1. How and why did the rumor mill develop at the *Gazette*? Why is morale a problem at the *Gazette*? Review chapters 2 and 3, using them as a guide for answering this question.

2. Assume Amber is Black, that Jose is Hispanic and that the rest of the characters mentioned are White. Identify and describe the major diversity issues that exist at the *Gazette* and *Noticias*. For example, identify the major cultures that exist and explain why they developed. How have differences among managers and employees in gender, race, family issues, and other factors contributed to the development of these cultures? Provide detail and examples. Review chapters 2 and 6 before answering.

3. What can you do as a manager to avoid fostering the development of separate cultures in an organization? Review chapters 1, 2, 3, 4, and 6 before answering. Also, review your answers to questions 1 and 2 before completing this answer. Then consider whether and how your own gender, race, ethnic background, and/or religious or atheistic beliefs may have affected your answer to this question. In other words, do your own experiences and background affect your perceptions? If yes, how? Finally, after reading the relevant chapters and completing your self-assessment, answer this question by describing what can you do when you are a manager (such as Amber) to avoid fostering the development of separate cultures in an organization.

4. Identify and describe Arthur's, William's, Jose's, and Amber's leadership styles. What is positive about the way each leads? What is negative about the way each leads? What did each manager do that led to the problems each is facing now? What other comments do you have

about each manager? How could each manager improve his or her own leadership and communication? Explain your answers. Review chapters 1, 2, 3, and 4 before answering.

5. Briefly identify and describe the pros and cons of family-owned media organizations. How do they differ from non-family-owned media organizations or media conglomerates? How has the organization type and structure led to the problems outlined in the case? Review chapter 4 before answering this question.

6. Why has William been replaced as managing editor? Why has Bobby Joe been asked to step down? Why is there uncertainty about whether Bobby Joe will accept the buyout? What other reasons might there be for not removing William and Bobby Joe outright or firing them? In other words, what are the factors that are or may be underlying all of these actions? What might be going on behind the scenes but is not discussed outright in the case? What else could be inferred from a careful reading of the case? Review chapters 6, 7, and 10 before answering.

7. What steps should Jose take? What should he do to help the *Gazette* regain its editorial prominence? How should he handle William's retirement? Why? Did he discuss his partnership with Amber appropriately? Why or why not? What should Jose do to ensure a good partnership with Amber and maintain their independence and mutual respect? What else should he do to ease the fears of newsroom employees and deal with the rumor mill?

8. What steps should Amber take? Did she respond to Jose's statements about their partnership appropriately? Why or why not? What should Amber do to ensure a good partnership with Jose and maintain their independence and mutual respect? How should she deal with the uncertainly of whether she will become the managing editor? What should she do if and when she becomes managing editor? What should she then do to ease the fears of newsroom employees and deal with the rumor mill? What should she do if she does not become managing editor? How should she try to improve her working relationship with Bobby Joe? Why? Review chapters 1, 2, 3, 4, and 6 before answering.

9. Conduct a market analysis of Dallas-Fort Worth (or the major city you've been assigned or selected). Review chapters 7, 8, and 9 before answering. Use the information in those chapters as a guide for what to include in your market analysis. (See pp. 378–379.)

10. Write the section of Jose's report recommending how the organizational structure should be changed to meet the firm's goals and change the organization's culture. Use the organizational structure and chain of command of your local paper or find others online or use those provided by your professor and pretend they are the *Gazette*'s.

If you can, evaluate the organization structure of all outlets owned by the Granger Group. (In other words, try to find relevant organizational charts or documents from actual local outlets to serve as the organizational structure of the *Gazette*, *Noticias*, local television and radio stations and Web sites owned by the Granger Group.) Review chapter 4 and analyze the structure of the organization, which outlets and the departments each has, how and why they are set up, the chain of command, etc. (Or your professor may assign only one or two outlets for this question.) Consider whether and how the print, TV, radio, Hispanic and online outlets should be interrelated or remain separate. Consider how to improve communication between the owner and CEO and all Granger outlets. Outline a chain of command for all outlets, as well as each individual outlet. Then write a report that identifies whether and how the Granger Group and its outlets should be changed. Make sure your recommendations fit the organizational goals outlined in the case. Also, be sure your recommendations will ensure good communication within and between all Granger outlets and the group owner.

11. Write the section of Jose's report on the new personnel and legal documents that the *Gazette* may need. Review chapter 6. Use the appropriate documents for your local paper. If unavailable, find others online or use those provided by your professor and pretend they are the *Gazette*'s. If you can, evaluate all the personnel and legal documents of the other outlets owned by the Granger Group (in other words, try to find relevant documents from actual local outlets to serve as the personnel and other legal documents relating to the *Gazette*, *Noticias*, local television and radio stations and Web sites owned by the Granger Group. Or, try to find the personnel and legal documents or an employee handbook of a group owner). Review chapter 6 and then review the appropriate documents and employee handbook(s), focusing on the documents or outlets your professor assigns. Then write a report identifying what should be changed in these documents and why. Make sure your recommendations fit the organizational goals outlined in the case.

12. Develop a research proposal to help the *Gazette*'s managers decide what new media sites or services to offer and to whom those services should be targeted. Review chapters 5 and 9 before answering this question. Be sure the research encompasses the various new media, digital, Internet, video streaming, podcasting, and other possibilities. Be sure the major demographic, psychographic, and geographic factors are included. (See pp. 378–379.) Be sure to provide suggestions for testing new ideas before they are fully implemented to save the company money. In other words, evaluate reactions to the new content or services before they are fully implemented and introduced to

the general public. The research proposal must also evaluate the success of the new content and/or services after introduction. In other words, develop a research plan for evaluating the new content before it is made available to the general public. Also, develop a research proposal to gauge reaction to the new content after it appears. Be sure to develop a research plan that allows the managers to adjust the content, if needed after its introduction.

13. Propose one to three new content or services or outlet ideas that the Granger Group should offer. These could be anything realistic including podcasting, video streaming, cell phone services or content, MP3 player services or content, PDA services or content, or any other technology that is available. These new content or services could be an entirely new outlet owned by the Granger Group. What new media outlets or services should the *Gazette* offer? Why? To whom should each be targeted? Why? Explain your ideas in as much detail as possible. Be sure to describe the demographics and psychographics of each target segment and estimate their size.

14. Select your best new content or service or outlet idea. What would be the best decision-making process to develop it once it is identified through the market analysis and research? Who should make the decision about implementing it? Why? Which persons, managers, organizations, outlets, etc., should be involved? Why? In other words, should this be an individual or group decision? Who should be involved? Why? Explain your answer in detail. Review chapters 1, 2, 3, 4, and 5 before answering.

15. Develop a preliminary budget for implementing your best content or service or outlet idea. Use chapters 5 and 10 as guides for what to include. Provide whatever cost estimates you can. Realize that you will not have the information you need, so ask your professor what to include before working on your budget. In other words, provide and explain your best guess as to how much your idea might cost and why. The goal here is to provide practice in thinking through budgets and the cost of new technologies as best you can.

16. Develop a plan to implement the introduction of the new content or service or outlet. Develop steps, a timetable, alternatives, etc., and so on to show how and when the new offering will be introduced. Include short-, intermediate- and long-term planning. Identify steps in succession to show what must be done to ensure that the section is introduced as planned. Review chapters 5 and 7 before answering.

17. Assume your best new content or service idea is approved and implemented. How should it be promoted? Why? When? For how long? Should it be cross-promoted by the *Gazette*, *Noticias*, and the television station owned by the Granger Group as well as their Web sites? Why or why not? If yes, how should the new content and/or services

be cross promoted? How could the new offering itself be used in this promotional effort? Why? Review chapter 9 before answering this question. Also explain what the brand identity and position of the new offering, as well as all the Granger Group outlets should be and why.

18. Once the new content for the paper and Internet is selected, should the newsroom or other departments be reorganized, or new departments added, to handle the new assignments? Should any new newsroom managerial positions be developed? If yes, who should be promoted? Why? Suggest organizational changes to make implementation of the content and promotional plans easier. Review chapters 4 and 5 before answering.

Extended Case 2: Planning for the Future at the LA Independent

Brandon Wang, editor of LA Independent, a Web site providing a unique look at news, politics, sports, entertainment, and happenings in Los Angeles, had been thinking about how to create a stronger presence in the market. He and his staff had met regularly over the past year and decided they wanted to be the alternative voice for original coverage of news stories and investigative reporting of major issues important to primarily Los Angeles and secondarily California.

His reporting staff was relatively small with only 10 full-time reporters. He had two top-notch health reporters on his staff: Rosa Martinez, who specialized in health issues in the Latino community, and Stanton Rogers, who covered health issues in general. His other eight full- and part-time reporters specialized in technology, state and local government, politics, sports, entertainment, and business, with the other two being general assignment reporters who covered a variety of issues and topics. He wondered whether it was time to change the way the Independent was organized.

The LA Independent had brief, written department and job descriptions but they hadn't been updated since the site started up with eight employees five years ago. They'd been doing well and descriptions had been added as employees were hired so it probably was time to reorganize and write new descriptions. Sometimes he'd given employees a new title when he couldn't give them the raises he'd like to. He wondered if he should shift positions from one department to another if someone left. Over the years, employees pretty much took on the responsibilities they wanted that were appropriate for their departments.

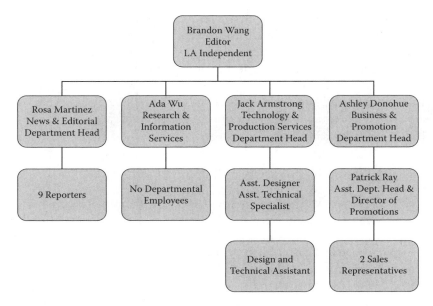

FIGURE 1 The LA Independent organization chart.

Brandon also had been thinking about a redesign and restructuring of the site itself. He'd checked out Poynteronline for ideas for design and trends (www.poynter.org), the Newspaper Association of America's Electronic Publishing link (www.naa.org/Electronic-Publishing.aspx) and its Digital Edge site (www.digitaledge.org) and cyberjournalist. net. He'd also asked the head of his tech and production department to think about how to update the site. Jack wanted to reorganize his department as well as the site and said he'd think about it and get back to Brandon.

Just as he'd done with Jack, Brandon chatted with the different department heads or employees to inform them of changes or policies. But with about 20 employees, this was getting hard. He also communicated regularly with everyone by e-mail, but it seemed a good time to consider whether organizational changes were needed.

It would be nice if he could delegate some of his business and technical responsibilities to others who had more expertise in those areas. He wondered if they needed new equipment or software. He wished he could spend more time on the editorial direction of the site and even do a little reporting sometimes. He and the entire staff shared the

same receptionist/secretary. She also handled general e-mail corre-
spondence, so he often didn't ask her for help because he knew how
swamped she was. How could they afford more support staff and maybe
another reporter or technical person or promotion specialist? And how
should they all decide what type of employee to hire first or second? The
Independent staff had decided to pursue the goal of being Los Angeles's
alternative voice, so it seemed a good time to think about all of these
kinds of things. However, the staff was cohesive and shared the same
journalistic values, and he didn't want to mess that up. He hadn't yet
shared these thoughts and hadn't yet decided how to approach the staff
about it.

Brandon also wanted to figure out which demographic, psychographic, or ethnic groups he should target to increase readership. He
knew he needed to see what was already being done in the Los Angeles market before he and his reporting team finalized their plans. His
research director, Ada Wu, would help him conduct a market analysis
and evaluate coverage of the major outlets to determine what opportunities might exist. With so many media outlets owned by groups, he
had a hunch many of his competitors were hesitant to take on local and
state corporations. Yet, he wanted to check out that hunch.

A prime example was the child obesity issue in California. While
many outlets covered it, including the *Los Angeles Times* in its Monday Health Watch section, there did not seem to be much coverage of
how food and beverage companies might be affected by or contributing to the problem. With all the state initiatives about child obesity
and the problems in Los Angeles, he was surprised more companies
had not developed programs with the schools. Rosa and Stanton had
approached him about investigating the child obesity issue in-depth.

Rosa said "Can you believe among 5th, 7th, and 9th graders in Los
Angeles County, 31.3% of children were overweight? And, the local
rates ranged from 8.0% in Manhattan Beach to 41.2% in Wilmington.
That's a pretty dramatic difference between those towns. Why is that? I
haven't seen anybody looking into that yet. And it's been estimated that
obesity and physical inactivity cost the state $28 billion" (California
Center for Public Health Advocacy, 2006b).

Stanton added, "The occurrence of child obesity increased among
girl and boys of all ethnic backgrounds. The Los Angeles Unified School
District, which enrolls 741,367 children, was not in compliance with
the requirement of 200 minutes of physical education every 10 days"
(California Center for Public Health Advocacy, 2006a).

Stanton continued, "While there are numerous factors involved, one problem seems to be that a lot of Californians may not realize they and their children are overweight. A study reported many residents think they're in good health, but more than half of California adults are overweight or obese. There's probably been a perceptual shift over time in that what is actually overweight might now be perceived as normal because so many people are overweight. Latinos, Indian and Alaska native and African Americans had the highest percentages of being overweight or obese."

Rosa concluded, "What makes all of that more ominous is the most important factor in a teenager's likelihood of being overweight is having an overweight parent (Griffith, 2006). Despite the laws that have been passed banning soft drinks and encouraging healthier food at schools, the problem seems to be getting worse. No wonder folks are calling the state Fatafornia."

Stanton said, "Obviously, everyone's covering the story, but I really haven't seen any hard-hitting, investigative reporting looking at these and other important questions. We've already got two health reporters anyway so it seems logical to make health reporting, including stories on child obesity, a part of our focus in the future. But we'll really need help with research if we're going to do quality coverage. There's so much online and we haven't even had time to conduct the interviews needed or hit the library. And we've got experts and USC and UCLA, etc. So we'd have to figure out how to do this. "

Brandon wondered whether the major local outlets avoided hard-hitting stories because they didn't want to alienate advertisers with large budgets. He figured his site could fill that gap. He didn't think it would be a problem with his current advertisers anyway. Some of these advertisers such as the Kashi Company (www.kashi.com), the Whole Foods Markets (www.wholefoodsmarket.com/stores/list_allstores.html), Alta Dena Dairy (www.altadenadairy.com), Muir Glen Organic (www.muirglen.com), Straus Family Creamery (www.strausmilk.com), Annie's (www.annies.com), Barbara's Bakery (www.barbarasbakery.com), Blue Diamond Almonds (www.bluediamond.com), Newman's Own Organics (www.newmansownorganics.com), Patagonia (www.patagonia.com), and ShiKai (www.shikai.com) offered health-oriented products anyway. He wondered about adding to his site special pages with games and information for kids that these advertisers might sponsor or help to develop. Or the Independent might work with these and other advertisers to develop community or public service or child health programs.

Ada had already broached the idea with him. "If we're going to have a visible presence in a market like Los Angeles, we've got to be involved in improving the community just like the major media outlets locally. I think we need to check out what they're doing in community service, too. If we're going to have our own editorial identity, I think it's only right to put our money where our coverage is and help solve those problems in the community. I don't know if any of our advertisers would want to do that. We should check out what kinds of community programs and public service promotions they're doing."

The business and promotion management team was on board with this idea. Ashley Donohue, the business and promotion manager, and Patrick Ray liked the idea of helping to solve problems in the community and saw this as a good way to promote and brand the site.

Patrick said, "We'll need to promote all of this as cheaply and efficiently as possible so we can check out why Universal McCann won for the best Internet media plan (Shields, 2006a) and Grupo Gallegos won for multicultural (Frutkin, 2006). Maybe that will give us ideas to include in our promotion plan. Ashley and the sales reps know some people who work at those agencies. But before we formalize any of this we need to talk to the reporting staff about it. We can get our ideas together and then approach them again in a staff meeting."

Brandon knew several reporters didn't like the idea of promoting the site based on its major editorial areas. He'd already had conversations with Rosa, Stanton, and all the other reporters individually. While no one said not to check it out, several noted they'd strenuously object if anything was done to jeopardize editorial integrity. "There better be an absolute brick wall between editorial and advertising," Rosa had said. "Besides, many of these companies advertise with us because we're known for our integrity, objectivity, and community spirit. We cannot do anything to damage the reputation we've worked so hard to get."

Brandon understood and agreed with Rosa's concerns. But he also had to make sure they stayed in business. He'd heard rumors that Tribune Interactive might want to buy the Independent (www.tribune interactive.com). He feared if that happened they wouldn't be able to do the kind of investigative journalism that they set as their goal.

He felt there were way too few voices like the Independent's left in journalism. It had been a source of pride among the staff over the years that they'd been lauded and chastised by politicians and groups from the left and right. He and his staff were well respected in Los Angeles's journalistic community. He and his reporters had had job offers but stayed to do the kind of journalism they wanted. Maybe there was a buyer in Los Angeles who could provide the capital to help them grow and support their editorial independence. And if the Independent were stronger financially they could resist advertiser pressure if one of their major advertisers did threaten to cancel its contract due to editorial coverage. So he felt like he was between a rock and a hard place. But he knew he would do everything he could to develop the Independent and take care of his employees.

Assignment

Read the most recent market profile of Los Angeles, California, in *Mediaweek* (Hudson, 2005a, or a newer version) to get an idea of the major media outlets there. Search online for alternative sites, direct or indirect competitors, or other online sites in Los Angeles. Use the suggestions from Backgrounder 2 as appropriate for the questions below.

1. What do you see as the main problems the LA Independent is facing? Identify each problem, explain it, and rank each problem from most important to least important. Then present your written or verbal answer in this order.
2. Identify Brandon's leadership style. What is positive about the way he leads? What is negative about the way he leads? Review chapters 1, 2, 3, and 4 before answering.
3. Identify and describe the culture of the Independent. What motivates Brandon and the other employees? How does the organization of the Independent affect the employees? What groups have formed in the organization? What are the differences between those groups? Write a report that describes the culture, motivation, groups, and other factors that explain why the Independent developed its culture. Review chapters 2 and 3 before answering.
4. Conduct a market analysis as well as an analysis of the major editorial departments, sections, and beats of the major media outlets in Los Angeles. Try to identify reporting niches that are neglected or ignored in the Los Angeles market. Identify and describe the editorial areas of specialization on which the Independent should focus and explain why. Review chapter 8 before answering.
5. After selecting the editorial areas of specialization in question 4, analyze the demographics, psychographics, geographics, ethnicity, and other major characteristics of the Los Angeles market. (See pp. 380–381.) First, identify and describe the segment or segments of consumers who might consume these new editorial offerings. Second, describe any other potential segments of readers based on other criteria. For example, check to see whether there are major compa-

nies or industries in Southern California that are associated with the new editorial offerings. In other words, are there also major firms or industries in the area that would naturally provide many readers of this new editorial content? Provide as much detail as you can about all segments you identify. Provide actual audience data and numbers if you can. Review chapter 9 before answering.

6. After selecting the editorial areas of specialization in question 4, analyze the Web sites of the newspapers, radio stations, and television stations and other online outlets in Los Angeles. Which sections do most have? Which areas or topics or sections are neglected? What online content or pages might the Independent adopt as a result of this analysis? How might the Independent's site be redesigned? Why? What approaches such as podcasting, video streaming , etc., might be incorporated into the site? Featuring what content or beats? Why? Review chapter 5 before answering.

7. After selecting the editorial areas of specialization in question 4, look for potential new advertisers for the Independent. What types of advertisers would want to advertise on these new pages or sections? Which new advertisers would be consistent with the Independent's image and editorial offerings? Which new advertisers are less likely to be alienated by the site's goal of quality investigative journalism? Identify at least five companies or advertisers and explain why they are appropriate for the Independent. Review chapter 9 before answering.

8. After selecting the editorial areas of specialization in question 4, analyze the present organizational structure of the Independent. Should the structure change? In other words, consider these and other questions related to the structure of the Independent. Should new departments be formed? Should some departments be dropped or renamed? Should an existing department be split into two or more departments? Should some employees be laid off? Should some employees be shifted from full time to part time? Should some employees not be replaced when they leave, and those positions shifted to other departments? Can the employee's motivation and the culture be improved through structural change? After analyzing the problems you identified in question 1 and the present structure, recommend a new organizational structure for the Independent or explain why the old structure should be retained. Review chapters 3, 4, and 5 before answering.

9. After establishing the recommended organizational structure from question 8, write new job descriptions for the departments and major positions in each department. Identify the chain of command and explain how communication should flow between managers and employees within the organization. Identify as best you can the major

responsibilities of the major managers and employees, if possible. Review chapters 4, 5, and 6 before answering.

10. Using the organizational structure and job descriptions you recommended in questions 8 and 9 (or assigned by your professor), develop short-run, intermediate, and strategic plans for the Independent. Base these plans on chapter 7, being sure to include goals, editorial, technological, marketing, human resources, business, and other factors.

11. After completing your plans from question 10, search for potential investors or buyers of the Independent in Los Angeles, Southern California, or anywhere else in the state of California. Look for buyers or investors who appear likely to support the editorial approach and investigative reporting mission of the Independent. Prepare a report identifying at least five potential buyers or investors and explain why they are suited to the Independent. Review chapters 7 and 8 before completing this question.

12. Read and analyze the data from the content analysis of television advertising in Backgrounder 4. Also, review the relevant Web sites listed there or any materials assigned by your professor. Figure out who the major advertisers to children are, the techniques they use, as well as the major concerns critics have about advertising to children. Now reconsider the list of present advertisers in the case, the new advertisers you recommended in question 7, and the potential investors you identified in question 11. What potential conflicts of interest, if any, do you see between these advertisers and investors and the guidelines generally recommended for advertising to children? Do any of these companies sell products that are unhealthy and may contribute to childhood obesity? Do any of these investors accept significant amounts of advertising revenue from advertisers who sell unhealthy products? What other potential problems do you see? Consider these factors and then write a report explaining which advertisers and investors would be best suited to the Independent, based on the child obesity information, and explain why.

13. Read and analyze Backgrounder 3 and 4. Also, review the relevant Web sites listed there or any materials assigned by your professor. Figure out who the major advertisers to children are, the techniques they use, as well as the major concerns critics have about advertising to children. Review your list of present and potential advertisers and investors for the Independent. Select the best three companies or brands (e.g., go to www.kashi.com or www.kashikids.com and www.kashikids.com/mightybites.asp and select a product to use for this question or use another company or product from your list). Review the advertiser's and brand's Web site for any current promotions. Examine the information they present about children or their health issues. After reviewing the sites, select 1 to 3 of these brands to use

for a promotion with the Independent to help solve the child obesity problem. Come up with an event or program or idea that can be sponsored by the advertiser and the Independent to educate children and their parents about healthy eating habits and exercise in a way that is fun and interesting. Consider the programs developed by Coca-Cola and Nickelodeon. Look for articles using online databases that feature other ideas to curb child obesity (e.g., see Borja, 2006; DeGuevara, 2006). Check the sites of the major media outlets in Los Angeles to see if they already have such programs. Search for other such programs or ideas online, too. Use these examples to help you come up with and describe in detail a program the Independent and one or more of its advertisers could sponsor that has not already been implemented in California.

14. Develop a budget, plan, and timetable for implementing the program you developed in question 13. Explain in as much detail as you can when, where, how, the cost, etc., of the program you propose. Ask your professor for any materials he or she can provide to help. Ask your professor for the level of detail required. Also use chapters 7 and 10 as guides for what to include in your answer.

15. Explain in detail how you will promote the program you recommended for dealing with child obesity in questions 13 and 14. How should the Independent and the advertiser(s) feature the program on their Web sites? Where else should messages about the program appear? Why? When? How often? What other clever and inexpensive ways could be used to promote the program and make as many Los Angeles area residents aware of it and participate? Be sure to develop promotional plans that are consistent with the cultures and images of the Independent and the advertiser(s). Review chapters 7, 8, 9, and 10 before answering.

16. What legal or ethical concerns may arise from implementing and promoting the program you recommended in questions 13, 14, and 15? What legal issues must be considered beforehand? What plans must be made for dealing with any legal issues that arise after the program is implemented? What other internal or external problems could arise that are associated with this program? Review chapter 6 before answering.

Acknowledgments

The author gratefully acknowledges Donna Daniels, the Business/Journalism Reference and Collection Development Librarian in Mullins Library at the University of Arkansas, who provided invaluable advice for this section and locating sources of information as well as aiding my classes over the years. She and the Reference Staff at Mullins Library have provided excellent advice and assistance to my classes. There are helpful reference librarians at your school, too.

The author gratefully acknowledges Dr. Ron Warren of the Communication Department at the University of Arkansas for providing the data used in Extended Case 2.

Dallas-Fort Worth, TX

Demographics
Base Index US = 100

Total Adult Population   4,630,074

Occupation	Population	%	Index
Administrative	819,523	17.7	117
Blue Collar	416,707	9.0	73
Clerical	430,597	9.3	98
Homemaker	620,430	13.4	100
Professional/Technical	1,402,912	30.3	113
Retired	481,528	10.4	69
Sales/Marketing	333,365	7.2	133
Self Employed	60,191	1.3	100
Student	69,451	1.5	115

Education (2000 Census)

Elementary (0-8 years)	312,138	8.7	116
High School (1-3 years)	430,535	12.0	99
High School (4 years)	846,718	23.6	83
College (1-3 years)	1,029,695	28.7	105
College (4+ years)	965,115	26.9	110

Race/Ethnicity

White	2,643,772	57.1	85
Black	601,910	13.0	107
Asian	185,203	4.0	95
Hispanic	1,111,218	24.0	169
American Indian	18,520	0.4	57
Other	74,081	1.6	80

Total Households   2,332,293

Age of Head of Household	Households	%	Index
18-24 years old	146,934	6.3	121
25-34 years old	464,126	19.9	124
35-44 years old	550,421	23.6	115
45-54 years old	489,782	21.0	100
55-64 years old	331,186	14.2	90
65-74 years old	195,913	8.4	78
75 years and older	153,931	6.6	63
Median Age	**45.1 years**		

Sex/Marital Status

Single Male	501,443	21.5	100
Single Female	513,104	22.0	91
Married	1,317,746	56.5	104

Children At Home

At Least One Child	776,654	33.3	110
Child Age Under 2	116,615	5.0	116
Child Age 2-4	202,909	8.7	119
Child Age 5-7	198,245	8.5	115
Child Age 8-10	193,580	8.3	115
Child Age 11-12	137,605	5.9	107
Child Age 13-15	200,577	8.6	104
Child Age 16-18	184,251	7.9	101

Home Ownership

Owner	1,460,015	62.6	93
Renter	872,278	37.4	115

Stage in Family Lifecycle	Households	%	Index
Single, 18-34, No Children	270,546	11.6	114
Single, 35-44, "	156,264	6.7	114
Single, 45-64, "	265,881	11.4	92
Single, 65+ "	125,944	5.4	64
Married, 18-34, "	114,282	4.9	148
Married, 35-44, "	86,295	3.7	123
Married, 45-64, "	345,179	14.8	96
Married, 65+ "	191,248	8.2	73
Single, Any Child at Home	195,913	8.4	97
Married, Child Age Under 13	340,515	14.6	123
Married, Child Age 13-18	237,894	10.2	106

Household Income

Under $20,000	363,838	15.6	81
$20,000-$29,999	247,223	10.6	91
$30,000-$39,999	263,549	11.3	98
$40,000-$49,999	242,558	10.4	100
$50,000-$74,999	457,129	19.6	101
$75,000-$99,999	289,204	12.4	109
$100,000 and over	468,791	20.1	123
Median Income	**$52,736**		

Income Earners

Married, One Income	499,111	21.4	100
Married, Two Incomes	818,635	35.1	107
Single	1,014,547	43.5	95

Dual Income Households

Children Age Under 13 years	205,242	8.8	117
Children Age 13-18 years	167,925	7.2	104
No Children	447,800	19.2	104

Age By Income

18-34, Income under $30,000	207,574	8.9	107
35-44, "	100,289	4.3	96
45-64, "	163,261	7.0	84
65+ "	137,605	5.9	60
18-34, Income $30,000-$49,999	156,264	6.7	129
35-44, "	114,282	4.9	114
45-64, "	153,931	6.6	89
65+ "	81,630	3.5	71
18-34, Income $50,000-$74,999	116,615	5.0	128
35-44, "	114,282	4.9	109
45-64, "	167,925	7.2	91
65+ "	60,640	2.6	81
18-34, Income $75,000 and over	130,608	5.6	144
35-44, "	221,568	9.5	132
45-64, "	338,182	14.5	110
65+ "	67,636	2.9	85

Credit Card Usage

Travel/Entertainment	394,158	16.9	117
Bank Card	1,793,533	76.9	98
Gas/Department Store	557,418	23.9	95
No Credit Cards	440,803	18.9	109

"The Lifestyle Market Analyst, 2006 Edition, published by SRDS in conjunction with Equifax Marketing Services."

Lifestyles

Base Index US = 100

Dallas-Fort Worth, TX

The Top Ten Lifestyles Ranked by Index

Own a Blackberry	153	Horseback Riding	123
Own a Satellite Dish	133	Electronics	123
Own a HDTV	130	Use a Wireless Internet	118
Frequent Flyer	128	Running/Jogging	117
Bible/Devotional Reading	127	Science/New Technology	116

Home Life	Households	%	Index	Rank
Avid Book Reading	865,281	37.1	96	166
Bible/Devotional Reading	725,343	31.1	127	65
Flower Gardening	699,688	30.0	85	198
Grandchildren	499,111	21.4	86	188
Home Furnishing/Decorating	776,654	33.3	101	91
Own a Cat	608,728	26.1	92	182
Own a Dog	1,030,874	44.2	115	88
Shop by Catalog/Mail	1,093,845	46.9	90	198
Vegetable Gardening	419,813	18.0	75	194

Good Life				
Attend Cultural/Arts Events	398,822	17.1	102	46
Cruise Ship Vacations	417,480	17.9	102	47
Fashion Clothing	433,806	18.6	104	48
Fine Art/Antiques	305,530	13.1	104	67
Foreign Travel	438,471	18.8	109	37
Frequent Flyer	713,682	30.6	128	22
Gourmet Cooking/Fine Foods	513,104	22.0	100	61
Travel for Pleasure/Vacation	237,894	10.2	92	90
Travel in USA	872,278	37.4	99	75
Wines	487,449	20.9	105	43

Hobbies & Interests				
Automotive Work	342,847	14.7	95	182
Buy Pre-Recorded Videos	550,421	23.6	105	75
Coin/Stamp Collecting	223,900	9.6	95	169
Collectibles/Collections	352,176	15.1	92	178
Community/Civic Activities	370,835	15.9	88	177
Crafts	573,744	24.6	91	192
Current Affairs/Politics	249,555	10.7	104	63
Donate to Charitable Causes	1,233,783	52.9	100	58
Home Workshop	702,020	30.1	98	183
Needlework/Knitting	303,198	13.0	82	201
Our Nation's Heritage	156,264	6.7	100	125
Self-Improvement	566,747	24.3	104	58
Sewing	361,505	15.5	91	193

Investing & Money				
Casino Gambling	398,822	17.1	104	89
Entering Sweepstakes	324,189	13.9	99	132
Moneymaking Opportunities	307,863	13.2	109	51
Real Estate Investments	221,568	9.5	95	80
Stock/Bond Investments	468,791	20.1	100	65

Sports, Fitness & Health	Households	%	Index	Rank
Bicycling Frequently	431,474	18.5	85	131
Dieting/Weight Control	660,039	28.3	102	101
Extreme Sports	233,229	10.0	101	88
Golf	422,145	18.1	95	110
Health/Natural Foods	569,079	24.4	100	70
Improving Your Health	816,303	35.0	105	42
Physical Fitness/Exercise	1,002,886	43.0	103	41
Running/Jogging	382,496	16.4	117	26
Snow Skiing Frequently	181,919	7.8	96	78
Tennis Frequently	179,587	7.7	108	29
Walking for Health	683,362	29.3	92	196
Watching Sports on TV	855,952	36.7	98	110

Great Outdoors				
Boating/Sailing	216,903	9.3	84	151
Camping/Hiking	566,747	24.3	90	161
Fishing Frequently	632,051	27.1	92	178
Horseback Riding	172,590	7.4	123	67
Hunting/Shooting	412,816	17.7	95	164
Recreational Vehicles	219,236	9.4	90	171
Wildlife/Environmental	319,524	13.7	85	196

High Tech Activities				
Electronics	517,769	22.2	123	4
Listen to Records/Tapes/CDs	1,142,824	49.0	98	154
Own a Blackberry	60,640	2.6	153	8
Own a CD Player	1,655,928	71.0	102	49
Own a CD Rom	1,485,671	63.7	112	8
Own a Cellular Phone	1,753,884	75.2	106	6
Own a Digital Camera	1,105,507	47.4	108	29
Own a Digital Video Recorder	419,813	18.0	115	17
Own a DVD Player	1,760,881	75.5	104	9
Own a HDTV	342,847	14.7	130	6
Own an Apple/Macintosh PC	130,608	5.6	90	63
Own an IBM Compatible PC	1,420,366	60.9	111	8
Own a Satellite Dish	851,287	36.5	133	34
Photography	576,076	24.7	101	65
Science Fiction	258,885	11.1	110	35
Science/New Technology	277,543	11.9	116	22
Subscribe to Online Service	1,637,270	70.2	111	3
Use a Wireless Internet	431,474	18.5	118	24
VCR Recording	391,825	16.8	102	75

"The Lifestyle Market Analyst, 2006 Edition, published by SRDS in conjunction with Equifax Marketing Services."

Los Angeles, CA

Demographics
Base Index US = 100

Total Adult Population	12,617,290		
Occupation	Population	%	Index
Administrative	2,195,408	17.4	115
Blue Collar	1,122,939	8.9	72
Clerical	1,249,112	9.9	104
Homemaker	1,577,161	12.5	93
Professional/Technical	3,734,718	29.6	111
Retired	1,476,223	11.7	78
Sales/Marketing	845,358	6.7	124
Self Employed	214,494	1.7	131
Student	201,877	1.6	123

Education (2000 Census)			
Elementary (0-8 years)	1,368,674	13.8	184
High School (1-3 years)	1,299,249	13.1	108
High School (4 years)	1,963,750	19.8	69
College (1-3 years)	2,856,364	28.8	105
College (4+ years)	2,429,893	24.5	100

Race/Ethnicity			
White	4,580,076	36.3	54
Black	895,828	7.1	59
Asian	1,400,519	11.1	264
Hispanic	5,387,583	42.7	301
American Indian	50,469	0.4	57
Other	302,815	2.4	120

Total Households	5,613,426		
Age of Head of Household	Households	%	Index
18-24 years old	246,991	4.4	85
25-34 years old	999,190	17.8	111
35-44 years old	1,335,995	23.8	116
45-54 years old	1,229,340	21.9	104
55-64 years old	825,174	14.7	94
65-74 years old	505,208	9.0	83
75 years and older	477,141	8.5	81
Median Age	46.9 years		

Sex/Marital Status			
Single Male	1,364,063	24.3	113
Single Female	1,431,424	25.5	106
Married	2,817,940	50.2	92

Children At Home			
At Least One Child	1,768,229	31.5	104
Child Age Under 2	263,831	4.7	109
Child Age 2-4	404,167	7.2	99
Child Age 5-7	415,394	7.4	100
Child Age 8-10	426,620	7.6	106
Child Age 11-12	331,192	5.9	107
Child Age 13-15	499,595	8.9	107
Child Age 16-18	465,914	8.3	106

Home Ownership			
Owner	3,059,317	54.5	81
Renter	2,554,109	45.5	140

Stage in Family Lifecycle	Households	%	Index
Single, 18-34, No Children	645,544	11.5	113
Single, 35-44, "	443,461	7.9	134
Single, 45-64, "	757,813	13.5	109
Single, 65+ "	426,620	7.6	89
Married, 18-34, "	196,470	3.5	106
Married, 35-44, "	190,856	3.4	113
Married, 45-64, "	707,292	12.6	82
Married, 65+ "	471,528	8.4	75
Single, Any Child at Home	516,435	9.2	106
Married, Child Age Under 13	690,451	12.3	103
Married, Child Age 13-18	561,343	10.0	104

Household Income			
Under $20,000	1,027,257	18.3	95
$20,000-$29,999	600,637	10.7	92
$30,000-$39,999	583,796	10.4	90
$40,000-$49,999	533,275	9.5	91
$50,000-$74,999	1,027,257	18.3	94
$75,000-$99,999	673,611	12.0	105
$100,000 and over	1,161,979	20.7	127
Median Income	$51,391		

Income Earners			
Married, One Income	1,055,324	18.8	87
Married, Two Incomes	1,762,616	31.4	96
Single	2,795,486	49.8	109

Dual Income Households			
Children Age Under 13 years	426,620	7.6	101
Children Age 13-18 years	387,326	6.9	100
No Children	948,669	16.9	92

Age By Income			
18-34, Income under $30,000	471,528	8.4	101
35-44, "	291,898	5.2	116
45-64, "	449,074	8.0	96
65+ "	421,007	7.5	76
18-34, Income $30,000-$49,999	286,285	5.1	98
35-44, "	258,218	4.6	107
45-64, "	364,873	6.5	88
65+ "	218,924	3.9	80
18-34, Income $50,000-$74,999	213,310	3.8	97
35-44, "	263,831	4.7	104
45-64, "	404,167	7.2	91
65+ "	151,563	2.7	84
18-34, Income $75,000 and over	275,058	4.9	126
35-44, "	527,662	9.4	131
45-64, "	836,400	14.9	113
65+ "	196,470	3.5	103

Credit Card Usage			
Travel/Entertainment	1,212,500	21.6	150
Bank Card	4,496,354	80.1	102
Gas/Department Store	1,403,357	25.0	100
No Credit Cards	842,014	15.0	86

"The Lifestyle Market Analyst, 2006 Edition, published by SRDS in conjunction with Equifax Marketing Services."

Lifestyles
Base Index US = 100

Los Angeles, CA

The Top Ten Lifestyles Ranked by Index

Own an Apple/Macintosh PC	177	Tennis Frequently	131
Own a Blackberry	176	Running/Jogging	128
Foreign Travel	142	Own a Digital Video Recorder	127
Use a Wireless Internet	140	Extreme Sports	126
Real Estate Investments	133	Own a HDTV	126

Home Life	Households	%	Index	Rank
Avid Book Reading	1,975,926	35.2	91	199
Bible/Devotional Reading	1,195,660	21.3	87	161
Flower Gardening	1,627,894	29.0	83	201
Grandchildren	1,094,618	19.5	79	204
Home Furnishing/Decorating	1,633,507	29.1	88	198
Own a Cat	1,347,222	24.0	85	198
Own a Dog	1,874,884	33.4	87	196
Shop by Catalog/Mail	2,542,882	45.3	87	205
Vegetable Gardening	959,896	17.1	72	198

Good Life	Households	%	Index	Rank
Attend Cultural/Arts Events	1,150,752	20.5	123	17
Cruise Ship Vacations	1,089,005	19.4	111	25
Fashion Clothing	1,167,593	20.8	117	12
Fine Art/Antiques	718,519	12.8	102	90
Foreign Travel	1,369,676	24.4	142	9
Frequent Flyer	1,611,053	28.7	120	31
Gourmet Cooking/Fine Foods	1,380,903	24.6	112	19
Travel for Pleasure/Vacation	757,813	13.5	122	17
Travel in USA	2,060,127	36.7	98	93
Wines	1,234,954	22.0	110	34

Hobbies & Interests	Households	%	Index	Rank
Automotive Work	791,493	14.1	91	194
Buy Pre-Recorded Videos	1,229,340	21.9	97	164
Coin/Stamp Collecting	516,435	9.2	91	191
Collectibles/Collections	813,947	14.5	88	190
Community/Civic Activities	1,060,938	18.9	105	68
Crafts	1,302,315	23.2	86	203
Current Affairs/Politics	634,317	11.3	110	35
Donate to Charitable Causes	2,885,301	51.4	98	87
Home Workshop	1,476,331	26.3	86	204
Needlework/Knitting	729,745	13.0	82	200
Our Nation's Heritage	319,965	5.7	85	195
Self-Improvement	1,392,130	24.8	106	30
Sewing	802,720	14.3	84	202

Investing & Money	Households	%	Index	Rank
Casino Gambling	1,161,979	20.7	125	17
Entering Sweepstakes	679,225	12.1	86	193
Moneymaking Opportunities	729,745	13.0	107	59
Real Estate Investments	746,586	13.3	133	14
Stock/Bond Investments	1,077,778	19.2	95	106

Sports, Fitness & Health	Households	%	Index	Rank
Bicycling Frequently	1,274,248	22.7	104	81
Dieting/Weight Control	1,425,810	25.4	91	194
Extreme Sports	701,678	12.5	126	30
Golf	892,535	15.9	84	149
Health/Natural Foods	1,538,079	27.4	113	13
Improving Your Health	1,953,472	34.8	105	46
Physical Fitness/Exercise	2,469,907	44.0	106	26
Running/Jogging	1,004,803	17.9	128	9
Snow Skiing Frequently	538,889	9.6	119	54
Tennis Frequently	522,049	9.3	131	8
Walking for Health	1,801,910	32.1	101	105
Watching Sports on TV	1,959,086	34.9	94	161

Great Outdoors	Households	%	Index	Rank
Boating/Sailing	533,275	9.5	86	140
Camping/Hiking	1,453,877	25.9	96	148
Fishing Frequently	1,060,938	18.9	64	207
Horseback Riding	314,352	5.6	93	130
Hunting/Shooting	510,822	9.1	49	206
Recreational Vehicles	555,729	9.9	94	149
Wildlife/Environmental	757,813	13.5	83	199

High Tech Activities	Households	%	Index	Rank
Electronics	1,167,593	20.8	116	9
Listen to Records/Tapes/CDs	2,857,234	50.9	101	57
Own a Blackberry	168,403	3.0	176	6
Own a CD Player	3,890,104	69.3	99	110
Own a CD Rom	3,379,282	60.2	105	32
Own a Cellular Phone	4,153,935	74.0	104	16
Own a Digital Camera	2,789,873	49.7	113	18
Own a Digital Video Recorder	1,122,685	20.0	127	7
Own a DVD Player	4,165,162	74.2	102	32
Own a HDTV	797,106	14.2	126	7
Own an Apple/Macintosh PC	617,477	11.0	177	5
Own an IBM Compatible PC	3,194,039	56.9	104	37
Own a Satellite Dish	1,611,053	28.7	104	114
Photography	1,453,877	25.9	106	41
Science Fiction	617,477	11.0	109	39
Science/New Technology	684,838	12.2	118	19
Subscribe to Online Service	3,693,634	65.8	104	34
Use a Wireless Internet	1,234,954	22.0	140	6
VCR Recording	976,736	17.4	106	55

"The Lifestyle Market Analyst, 2006 Edition, published by SRDS in conjunction with Equifax Marketing Services."

REFERENCES

Aaker, D. A. (1995). *Developing business strategies* (4th ed.). New York: John Wiley & Sons.

About Case Assignments. (2006). Retrieved August 16, 2006, from Pennsylvania State University Teaching and Learning with Technology, http://tlt.its.psu.edu/suggestions/cases/studenttips/index.html

About Case Studies. (2006). Retrieved August 16, 2006, from Pennsylvania State University Teaching and Learning with Technology, http://tlt.its.psu.edu/suggestions/cases.

Abraham, R. (1999). Emotional dissonance in organizations: Conceptualizing the roles of self-esteem and job-induced tension. *Leadership & Organization Development Journal, 20*, 18–25.

Adams, J. S. (1963). Toward an understanding of inequity. *Journal of Abnormal and Social Psychology, 67*, 422–436.

Adams, R. C., & Fish, M. J. (1987). TV news directors' perceptions of station management style. *Journalism Quarterly, 64*, 154–162, 276.

Adams, W. J., & Eastman, S. T. (2002). Prime-time network entertainment programming. In S. T. Eastman, & D. A. Ferguson (Eds.), *Broadcast/cable/Web/programming* (6th ed., pp. 111–150). Belmont, CA: Wadsworth.

Advertising Research Foundation. (2003, August). *Advertising Research Foundation's guidelines for market research.* New York: Author. Retrieved August 16, 2006, from http://www.arfsite.org/downloads/GuidelinesForMarketResearch.pdf

Albarran, A. B. (1996). *Media economics: Understanding markets, industries and concepts.* Ames, IA: Iowa State University Press.

Albarran, A. B. (1998). The coalescence of power: The transformation of the communication industries. In R.G. Picard (Ed.), *Evolving media markets: Effects of economic and policy changes* (pp. 8–24). Turku, Finland: The Economic Research Foundation for Mass Communication.

Aldag, R. J., & Brief, A. P. (1978). *Task design and employee motivation.* Glenview, IL: Scott, Foresman & Co.

Alderfer, C. P. (1972). *Existence, relatedness, and growth.* New York: Free Press.

Allen, M. W., Seibert, J. H., Haas, J. W., & Zimmermann, S. (1988). Broadcasting departmental impact on employee perceptions and conflict. *Journalism Quarterly, 65*, 668–677.

AMA board approves new marketing definition. (1985, March 1). *Marketing News.*

Amari, J. (2000). Toto, we're not in Kansas anymore. In ASNE Interactive Media Committee (Eds.), *The new journalists: A report from ASNE's interactive media committee* (p. 2). Reston, VA: American Society of Newspaper Editors Foundation.

American Society of Newspaper Editors. (2006, April 26). *ASNE census shows newsroom diversity grows slightly.* Retrieved July 15, 2006, from http://www.asne.org/

Arbitron Persons Using Radio Report. (2006). Retrieved July 3, 2006, from http://wargod.arbitron.com/scripts/ndb/ndbradio2.asp

Argyris, C. (1962). *Interpersonal competence and organizational effectiveness.* Homewood, IL: Dorsey.

Argyris, C. (2000). *Flawed advice and the management trap.* New York: Oxford University Press.

Argyris, C. (2001). *Reasons and rationalizations: The limits to organizational knowledge.* New York: Oxford University Press.

Argyris, C., & Schön, D. A. (1974). *Theory in practice: Increasing professional effectiveness.* San Francisco: Jossey-Bass.

Argyris, C., & Schön, D. A. (1978). *Organizational learning.* Reading, MA: Addison-Wesley.

Arnas, Y. A. (2006). The effects of television food advertisement on children's food purchasing requests. *Pediatrics International, 48,* 138–145.

Arnold, M., & Nesbitt, M. (2006). *Women in media 2006: Finding the leader in you.* Evanston, IL: Media Management Center, Northwestern University.

Aronson, E. (1969). The theory of cognitive dissonance: A current perspective. In L. Berkowitz (Ed.), *Advances in experimental social psychology* (Vol. 4, pp. 1–34). New York: Academic Press.

Associated Press. (2006a, June 14). DOJ seeks info on California newspaper deals. *PhillyBurbs.com.* Retrieved July 2, 2006, from http://www.phillyburbs.com/pb-dyn/news/24-06142006-670094.html

Associated Press. (2006b, June 20). *Alleged assault brings $30 million suit against MySpace.com.* Associated press state and local wire—News briefs from around Texas, p. 1.

Associated Press v. U.S. (1945). Dist. Court, 705 F.2d 1143.

Babbie, E. (2004). *The practice of social research* (10th ed.). Belmont, CA: Wadsorth.

Babbie, E. (2005). *The basics of social research* (3rd ed.). Belmont, CA: Wadsworth.

Bandura, A. (1997). *Self-efficacy: The exercise of control.* New York: Freeman.

Barkin, S. M. (2001, September). Satellite extravaganza. *American Journalism Review, 23*(7), 48–51.

Barnett, R. (2006, July). Is this child overweight? *Parenting, 20,* 34.

Bass, B. M. (1983). *Organizational decision making.* Homewood, IL: Irwin.

Baxter, R. (1983, September 12). Managing the risks in firing employees. *The National Law Journal,* pp. 20–21.

Beam, R. A. (2006). Organizational goals and priorities and the job satisfaction of U.S. journalists. *Journalism & Mass Communication Quarterly, 83*(1), 169–185.

Becker, L. B., Vlad, T., & Coffey, A. J. (2005). *2004 Annual survey of journalism and mass communication graduates.* Retrieved July 16, 2006, from http://www.grady.uga.edu/service_&_outreach.php?page=frame|http://www.grady.uga.edu/coxcenter/

Beckhard, R., & Harris, R. (1987). *Organizational transitions: Managing complex change.* Reading, MA: Addison-Wesley.

Bergen, L. A., & Weaver, D. (1988). Job satisfaction of daily newspaper journalists and organization size. *Newspaper Research Journal, 9* (2), 1–13.

Blackler, F., & Brown, C. (1985). Evaluation and the impact of information technologies on people in organizations. *Human Relations, 38*(3), 213–231.

Boczkowski, P. J. (2004) *Digitizing the news.* Cambridge, MA: MIT Press.

Boehrer, J., & Linsky, M. (1990). Teaching with cases: Learning to question. In M. D. Svinicki (Ed.), *The changing face of college teaching: New directions for teaching and learning* (No. 42, 41–57). San Francisco: Josey-Bass.

Boisot, M. H. (1998). *Knowledge assets: Securing competitive advantage in the information economy.* New York: Oxford University Press.

Bok, S. (1989). *Lying: Moral choice in public and private life.* New York: Random House.

Borja, R. R. (2006). Dance video games hit the floor in schools. *Education Week, 25,* 1–2.

Bormann, E. G., & Bormann, N. C. (1992). *Effective small group communication* (5th ed.). Edina, MN: Burgess International Group.

Bramlett-Solomon, S. (1992). Predictors of job satisfaction among black journalists. *Journalism Quarterly, 69,* 703–712.

Bramlett-Solomon, S. (1993). Job appeal and job satisfaction among Hispanic and black journalists. *Mass Communication Review, 20* (3–4), 202–212.

Braus, P. (1992). What workers want. *American Demographics, 14* (8), 30–35.

Bressers, B., & Meeds, R. (1995, August). *Executives' perceptions of print/online integration factors that influence major newspapers.* Paper presented at the Association for Education in Journalism and Mass Communication, San Antonio, Texas.

Broadcasting & Cable. (2003–2004). *Broadcasting & cable yearbook 2003–2004.* New York: Author.

Brockner, J., Grover, S., Reed, T., DeWitt, R., & O'Malley, M. (1987). Survivors' reaction to layoffs: We get by with a little help from our friends. *Administrative Sciences Quarterly 32,* 526–541.

Brown, D. (2002, March). Back to Earth. *American Journalism Review, 24,* 42–47.

Brown, S. L., & Eisenhardt, K. M. (1998). *Competing on the edge: Strategy as structured chaos.* Boston, MA: Harvard Business School Press.

Buchanan, D. A. (1985). Using the new technology. In T. Forester (Ed.), *The information technology revolution* (pp. 454–465). Cambridge, MA: MIT Press.

Burnes, B., & James, H. (1995). Culture, cognitive dissonance and the management of change. *International Journal of Operations & Production Management, 15,* 14–33.

Butler, J. M., Broussard, E. J., & Adams, P. (1987). Stress and the public relations practitioner. *Southwestern Mass Communication Journal, 3,* 60–79.

Buzzell, R. D., & Cook, V. (1969). *Product life cycles.* Cambridge, MA: Marketing Science Institute.

California Center for Public Health Advocacy. (2003). *LAUSD school food policy reforms.* Davis, CA: Author. Retrieved August 16, 2006, from http://www.publichealthadvocacy.org/limits/LAUSD2003.html

California Center for Public Health Advocacy. (2005a). *California legislature votes to limit school soda and junk food sales (K–12).* Davis, CA: Author. Retrieved August 16, 2006, from http://www.publichealthadvocacy.org/

California Center for Public Health Advocacy. (2005b, August). The growing epidemic: Child overweight rates on the rise in California assembly districts. *Rates of childhood overweight in California counties, cities and communities September 2005.* Davis, CA: Author. Retrieved August 16, 2006, from http://www.publichealthadvocacy.org/policy_briefs/overweight2004.html

California Center for Public Health Advocacy. (2006a). *District compliance summary in California elementary school PE requirements 2004–05/2005–06.* Davis, CA: Author. Retrieved August 16, 2006, from http://www.publichealthadvocacy.org/policy_briefs/DistrictComplianceChart.pdf

California Center for Public Health Advocacy. (2006b). *Overweight children in California counties & communities, 2004: Los Angeles County.* Davis, CA: Author. Retrieved August 16, 2006, from http://www.publichealthadvocacy.org/policy_briefs/county/Los_Angeles_Fact_Sheet.pdf

California Center for Public Health Advocacy. (2006c, June 6). *Dropping the ball: Schools fail to meet physical education mandates.* Davis, CA: Author. Retrieved August 16, 2006, from http://www.publichealthadvocacy.org/policy_briefs/index.html

Central Hudson Gas & Electric v. Public Service Commission of New York. (1980). 447 U.S. 557.

Central Intelligence Agency. (2006). *CIA world factbooks.* Retrieved June 14, 2006, from http://www.cia.gov/cia/publications/factbook/

Chan-Olmstead, S. M. (2006). Issues in strategic management. In A. B. Albarran, S. M. Chan-Olmsted, & M. O. Wirth (Eds.), *Handbook of media management and economics* (pp. 161–180). Mahwah, NJ: Lawrence Erlbaum Associates.

Chandy, K. T. (2004). *Case writing guide.* Retrieved August 16, 2006, from http://bingweb.binfhamton.edu/(tilda)tchandy/Mgmt411/case_guide .html

Chang, L. A., & Sylvie, G. (1999, August). *Job satisfaction, dissatisfaction of Texas newspaper reporters.* Paper presented at the meeting of the Association for Education in Journalism and Mass Communication, New Orleans, Louisiana.

Child obesity leads to new marketing campaigns, industry regulations. (2005, December 15). *Marketing News,* p. 22.

Christakis, D. (2006). The hidden and potent effects of television advertising. *Journal of the American Medical Association, 295,* 1698–1699.

Christensen, C. R., with Hansen, A. J. (1987). *Teaching and the case method: Text, cases, and readings.* Boston: Harvard Business School.

Chyi, H. I., & Sylvie, G. (1998). Competing with whom? Where? And how? A structural analysis of the electronic newspaper market. *Journal of Media Economics, 11*(2), 1–18.

Clark, C. V. (2005, February). Memos from CEOs: Marked "urgent": Richard Parsons, Ann Fudge, and Ken Chenault offer powerful lessons in leadership. *Black Enterprise.* Retrieved July 14, 2006, from http://www.find articles.com/p/articles/mi_m1365/is_7_35/ai_n9485662/pg_2

Cleary, J. (2005, August). *"Walking the walk?": The disconnect over minority professional development in the newsroom.* Paper presented at the Association for Education in Journalism and Mass Communication, San Antonio, Texas.

Coleman, R., & Colbert, J. (1999, August). *Grounding the teaching of journalistic design in creativity theory: 10 steps to a more creative curriculum.* Paper presented at the Association for Education in Journalism and Mass Communication, New Orleans, Louisiana.

Collins, B., & Guetzkow, H. (1964). *Social psychology of group processes for decision making.* New York: Wiley.

Commission on the Freedom of the Press. (1947). *A free and responsible press.* Chicago: University of Chicago Press.

Compaine, B., & Gomery, D. (2000). *Who owns the media?* (3rd ed.). Mahwah, NJ: Lawrence Erlbaum Associates

The Congressional International Anti-Piracy Caucus. (2006). *2006 country watch list.* Retrieved July 17, 2006, from http://schiff.house.gov/antipiracy caucus/pdf/IAPCpercent202006percent20Watchpercent20List.pdf

Cook, B. B., Banks, S. R., & Turner, R. J. (1993). The effects of work environment on burnout in the newsroom. *Newspaper Research Journal, 14* (3–4), 123–136.

Covington, W. G., Jr. (1997). *Systems theory applied to television station management in the competitive marketplace.* Lanham, MD: University Press of America.

Crable, C., Morelock, A., & Willard, A. (2005, August). *Newsroom leaders' perceptions of the role and value of copy editors at community newspapers.*

Paper presented at the Association for Education in Journalism and Mass Communication, San Antonio, Texas.

Cummings, D. G., & Worley, C. (1993). *Organization development and change.* New York: West Publishing.

Cutler, Galeser, & Shapiro. (2003). Why have Americans become obese? *Harvard Institute of Economic Research* (Discussion paper No. 1994, January). Cambridge, MA: Harvard University. Retrieved August 16, 2006, from http://post.economics.harvard.edu/hier/2003papers/HIER1994.pdf

Cyert, R. M., & March, J. G. (1963). *A behavioral theory of the firm.* Englewood Cliffs, NJ: Prentice Hall.

Daniels, D. E. (2005). *Journalism sources: Library quick guide.* Fayetteville, AR: University of Arkansas.

Daniels, G., & Hollifield, C. A.(2002). Times of turmoil: Short- and long-term effects of organizational change on newsroom employees. *Journalism and Mass Communication Quarterly, 79,* 661–680.

Day, G. S., & Schoemaker, P. J. H. (2000). A different game. In G. S. Day, P. J. H. Schoemaker, & R. E. Gunther (Eds.), *Wharton on managing emerging technologies* (pp. 1–23). New York: John Wiley & Sons.

Dedinsky, M. L. (2000). An editor's primer: Lessons learned at the Chicago Tribune. In Zeeck, D. A. (Ed.), *Extending the brand* (pp. 43–46). Reston, VA: American Society of Newspaper Editors.

Deeken, A. (2005, October 10). Viacom expands Dallas outdoor presence. *Mediaweek, 15,* 48.

Deeken, A. (2006a, April 10). G4 net plugs into YouTube.com. *Mediaweek, 16,* 71.

Deeken, A. (2006b, April 10). Satellite radio hits 10 million subs. *Mediaweek, 16,* 72.

Deggans, E. (2006, May 24). TV reporter painted into a corner. *St. Peterburg (FL) Times Online.* Retrieved August 16, 2006, from http://www.sptimes.com/2006/05/24/Tampabay/TV_reporter_painted_i.shtml

DeGuevara, M. L. (2006, May 16). At a park near you: Recreation and education. *The Press Enterprise,* p. B01.

Demographics U.S.A.—County edition. (2005). Survey of buying power demographics. New York: Market Statistics.

Denison, D. R. (1990). *Corporate culture and organizational effectiveness.* New York: Wiley.

Deutsch, M. (1949, February). A theory of cooperation and competition. *Human Relations, 2,* 129–152.

Deutschman, A. (2005, July). Is your boss a psychopath? [Electronic version]. *Fast Company, 96,* 44.

Downie, L., Bennett, P., & Coleman, M. (2006). *A report on diversity in the Washington Post newsroom.* Retrieved June 30, 2006, from http://www.mediabistro.com/fishbowlDC/original/05newsroomdiversityreport.pdf

Driver, M. J., Brousseau, K. R., & Hunsaker, P. L. (1993). *The dynamic decision maker.* San Francisco: Jossey-Bass.

Drucker, P. F. (1983). The effective decision. In E. Collins (Ed.), *Executive success: Making it in management* (pp. 464–475). New York: Wiley.

Elliott, P., & Chavez, D. (1969, November). A sociological framework for the study of television production. *Sociological Review, 17*, 355–337.

Ellis, S. L., & Jabro, A. D. (1997). *Television newsroom training for the 21st century.* Paper presented at the Annual Convention of the Association for Education in Journalism and Mass Communication, Chicago, Illinois.

Ellison, S. (2005, October 31). Small bites: Why Kraft decided to ban some food ads to children. *Wall Street Journal*, p. A1.

Ellison, S., & Adamy, J. (2005, December 7). Panel faults food packaging for kid obesity. *Wall Street Journal*, p. B1.

Emling, S. (2002, July 7). DVDs ejecting VCRs from the scene. *The Austin-American Statesman*, pp. J1, J6.

Endres, F. (1988). Stress in the newsroom at Ohio dailies. *Newspaper Research Journal, 10* (1), 1–14.

Endres, F. (1992). Stress in professional classes: Causes, manifestations, coping. *Journalism Educator, 47* (1), 16–30.

Endres, F., Schierhorn, A. B., & Schierhorn, C. (1999, August). *Newsroom teams: A baseline study of prevalence, organization and effectiveness.* Paper presented at the Association for Education in Journalism and Mass Communication, New Orleans, Louisiana.

Esterberg, K. (2002). *Qualitative methods in social research.* Boston: McGraw Hill.

European Audiovisual Observatory. (1997). *Statistical yearbook.* Strasbourg, France: Council of Europe.

European Federation of Journalists. (2004). *Eastern empires: Foreign ownership in eastern and central European media: Ownership, policy issues and strategy.* Retrieved June 15, 2006, from http://www.ifj-europe.org/pdfs/MedconJune2003.pdf

Evans, M. G. (1970). The effects of supervisory behavior on the path-goal relationship. *Organizational Behavior and Human Performance, 5*, 277–298.

Fagerling, M., & Norbäck, M. (2005, August). *Managing professionals versus managing experts—A narrative of newsroom groups during the development of a Web edition.* Paper presented at the Scandinavian Academy of Management, Aarhus, Denmark.

Fagerling, M., & Norbäck, M. (2005). Newsroom identities: Group configurations and transforming boundaries during the introduction of a Web edition. *Intervention Research, 1*, 191–207.

Falcone, P. (1997, February). The fundamentals of progressive discipline; employee discipline. *HR Magazine, 42*, 90.

Federal Communication Commission. (2005, December 1). *FCC's review of the broadcast ownership rules.* Retrieved July 3, 2006 from http://www.fcc.gov/cgb/consumerfacts/reviewrules.html

Fedler, F., Buhr, T., & Taylor, D. (1988). Journalists who leave the news media seem happier, find better jobs. *Newspaper Research Journal, 9* (2), 15–23.

Feinstein, A., & Owen, J. (2002, July/August). Exposure to light: War photographers and stress. *Columbia Journalism Review 41,* 51.

Fentin, S. (2002). Documenting performance problems — no surprises, please! *Massachusetts Employment Law Letter, 13,* 1.

Festinger, L. (1957). *A theory of cognitive dissonance.* Stanford, CA: Stanford University Press.

Fiedler, F. E. (1967). *A theory of leadership effectiveness.* New York: McGraw-Hill.

Fink, S. L. (1993). Managing individual behavior: Bringing out the best in people. In A. R. Cohen (Ed.), *The portable MBA in management* (pp. 71–112). New York: Wiley.

Fisher, R., Ury, W. L., & Patton, B. (1991). *Getting to yes: Negotiating agreement without giving in* (2nd ed.). London: Penguin Books.

Folkerts, J., & Lacy, S. (2004). *The media in your life* (3rd ed.). Boston: Allyn & Bacon.

Food marketers hope veggies look fun to kids. (2005, July 15). *USA Today,* Money, p. 05b.

Foran, J. (2002). *University of California—Santa Barbara case method—Student guidelines.* Retrieved August 16, 2006, from http://www.soc.ucsb.edu/projects/casemethod/guidelines.html

Foucault, M. (1980). *Power/knowledge: Selected interviews and other writings 1972–1977.* London: Harvester Wheatsheaf.

Freedom House. (2005). *Freedom of the press 2005: A global survey of media independence.* New York: Rowman & Littlefield Publishers.

Frutkin, A. J. (2006, June 19). Best use of multicultural: Grupo Gallegos. *Mediaweek,* 16, SR25.

Funk, L., & Lesch, H. (2005, March 8). Minimum wages in Europe. *EIROnline.* Retrieved July 3, 2006, from http://www.eiro.eurofound.eu.int/2005/07/study/tn0507101s.html

Gade, P. (2004). Newspapers and organizational development: Management and journalist perceptions of newsroom cultural change. *Journalism & Communication Monographs, 6,* 1–55.

Gade, P. (2005, August). *Journalism guardians in a sea of change: U.S. newspaper editors' perceptions of their organizational roles, organizational integration and perceived organizational support.* Paper presented at the Association for Education in Journalism and Mass Communication, San Antonio, Texas.

Gade, P., Perry, E.L., & Coyle, J. (1997, August). *Predicting the future: How St. Louis Post-Dispatch journalists perceive a new editor will affect their jobs.* Paper presented at the Association for Education in Journalism and Mass Communication, Chicago, Illinois.

Gannett. (2006). *Vision mission.* Retrieved August 16, 2006, from http://www
.gannett.com/about/visionmission.htm

Gardner, H., Csikszentmihalyi, M., & Damon, W. (2001). *Good work: When
excellence and ethics meet.* New York: Basic Books.

Gaziano, C., & Coulson, D. C. (1988). Effect of newsroom management styles
on journalists: A case study. *Journalism Quarterly, 65,* 869–880.

George, E., Chattopadhyay, P., Sitkin, S. B., & Barden, J. (2006). Cognitive
underpinnings of institutional persistence and change: A framing perspective. *Academy of Management Review, 31,* 347–365.

Gershon, R. A. (2001). *Telecommunications management: Industry structures
and planning strategies.* Mahwah, NJ: Lawrence Erlbaum Associates.

Giles, R. H. (1983). *Editors and stress.* New York: Associated Press Managing
Editors Association.

Gillmor, D., Barron, J., & Simon, T. (1998). *Mass communication law: Cases
and comment* (6th ed.). Belmont, CA: Wadsworth.

Gillmor, D. M., Barron, J. A., Simon, T. F., & Terry, H. A. (1990). *Mass communication law: Cases and comment* (5th ed.). St. Paul, MN: West Publishing Co.

Goodwin, H. E. (1987). *Groping for ethics in journalism* (2nd ed.). Ames, IA:
Iowa State University.

Green, A. (2002, June 17). The amazing game. *Advertising Age, 73,* 30.

Greene, C. N. (1972, October). The satisfaction-performance controversy.
Business Horizons, pp. 32–40.

Greve, H. R. (1998). Managerial cognition and the mimetic adoption of market positions: What you see is what you do. *Strategic Management Journal 19,* 967–988.

Griffin, R. W., & Moorhead, G. (1986). *Organizational behavior.* Boston:
Houghton-Mifflin.

Griffith, D. (2006, July 7). Think you're healthy? Most do; But some trends may
contradict that belief, state survey finds. *Sacramento Bee,* p. A1.

Gubman, J., & Greer, J. (1997, August). *An analysis of online sites produced by
U.S. newspapers: Are the critics right?* Paper presented at the meeting of
the Association for Journalism and Mass Communication, Chicago.

Hall, G. E., & Hord, S. M. (2006). *Implementing change: patterns, principles
and potholes.* Boston: Pearson Education, Inc.

Harrison, E. F. (1987). *The managerial decision-making process* (3rd ed.). Boston: Houghton-Mifflin.

Harrison, K., & Marske, A. L. (2005). Nutritional content of foods advertised
during the television programs children watch most. *American Journal
of Public Health, 95,* 1568–1574.

Hein, K. (2005, December 12). Do top shows prime kids for obesity-inducing
fare? *Brandweek, 46,* 12.

Hersey, P., & Blanchard, K. H. (1982). *Management of organizational behavior:
Utilizing human resources* (4th ed.). Englewood Cliffs, NJ: Prentice Hall.

Herzberg, F., Mausner, B., & Snyderman, B. (1968). *The motivation to work.* New York: Wiley.

Hickey, N. (May/June 2002). Q & A: Media monopoly: Behind the mergers. *Columbia Journalism Review,* 41, 50–54.

Hinkle, Hensley, Shanor, & Martin, L. L. P. (2002). Question corner: Performance evaluation can contribute positively. *New Mexico Employment Law Letter, 8,* 1–3.

Hislop, D. (2005). *Knowledge management in organizations.* New York: Oxford University Press.

Hoag, A., Brickley, D. J., & Cawley, J. M. (2001). Media management education and the case method. *Journalism & Mass Communication Educator, 55,* 49–59.

Hofstede, G. (1980). *Culture's consequences.* Newbury Park, CA: Sage.

Holland, B. (2006, June 22). FCC votes to review ownership rules. *The Hollywood Reporter.com.* Retrieved July 3, 2006, from http://www.hollywood reporter.com/thr/article_display.jsp?vnu_content_id=1002725666

Hollifield, C. A., Vlad, T., & Becker, L. B. (2004). Market, organizational, and strategic factors affecting media entrepreneurs in emerging economies. In R. Picard (Ed.), *Proceedings from the International Conference on Strategic Responses to Media Market Changes* (pp. 133–153). Jönköping, Sweden: Media Management and Transformation Centre, Jönköping International Business School, Jönköping University, Sweden.

Hollifield, C. A., Becker, L. B., & Vlad, T. (2006, July). *The effects of political, economic and organizational factors on the performance of broadcast media in developing countries.* Paper presented at the International Association for Media and Communication Research, Cairo, Egypt.

Holloway, D. (2006, June 3). Ready to trade the remote for a mouse? *Austin American-Statesman,* p. A1.

House, R. J., & Dessler, G. (1974). The Path-Goal theory of leadership: Some posthoc and a priori tests. In J. G. Hunt, & L. L. Larson (Eds.), *Contingency approaches to leadership* (pp. 29–55). Carbondale, IL: Southern Illinois University Press.

How parents view their child's weight. (2006, May). *Child Health Alert, 24,* 5.

How to align performance management with corporate goals (News you can use). (2002). *Business and Management Practices,* T[plus]D, 56, 19.

How to remake a sub-par performance management process. (2002, February). *Design Firm Management & Administration Report,* p. 6.

Huber, G. P. (1980). *Managerial decision making.* Glenview, IL: Scott, Foresman.

Hudson, E. D. (2005a, September 19). Los Angeles. *Mediaweek, 15,* 9–12.

Hudson, E. D. (2005b, October 3). Dallas. *Mediaweek, 15,* 9–12.

Hughes, R. L., Ginnett, R. C., & Curphy, G. J. (1999). *Leadership: Enhancing the lessons of experience* (3rd ed.). Boston: Irwin McGraw Hill.

Interactive Advertising Bureau. (2004, September). *IAB interactive audience measurement and advertising campaign reporting and audit guidelines*

(United States Version 6.0b). Retrieved August 16, 2006, from http://www.iab.net/standards/pdf/2292%20IAB%20spreads.pdf

Interactive Advertising Bureau, & PricewaterhouseCoopers. (2006). *IAB Internet advertising revenue report*. Retrieved July 15, 2006, from http://www.iab.net/resources/adrevenue/pdf/IAB_PwC_2005.pdf

Iorio, S. H. (Ed.). (2004). *Qualitative research in journalism: Taking it to the streets*. Mahwah, NJ: Lawrence Erlbaum Associates.

Ivancevich, J. M., Lorenzi, P., Skinner, S. J., & Crosby, P. B. (1994). *Management: Quality and competitiveness*. Burr Ridge, IL: Irwin.

Ives, N. (2006, May 22). Study rebuts 'engagement' assumptions. *Advertising Age, 77*, 4.

Janis, I. L. (1982). *Groupthink* (2nd ed.). Boston: Houghton Mifflin.

Jaksa, J. A., & Pritchard, M. S. (1988). *Communication ethics: Methods of analysis*. Belmont, CA: Wadsworth Publishing, Co.

Jung, J. (2003). The bigger, the better? Measuring the financial health of media firms. *International Journal of Media Management, 5*, 237–250.

Jurczak, P. R. (1996, August). *Newsroom cultures, newspaper acquisitions and the community: A case study of Pittsburgh newspapers*. Paper presented at the Association for Education in Journalism and Mass Communication, Anaheim, California.

Kahneman, D., & Tversky, A. (1979). Prospect theory: An analysis of decision under risk. *Econometrica, 47*, 263–292.

Kanter, R. M. (2001, February). A more perfect union. *Inc.*, pp. 93–98.

Katz, D., & Kahn R. L. (1978). *The social psychology of organizations*. New York: Wiley.

Katz, H. (2007). *The media handbook* (3rd ed.). Mahwah, NJ: Lawrence Erlbaum Associates.

Keppel, G., & Wickens, T. D. (2004). *Design and analysis: A researcher's handbook* (4th ed.). Englewood Cliffs, NJ: Prentice-Hall.

Keyt Law. (2006, April 24). *Sono Bono term extension act extends copyright terms*. Retrieved July 17, 2006, from http://www.keytlaw.com/Copyrights/sonybono.htm

Kiesler, C. A., & Kiesler, S. B. (1969). *Conformity*. Reading, MA: Addison-Wesley.

Killebrew, K. C. (2001, August). *Managing in a converged environment: Threading camels through newly minted needles*. Paper presented at the meeting of the Association for Education in Journalism and Mass Communication, Washington, DC.

Klieman, H. (2005). Equal time rule. *Museum of Broadcast Communications*. Retrieved July 15, 2006, from http://www.museum.tv/archives/etv/E/htmlE/equaltimeru/equaltimeru.htm

Kluth, A. (2006, April 20). It's the links, stupid: Blogging is just another word for having a conversation. Surveys: A Survey of new media. *The Economist*, 3–4.

Kodrich, K. P., & Beam, R. A. (1997, August). *Job satisfaction among journalists at daily newspapers: Does size of organization make a difference?* Paper presented at the Association for Education in Journalism and Mass Communication, Chicago, Illinois.

Koenig, D. (2006a, June 22). AT&T to own customer data, track some Internet use. *Associated press state and local wire, Business News,* p. 1.

Koenig, D. (2006b, May 28). Texas Instruments expects video to drive semiconductor sales. *Associated press state and local wire, State and Regional,* p. 1.

Kogut, B. (1989). The stability of joint ventures: Reciprocity and competitive rivalry. *The Journal of Industrial Economics, 38,* 183–198.

Kolo, C., & Vogt, P., (2003). Strategies for growth in the media and communication industries: Does size really matter? *International Journal of Media Management, 5,* 251–261.

Kolodny, H., & Stjernberg, T. (1993). Self-managing teams: The new organization of work. In A. R. Cohen (Ed.), *The portable MBA in management* (pp. 29–314). New York: Wiley.

Kovarik, B. (2003). *Interactive notes on global media and law.* Retrieved July 1, 2006, from http://www.runet.edu/~wkovarik/class/law/1.0.lawbook.html

Krippendorff, K. (2004). *Content analysis: An introduction to its methodology* (2nd ed.). Thousand Oaks, CA: Sage.

Kuhn, T. S. (1996). *The structure of scientific revolutions.* Chicago: University of Chicago Press.

Küng, L. (2004). What makes media firms tick? Exploring the hidden drivers of performance. In R. Picard (Ed.), *Proceedings from the International Conference on Strategic Responses to Media Market Changes* (pp. 65–82). Jönköping, Sweden: Media Management and Transformation Centre, Jönköping International Business School, Jönköping University, Sweden.

Lacy, S., & Martin, H. J. (2005). Circulation and advertising competition: Implications of research. *Newspaper Research Journal, 25,* 18–39.

Lacy, S., & Simon, T. (1993). *The economics and regulation of United States newspapers.* Norwood, NJ: Ablex.

Lafayette, J. (2006, May 15). Flat kids upfront seen by buyers. *TelevisionWeek, 25,* 3.

Lawson-Borders, G. (2003). Integrating new media and old media: Seven observations of convergence as a strategy for best practices in media organizations. *The International Journal on Media Management, 5,* 91–99.

Learned, E. P. (1987). Reflections of a case method teacher. In C. R. Christensen, with A. J. Hansen (Eds.), *Teaching and the case method: Text, cases, and readings* (pp. 9–15). Boston: Harvard Business School. (Original work published 1980)

Leavitt, H. (1965). Applied organizational change in industry. In J. March (Ed.), *Handbook of organizations* (pp. 1144–1170). Chicago: Rand McNally.

Lenhart, A., & Madden, M. (2005). *Teen content creators and consumers.* Pew Internet and American Life Projects. Retrieved July 15, 2006, from http://www.pewinternet.org/pdfs/PIP_Teens_Content_Creation.pdf

Leonard, D. (1995). *Wellsprings of knowledge: Building and sustaining the sources of innovation.* Boston: Harvard Business School Press.

Lewis, M. (2000, September 10). The end of TV as we know it? *The Austin American-Statesman*, pp. J1, J5.

Limburg, V. E. (2005). Fairness doctrine. *Museum of Broadcast Communications.* Retrieved July 15, 2006 from http://www.museum.tv/archives/etv/F/htmlF/fairnessdoct/fairnessdoct.htm

Lin, C. A., & Jeffres, L. W. (2001). Comparing distinctions and similarities across websites of newspapers, radio stations and television stations. *Journalism and Mass Communication Quarterly, 78*(3), 555–573.

Lindlof, T. R., & Taylor, B. C. (2002). *Qualitative communication research methods* (2nd ed.). Thousand Oaks, CA: Sage.

Lindstrom, P. B. (1997). The Internet: Nielsen's longitudinal research on behavioral chanes in use of this counterintuitive medium. *Journal of Media Economics, 10*(2), 35–40.

Lippmann, W. (1922). *Public opinion.* New Brunswick, NJ: Transaction Publishers.

Livingston, C., & Voakes, P. S. (2005). *Working with numbers and statistics: A handbook for journalists.* Mahwah, NJ: Lawrence Erlbaum Associates.

Locke, E. A. (1968). Toward a theory of task motivation and incentives. *Organizational Behavior and Human Performance, 3*, 157–189.

Lowrey, W. (2005). Commitment to newspaper-TV partnering: A test of the impact of institutional isomorphism. *Journalism and Mass Communication Quarterly, 82*, 495–515.

Lucan, A. N. (2004, September). Overtime for journalists? It depends. *Association of Alternative Newsweeklies.* Retrieved July 15, 2006, from http://aan.org/gyrobase/Aan/viewArticle?oid=138697

Machkovech, S. (2006, June 22). More Plugs; after reading this week's feature discover more of the local blogosphere here. *Dallas Observer*, p. 1.

MacLeod, W. (2006, February 20). Does advertising make us fat? No! *Brandweek, 47*, 19.

Mankins, M., & Steele, R. (2006). Stop making plans start making decisions. *Harvard Business Review, 84*, 76–84.

March, J. G. (1997). Understanding how decisions happen in organizations. In Z. Shapira (Ed.), *Organizational decision making* (pp. 9–32). Cambridge, MA: Cambridge University Press.

Marshall, J. L. (2005, Winter). How to build a fruitful relationship with the boss [Electronic version]. *Fusion*: 10–11.

Martel, J. (2006, March/April). Reorganizing to build winning teams. *Newspaper Marketing, 4*(2), 14–17.

Maslow, A. H. (1954). *Motivation and personality.* New York: Harper & Row.

McClellan, S. (2005, December 5). In-game integration reaps consumer recall. *Adweek, 46*, 9.

McClellan, S. (2006a, March 20). More time with media means less patience for ads. *Adweek, 47*, 10.

McClellan, S. (2006b, May 8). Setting the bar higher. *Mediaweek, 16*, 6.

McClelland, D. (1961). *The achieving society.* Princeton, NJ: Van Nostrand.

McConnell, B. (2002, March 4). New rules for risqué business. *Broadcasting & Cable.* Retrieved July 15, 2006, from http://www.broadcastingcable.com

McDevitt, M., Gassaway, B. M., & Perez, F. G. (2002). The making and unmaking of civic journalists: Influences of professional socialization. *Journalism and Mass Communication Quarterly, 79*(1), 87–100.

McGill, L. (2002, April). Surveys on retention are in agreement. *The American Editor,* Retrieved August 16, 2006, from http://www.asne.org/index.cfm?id3646

McGill, L. T. (2000). *Newsroom diversity: Meeting the challenge.* Arlington, VA: The Freedom Forum. Retrieved June 30, 2006, from http://www.freedomforum.org/publications/diversity/meetingthechallenge/meetingthechallenge.pdf

McGinnis, J. M., Appleton Gootman, J., & Kraak, V. I. (Eds.). (2006). *Food marketing to children and youth: Threat or opportunity?* [Electronic version]. Washington, DC: The National Academies Press.

McGregor, D. (1960). *The human side of enterprise.* New York: McGraw-Hill Book Company, Inc.

McGregor, D. (2006). *The human side of enterprise: Annotated edition; Updated and with a new commentary by Joel Cutcher-Gershenfeld.* New York: McGraw Hill. (Original work published 1960)

McKean, R. N. (1975). Cost-benefit analysis. In E. Mansfield (Ed.), *Managerial economics and operational research* (3rd ed., pp. 549–561). New York: Norton.

McQuarrie, F. (1992). Dancing on the minefield: Developing a management style in media organizations. In S. Lacy, A. B. Sohn, & R. H. Giles (Eds.), *Readings in media management* (pp. 229–239). Columbia, SC: Media Management & Economics Division of the Association for Education in Journalism and Mass Communication.

McQuarrie, F. (1999). Professional mystique and journalists' dissatisfaction. *Newspaper Research Journal, 20*(3), 20–28.

The Media Center. (2006). Convergence tracker search page. (2006). *The media center at the American Press Institute.* Retrieved August 16, 2006, from http://www.mediacenter.org/convergencetracker/search/

Media management and economics: Theory and practice. (2006, May 14). Paper presented at workshop at the University of Belgrade, Serbia.

Mediamark Research. (2006). *Mediamark research to launch comprehensive survey of 24-hour-day media consumption.* Retrieved August 16, 2006, from http://www.mediamark.com/mri/docs/press/pr_04-04-06_Media Day.htm

Merrill, J. C. (1974). *The imperative of freedom: A philosophy of journalism autonomy.* New York: Hastings House, Publishers.

Middleton, K. R., Trager, R., & Chamberlin, B. F. (2001). *The law of public communication* (5th ed.). New York: Longman.

Miller v. California. (1973). 413 U.S. 22.

Miller, S. J., Hickson, D. J., & Wilson, D. C. (1996). Decision making in organizations. In S. R. Clegg, C. Hardy, & W. R. Nord (Eds.), *Handbook of organization studies* (pp. 293–312). London: Sage.

Miller, P., & Miller, R. (1995). The invisible woman: Female sports journalists in the workplace. *Journalism & Mass Communication Quarterly, 72,* 883–889.

Miller, K. I., & Monge, P. R. (1985). Social information and employee anxiety about organizational change. *Human Communication Research, 11,* 365–386.

Mitchell, R. R., Smyser, C. M., & Weed, S. E. (1975). Locus of control: Supervision and work satisfaction. *Academy of Management Journal, 18,* 623–631.

Mobile Marketing Association. (2006a, February 27). *Use of wireless features among subscribers in Japan and the U.S.* Retrieved August 16, 2006, from http://mmaglobal.com/modules/wfsection/print.php?articleid=211

Mobile Marketing Association. (2006b, June 20). *Camera phone statistics* (The NPD Group). Retrieved August 16, 2006, from http://mmaglobal.com/modules/wfsection/article.php?articleid=445

Mobile Marketing Association, & The NPD Group. (2006, May 21). *Mobile video research and statistics.* Retrieved August 16, 2006, from http://mmaglobal.com/modules/wfsection/article.php?articleid=378

Mobilizing the magazines: Maxim and Cosmo phone it in (2006, April 6). *Wireless Business Forecast, 14,* 1.

Moore, G. (2002, Summer). We must win the battle—now. *Paynter Report,* p. 8.

Moore, R. L. (1999). *Mass communication law and ethics* (2nd ed.). Mahwah, NJ: Lawrence Erlbaum Associates.

Moses, L. J., & Baldwin, D. A. (2005). What can the study of cognitive development reveal about children's ability to appreciate and cope with advertising? *Journal of Public Policy and Marketing, 24,* 186–201.

Moss, L. (2005, December 5). Cable gobbles up sweep. *Multichannel News,* 6.

Munk, N. (2002, July). Power failure. *Vanity Fair, 503,* 128–131,167–170.

Nanus, B. (1992). *Visionary leadership.* San Francisco: Jossey-Bass.

Napoli, P. (1997). The media trade press as technology forecaster: A case study of the VCR's impact on broadcast. *Journalism and Mass Communication Quarterly, 74*(2), 417–430.

National Association of Broadcasters. (2004). *Television financial report.* Washington, DC: Author.

Nelson, B., & Economy, P. (1996). *Managing for dummies.* New York: Wiley Publishing.

Neuendorf, K. A. (2002). *The content analysis guidebook*. Thousand Oaks, CA: Sage.

Newman, S. (2002, April 5). Remarks made at 3rd Symposium on Online Journalism, The University of Texas at Austin.

New York Times v. Sullivan. (1964). 376 U.S. 254.

Newspaper Association of America. (2004). *2004 Horizon Watching Initiative: Board Committee on Industry Development: Cable TV*. Retrieved June 15, 2006, from http://www.naa.org/horizon/mt/cabletv.ppt#518,1,Slide 1

Newspaper Association of America. (2005, November). *Top 100 newspaper Web sites*. Nielsen//NetRatings MegaPanel Custom Analysis. Retrieved August 16, 2006, from http://www.naa.org/nadbase/Top_100_Newspaper_Web_Sites.pdf

Newspaper Association of America. (2006). *U.S. Daily Newspaper Trends*. Retrieved July 3, 2006, from http://www.naa.org/thesource/14.asp#circulation

Noon, M. (1994). From apathy to alacrity: Managers and new technology in provincial newspapers. *Journal of Management Studies, 31*(1), 19–32.

The NPD Group. (2006, March 19). Bluetooth capable phones. *Mobile Marketing Association Research Reports & Publications*. Retrieved August 16, 2006, from http://mmaglobal.com/modules/wfsection/article.php?articleid=351

O'Guinn, T. C., Allen, C. T., & Semenik, R. J. (2006). *Advertising and integrated brand promotion* (4th ed.). Mason, OH: Thomson South-Western.

Okada, B. (2006, June 13). How dirty is that diner? Go online to find out. *Fort Worth Star-Telegram*, p. 1

Ouichi, W. G. (1981). *Theory Z*. Reading, MA: Addison-Wesley.

Overholser, G. (2003, August 21). Reinforcing the stigma of rape: Is that what we do when we withhold victims' names? *Tampa Weekly Planet.com*. Retrieved July 11, 2006, from http://www.weeklyplanet.com/gyrobase/PrintFriendly?oid=oid percent3A2942

Paskowski, M. (2006, May 8). Curbing kids' TV appetite. *Television Week, 25*, 10.

Pearce, J. A., & Robinson, R. B. (1997). *Strategic management: Formulation, implementation and control* (6th ed.). Boston: Irwin McGraw-Hill.

Pease, T. (1992). Race, gender and job satisfaction in newspaper newsrooms. In S. Lacy, A. B. Sohn, & R. H. Giles (Eds.), *Readings in media management* (pp. 97–122). Columbia, SC: Media Management & Economics Division of the Association for Education in Journalism and Mass Communication.

Pediatric obesity: Too much TV could put extra pounds on your preschooler. (2006, April 28). *Medicine & Law Weekly*, 338.

Pember, D. R. (2000). *Mass media law*. Boston: McGraw-Hill.

Petersen, B. K. (1992). The managerial benefits of understanding organizational culture. In S. Lacy, A. B. Sohn, & R. H. Giles (Eds.), *Readings in media management* (pp. 123–152). Columbia, SC: Media Management & Economics Division of the Association for Education in Journalism and Mass Communication.

Pfanner, E. (2006, May 17). Hollywood writing new profit scenarios [Electronic version]. *International Herald Tribune.* Retrieved June 15, 2006, from Factiva Database Web site: http://www.iht.com/articles/2006/05/16/your money/movies.php

Piaget, J. (1970). *Genetic epistemology* (E. Duckworth, Trans.). New York: Columbia University Press.

Piaget, J. (1977). Problems in equilibration. In M. Appel, & S. Goldberg (Eds.), *Topics in cognitive development: Vol. 1. Equilibration: Theory, research, and application* (pp. 3–13). New York: Plenum.

Picard, R. G. (2002). *The economics and financing of media companies (Business, economics and legal studies,* 1). New York: Fordham University Press.

Phillips, C. L. (1991). Evaluating and valuing newsroom diversity. *Newspaper Research Journal, 12*(2), 28–37.

Policy Statement on Deception. (1983, October 14). *Letter from then Federal Trade Commission Chairman James C. Miller III to Congressman John D. Dingell.* (Reprinted as an appendix to Cliffdale, 103 FTC 110 at 174, 1984)

Powers, A. (1990). The changing market structure of local television news. *Journal of Media Economics, 3*(1), 37–55.

Powers, A. (2006). An exploratory study of the impact of leadership behavior on levels of news convergence and job satisfaction. In L. Küng (Ed.), *Leadership in the media industries: Changing context, emerging challenges* (pp. 11–28). Jonkoping, Sweden: Media Management and Transformation Centre.

Preparing an effective case analysis. (1998). Belmont, CA: South-Western College Publishing. Retrieved August 16, 2006, from http://www.swlearning .com/management/hitt/hitt_student/case_analysis_1.html

Preston, I. L. (1994). *The tangled web they weave: Truth, falsity and advertisers.* Madison, WI: University of Wisconsin Press.

Preston, I. L. (1996). *The great American blow-up: Puffery in advertising and selling* (Rev. ed.). Madison, WI: University of Wisconsin Press.

Priest, C. (1994). *The character of information: Characteristics and properties of information related to issues concerning intellectual property.* Center for Information, Technology, and Society. Retrieved August 16, 2006, from http://www.eff.org/Groups/CITS/Reports/cits_nii_framework_ota.report

Priest, W. C. (1994). *An information framework for the planning and design of "information highways."* Retrieved June 15, 2006, from http://www.eff .org/Groups/CITS/Reports/cits_nii_framework_ota.report

Rabasca, L. (2001, June). The next newsrooms: Benefits, costs & convergence. *Presstime 23*(7), 44–48.

Reca, A. A. (2005). Issues in media product management. In A. B. Albarran, S. M. Chan-Olmsted, & M. O. Wirth (Eds.), *Handbook of media management and economics* (pp. 181–201). Mahwah, NJ: Lawrence Erlbaum Associates.

Reno v. ACLU. (1997). 521 U.S. 844.

Reyes, S. (2006a, May 8). Fed obesity report seen as boon to self-regulation. *Brandweek, 47,* 5.

Reyes, S. (2006b, January 2). Kellogg, Kraft, Knorr cater to consumer needs. *Brandweek, 47,* 8.

Reyes, S. (2005, December 12). Battle lines drawn over kid marketing food fight. *Brandweek, 46,* 5.

Richards, J. (1990). *Deceptive advertising: Behavioral study of a legal concept.* Hillsdale, NJ: Lawrence Erlbaum Associates.

Riffe, D., Lacy, S., & Fico, F. G. (2005). *Analyzing media messages: Using quantitative content analysis in research* (2nd ed.). Mahwah, NJ: Lawrence Erlbaum Associates.

Rivers, W. L., & Mathews, C. (1988). *Ethics for the media.* Englewood Cliffs: Prentice-Hall.

Rogers, E. (1983). *Diffusion of innovation* (3rd ed.). New York: Free Press.

Rogers, E. (1986). *Communication technology: The new media in society.* New York: Free Press.

Roth v. U.S. (1957). 354 U.S. 476.

Rubin, R. B., Palmgreen, P., & Sypher, H. E. (Eds) (2004). *Communication research measures: A sourcebook.* Mahwah, NJ: Lawrence Erlbaum Associates.

Ruskin, G. (2006, February 20). Does advertising make us fat? Yes! *Brandweek, 47,* 18.

Russial, J. T. (1997). Topic-team performance: A content study. *Newspaper Research Journal, 18*(1–2), 126–144.

Saba, J. (2005, November). Evening the score. *Editor & Publisher, 138,* 39–40, 42, 44–46.

Saksena, S., & Hollifield, C. A. (2002). U.S. newspapers and the development of online editions. *International Journal of Media Management, 4,* 75–84.

Schein, E. H. (1985). *Organizational culture and leadership: A dynamic view.* San Francisco: Jossey-Bass.

Schein, E. H. (1995). *Career survival.* San Francisco: Jossey-Bass.

Schein, E. H. (2004). *Organizational culture and leadership.* San Francisco: Jossey-Bass.

Screen Digest. (2001, November 1). Generation of change: Thirty years of *Screen Digest.* Retrieved November 12, 2003, from Dow Jones Interactive Publications Library Web site.

Severin, W. J., & Tankard, J. W., Jr. (1992). *Communication theories: Origins, methods, and uses in mass media* (3rd ed.). New York: Longman.

Shaver, M. (1995). *Making the sale: How to sell media with marketing.* Chicago: Copy Workshop.

Sherif, M. (1962). *Intergroup relations and leadership*. New York: Wiley.

Shields, M. (2005, November 14). Counting podcast people. *Mediaweek, 15*, 6.

Shields, M. (2006a, June 19). Best use of Internet: Universal McCann. *Mediaweek, 16*, SR23.

Shields, M. (2006b, April 10). Planting podcasting seed. *Mediaweek, 16*, 7.

Shields, T. (2003, June 2). FCC relaxes ownership rules. *Adweek*. Retrieved July 3, 2006, from http://www.adweek.com/aw/national/article_display .jsp?vnu_content_id=1899609

Shlachter, B. (2006, June 27). Dallas morning news planning buyout offers. *Fort Worth Star-Telegram*, p. 1.

Simon, D. H. (2006, August). *Competitive threat, learning or legitimacy: Understanding the adoption and diffusion of Web sites by consumer magazines.* Paper presented at the Academy of Management, Honolulu, Hawaii.

Simon, H. (1957). *Models of man*. New York: Wiley.

Simon, H. (1960). *New science of management decisions*. New York: Harper & Row.

Singer, J. B. (2003). Who are these guys? The online challenge to the notion of journalistic professionalism. *Journalism, 4*, 139–163.

Singer, J. B. (2004a). More than ink-stained wretches: The resocialization of print journalists in converged newsrooms. *Journalism &Mass Communication Quarterly 81*, 838–856.

Singer, J. B. (2004b). Strange bedfellows? The diffusion of convergence in four news organizations. *Journalism Studies 5*, 3–18.

Sissors, J., & Baron, R. (2002). *Advertising media planning* (6th ed.). New York: McGraw-Hill.

Skinner, B. F. (1971). *Beyond freedom and dignity*. New York: Alfred A. Knopf.

Skoler, Abbott, & Presser, L.L.P. (2002, January). Guidance for employee performance evaluations. *Massachusetts Employment Law Letter, 12*, 1–3.

Smith, C. (1992). Models of social responsibility for news media managers. In S. Lacy, A. B. Sohn, & R. H. Giles (Eds.), *Readings in media management* (pp. 241–260). Columbia, SC: Association for Education in Journalism & Mass Communication.

Smith, G. D., Arnold, D. R., & Bizell, B. G. (1985). *Strategy and business policy*. Boston: Houghton-Mifflin.

Society of Professional Journalists Code of Ethics. (1996). In J. Folkerts, & S. Lacy. (2004), *The media in your life* (3rd ed., pp. 353). Boston: Allyn & Bacon.

Stein, J. (2006, May 15). Sporty teens refuel best. *Los Angeles Times*, p. 13.

Stevens, R. E., Sherwood, P. K., & Dunn, P. (1993). *Market analysis: Assessing your business opportunities*. New York: Haworth Press.

Stigler, G. J., (1952). *The theory of price* (Rev. ed.). New York: Macmillan.

Straub, J. T. (1984). *Managing: An introduction*. Boston: Kent.

Straubhaar, J. (1991). Beyond media imperialism: Asymmetrical interdependence and cultural proximity. *Critical Studies in Mass Communication, 8*, 1–11.

Straus, B. (2005, May). Negating newsroom negativity. *Presstime, 27,* 57.

Strupp, J. (2000, August 21). Three-point play: Print, Web, and TV operations now live under the same roof in Tampa. Big Brother may not be watching, but everyone else is. *Editor & Publisher,* pp. 18–23.

Student tips for solving case problems. (2006). Retrieved August 16, 2006, from Penn State University, Teaching and Learning with Technology Web site: http://tlt.its.psu.edu/suggestions/cases/studenttips/index.html

Sundar, S. S., Narayan, S., Obregon, R., & Uppal, C. (1997, August). *Does Web advertising work? Memory for print vs. online media.* Paper presented at the meeting of the Association for Journalism and Mass Communication, Chicago.

Sylvie, G. (1995). Editors and pagination: A case study in management. *Journal of Mediated Communication, 10*(1), 1–20.

Sylvie, G. (1996). Departmental influences on interdepartmental cooperation in daily newspapers. *Journalism and Mass Communication Quarterly, 73,* 230–241.

Sylvie, G., & Danielson, W. (1989). *Editors and hardware: Three case studies in technology and newspaper management.* Austin, TX: The University of Texas at Austin.

Sylvie, G., & Huang, J. S. (2006, May). *Decision-making by newspaper editors: Understanding values and change.* Paper presented at the International Communication Association, Dresden, Germany.

Sylvie, G., & Witherspoon, P. D. (2002). *Time, change, and the American newspaper.* Mahwah, NJ: Lawrence Erlbaum Associates.

Taylor, R. N. (1984). *Behavioral decision making.* Glenview, IL: Scott, Foreman.

Third of kids tip scales wrong way. (2006, April 5). *USA Today,* p. 1A.

Triandis, H. C., & Albert, R. D., (1987). Cross-cultural perspectives. In F. M. Jablin, L. L. Putnam, K. H. Roberts, & L. W. Porter (Eds.), *Handbook of organizational communication* (pp. 264–295). Newbury Park, NJ: Sage.

Two tools to boost a sub-par performance management process. (2002, January). *Pay for Performance Report,* 1–4.

Two ways you can improve the impact of performance management programs. (2002, April). *Managing Training & Development,* 1–2.

UNESCO. (2005). *International flows of selected cultural goods and services, 1994–2003.* Retrieved June 15, 2006, from http://www.uis.unesco.org/template/pdf/cscl/IntlFlows_EN.pdf

University of Minnesota: Dieting may indicate other unhealthy behaviors and depression in youth regardless of weight. (2006, July 2). *Managed Care Law Weekly,* 189.

U.S. Census Bureau. (1994). *Statistical abstract of the United States* (114th ed.). Washington, DC: U.S. Government Printing Office.

U.S. Census Bureau. (2000). *Statistical abstract of the United States* (120th ed.). Washington, DC: U.S. Government Printing Office.

U.S. Census Bureau. (2001). *Statistical abstract of the United States* (121st ed.) [Electronic version]. Washington, DC: U.S. Government Printing Office.

U.S. Department of Labor. (2006, April 3). *Minimum wage laws in the states.* Retrieved July 23, 2006, from http://www.dol.gov/esa/minwage/america .htm#Wisconsin

Using cases in teaching. (2006). Retrieved August 16, 2006, from Penn State University, Teaching and Learning with Technology Web site: http://tlt .its.psu.edu/suggestions/cases

Valenti, J. (2002, April 23). *A clear present and future danger: The potential undoing of America's greatest export trade prize.* Statement by Jack Valenti, chairman and CEO, Motion Picture Association, to the House Appropriations Committee, Subcommitee on Commerce, Justice, State, the Judiciary, and Related Agencies. Retrieved August 16, 2006, from http://www.mpaa.org.jack/2002/2002_04_23b.htm

Valentine v. Chrestensen. (1942). 316 U.S. 52.

van Evra, J. (2004). *Television and child development* (3rd ed). Mahwah, NJ: Lawrence Erlbaum Associates.

Van Maanen, J., & Barley, S. R. (1984). Occupational communities: Culture and control in organizations. In B. M. Staw, & L. L. Cummings (Eds.), *Research in organizational behavior* (pp. 287–365). Greenwich, CT: JAI Press.

Viral Marketing: The buzzword du jour in digital marketing universe. (2006, June 5). *Mediaweek, 16,* S6.

Voakes, P. (1995). *"Living Law" in the newsroom: A study of social influences.* Paper presented at the Annual Convention of the Association for Education in Journalism and Mass Communication, Atlanta, Georgia.

Vroom, V. H. (1964). *Work and motivation.* New York: Wiley.

Vroom, V. H., & Yetton, P. W. (1973). *Leadership and decision making.* Pittsburg, PA: University of Pittsburg Press.

Walsh, C. M. (2006). The race to measure radio is on. *Billboard, 118,* 10.

Wanberg, C. R., & Banas, J. T. (2000). Predictors and outcomes of openness to changes in a reorganizing workplace, *Journal of Applied Psychology, 85,* 132–142

Warren, R., Wicks, R., Chung, H., Wicks, J., & Fosu, I. (2006). *Food beverage advertising on U.S. Television: A comparison of child-targeted versus general audience commercials.* Unpublished manuscript.

Weaver, D., Beam, R., Brownlee, B., Voakes, P., & Wilhoit, G. C. (2003). *The face and mind of the American journalist.* Retrieved July 12, 2006, fromhttp://www.poynter.org/content/content_view.asp?id=28235

Weaver, D. H., & Wilhoit, G. C. (1996). *The American journalist in the 1990s: U.S. news people at the end of an era.* Mahwah, NJ: Lawrence Erlbaum Associates.

Weaver, J. (2000). Orlando: Values are central to convergence strategy. In D.A. Zeeck (Ed.), *Extending the brand* (pp. 22–25). Reston, VA: American Society of Newspaper Editors.

Weber, M. M., & Kirk, D. J. (2000). Teaching teachers to teach cases: It's not what you know, it's what you ask. *Marketing Education Review, 10,* 59–67.

Webster, J., Phalen, P., & Lichty, L. W. (2006). *Ratings analysis: The theory and practice of audience research* (3rd ed.). Mahwah, NJ: Lawrence Erlbaum Associates.

Weick, K. E. (1995). *Sensemaking in organizations.* Thousand Oaks, CA: Sage.

Wertheim, E. G. (2006). *A model for case analysis and problem solving.* Retrieved August 16, 2006, from College of Business Administration, Northeastern University Web site: http://web.cba.neu.edu/(tilda)ewertheim/introd/cases.htm

Whiting, C. S. (1995, October). Operational techniques and creative thinking. *Advanced Management,* 24–30.

Wilhoit, G. C., & Weaver, D. (1994, August). *U.S. journalists at work, 1971–1992.* Paper presented at the meeting of the Association for Education in Journalism and Mass Communication, Atlanta, Georgia.

Williams, F., & Monge, P. R. (2001). *Reasoning with statistics: How to read quantitative research* (5th ed.). New York: Harcourt.

Wimmer, R., & Dominick, J. (2006). *Mass media research: An introduction* (8th ed.). Belmont, CA: Wadsworth.

Witcover, J. (1971, September/October). Two weeks that shook the press. *Columbia Journalism Review, 10,* 7–15.

Woods, K. (2005). *Looking inward, going forward.* McLean, VA: National Association of Minority Media Executives.

Zachary, M. (2000, August). Performance evaluations trigger many lawsuits. *Supervision, 61,* 23–26.

Zavoina, S., & Reichert, T. (2000). Media convergence/management change: The evolving workflow for visual journalists. *The Journal of Media Economics 13*(2), 143–151.

Zikmund, W. G., & Babin, B. J. (2007). *Exploring marketing research* (9th ed.). Belmont, CA: Thomson South-Western.

AUTHOR INDEX

SUBJECT INDEX

302.230868 SYL
1WL

Fourth Edition

Media
Management

Southampton
SOLENT

oach

George Sylvie
Jan LeBlanc Wicks • C. Ann Hollifield
Stephen Lacy • Ardyth Broadrick Sohn

LEA Lawrence Erlbaum Associates
Taylor & Francis Group

New York   London